Communications in Computer and Information Science   2697

Series Editors

Gang Li, *School of Information Technology, Deakin University, Burwood, VIC, Australia*

Joaquim Filipe, *Polytechnic Institute of Setúbal, Setúbal, Portugal*

Zhiwei Xu, *Chinese Academy of Sciences, Beijing, China*

Rationale

The CCIS series is devoted to the publication of proceedings of computer science conferences. Its aim is to efficiently disseminate original research results in informatics in printed and electronic form. While the focus is on publication of peer-reviewed full papers presenting mature work, inclusion of reviewed short papers reporting on work in progress is welcome, too. Besides globally relevant meetings with internationally representative program committees guaranteeing a strict peer-reviewing and paper selection process, conferences run by societies or of high regional or national relevance are also considered for publication.

Topics

The topical scope of CCIS spans the entire spectrum of informatics ranging from foundational topics in the theory of computing to information and communications science and technology and a broad variety of interdisciplinary application fields.

Information for Volume Editors and Authors

Publication in CCIS is free of charge. No royalties are paid, however, we offer registered conference participants temporary free access to the online version of the conference proceedings on SpringerLink (http://link.springer.com) by means of an http referrer from the conference website and/or a number of complimentary printed copies, as specified in the official acceptance email of the event.

CCIS proceedings can be published in time for distribution at conferences or as post-proceedings, and delivered in the form of printed books and/or electronically as USBs and/or e-content licenses for accessing proceedings at SpringerLink. Furthermore, CCIS proceedings are included in the CCIS electronic book series hosted in the SpringerLink digital library at http://link.springer.com/bookseries/7899. Conferences publishing in CCIS are allowed to use our online conference service (Meteor) for managing the whole proceedings lifecycle (from submission and reviewing to preparing for publication) free of charge.

Publication process

The language of publication is exclusively English. Authors publishing in CCIS have to sign the Springer CCIS copyright transfer form, however, they are free to use their material published in CCIS for substantially changed, more elaborate subsequent publications elsewhere. For the preparation of the camera-ready papers/files, authors have to strictly adhere to the Springer CCIS Authors' Instructions and are strongly encouraged to use the CCIS LaTeX style files or templates.

Abstracting/Indexing

CCIS is abstracted/indexed in DBLP, Google Scholar, EI-Compendex, Mathematical Reviews, SCImago, Scopus. CCIS volumes are also submitted for the inclusion in ISI Proceedings.

How to start

To start the evaluation of your proposal for inclusion in the CCIS series, please send an e-mail to ccis@springer.com

Luiz Antonio Rodrigues · Rui Oliveira

Editors

Dependable and Secure Computing

14th Latin-American Symposium, LADC 2025
Valparaíso, Chile, October 27–31, 2025
Proceedings

 Springer

Editors
Luiz Antonio Rodrigues
Western Parana State University
Cascavel, Brazil

Rui Oliveira
INESC TEC and University of Minho
Braga, Portugal

ISSN 1865-0929   ISSN 1865-0937 (electronic)
Communications in Computer and Information Science
ISBN 978-3-032-11538-6   ISBN 978-3-032-11539-3 (eBook)
https://doi.org/10.1007/978-3-032-11539-3

This Springer imprint is published by the registered company Springer Nature Switzerland AG
The registered company address is: Gewerbestrasse 11, 6330 Cham, Switzerland

If disposing of this product, please recycle the paper.

Preface

It is our pleasure to present the proceedings of the 14th Latin-American Symposium on Dependable and Secure Computing (LADC 2025), the major event on computer system dependability and secure computing in Latin America. LADC 2025 provided a forum for researchers, practitioners, and students to discuss recent advances, share experiences, and foster collaboration in this critical area of computing.

The symposium featured a rich program, including technical sessions, workshops, tutorials, fast abstracts, keynote talks from international experts, a student forum, and an industrial track. The scope of LADC encompasses software and system dependability, security foundations, fault-tolerant and self-adaptive systems, verification and validation techniques, intrusion detection, and practical applications in secure computing environments.

LADC 2025 was held in Valparaíso, Chile, from October 27–31, co-located with CLEI 2025 (Conferencia Latinoamericana de Informática). The co-location offered a unique opportunity to strengthen collaborations within the broader Latin-American informatics community.

For this edition, we received 34 full-paper submissions. Each submission underwent a single-blind peer review process, with at least four independent reviews per paper to ensure the quality and technical soundness of the accepted contributions. In total, 17 papers were accepted for presentation, reflecting a 50% acceptance rate. For submissions co-authored by any program committee members, an objective procedure was followed: the co-authored papers were reviewed independently by reviewers with no conflict of interest, and decisions were made without the involvement of the conflicted committee member.

The accepted papers were presented in six technical sessions, grouped by related topics, highlighting both theoretical and practical advances in dependable and secure computing: Advances in Dependable and Secure Computing (Best Paper Candidates); Security Foundations and Compliance; AI for Security and Dependability; Consensus, Cryptography, and Blockchain; Modeling and Dependability Evaluation; Monitoring and Critical Infrastructures. This organization allowed attendees to follow coherent streams of research and facilitated discussions among participants working on similar themes.

We would like to extend our sincere gratitude to all authors, reviewers, program committee members, and supporting organizations whose dedication and effort made LADC 2025 possible. We hope that the readers of these proceedings will find the contributions inspiring, thought-provoking, and valuable for advancing the science and practice of dependable and secure computing.

October 2025

Luiz A. Rodrigues
Rui Oliveira

Organization

General Chairs

Edson Tavares de Camargo	Federal Technological University of Paraná, Brazil
Odorico Mendizabal	Federal University of Santa Catarina, Brazil
Sebastián Berríos Vásquez	Pontifical Catholic University of Valparaíso, Chile

Program Committee Chairs

Luiz Antonio Rodrigues	Western Paraná State University, Brazil
Rui Oliveira	INESC TEC & University of Minho, Portugal

Workshop Chair

Jamilson Ramalho Dantas	Federal University of Pernambuco, Brazil

Industry Track Chair

Lásaro Jonas Camargos	Weilliptic Inc., USA

Fast Abstract Chair

Nicolás Hidalgo Castillo	Diego Portales University, Chile

Student Forum Chair

Rafael Obelheiro	Santa Catarina State University, Brazil

Publicity Chair

Regina Moraes   University of Campinas, Brazil

Publication Chair

Leonardo Montecchi   Norwegian University of Science and Technology,
                                Norway

Patronage Chairs

Vinicius Fulber-Garcia   Federal University of Paraná, Brazil
José Flauzino   Federal University of Paraná, Brazil

Webmaster and Social Media

José Flauzino   Federal University of Paraná, Brazil

Steering Committee

Elias P. Duarte Jr.   Federal University of Paraná, Brazil
  (Permanent Member)
Marco Vieira   University of North Carolina at Charlotte, USA
  (Permanent Member)
Felicita Di Giandomenico   ISTI-CNR, Italy
  (Permanent Member)
Allan Edgard Silva Freitas   Federal Institute of Bahia, Brazil
  (CE-TF Coordinator
  2025–2026)
Paulo R. da Silva L. Coelho   Federal University of Uberlândia, Brazil
  (CE-TF Vice-Coordinator
  2025–2026)
Fernando Dotti   Pontifícia Universidade Católica do Rio Grande
  (PC Co-Chair LADC 2024)   do Sul, Brazil
Nuno Laranjeiro   University of Coimbra, Portugal
  (PC Co-Chair LADC 2024)
Roberto Natella   Università degli Studi di Napoli Federico II, Italy
  (PC Co-Chair LADC 2023)

Fabíola Greve (in memoriam)   Federal University of Bahia, Brazil
  (PC Co-Chair LADC 2023)
Eduardo Alchieri   University of Brasília, Brazil
  (PC Co-Chair LADC 2022)
José Orlando Pereira   University of Minho, Portugal
  (PC Co-Chair LADC 2022)

Program Committee

Allan Edgard Silva Freitas   Instituto Federal da Bahia, Brazil
Andrey Brito   Universidade Federal de Campina Grande, Brazil
Antonio Augusto Frohlich   Universidade Federal de Santa Catarina, Brazil
Cecilia Mary Fischer Rubira   Universidade Estadual de Campinas, Brazil
David Alvarez Martinez   Universidad de Los Andes, Colombia
Edson Tavares de Camargo   Universidade Tecnológica Federal do Paraná,
                                        Brazil
Eliane Martins   Universidade Estadual de Campinas, Brazil
Elias P. Duarte Jr.   Universidade Federal do Paraná, Brazil
Erica Sousa   Universidade Federal Rural de Pernambuco,
                                        Brazil
Erwan Mahe   CEA LIST, France
Fatima Mattiello-Francisco   INPE, Brazil
Felicita Di Giandomenico   ISTI-CNR, Italy
Fernando Pedone   University of Lugano, Switzerland
Francisco Airton Silva   Federal University of Piauí, Brazil
Gustavo Callou   Federal Rural University of Pernambuco, Brazil
Gustavo Betarte   Universidad de la República, Uruguay
Hans P. Reiser   Reykjavik University, Iceland
Hector Cancela   Universidad de la República, Uruguay
Horst Schirmeier   TU Dresden, Germany
João R. Campos   University of Coimbra, Portugal
José Alexandre D'Abruzzo Pereira   University of Coimbra, Portugal
Juan Pablo Carvallo   Universidad del Azuay, Ecuador
Kadna Camboim   Universidade Federal do Agreste de Pernambuco,
                                        Brazil
Leonardo Montecchi   Norwegian University of Science and Technology,
                                        Norway
Lourenco Alves Pereira Jr.   Instituto Tecnológico de Aeronáutica, Brazil
Luciana Arantes   Sorbonne Université, France
Luiz Fernando Rust da Costa   Inmetro, Brazil
  Carmo

Marco Vieira	University of North Carolina at Charlotte, USA
Maximiliano Cristia	CIFASIS, Argentina
Naghmeh Ramezani Ivaki	University of Coimbra, Portugal
Nuno Neves	LASIGE/UL, Portugal
Odorico M. Mendizabal	Universidade Federal de Santa Catarina, Brazil
Paulo Coelho	Universidade Federal de Uberlândia, Brazil
Paulo Romero Martins Maciel	Universidade Federal de Pernambuco, Brazil
Pietro Liguori	University of Naples Federico II, Italy
Raimundo José de Araújo Macêdo	Universidade Federal da Bahia, Brazil
Raul Ceretta Nunes	Federal University of Santa Maria, Brazil
Regina Lúcia de Oliveira Moraes	Universidade Estadual de Campinas, Brazil
Roberto Palmieri	Lehigh University, USA
Rogerio de Lemos	University of Kent, UK
Roman Vitenberg	University of Oslo, Norway
Sérgio Gorender	Universidade Federal da Bahia, Brazil

Contents

Security Foundations and Compliance

Applying DevSecOps Approach in Legacy Computing Infrastructures:
A Case Study in Public Sector of Brazil 3
   João C. C. Lima, Francisco R. M. Campos, Rafael L. Gomes,
   Emanuel B. Rodrigues, Rossana M. C. Andrade, Clenival L. Silva,
   Daniel C. Bentes, and Alexandre S. Cialdini

SPIRE-Based Remote Attestation for Secure VPN Access 20
   Davi Pontes and Andrey Brito

Towards a Minimum Security Baseline for Cyber-Physical Systems
Through Security Standards Harmonization 37
   Henrique A. Fonseca, João R. Campos, and Regina Moraes

Towards LGPD Compliance: Analysis and Support to Prepare Your
Computing Environment 54
   Aldrey Pedrazoli, Naghmeh Ivaki, and Regina Moraes

AI for Security and Dependability

An Empirical Study of Large Language Models as Experts in Software
Trustworthiness Assessment 75
   Saeed Javani Jananloo, José D'Abruzzo Pereira, and Marco Vieira

FlowMon: A Workflow-Driven Visual Tool for Automated Monitoring
Script Generation 94
   Eduardo Lima, Igor Vanderlei, and Jean Araujo

Reasoning over Vulnerabilities via LogiSec of Thoughts: A Reductio Ad
Absurdum-Based LLM Framework 112
   Claudio A. S. Lelis, Cesar A. C. Marcondes, and Kevin Fealey

Consensus, Cryptography, and Blockchain

A Blockchain-Based Architecture for Communication Between Spectrum
Access Systems 133
   Alan Veloso, Jeffson Sousa, Diego Abreu, Allan Freitas,
   and Antônio Abelém

Byzantine Consensus with Secure and Intrusion-Tolerant In-Network
Ordering   148
*Gabriel Faustino Lima da Rocha, Eduardo A. P. Alchieri,
Giovanni Venâncio, Vinicius Fulber-Garcia, and Elias P. Duarte Jr.*

Thetacrypt: A Distributed Service for Threshold Cryptography   163
*Mariarosaria Barbaraci, Michael Senn, Noah Schmid, Orestis Alpos,
and Christian Cachin*

Modeling and Dependability Evaluation

A Practical TLA+ Library for Designing and Verifying Distributed Systems . . .   183
Diogo Canut Freitas Peixoto and Odorico Machado Mendizabal

Long-Term Experimental Evaluation of Software Aging Effects in NoSQL
Database   201
Paulo Amaral and Jean Araujo

**Advances in Dependable and Secure Computing (Best Paper
Candidates)**

Addressing Cryptographic Overheads in Low-Latency File Systems
Through Ahead-of-Time Encryption   221
Jorge Pires Correia and Wagner Machado N. Zola

Evaluating eBPF as an Alternative to Virtual Machine Introspection
for High-Interaction Honeypot Implementation   238
*Niku Waltteri Saulinpoika Nuutinen, Miguel Faísco, Milan Petrusic,
Ibéria Medeiros, and Hans P. Reiser*

Source Code Vulnerability Detection and Interpretability with Language
Models   255
*Leonardo Silveira, Claudio A. S. Lelis, Cesar A. C. Marcondes,
and Filipe A. N. Verri*

Monitoring and Critical Infrastructures

Impact of Image Resolution on Drone Surveillance System Availability:
A Stochastic Petri Net Approach   275
Ivson Borges, Luan Lins, Gustavo Callou, and Paulo Maciel

Quantitative Availability Analysis of Fog-Edge Monitoring Architectures
in Bus Rapid Transit Station   291
Raquel F. Trajano, Carlos Melo, and Jamilson Ramalho

Industry Track

Malware Detection in Windows Operating Systems Using AI
and In-Memory Process Analysis 311
*Jessica C. C. Patricio, Carlos H. Paiva, Renan L. Rodrigues,
Vanessa C. Lima, and Rafael L. Gomes*

Risk Classification of IP Addresses Using Machine Learning
with Weighted Voting Approach 320
*Francisco V. J. Nobre, Davi O. Alves, Ramon S. Araujo,
Gustavo A. Campos, and Rafael L. Gomes*

Student Forum

Improving Safety in Industry 4.0 Using an IoT-Helmet 331
Evellin S. de Moura, Antônio M. B. Neto, and Rafael L. Gomes

Forecasting-Oriented Management of Software-Defined Fabric
Environments 342
Ariel L. C. Portela, Maria C. M. M. Ferreira, and Rafael L. Gomes

Service Level Agreements Compliance in 5G Network Slicing:
An Analysis of Resource Allocation Strategies 353
Wanderson L. Costa and Rafael L. Gomes

Towards Hierarchical Byzantine Distributed Replication 364
Gabriela Stein, Luiz Antonio Rodrigues, and Elias P. Duarte Jr.

Author Index 377

Security Foundations and Compliance

Applying DevSecOps Approach in Legacy Computing Infrastructures: A Case Study in Public Sector of Brazil

João C. C. Lima[1(✉)], Francisco R. M. Campos[1], Rafael L. Gomes[2], Emanuel B. Rodrigues[1], Rossana M. C. Andrade[1], Clenival L. Silva[3], Daniel C. Bentes[3], and Alexandre S. Cialdini[3]

[1] Federal University of Ceará (UFC), Fortaleza, Ceará, Brazil
`{jcarloslima,ramon}@alu.ufc.br`, `{emanuel,rossana}@dc.ufc.br`
[2] State University of Ceará (UECE), Fortaleza, Ceará, Brazil
`rafa.lopes@uece.br`
[3] State Secretariat of Planning and Management of Ceará (SEPLAG), Fortaleza, Ceará, Brazil
`{clenival.lopes,daniel.bentes,alexandre.cialdini}@seplag.ce.gov.br`

Abstract. Legacy computing environments in the public sector present significant cybersecurity challenges due to outdated systems, technological heterogeneity and complex operational demands. In this context, this paper presents an initial study within a real-world case at a Brazilian governmental institution that applies the DevSecOps methodology in the CI/CD pipeline with two distinct security tools: Static Application Security Testing (SAST) and Vulnerability Management (VM). SAST was applied to assess application security at code level, while VM targeted infrastructure-level risks using metrics such as CVSS and EPSS. The results demonstrate the value of each approach in improving risk visibility and mitigation and the possibility of integrating both tools into a unified DevSecOps workflow, aiming for continuous security and greater operational resilience. This work provides practical insights for public institutions seeking to modernize their cybersecurity posture while addressing the constraints inherent to legacy systems, in alignment with frameworks such as NIST CSF and CIS Controls.

Keywords: Cybersecurity · DevSecOps · CI/CD Pipeline · Application Security Testing · Vulnerability Management · Risk Mitigation

1 Introduction

The landscape of cyber threats in Brazil is rapidly evolving, characterized by increasingly sophisticated tactics that target individuals and institutions alike. Data from Serasa Experian's 2025 Digital Identity and Fraud Report reveals a stark reality: 51% of Brazilians fell victim to fraud in the last year, with a significant portion (54%) experiencing financial losses [28]. This pervasive insecurity underscores the critical need for robust cybersecurity measures, particularly within government institutions.

L. A. Rodrigues and R. Oliveira (Eds.): LADC 2025, CCIS 2697, pp. 3–19, 2026.
https://doi.org/10.1007/978-3-032-11539-3_1

Concurrently, the push for digital transformation in public services has led government agencies to develop numerous software solutions. This rapid growth has created highly heterogeneous technological environments, involving a wide range of libraries, platforms, and frameworks [2,12]. While this fosters innovation, it also increases maintenance complexity, complicates system integration, and heightens information security risks such as update failures and vulnerability exposure [30]. These risks are particularly critical in public institutions like the Secretariat of Planning and Management of Ceará (SEPLAG)[1], which handles sensitive data including personal, fiscal, judicial, and health information. The rising incidence of cyberattacks globally especially in Latin America and Brazil further intensifies the threat landscape [21]. In this context, mitigating vulnerabilities, ensuring service continuity, and complying with data protection regulations such as the LGPD are strategic imperatives [20].

In this complex environment, adopting a DevSecOps methodology becomes essential, as it integrates security practices throughout the Software Development Life Cycle (SDLC), promoting a proactive "security-by-design" approach. This continuous security integration is crucial for managing vulnerabilities in diverse and dynamic public sector infrastructures, aligning with internationally recognized best practices such as the National Institute of Standards and Technology (NIST) Cybersecurity Framework (CSF) [15], which emphasizes continuous risk assessment, protection, and response, and the Center for Internet Security Critical Security Controls (CIS Controls) [3], which provide a prioritized set of defensive measures against common attack vectors.

Within the DevSecOps framework, the Static Application Security Testing (SAST) technique is a integral component of a robust Continuous Integration/Continuous Delivery (CI/CD) pipeline. Since it enables the identification of vulnerabilities directly within the source code [4], SAST allows for early detection of security flaws, adhering to the "shift-left" principle of DevSecOps. This proactive approach is particularly valuable in the early stages of development, minimizing the cost and effort associated with fixing vulnerabilities later in the cycle.

Additionaly, Vulnerability Management (VM) plays a fundamental strategic role, especially given the aforementioned complexity and heterogeneity of public agency computing environments [26]. Unlike homogeneous setups, public institutions contend with a diverse ecosystem of legacy systems, modern applications, varied hardware, and a wide spectrum of user profiles. This process allows for the systematic identification of technical flaws and configuration gaps that could be exploited by malicious actors, safeguarding sensitive data confidentiality, critical system integrity, and public service continuity [7].

Within this context, this paper presents a case study on the application of critical security practices of DevSecOps (in particular SAST and VM) in the context of the Secretariat of Planning and Management of Ceará (SEPLAG) in Brazil. These practices were applied in the IT processes, allowing the evaluation

---

[1] https://www.seplag.ce.gov.br.

of their effectiveness in identifying and mitigating security risks within legacy public sector environments.

The remainder of this paper is organized as follows. Section 2 presents some existing work about DevSecOps and security solutions. Section 3 describes the methodology applied, while Sect. 4 outlines the experimental setup and discusses the results. Finally, Sects. 5 and 6 present the final discussion, conclusions and perspectives of future work.

2   Related Work

This section presents some work on the combined use of SAST, VM and other security tools in DevSecOps pipelines, emphasizing how this combined strategy can strengthen the cybersecurity posture of digital public services.

Riaz et al. [25] analyze the integration of VM, SAST and DAST within the DevSecOps framework as essential strategies to strengthen software security throughout the development lifecycle. By embedding security practices into every phase of DevOps, the study emphasizes the importance of identifying, assessing, and remediating vulnerabilities proactively to prevent security breaches and ensure compliance with industry standards. Through a Multivocal Literature Review (MLR), the authors analyze both academic and industry sources to highlight key metrics for evaluating the effectiveness of DevSecOps implementations. The paper ultimately reinforces the critical role of structured VM and automated testing tools like SAST and DAST in building secure, resilient systems especially in environments where rapid, automated deployments are the norm.

Marandi et al. [13] present a practical approach to integrating VM with SAST and DAST within DevSecOps pipelines, specifically in the context of containerized applications and CI/CD environments. Recognizing the increased security risks introduced by containerization and automated deployments, the research focuses on automated security scanning of software images deployed in cloud infrastructures. It proposes a method using Snyk (for SAST) and StackHawk (for DAST) to scan application images during the build process, providing a dashboard for tracking vulnerabilities and automating fixes. The tools are integrated with GitHub, enabling continuous vulnerability detection and remediation as part of the CI/CD workflow. The study demonstrates that this integration improves security by reducing the time required to identify and address vulnerabilities, thereby strengthening the overall security posture of applications in DevSecOps environments.

A relevant study conducted in a Mexican government organization [5] presents the implementation of a DevSecOps strategy within a responsive infrastructure designed to ensure high availability, cybersecurity, and risk management. The initiative aimed to support the automation of critical processes by leveraging modern technologies such as microservices and container-based architectures, allowing for scalable and fault-tolerant systems. The authors emphasize the use of DevSecOps as an integral solution to reduce project delivery times while enhancing the quality and security of public digital services. Rooted in agile and lean principles, the DevSecOps approach in this case promotes strong collaboration between IT professionals and developers, enabling continuous and secure deployment in complex public-sector environments. This study demonstrates how DevSecOps can be effectively adapted to the specific needs of government data centers to improve both operational efficiency and service delivery to citizens.

Efendi et al. [6] explore the integration of the DevSecOps approach within a public-sector organization, specifically the Public Company Logistic Agency (PCLA), to address challenges in application development such as project delays, frequent late-stage changes, and high vulnerability levels. Through a Systematic Literature Review (SLR) and a mixed-method research approach, the authors identified DevSecOps transformation phases and best practices from various case studies. The study highlights how DevSecOps can help public institutions like PCLA reduce operational costs, enhance software quality, and strengthen security throughout the software development lifecycle. By adopting DevSecOps, PCLA aims to modernize its development processes and align them with industry standards, offering valuable insights for both academics and practitioners in the digital transformation of state-owned enterprises.

As presented by [10], the NIST CSF was applied to assess the cybersecurity posture of a local government organization in Western Australia. Their methodology enabled the quantification of risk across the CSF's core functions and categories, helping to identify specific gaps in people, processes, and technologies. Based on this assessment, strategic recommendations were provided to guide mitigation efforts and strengthen future security capabilities. The authors emphasize the comparative advantages of the NIST CSF over other frameworks, particularly in facilitating structured evaluations. They also note that, despite some implementation challenges, the framework is effective in guiding organizations toward measurable improvements. Future work aims to enhance the assessment tool used in the study, making it more adaptable and accessible for broader adoption.

The main contribution of the present study, in comparison to the cited works, lies in the practical and structured application of security techniques SAST and VM within the legacy infrastructure of a real public-sector organization (SEPLAG), a context still underexplored in the literature. Unlike prior studies that focus on generic DevSecOps strategies or implementations in cloud-native and highly automated environments, this work demonstrates the technical feasibility of adopting DevSecOps practices in traditional legacy systems by integrating tools such as Trivy, Semgrep, and OpenVAS into an existing CI/CD pipeline. It also provides concrete performance and risk metrics (e.g., execution times, CVSS severities, and EPSS scores), while adopting a prioritization approach aligned with the NIST CSF and CIS Controls. By combining empirical evidence with internationally recognized best practices, this study offers a replicable model for public institutions seeking to modernize legacy systems with a strong cybersecurity posture.

3   Methodology

Figure 1 presents the DevSecOps methodology adopted in this work for incorporating security practices into the software development process at SEPLAG, with a focus on two distinct approaches: SAST and VM.

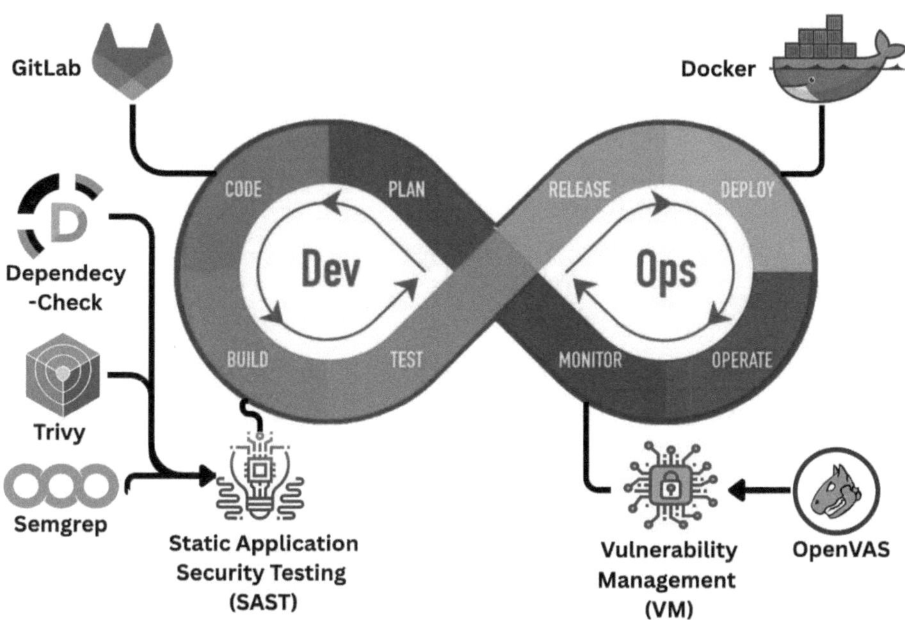

Fig. 1. DevSecOps methodology and security tools used in the case study.

The DevSecOps loop integrates security practices throughout all stages of the software development life cycle, ensuring that security is a continuous and automated concern. During the Plan phase, teams can incorporate threat modeling to anticipate potential risks and define mitigation strategies early. In the Code phase, security starts with developer awareness and secure coding practices, complemented by tools such as Semgrep for SAST. The Build phase benefits from dependency checks (e.g., using tools like Trivy or Dependency-Check) to detect known vulnerabilities in third-party libraries. In the Test phase, automated security testing, including SAST, ensures that vulnerabilities are caught before deployment. The Release and Deploy phases involve secure configuration practices and container scanning (e.g., with Trivy) to validate the runtime environment. Once in Operate and Monitor, VM practices are applied, such as scanning infrastructure with OpenVAS, enabling continuous risk assessment and remediation. While intrusion testing is traditionally manual and periodic, it can complement this continuous model by validating the effectiveness of protections under real-world attack scenarios. In our implementation, SAST tools were used to detect vulnerabilities in the application's source code, while VM targeted infrastructure-level weaknesses.

Our objective was to explore how they might be integrated into a unified and automated security workflow, aiming to promote continuous and comprehensive security throughout the software development life cycle.

Although the current work focuses on the public sector within a governmental institution, the processes and methods discussed are equally applicable to private sector environments, where security demands and development practices often mirror those found in public organizations.

The subsequent subsections detail the techniques, tools, and procedures employed in the current DevSecOps implementation.

3.1   Static Application Security Testing (SAST)

The SAST technique was integrated directly into the CI/CD pipeline, promoting a preventive and continuous security approach in the software development cycle. This integration allows for early detection of flaws, optimizing the cost and time of correction.

The following tools were used for static analysis:

- **Trivy**[2]: A scanner for vulnerabilities in containers, code repositories, and packages.
- **Semgrep**[3]: A customizable static analysis tool applicable to various programming languages.
- **Dependency Check**[4]: Detects publicly disclosed vulnerabilities in project dependencies, utilizing an extensive database (National Vulnerability Database - NVD) for its analysis.

These tools provide detailed and standardized results, with the ability to integrate into CI/CD pipelines, facilitating rapid identification and correction of vulnerabilities throughout development. In addition, they were chosen because they are widely adopted by the development and security communities, including major companies and open-source projects. They are also actively updated to better respond to emerging security threats. Their use in academic and educational settings further reinforces their credibility and technical value.

For the classification of vulnerabilities found by SAST tools, the *Common Vulnerabilities and Exposures* (CVE)[5] and *Common Weakness Enumeration* (CWE)[6] lists were used.

- **CVE**: Managed by MITRE, this list organizes information on publicly known vulnerabilities, serving as a widely used standard in cybersecurity research and studies [29]. Each vulnerability has a severity score calculated by the CVSS [8].

---

[2] https://github.com/aquasecurity/trivy.
[3] https://github.com/semgrep/semgrep.
[4] https://github.com/dependency-check/DependencyCheck.
[5] https://cve.mitre.org.
[6] https://cwe.mitre.org.

- **CWE**: Also managed by MITRE, CWE provides information on common types of software weaknesses, along with mitigation strategies and good development practices to avoid introducing these weaknesses [11, 27].

The CVE focuses on documenting specific security flaws in systems and applications that can then each be linked to one or more CWE classifications, which are a more general type of categorization, with one CWE being associated with any CVE that fits the category. This association between the two lists ensures that, when used together, a comprehensive and standardized assessment of flaws is achieved, promoting greater traceability and effective prioritization of fixes.

The phases of a CI/CD pipeline bring together practices and tools aimed at automating the software development process, from code integration to its deployment in production [13, 23]. The secure CI/CD pipeline in this work was designed to integrate the aforementioned SAST tools, ensuring that each code update in the repository triggers an automatic analysis. For the pipeline's execution environment, a local GitLab docker instance was created to run the pipeline on GitLab CI/CD. The integration begins in the Build phase, where static security analysis is performed with the following configurations:

- **Trivy**: Configured to scan the container created in the build phase while filtering for high and critical vulnerabilities. It generates a report in HTML format.
- **Semgrep**: Configured to automatically identify the programming language of code base and use the appropriate ruleset. It generates a report in JSON format.
- **Dependency-Check**: Under default configurations, database download is very slow, so to optimize the download process and reduce latency, an NVD API key was used [16]. It generates a report in HTML format.

Because the pipeline was designed for the three tools to generate their own report, there may be situations where overlapping information appears across the reports. In such cases, the technical team of the government institution will perform a cross-analysis. In addition, all generated reports are set to expire after one day.

3.2   Vulnerability Management (VM)

Vulnerability management followed a cycle of continuous improvement and risk-based prioritization, adapting to the operational constraints and technological environment of the institution. In this work, the main steps were:

1. **Information Collection and Asset Mapping**:
   Initially, a collaborative survey was conducted with the institution's technical team to identify available network ranges, the most relevant assets, and appropriate periods for conducting tests. This step is crucial for contextualizing security analyses and efficiently directing efforts. The prioritization of

hosts for analysis considered the viability of execution under network constraints, such as firewall rules and access restrictions to servers. Additionally, hosts with associated PTR (Pointer) records were prioritized, as they were more likely to be exposed to external networks and thus represented potentially higher risk. These criteria helped optimize resource allocation while focusing on targets with greater exposure and feasibility of assessment.

2. **Vulnerability Scanning**: The analysis was performed using the open-source tool OpenVAS[7], which is widely recognized in the security community for vulnerability detection. Tests were run in unauthenticated mode, simulating the behavior of an external attacker without valid credentials. This approach allowed us to identify flaws exposed directly on the network surface, respecting operational limitations and avoiding impacts on production systems. These actions were performed outside of business hours to mitigate any impact on the institution's production network.

3. **Vulnerability Analysis, Classification, and Prioritization**: Detected vulnerabilities were classified based on CVSS (Common Vulnerability Scoring System) [8], assigning severity levels (Low, Medium, High and Critical). This classification, automatically provided by OpenVAS based on the Common Vulnerabilities and Exposures (CVE) database, considers aspects such as attack vector, exploitation complexity, required privileges, and impact on confidentiality, integrity, and availability. For more assertive prioritization, the CVSS classification was complemented with the EPSS (Exploit Prediction Scoring System) metric [9], which estimates the actual probability of exploitation for each flaw. EPSS, expressed as a score between 0 and 1, indicates the likelihood that a vulnerability will be exploited by malicious agents within 30 days of its disclosure. Additionally, the existence of a publicly available exploit (software, data block, or exploitation script) in repositories such as Exploit-DB [18] or Metasploit [24] was considered an additional risk factor, as it significantly increases the likelihood that the vulnerability will be exploited by low-sophisticated attackers. The context of the affected asset (function, exposure to Internet, criticality) was also evaluated to refine prioritization.

4. **Consolidation and Continuous Monitoring**: The data generated in the previous steps was consolidated into a document containing an action plan, allowing the agency's technical team to monitor the progress of corrections and implement a continuous remediation cycle.

---

[7] https://www.openvas.org.

4   Results and Discussion

This section presents the results obtained from the case study conducted at SEPLAG, aiming to evaluate the effectiveness of the security practices applied by two distinct but complementary techniques: SAST and VM.

The findings serve as proof of concept, providing an initial assessment of the integration of both approaches into a unified security workflow aligned with DevSecOps principles. This evaluation ensures a solid methodological foundation for subsequent iterations and broader application in real production environments.

4.1   SAST Analysis Results

This section presents the results of applying the CI/CD pipeline with SAST at SEPLAG.

Regarding execution time, the Trivy and Semgrep tools had an execution time of less than 30 s each, while the Dependency Check tool, using the NVD API key, took around 3 min. Thus, the total execution time of the SAST tools in the CI/CD pipeline was around 4 min for a repository with around 23000 lines of code written, making its execution feasible in a real-world scenario and demonstrating that it can be successfully applied to repositories of similar size.

Throughout the analysis, several security vulnerabilities were identified in the application's source code, such as *misconfigurations* and critical flaws, which could be exploited by attackers to gain unauthorized access to sensitive data. A total of 8 vulnerabilities were found during the SAST analysis of an application chosen by SEPLAG, with the following severity distribution (calculated using CVSS): 1 High (CVSS between 7.0 and 8.9), 6 Medium (between 4.0 and 6.9), and 1 Low (between 0.1 and 3.9). This CVSS-based severity categorization was essential for strategically prioritizing fixes, allowing SEPLAG's workforce to be used more effectively. Additionally, Table 1 divides the vulnerabilities found by an assigned number - omitting direct mentions of related CVEs at the request of the institution - their associated CWE and their overall severity, exploitability, and impact scores, calculated using the CVSS v3.1 calculator from NIST [17].

It is noted that most of the vulnerabilities found have an exploitability score lower than 5.0, indicating a low probability of a malicious attack. However, half of the vulnerabilities have an impact score greater than 6.0, with emphasis on vulnerability 01, classified with CWE-200, which has the maximum impact on the application as it is related to the exposure of sensitive information to an unauthorized actor. This fact indicates that, if exploited, this vulnerability could cause significant damage to SEPLAG's assets. These results demonstrate the importance of the CI/CD pipeline with applied SAST, enabling the discovery and correction of vulnerabilities.

The found vulnerabilities can be divided into three categories: (1) Sensitive Data Exposure; (2) Insecure Service Configuration; and (3) Improper Configurations.

Table 1. Vulnerabilities with severity, exploitability, and impact scores.

Vulnerability Number	Common Weakness Enumeration (CWE)	Severity	Exploitability	Impact
01	CWE-200: Exposure of Sensitive Information to an Unauthorized Actor	7.5	5	10
02	CWE-863: Incorrect Authorization	6.8	6.7	6.9
03	CWE-321: Use of Hard-coded Cryptographic Key	6.4	4.8	8
04	CWE-35 Path Traversal	6.3	5.6	7
05	CWE-732: Incorrect Permission Assignment for Critical Resource	4.2	3.4	5
06	CWE-732: Incorrect Permission Assignment for Critical Resource	4.2	3.4	5
07	CWE-209: Generation of Error Message Containing Sensitive Information	4.2	3.4	5
08	CWE-358: Improperly Implemented Security Check for Standard	2	2	2

The first one refers to problems of exposing confidential information in improper locations or to unauthorized users, as in vulnerabilities 01 and 03, classified with CWE-200 and CWE-321 respectively. Furthermore, excessively descriptive error messages, as in vulnerability 07, classified with CWE-209, can reveal sensitive information about the application's structure. To mitigate these risks, confidential data must be stored and managed in secure locations, and for more generic messages to be used to communicate application errors to users.

The second category refers to services used or implemented that were not configured securely, as in the case of vulnerabilities 06 and 07, both classified with CWE-732, where there is incorrect permission assignment, and in the case of vulnerability 08, classified with CWE-358, where there is an improperly implemented security check for a pre-established standard, increasing the risk of application compromise. To mitigate them, it is necessary to remove the incorrect assignments and follow good security practices for the services.

Finally, the third category comprises improper configurations in the application. This includes vulnerability 02, classified with CWE-863, where improper configuration of authorization checks allows unauthorized actions to be performed, as well as vulnerability 04, classified with CWE-35, which indicates the possibility of externally manipulating the path of the file being accessed by the application, allowing access to restricted files and directories. To reduce these risks, it is necessary to reinforce access control and data input validation policies.

Alternatively, we can also divide them using the OWASP Top 10 2021 list because each category is mapped to a set of CWEs [19]. However, not all CWEs are contemplated in OWASP top 10 2021, and thus not all 8 vulnerabilities can be classified using it. In this list, vulnerabilities 01, 02 and 04 are classified as A01:2021 Broken Access Control, while vulnerabilities 03 and 07 are A02:2021 Cryptographic Failures and A04:2021 Insecure Design, respectively. Vulnerabilities 05, 06 and 08's CWE are not mapped to any OWASP Top 10 classification.

From the presented results, although the SAST tools used in this work are already widely known in the industry and thus not innovative by themselves, it is clear that the application of SAST techniques by integrating these tools in SEPLAG's CI/CD pipeline represents an innovation in the context of public administration, which has historically faced challenges implementing security automation and DevSecOps culture. The introduction of these tools represents, when compared to the application's previous pipeline, an improvement in coverage and standardization in vulnerability detection that outweighs the increase in pipeline execution time to around 4 min. It reinforces the importance of adopting continuous security practices in the SSDLC, promoting a preventive and sustainable culture of protecting public sector digital assets while adhering to the operational constraints common in the sector. Furthermore, the application of the CI/CD pipeline with SAST directly aligns with international security best practices, such as the NIST CSF and the CIS Controls, by incorporating automated and continuous mechanisms for identifying and mitigating vulnerabilities throughout the development cycle [1].

4.2   VM Analysis Results

The results of the case study presented in this section represent a proof of concept of the VM process, conducted at SEPLAG to obtain results that serve as a basis for validating the approaches and techniques used. This stage aims to ensure the effectiveness of the process before its full application in the real environment analyzed, ensuring greater accuracy and reliability in future results.

The analysis of the identified vulnerabilities is essential to understand the criticality of each one of them, and the CVSS score plays a crucial role in this process. In total, 82 vulnerabilities were identified during the scanning process, with severities (High, Medium, and Low) distributed as follows: 19 High (23.17%), 33 Medium (40.24%) and 30 Low (36.59%). Vulnerabilities classified as high should be treated with top priority, while those of medium and low severity can be scheduled for correction in a medium/long-term mitigation schedule.

OpenVAS identifies several network protocols to detect vulnerabilities in services, including TCP (Transmission Control Protocol), UDP (User Datagram Protocol), and ICMP (Internet Control Message Protocol) for basic communication and host discovery, as well as several application protocols, such as HTTP (Hypertext Transfer Protocol), SSH (Secure Shell), and RDP (Remote Desktop Protocol) [22].

For a more in-depth analysis of asset exposure, Fig. 2 shows the distribution of vulnerabilities identified by service port, segmented according to CVSS severity. The five services/ports with the highest number of occurrences were considered, allowing a clear visualization of the criticality associated with each exposed service. This approach allows for the visualization of which services are most vulnerable, facilitating the prioritization of mitigation actions in critical areas.

Among the vulnerabilities with ports identified, critical services stand out, such as SSH (port 22), HTTPS (port 443), and RDP (port 3389), which should be prioritized due to their operational relevance and potential impact in case of

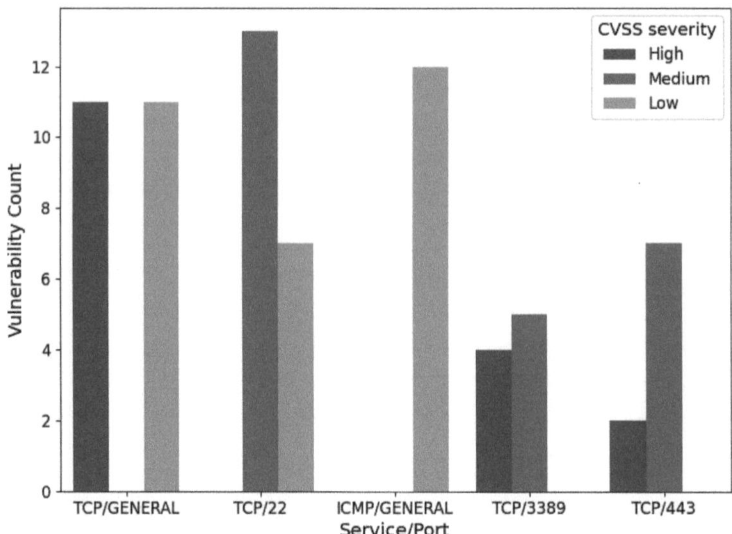

Fig. 2. Analysis by port/service.

exploitation. In addition, vulnerabilities related to Windows network services, such as RPC (Remote Procedure Call) and SMB (Server Message Block) protocols, were also detected, reinforcing the need for specific assessments in these areas. Additionally, OpenVAS may indicate that some occurrences were classified as "GENERAL", which means that the tool was unable to determine the source port of the vulnerability directly. In these cases, it is essential that the reported vulnerability be assessed on the server to identify which ports are effectively impacted. This distribution of vulnerabilities allows mitigation actions to be directed to the most critical services and ports susceptible to attacks, optimizing the use of resources and increasing the effectiveness of the security measures implemented.

Figure 3 presents a joint analysis of the CVSS and EPSS metrics of a set of identified vulnerabilities, allowing a more accurate assessment of both the potential impact and the practical exploitability of each vulnerability. For example, CVEs 3, 4, and 5 are highly critical because they have a High severity (CVSS 9.8, 9.3, and 8.8, respectively) and high exploitability (EPSS 0.975, 0.795, and 0.968, respectively). On the other hand, the vulnerability represented as CVE-1 presented a CVSS of 7.5 (High severity) and an extremely low EPSS (0.001), indicating a technically severe flaw, but with a low probability of exploitation in the current scenario. CVEs 2 and 6 deserve attention because, despite having low severity, they have high exploitability and may be initial or intermediate stages in the chain of events of a cyberattack.

Figure 4 shows the distribution of the number of vulnerabilities associated with each asset identified in the environment. This graph provides a clear view of which assets have the highest number of vulnerabilities. In this analysis, it is

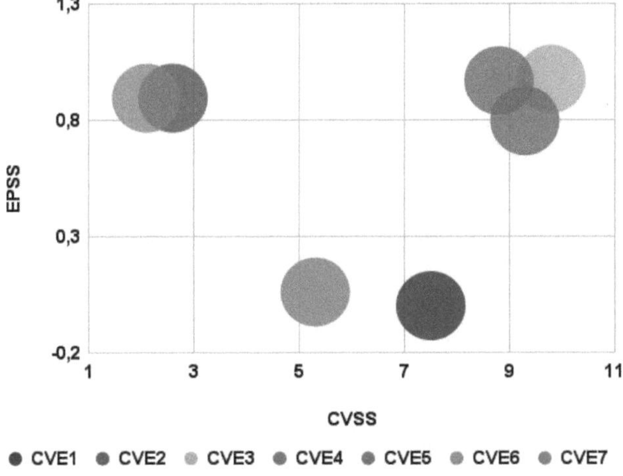

Fig. 3. Analysis by severity and exploitability.

important to consider the type and context of the asset, for example, whether it is a server or a common workstation, whether it is exposed to the Internet or not, whether it contains databases that are critical to the organization, etc. This contextualized analysis allows for a correct classification of the risk of vulnerabilities and a more assertive prioritization of the corrections that will need to be made. By analyzing this information, security teams can direct efforts to the most exposed assets, optimizing the use of resources and reducing the risk of critical infrastructure compromises.

The results obtained demonstrate the effectiveness of VM, integrating severity (CVSS), exploitability (EPSS), the existence of public exploits, and the environment context. In addition, it is worth noting that the study aligns with international security best practices, such as the NIST CSF and CIS Controls [1], by structuring a process for identifying and prioritizing vulnerabilities based on risk metrics and operational context. Regarding the NIST CSF, the functions "Identify", "Protect", and "Detect" are used through asset mapping, vulnerability scanning with OpenVAS, and the use of indicators such as CVSS and EPSS. Similarly, about CIS Controls, the highlights are asset inventory controls, continuous vulnerability management, and verification of the existence of public exploits. Thus, the work establishes a solid foundation for the prevention of cyberattacks and more effective incident response plans, aligned with widely recognized frameworks [14].

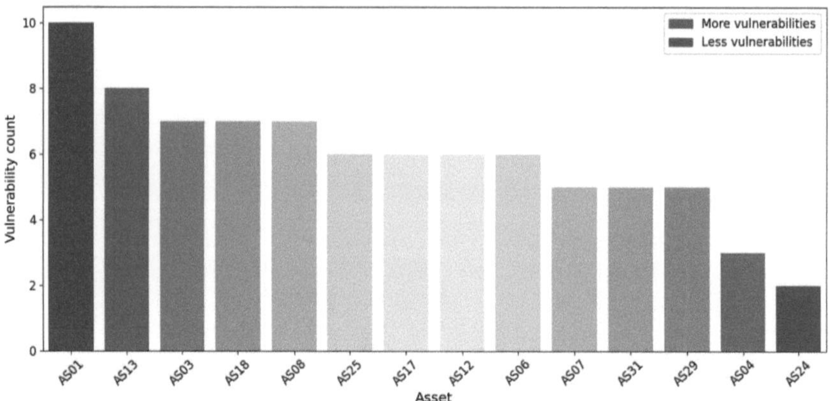

Fig. 4. Total vulnerabilities per asset.

5   Main Findings

This study evaluated the application of structured security techniques within SEPLAG's legacy environment, focusing on two complementary techniques: SAST at the application development level and VM at the infrastructure level. The findings validate the feasibility and effectiveness of these techniques and offer insights into their practical integration into a DevSecOps workflow. We present below the main findings in this research:

Static Application Security Testing (SAST)

- The CI/CD pipeline with integrated SAST tools (Trivy, Semgrep, and Dependency Check) achieved full execution in under 4 min, proving viable for real-world DevSecOps adoption.
- A total of 8 code-level vulnerabilities were identified, including 1 High, 6 Moderate, and 1 Low severity.
- Vulnerabilities fell into three main CWE categories: (1) Sensitive Data Exposure; (2) Insecure Service Configuration; and (3) Improper Configurations.
- Despite relatively low exploitability in most cases, several vulnerabilities had high impact scores, posing serious risk if exploited - especially the exposure of sensitive information.
- The approach reinforced international best practices by integrating automated security checks into the software development life cycle (SDLC).

Vulnerability Management (VM)

- A total of 82 vulnerabilities were identified through network scanning using OpenVAS, with the following severity distribution based on CVSS scores: 19 High, 33 Medium, and 30 Low.

- Critical services such as SSH (port 22), HTTPS (port 443), and RDP (port 3389) were among the most exposed, highlighting the need for prioritized mitigation.
- The analysis also incorporated EPSS metrics to assess exploitability, identifying vulnerabilities with high impact and high likelihood of exploitation (e.g., CVEs with CVSS > 8.8 and EPSS > 0.9).
- Asset-level mapping showed an uneven distribution of vulnerabilities, allowing targeted remediation strategies based on operational risk and system criticality.
- The process was aligned with best practices from the NIST CSF and CIS Controls, supporting structured risk-based prioritization.

6   Conclusion

This study demonstrated the feasibility and relevance of applying structured security methodologies to legacy environments in the public sector, where technological diversity and operational constraints demand adaptable and effective cybersecurity strategies. Adopting the DevSecOps methodology becomes crucial for protecting citizen data, keeping services running, and maintaining trust in online public offerings. In this context, two complementary approaches were applied independently in this work: SAST at the development pipeline level and VM at the infrastructure level. The results confirm that addressing vulnerabilities at both levels is essential for improving cyber resilience.

As part of the results, detailed reports were prepared and delivered to the management team, outlining the main findings from each individual analysis. These reports included specific mitigation recommendations for the vulnerabilities identified, as well as a proposed action plan to ensure continuity of security assessments. This plan is intended to support strategic decision-making, enabling managers to prioritize high-risk issues and take immediate corrective measures when necessary.

Although DAST was not implemented in this work due to limitations in SEPLAG's current infrastructure, its importance in runtime security analysis is well recognized. Future work intends to expand the security pipeline to include DAST, further aligning with DevSecOps principles and strengthening SEPLAG's proactive cybersecurity posture.

Acknowledgment. The authors would like to thank CNPq (Processes 306362/2021-0 and 303877/2021-9) and FUNCAP/SEPLAG, through the Chief Scientist program in the project "Vulnerability Testing and Cybersecurity Monitoring in SEPLAG Computer Systems and Networks", for the financial support.

References

1. Bashofi, I., Salman, M.: Cybersecurity maturity assessment design using NIST CSF, CIS Controls v8 and ISO/IEC 27002. In: 2022 IEEE International Conference on Cybernetics and Computational Intelligence (CyberneticsCom). pp. 58–62. IEEE (2022)
2. Bower, L.: Brazil as a leader in digital transformation. In: Proceedings of the 16th International Conference on Theory and Practice of Electronic Governance. pp. 80–85 (2023)
3. Center for Internet Security: CIS Critical Security Controls v8. https://www.cisecurity.org/controls/cis-controls-list (2023). Accessed 03 Jul 2025
4. Darus, M.Y., Bolhan, M.F.B., Kurniawan, A., Muliono, Y., Pardomuan, C.R., Hata, M.M.: Enhancing web application penetration testing with a static application security testing (SAST) tool. In: 2023 IEEE 8th International Conference on Recent Advances and Innovations in Engineering (ICRAIE). pp. 1–6. IEEE (2023)
5. Díaz, O., Muñoz, M., Mejía, J.: Responsive infrastructure with cybersecurity for automated high availability devsecops processes. In: 2019 8th International Conference On Software Process Improvement (CIMPS). pp. 1–9 (2019). https://doi.org/10.1109/CIMPS49236.2019.9082439
6. Efendi, M., Raharjo, T., Suhanto, A.: Devsecops approach in software development case study: Public company logistic agency. In: 2021 International Conference on Informatics, Multimedia, Cyber and Information System (ICIMCIS. pp. 96–101 (2021). https://doi.org/10.1109/ICIMCIS53775.2021.9699316
7. Ficco, M., Granata, D., Palmieri, F., Rak, M.: A systematic approach for threat and vulnerability analysis of unmanned aerial vehicles. Internet of Things **26**, 101180 (2024)
8. FIRST: Forum of Incident Response and Security Teams - Common Vulnerability Scoring System v3.1: Specification Document (2019). https://www.first.org/cvss/specification-document, acessado em: 17 maio 2025
9. FIRST: Forum of Incident Response and Security Teams - Exploit Prediction Scoring System (EPSS) – v2 Model Documentation (2022). https://www.first.org/epss/model, acesso em: 17 maio 2025
10. Ibrahim, A., Valli, C., McAteer, I., Chaudhry, J.: A security review of local government using nist csf: a case study. J. Supercomput. **74**, 5171–5186 (2018)
11. Kota, K., Manjunatha, A., et al.: CWE prediction using CVE description-the semantic similarity approach. Proc. Comput. Sci. **235**, 1167–1178 (2024)
12. Lanza, B.B.B., Ávila, T.J.T., Valotto, D.: An overview of rede.gov.br as a federative mechanism for digital government development in Brazil. In: Proceedings of the 23rd Annual International Conference on Digital Government Research. pp. 380–390 (2022)
13. Marandi, M., Bertia, A., Silas, S.: Implementing and automating security scanning to a devsecops ci/cd pipeline. In: 2023 World Conference on Communication and Computing (WCONF). pp. 1–6 (2023). https://doi.org/10.1109/WCONF58270.2023.10235015
14. Möller, D.P.F. et al.: NIST cybersecurity framework and MITRE cybersecurity criteria. In: Guide to Cybersecurity in Digital Transformation: Trends, Methods, Technologies, Applications and Best Practices, vol. 103, pp. 231–271, Springer, Cham (2023). https://doi.org/10.1007/978-3-031-26845-8_5
15. National Institute of Standards and Technology (NIST): Framework for Improving Critical Infrastructure Cybersecurity, Version 1.1. Tech. rep., NIST (April 2018).

https://nvlpubs.nist.gov/nistpubs/CSWP/NIST.CSWP.04162018.pdf, acesso em: 17 maio 2025

16. NIST: NVD API: keys, documentation, and request limits. National Institute of Standards and Technology. https://nvd.nist.gov/general/news/API-Key-Announcement (2023). acessado em: 25 de Maio de 2025

17. NIST: Common vulnerability scoring system (CVSS) calculator. National Institute of Standards and Technology. https://nvd.nist.gov/vuln-metrics/cvss/v3-calculator (2025). acessado em: 17 de maio de 2025

18. Offensive Security: Exploit Database (Exploit-DB) (2025). https://www.exploit-db.com. acesso em: 17 maio 2025

19. OWASP: Owasp top 10. Open Web Application Security Project https://owasp.org/Top10/ (2021). Accessed 04 Jul 2025

20. Pimenta, I., Silva, D., Moura, E., Silveira, M., Gomes, R.L.: Impact of data anonymization in machine learning models. In: Proceedings of the 13th Latin-American Symposium on Dependable and Secure Computing. p. 188–191. LADC '24, Association for Computing Machinery, New York, NY, USA (2024). https://doi.org/10.1145/3697090.3699865, https://doi.org/10.1145/3697090.3699865

21. Prabowo, Set al.: Privacy-preserving tools and technologies: Government adoption and challenges. IEEE Access (2025)

22. Rahalkar, S.: OpenVAS. In: Quick Start Guide to Penetration Testing: With NMAP, OpenVAS and Metasploit, pp. 47–71. Springer (2018). https://doi.org/10.1007/978-1-4842-4270-4

23. Rangnau, T., Buijtenen, R.v., Fransen, F., Turkmen, F.: Continuous security testing: A case study on integrating dynamic security testing tools in CI/CD pipelines. In: 2020 IEEE 24th International Enterprise Distributed Object Computing Conference (EDOC). pp. 145–154. IEEE (2020)

24. Rapid7: Metasploit Framework (2025). https://www.metasploit.com. acesso em: 17 maio 2025

25. Riaz, S., et al.: Software development empowered and secured by integrating a devsecops design. J. Comput. Biomed. Inf. **8**(02) (2025)

26. Safitra, M.F., Lubis, M., Widjajarto, A.: Security vulnerability analysis using penetration testing execution standard (PTES): case study of government's website. In: Proceedings of the 2023 6th international conference on electronics, communications and control engineering. pp. 139–145 (2023)

27. Santos, J.C., Tarrit, K., Sejfia, A., Mirakhorli, M., Galster, M.: An empirical study of tactical vulnerabilities. J. Syst. Softw. **149**, 263–284 (2019)

28. Serasa Experian: Relatório de identidade digital e fraude (2025), edição Especial Segmento Financeiro

29. Wang, T., Qin, S., Chow, K.P.: Towards vulnerability types classification using pure self-attention: A common weakness enumeration based approach. In: 2021 IEEE 24th International Conference on Computational Science and Engineering (CSE). pp. 146–153. IEEE (2021)

30. Zheng, Y., Li, Z., Xu, X., Zhao, Q.: Dynamic defenses in cyber security: Techniques, methods and challenges. Digital Commun. Netw. **8**(4), 422–435 (2022)

SPIRE-Based Remote Attestation
for Secure VPN Access

Davi Pontes$^{(\boxtimes)}$ and Andrey Brito

Federal University of Campina Grande, Campina Grande, PB 58429-900, Brazil
`davi.pontes@ccc.ufcg.edu.br`, `andrey@computacao.ufcg.edu.br`
`https://www.computacao.ufcg.edu.br/`

Abstract. This work proposes an intermediate solution between a full-fledged Zero-Trust Architecture (ZTA) for remote access and a conventional, less secure Virtual Private Network (VPN). Our approach enhances the authentication component of VPNs to help achieve some of the benefits of ZTA without requiring modifications to the VPN infrastructure or code. We leverage the Cloud Native Computing Foundation's open-source standard, SPIFFE, and its reference implementation, SPIRE, to build an attestation-based authorization for VPN access. The work proposes new node and workload attestors for SPIRE, enabling the verification of user and machine identity before granting access to the VPN. SPIRE also provides automatic credential rotation, which avoids long-term credentials and consequently minimizes the impact if the credentials are stolen. Finally, the paper provides an overview of the major security issues associated with traditional VPN authentication methods, such as credential or physical device theft, and how the proposed solution addresses these threats.

Keywords: Device Attestation · User Authentication · Zero Trust Security · Virtual Private Network (VPN) · Remote Attestation · SPIFFE · SPIRE · Multi-Factor Authentication (MFA)

1 Introduction

After the COVID-19 pandemic, organizations worldwide had to adopt the home-office system, causing many employees to use their personal computers (PCs) to work from home (or to use work PCs for personal usage). This shift introduced significant security concerns. Previously, organizations maintained a well-defined security perimeter around their managed workstations. However, after this change, the workstations were widely distributed, often beyond the organization's control, making it difficult to verify who accessed these machines and ensure a secure work environment. Even with the end of the pandemic, many of these companies have continued to maintain this work model.

A virtual private network (VPN) [8] helps solve some security issues associated with remote work. With it, the organization can protect sensitive resources

L. A. Rodrigues and R. Oliveira (Eds.): LADC 2025, CCIS 2697, pp. 20–36, 2026.
https://doi.org/10.1007/978-3-032-11539-3_2

within an emulation of a private network built upon a potentially unprotected network infrastructure, such as the Internet, granting access to these resources only to authenticated and authorized users. This solution gives the organization more control over its resource access. However, they still have problems with the security of the employees' PCs.

In the old, physical-office habits, the organizations had control over the workstations' physical and logical security, monitoring who had physical access to the machines and constantly applying security patches and critical updates on the Operating System (OS), but with the home office and the usage of PCs for work, this control has been lost. Although VPNs can help protect the communication channel between the employee's PC and the company's servers, they do not guarantee that the person using the credentials or the computer accessing the private resources is authorized to do so.

In addition to VPNs, Zero Trust Architectures (ZTAs) [2] also help solve the remote access to restricted resources. Unlike VPNs, ZT network security models do not emulate a private network over the original infrastructure; instead, they verify every access request, regardless of location, before granting access to resources. To do so, every component accessing the infrastructure must have its identity. With this, identity and permission verifications can be performed before granting access to any resources within the infrastructure. In this model, the components must be constantly verified, and one way to achieve this is through an attestation process; the component must present proof of identity and current state to obtain the necessary credentials. Although ZTAs solve the identity verification issues that VPNs face, they also require significant resource management and protection modifications, making ZTA implementations more complex than VPN implementations.

This work proposes a solution to address the VPN user identity verification challenge by modifying the process by which users obtain VPN credentials. Instead of relying on static credentials distributed by the organization, we propose an attestation-based approach to provide short-term credentials. The solution leverages the Cloud Native Computing Foundation's open-source standard, SPIFFE, and its reference implementation, SPIRE, to establish a reliable and scalable method for continuously verifying users and their devices. Through this identity verification process, users can obtain VPN credentials without relying on static, long-term credentials that could be stolen or misused. In the proposed solution, VPN credentials are tied not only to the user's identity but also to the physical machine's identity and state, which can be further verified through multi-factor authentication. By linking the computer and user and applying continuous verification, authentication policies are strengthened, making it more difficult for credentials to be exploited by unauthorized users. Additionally, the use of short-term credentials limits the impact of potential compromises, as any unauthorized access to the VPN would be time-limited. Furthermore, because the solution focuses on credential acquisition through attestation, it can be seamlessly integrated into modern ZTA frameworks, providing users with the necessary credentials to access resources within the architecture.

2   Background

2.1   Virtual Private Networks and Zero Trust Architecture

The Virtual Private Networks (VPN) architecture emulates private, secure networks over a public or less secure network, such as the Internet. The primary security features of a VPN are the encryption and authentication of data traffic through the use of tunneling mechanisms, thereby protecting data transmitted over potentially untrusted networks. With this, an organization can protect and guarantee access to its infrastructure for devices authenticated in the VPN.

One of the most commonly used VPN protocols is OpenVPN (OVPN) [12]. It allows remote clients to access resources protected inside the VPN. The advantage of OVPN over other protocols, such as Point-to-Point Tunneling Protocol (PPTP), which was used on past VPNs, is the support for Network Address Translation (NAT), firewalls, and modern encryption and authentication methods. OVPN also supports modern user authentication methods through user/-password or certificates to authenticate clients on the OVPN Server. In the context of this work, we will assume a certificate authentication method that uses X.509 certificates.

On the OVPN architecture, the organization will provide OVPN Access Servers where the clients will connect, and each client will be authenticated. After authentication, the OVPN Access Server will tunnel the client's communication, cryptographically protecting it using SSL/TLS. In addition to this protection, OVPN provides Internet Protocol Security (IPSec), providing privacy to the connected clients by securing the Internet Protocol (IP) packet, masking the client's original IP, and emulating a private network.

A more modern approach to secure networks is the Zero Trust (ZT) approach. ZT is a network security model based on principles that eliminate implicit trust in any user, application, or hardware without prior verification. It enforces the principle of least privilege by granting the minimum necessary access to all pieces of the system and continuously verifying and authenticating all communications [2].

Zero Trust Architecture (ZTA), in turn, is the implementation of Zero Trust (ZT) principles, applying them to design an organization's infrastructure and workflows [13]. ZTAs can also be used to secure communication between the devices and services of a single or different organizations. As ZTA follows ZT principles, the idea is to have all the devices inside this architecture constantly being verified. The goal of this work is to incorporate this constant verification into the VPN and leverage its security benefits. The advantage of ZTA is that it does not target perimeter-based security, such as VPNs. All the communication will be authenticated and encrypted, segmenting the network and removing single points of failure, as the communication is not concentrated in a single server.

2.2 SPIFFE and SPIRE

With modern automated infrastructure concepts and distributed services based on the cloud, and with the arrival of ZT [2] concepts, the need to provide identities to software components has increased. Moreover, generating these identities by hand poses some problems in terms of scalability, as it is impractical to create hundreds or maybe thousands of credentials manually, and security, as the manual method implies having long-term credentials, which is undesirable in ZTAs. SPIFFE proposes a solution to this by providing an automated mechanism to generate identities in a scalable and secure way, establishing trust in application identity [3]. This work leverages the continuous verification feature of ZTAs within VPNs using SPIFFE and SPIRE.

SPIFFE Standard. The Secure Production Identity Framework for Everyone (SPIFFE) [5] is a specification that describes how to provide identities to software components in a platform—and technology-agnostic fashion. SPIFFE's primary objective is to avoid leaving the last credential unprotected. For that, SPIFFE issues identities based on the software's attestation process.

In SPIFFE's vocabulary, a piece of software is called a workload. After attestation, the workload receives its identity as an SPIFFE Verifiable Identity Document (SVID), a cryptographically verifiable object representing the workload identity. This object can be, for instance, an X.509 certificate or a JSON Web Token (JWT). The SVID also contains the SPIFFE ID, a string representing the workload's identity. For the X.509 implementation, the SPIFFE ID is a Uniform Resource Identifier (URI) included in the Subject Alternative Name (SAN) extension. The SPIFFE ID contains the trust domain and the identifier for the workload. This identifier could be any string that identifies the workload, such as a name, a hash, or a unique ID. A valid SPIFFE ID looks like *spiffe://example.org/my-example-workload*.

To obtain its identity, the workload communicates with an API called the Workload API. This API is responsible for giving identities to the workloads. To avoid the need for bootstrap credentials, the Workload API does not require authentication. As it has no authentication, it must collect information about granting the workload's identity from a reliable source (which, depending on your threat model, could be the Operating System, secure processor, or a TPM chip, for example). Attestation consists of acquiring information about the workload to derive its identity. The properties used to derive the identity are called selectors.

SPIRE. The SPIFFE Runtime Environment (SPIRE) is the reference implementation[1] of SPIFFE. SPIRE has two main components: the SPIRE Server and the SPIRE Agent. The SPIRE Server is the root of trust in SPIRE architecture and must run in a secure and reliable environment. It is responsible for managing all the identities, attesting the nodes that run the workloads, and issuing

---

[1] https://github.com/spiffe/spire.

the SVIDs. It provides two APIs: the Registration API, which manages the creation of identities of the workloads by relating selector values to an SPIFFE ID; and the Node API, which provides the interface to attest a node. Each identity registration is called an entry. After being attested through the Node API and obtaining their own identities, Agents will provide the Workload API to deliver the SVIDs to the workloads.

The SPIRE Agent, in turn, runs in each node where workloads are running. It is responsible for attesting the workload's identity by using a reliable source to obtain information about it, e.g., the node's operating system (OS). The agent itself must also be attested within the Server. After successful attestation, the Agent receives its SVID and can issue the SVIDs of all the associated workloads.

To provide various attestation capabilities, SPIRE follows a plugin-oriented architecture, which permits the easy implementation of different forms of attestation for the Nodes and the Workloads. Node Attestor plugins manage the process of attesting a Node, while Workload Attestor plugins enable the attestation of workloads. Each plugin will generate selectors, which are used to create the identities through the Registration API on the SPIRE Server. Figure 1 shows what a CLI command to create a node and a workload identity looks like.

```
Node
spire−server  entry  create
   −node
   −spiffeID  spiffe :// ufcg . edu . br/pc01
   -selector tpm_ devid:issuer:cn:ufcg.edu.br
   -selector tpm_ devid:subject:cn:ufcg.edu.br
Workload
spire−server  entry  create
   -parentID spiffe://ufcg.edu.br/pc01
   −spiffeID  spiffe :// ufcg . edu . br/user/davi . pontes
   −selector  unix : uid :1001
   −selector  unix : user : davi
```

Fig. 1. Entries registration CLI commands.

In Fig. 1, the first command refers to the creation of a node identity, as the *-node* flag suggests, with the SPIFFE ID *spiffe://ufcg.edu.br/pc01*, which will be issued to the node with the Trusted Platform Module (TPM) device identity document with issuer common name equal to *ufcg.edu.br* and the subject common name equal to *ufcg.edu.br*, as the selectors describe.

The second command is for the workload entry registration. The *-parent* flag indicates that this workload identity is associated with Agent with the SPIFFE ID *spiffe://ufcg.edu.br/pc01*, and must be delivered by it, which also prevents the IDs from being accessible to less trusted nodes. The selectors describe that the workload must be a UNIX process owned by the user named *davi* with UID *1001*.

2.3   Single Sign On and OpenID Connect

Single Sign-On (SSO) is an authentication scheme that enables users to authenticate once using a single set of credentials and access multiple systems with the same credentials. SSO uses the concept of Identity as a Service (IDaaS), relying on an Identity Provider (IdP) to manage users' logins. The idea of SSO is that the user logs into the IdP using a set of credentials and receives an access token. This token is sent to applications to authenticate the user, and the applications verify the token and get the user's information through the IdP. Using SSO simplifies the user's experience by eliminating the need to store or remember multiple credentials and provides an easy way to implement secure authentication, as there will be only one IdP implementation, which can be better audited and maintained, including support for Multi-Factor Authentication (MFA) and other security functionalities.

Open ID Connect (OIDC) is an authentication protocol based on OAuth2. It simplifies users' identity verification based on the authentication performed by an Authorization Service. OIDC can be used to enable SSO in an application by relying on an IdP, named OpenID Provider (OP) in the OIDC context, to manage the authentication process and users' credentials. OIDC workflow is described in Fig. 2.

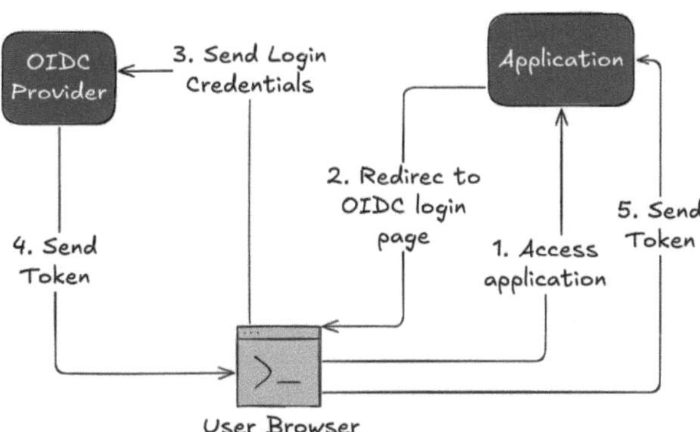

Fig. 2. OIDC protocol workflow [11].

The user accesses the application, redirecting them to the OIDC login page. The user then logs in using the credentials, receives the Access Token, and sends it to the application. The Access Token allows the client application to perform delegated authorization, granting access to a designated resource to carry out defined actions on behalf of the user after prior consent.

In this work, OIDC and SSO are used to manage users' identity verification and authentication within the implemented solution, which allows a simple integration and application of multi-factor authentication to manage user identity.

2.4 Trusted Platform Module

Trusted Platform Module (TPM) [1] is a security chip on a computer that stores secrets and verifies platform identity and integrity. To verify platform identity, TPM has an Endorsement Key (EK), stored in the TPM's hardware with the private key inaccessible by software. The EK is unique to each TPM chip and is signed by the vendor's certificate authority (CA) so it can be used to verify the platform's identity. The TPM also has registers that store hashes of measurements of software components running on the platform since its boot. These registers are called Platform Configuration Registers (PCRs), and there are 24 of them on the TPM chip. The PCRs can store hashes of the machine's boot process, such as kernel, Unified Extensible Firmware Interface (UEFI), and initial RAM file system (*initramfs*). The TPM can generate reports with the PCR values; these reports are signed by the Attestation Key (AK), a TPM's private key signed by the vendor's CA, and protected on the TPM's private memory. This enables the verification of TPM-generated reports, which are used in this work to verify the user's PC identity and state.

3 Problem Definition and Solution Requirements

This work considers the following initial scenario: an organization provides remote access to specific private resources for its employees and selected clients through a VPN connection. The organization's VPN uses the OVPN protocol and supports X.509 certificates for user authentication.

In such a scenario, common in current work environments, the organization issues the X.509 certificates and keys and delivers them to the employees through some secure channel (e.g., through company email or delivered in person on physical devices) to avoid leakage. The employees then store the certificates on their personal computers (PCs) to use them in the authentication process when connecting to the VPN. Once stored in the employees' PC, an attacker can focus on the employee's PC[2] to access the organization's infrastructure, as the employees are way more unprotected than the organization's servers. Leveraging this, the attacker can use this access as a door to start escalating privileges. Table 1 describes some of the attacks this scenario is vulnerable to.

To mitigate the threats, a proposed solution must meet specific requirements to protect against each attack vector. (Req.1) To prevent private key theft, the system should enforce device identity attestation to prevent credentials from being used on untrusted devices, and Multi-Factor Authentication (MFA) to strengthen security by not trusting in only one factor to authenticate. (Req.2) Countermeasures such as full disk encryption, session re-authentication, short-term credentials, and the ability to remotely revoke compromised devices' access can significantly reduce the risk if a physical device is stolen. (Req.3) To defend against session hijacking, the system should employ mutual TLS (mTLS) to

---

[2] E.g. through spearphishing attacks, which by meticulously researching their targets and crafting personalized emails deceive even experienced professionals.

Table 1. Threat Model for VPN Access Protection

Attack	Entry Point	Impact
Primary Key Theft	Malware, phishing, keyloggers	VPN access, impersonation
Physical Device Theft	Stolen laptop, unattended sessions	VPN access, further internal compromise
Session Hijacking	Weak TLS configs	Take over existing VPN session
Lateral Movement	Weak internal access control	Internal escalation, data breach
Persistent Backdoors	Malware on an employee PC	Long-term stealthy access & Endpoint detection

ensure strong, bidirectional authentication and use short-lived credentials to minimize the usefulness of stolen sessions. (Req.4) Addressing lateral movement within the infrastructure requires enforcing least-privilege access principles and implementing per-request authentication, ensuring users can only access necessary resources with re-verification. (Req.5) Lastly, detecting and containing persistent backdoors requires continuous monitoring and automated access revocation mechanisms for identifying anomalies and cutting off compromised devices' access.

4 Proposal

4.1 Architecture

This work proposes a solution to secure VPN access through attestation, replacing static, long-term credentials with prior verifications. The approach preserves the original VPN configuration, changing only how users obtain their credentials. Verifications are applied to both the physical device and the user, ensuring device identity and integrity while binding the user to authorized hardware. This prevents authenticated users from operating on unauthorized devices and mitigates internal impersonation.

Figure 3 describes the general architecture of the solution. The Attestor Module is installed on the user's PC and communicates with the organization's Attestation Server to request a remote attestation. In the first step, the hardware is attested, using TPM cryptographic keys and measurements to guarantee hardware identity and secure state. As the TPM identity is a hardware feature, it becomes harder for the attacker to corrupt it. After successful hardware attestation, the user authenticates within the OIDC provider and sends the token to the

Attestation Server. The Attestation Server then verifies user identity within the OIDC provider and provides the credentials to VPN access to the Attestor Module. The entire attestation process must use TLS to avoid message interception and reading by an attacker.

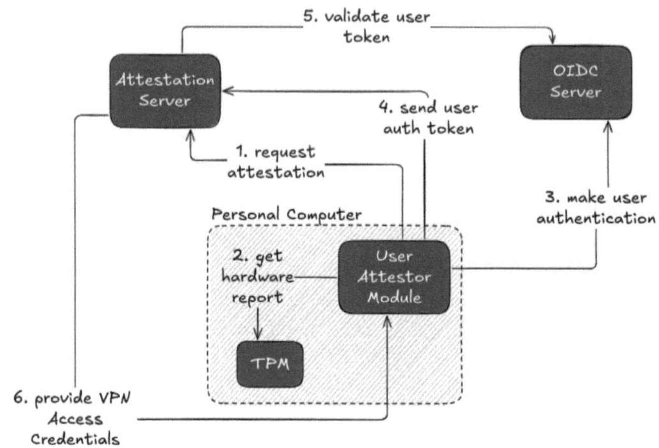

Fig. 3. Solution Architecture.

4.2   Implementation

The proposal is implemented using SPIRE plugins that attest the physical machine via TPM and the user identity through Auth0[3], a widely adopted OIDC provider with integration into social and enterprise IdPs. The infrastructure operator registers both the PC and user entries in the SPIRE Server, linking them by setting the PC SPIFFE ID as the parent of the user entry. The SPIRE Server attests the PC's identity using the Trusted Platform Module (TPM) [9], after which the SPIRE Agent verifies the user's identity through the User Attestation Module (UAM). The resulting SVID is then stored for VPN access[4].

Attesting the Machine To attest to the PC, a new SPIRE Node Attestor plugin was developed, utilizing TPM capabilities to verify device identity and boot integrity. This can ensure that the device receiving the identity is correct and in a trusted state (e.g., running a specific kernel version with disk encryption and secure boot enabled). Figure 4 describes the TPM Node attestation workflow.

---

[3] https://auth0.com/.
[4] The source code is available at https://github.com/Daviiap/SPIREPersonalComputing.

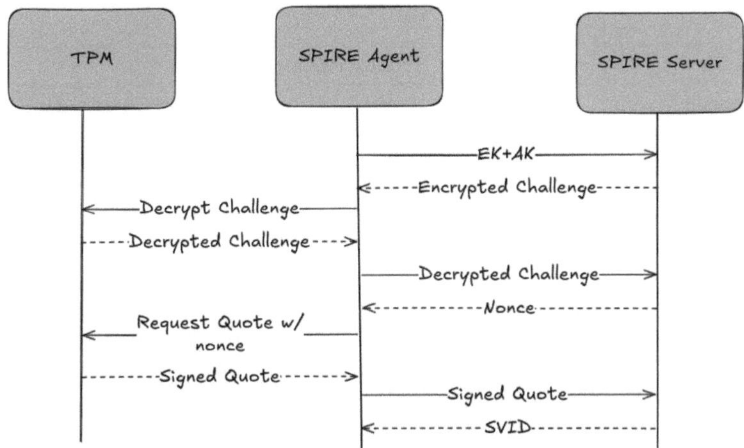

Fig. 4. Machine Attestation Workflow.

The SPIRE Agent starts requesting attestation to the SPIRE Server, providing the public part of the TPM's Endorsement Key (EK) and Attestation Key (AK). The SPIRE Server will respond with a challenge, encrypting a secret using the public part of the provided keys. The Agent asks for the TPM to decrypt the secret and sends the decrypted secret to the SPIRE Server, which will verify if the secret returned is the same as the one sent before. As the TPM is the only one with access to the private key of EK and AK, this proves the machine has the expected TPM hardware.

After verification, the server sends a nonce[5] to the Agent, which requests a TPM Quote using it. The TPM produces a cryptographic assertion, signed by the AK, attesting to the system's integrity and configuration. The Agent forwards this quote to the Server, which verifies the AK signature and, if valid, extracts platform information to generate selectors identifying the machine.

The selectors extracted from the quote capture the machine's identity and state, as shown in Table 2. PCR selectors identify key boot information, including the UEFI, kernel version, and *initramfs*, providing an overview of the machine's state at startup. According to the Trusted Computing Group (TCG) [14], Platform Configuration Registers (PCRs) store integrity measurements during the boot process: PCR0 records UEFI firmware, PCR1 the host configuration, PCRs 2–3 UEFI drivers, PCRs 4–5 Boot Manager and partition data, PCR6 the platform manufacturer, and PCR7 the Secure Boot policy. PCRs 8–15 are used by the operating system, PCR16 for debugging, PCR23 for application support, and PCRs 17–22 can be extended as needed.

---

[5] The nonce is a random data generated to guarantee report freshness.

Table 2. SPIRE TPM selectors.

Selector	Description
ek:<hash_value>	SHA256 of the EK certificate. It identifies the machine's identity.
pcr:[num]:[algorithm]:<pcr_value>	The value of PCR 0 to 23. It can be in SHA256 or SHA512.

To create an SPIRE entry for the machine, the administrator must require the TPM's EK certificate from the user machine, in Distinguished Encoding Rules (DER) form, take the SHA-256 digest, and set the value as the *ek* selector. This value reflects the machine's identity. For the machine state, PCR selectors can be used. As the PCRs are hard to predict and vary depending on many factors, the administrator can audit the user's machine to get initial PCRs to use as selectors. For instance, during the initial setup of the machine, the administrator can verify the boot state and then get the value of PCRs 1 to 7 to use as selectors. As the values were settled through audit, the administrator can guarantee that this initial value is reliable, and if some of these values change, the boot state has changed, and access must be re-evaluated.

As some non-malicious changes on the machine (e.g., kernel and BIOS updates) can also interfere with some of the PCR values, it is needed that in case of some of these changes occurring, the user should notify the administrator so he can update the SPIRE entry to reflect the new PCR values to be trusted. Otherwise, the machine will lose permission to obtain the credentials to access the VPN.

Attesting User's Identity. A new SPIRE workload attestor plugin and a User Attestation Module (UAM) were built to attest to user identity. The UAM is used to authenticate users; this module is responsible for managing the user login on the Auth0 API. The Auth0 API can be configured as the system administrator prefers. The usage of MFA is strongly recommended since it enhances security by relying on different factors to authenticate the user. The SPIRE workload attestor is responsible for communicating with the UAM to retrieve the authentication tokens, validate them, and fetch user information to build the selectors to identify the user. Figure 5 describes the user authentication and UAM attestation workflow.

The user starts the login process within the UAM, and the UAM redirects the user to the Auth0 login web interface, where the authentication is performed. The user then provides valid credentials, which are verified by Auth0. Once authentication is completed, Auth0 issues a token and redirects the user back to the UAM along with this token.

Upon receiving the token, the UAM requests attestation from the SPIRE Agent through the workload API. The SPIRE Agent retrieves the authentication token through a UNIX socket exposed by the UAM and verifies it within

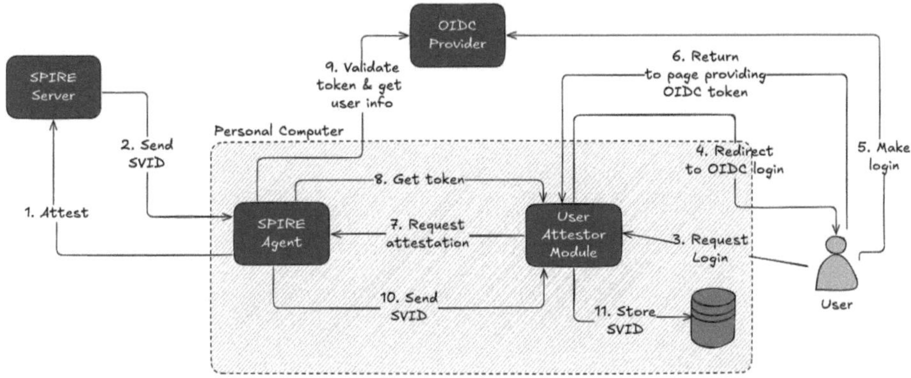

Fig. 5. Personal Computer and User Attestation Workflow.

the Auth0 API. After validating the token and fetching the user's information, the SPIRE Agent is responsible for generating selectors based on the user's attributes. Table 3 provides a listing of these selectors.

Table 3. SPIRE user selectors.

Selector	Description
sub:<value>	Value unique for each user, can be used as an ID.
given_name:<value>	The first name of the user.
family_name:<value>	User's family name.
nickname:<value>	User's nickname.
name:<value>	User's full name.
email:<value>	User's email address.
email_verified:<true/false>	Indicates if the user has verified the e-mail address.

If an identity has been registered that corresponds to the generated selectors, and if the SPIRE Agent is configured as the parent on this identity, the UAM subsequently receives its SVID. The UAM stores this SVID for later use in VPN authentication.

Figure 6 shows the workload attestor configuration. The *auth0_domain* is the Auth0 endpoint used to verify the authentication token and retrieve the user's information, the *client_id* is the client ID on the Auth0 provider, and the *socket_path* is the socket exposed by UAM to enable the token fetch.

```
WorkloadAttestor "user" {
    plugin_cmd = "/home/davi/.spire/configs/plugin"
    plugin_data {
        auth0_domain = "https://dev-87asgcbas97.us.auth0.com/"
        client_id = "abcdefghijkLMNOPQRSTUVwxyzaBcde"
        socket_path = "/tmp/uam.sock"
    }
}
```

Fig. 6. SPIRE User Workload Attestor configuration.

5   Evaluation

This section evaluates the proposed solution by analyzing how it fits the solution requirements described in Sect. 3. It also analyzes resource consumption to see if the solution impacts PC performance.

5.1   Requirements Satisfaction

Section 3 has described the problems with VPN protection and enumerated some requirements that a solution must achieve to enhance the security of VPN authentication. Table 4 presents the attacks identified in Sect. 3 and how the proposed solution helps mitigate them.

Table 4. Mitigation Strategies for VPN Threats

Attack	Mitigation Strategies
Private Key Theft	Device identity attestation, Multi-factor authentication (MFA), Constant certificate rotation
Physical Device Theft	Short-term credentials, Remote access revocation
Session Hijacking	Short-term credentials
Lateral Movement	—
Persistent Backdoors	Continuous attestation,Device integrity attestation

For Private Key Theft, the proposed solution provides MFA to strengthen the defense by requiring additional factors to authenticate the user, making it harder for an attacker to use stolen credentials. The device attestation guarantees that even if an attacker gains access to the user's credentials, they cannot authenticate into the VPN without access to the physical machine. The solution also relies on SPIRE to provide constant certificate rotation, reducing the damage in case of a successful private key theft.

In the case of Physical Device Theft, short-term credentials help prevent prolonged unauthorized access, as the machine will be valid, but the user credentials (e.g., MFA) will still be missing. SPIRE revocation of SVIDs enables administrators to disable access to the stolen device quickly.

To counter Session Hijacking, short-term credentials reduce the lifetime of active sessions. Any intercepted session tokens quickly become useless unless the attacker can continuously re-authenticate.

Lateral Movement attacks are out of the scope of the solution, as it aims to guarantee the security of the authentication process, not the authorization. Although the solution does not mitigate these attacks, good practices such as having least privilege access can help protect against them. They can be implemented in the VPN access control along with the proposed solution.

For Persistent Backdoors, device integrity attestation verifies that the system has not been tampered with, thereby preventing many malware-based persistence mechanisms from remaining undetected. It is recommended that users reboot their computer every day to ensure that the PCR values are updated and reflect a fresh state of the machine's boot. However, if some malware is infecting the PC and it does not interfere with any PCR value, or if the PCR value selectors are not used properly, it will remain undetected by the attestation process.

5.2   Resource Consumption and Time Overhead

To evaluate the resource consumption and time overhead of the solution, tests were run using a PC with an Intel Core i5-13450HX processor and 16 GB of RAM, running the UAM and the SPIRE Agent only. The machine had an Ubuntu 22.04.5 LTS (Jammy Jellyfish) installed and was running SPIRE Agent version 1.11.2.

The Linux *ps* command retrieved CPU and RAM usage. The command has been executed with the parameters *"-p <pid>"*, to identify the process, and *"-o %cpu,%mem"*, to retrieve CPU and RAM usage in percentage. The SVID renewals were set to occur every 15 min, and the executions were monitored for 1 h. The results are as follows: the SPIRE Agent consumed a mean of 0.1% of CPU and 0.2% of RAM (32 MB). The UAM consumed less than 0.01% of the CPU and 0.1% (16 MB) of RAM. This represents a total mean consumption of 48 MB of RAM and less than 0.3% of the CPU consumption. This indicates that the solution can be run on lightweight machines without becoming an overhead.

To evaluate the time overhead introduced by the attestation process for obtaining the credentials, we executed the procedure 30 times to calculate the mean time required for both the SPIRE Agent and the UAM to acquire the SVIDs. The SPIRE Agent attestation had a mean time of 688 ms with a standard deviation of 4 ms. The user identity attestation took a mean time of 1.86 s with a standard deviation of 0.2 s. This represents a total mean overhead of 2.54 s, which is not representative in the context of establishing a VPN connection.

6   Related Work

In [10], the authors proposed using the device's GPS information in addition to regular authentication information to grant access to VPNs. This method reduces the risk of intrusion from stolen credentials or devices, since the attacker would need to be in the authorized area to access the VPN. However, the geolocation solution does not perform any integrity verification on the device's state. In [16], the authors propose a framework that integrates existing VPNs with Zero Trust Network Access (ZTNA) to enhance access control through continuous verification and automatic revocation upon intrusion. In contrast, this work focuses on strengthening VPN authentication to prevent unauthorized initial access by applying stronger verifications than in a regular VPN authentication.

In [15], the authors gave an overview of Secure Access Service Edge (SASE) [7] and proposed a deployment strategy to enhance its security, providing device attestation with identity and environment verification and MFA on user authentication. Although [15] attests the device identity and state, it relies on software to do so, making it easier to corrupt. The SPIRE-based solution proposed in this work uses hardware features to perform the device attestation, making it more reliable.

In [6], the authors propose a Zero Trust Network Access Control (ZTNAC) system that validates user identity, assesses device security posture, verifies hardware integrity, and employs AI-based behavior profiling to detect and block anomalies. Although the system offers robust security, its deployment is highly complex and demands the addition of numerous components to the existing infrastructure. By contrast, the SPIRE-based approach enhances infrastructure security without requiring a complete overhaul of the existing infrastructure.

7   Concluding Remarks

This paper proposes a novel approach to enhancing VPN security by improving the authentication process through both personal computer and user identity verification. The solution utilizes hardware checks to verify device integrity and employs modern authentication methods for users. It can be integrated into traditional VPNs by using SPIRE to provide credentials, replacing less secure methods (e.g., email), thereby enabling ZT principles without modifying the VPN itself.

Despite its benefits, the solution lacks features common in modern ZTA implementations, such as behavior-based user profiling and automated access revocation. VPNs still assume a trusted perimeter: once inside, devices are considered reliable. However, our approach can be integrated with modern ZTA solutions like SDP, using proxies instead of VPNs to manage connections. Combined with minimal access privileges, continuous authentication, monitoring, and automated threat analysis, this integration could achieve a high maturity level for user identity in the CISA ZT Maturity Model [4].

Future work includes supporting Windows systems, as the current implementation is only supported by Unix-based systems. Enhancing hardware attestation is also possible by verifying software executing on the computer, using, for example, Integrity Measurement Architecture (IMA) to verify runtime.

Disclosure of Interests. The authors have no relevant competing interests to declare in the context of this article.

References

1. Arthur, W., Challener, D.: A Practical Guide to TPM 2.0: Using the Trusted Platform Module in the New Age of Security. A practical guide to TPM 2.0 / Arthur, Will, Apress (2015)
2. Campbell, M.: Beyond zero trust: Trust is a vulnerability. Comput. **53**(10), 110–113 (2020). https://doi.org/10.1109/MC.2020.3011081
3. Chandramouli, R., Chandramouli, R., Butcher, Z.: A zero trust architecture model for access control in cloud-native applications in multi-location environments. US Department of Commerce, National Institute of Standards and Technology (2023)
4. Cybersecurity, (CISA), I.S.A.: Zero trust maturity model version 2.0. Tech. rep., Cybersecurity and Infrastructure Security Agency (2023). https://www.cisa.gov/sites/default/files/2023-04/CISA_Zero_Trust_Maturity_Model_Version_2_508c.pdf. Accessed 9 Apr 2025
5. Feldman, D., et al.: Solving the bottom turtle: a spiffe way to establish trust in your infrastructure via universal identity. Sprint Lab, Nova Zelândia (2020)
6. García-Teodoro, P., Camacho, J., Maciá-Fernández, G., Gómez-Hernández, J., López-Marín, V.: A novel zero-trust network access control scheme based on the security profile of devices and users. Comput. Netw. **212**, 109068 (2022). https://doi.org/10.1016/j.comnet.2022.109068, https://www.sciencedirect.com/science/article/pii/S1389128622002109
7. Gartner, Inc.: The future of network security is in the cloud. https://www.gartner.com/en/documents/3957375 (2019). Accessed 09 Apr 2025
8. Hurkens, C.A.J., Keijsper, J.C.M., Stougie, L.: Virtual private network design: A proof of the tree routing conjecture on ring networks. SIAM J. Discrete Math. **21**(2), 482–503 (2007). https://doi.org/10.1137/050626259, https://doi.org/10.1137/050626259
9. ISO: ISO/IEC 11889-1:2015 – Information technology – Trusted Platform Module Library – Part 1: Architecture (2015). Accessed 9 Apr 2025
10. Jin, Y., Tomoishi, M., Matsuura, S.: Enhancement of vpn authentication using gps information with geo-privacy protection. In: 2016 25th International Conference on Computer Communication and Networks (ICCCN). pp. 1–6 (2016). https://doi.org/10.1109/ICCCN.2016.7568518
11. Open ID Connect: What is openid connect (nd), https://openid.net/developers/how-connect-works/. Accessed 20 May 2025
12. OpenVPN Project: Openvpn protocol (nd), https://openvpn.net/community-resources/openvpn-protocol/. Accessed 19 Mar 2025
13. Stafford, V.: Zero Trust Architect. NIST Spec. Publ. **800**(207), 800–207 (2020)
14. Trusted Computing Group: Tcg pc client platform firmware profile specification version 1.06 revision 52. https://trustedcomputinggroup.org/wp-content/uploads/TCG-PC-Client-Platform-Firmware-Profile-Version-1.06-Revision-52_pub-3.pdf (2018), Accessed 09 Apr 2025

15. Yiliyaer, S., Kim, Y.: Secure access service edge: A zero trust based framework for accessing data securely. In: 2022 IEEE 12th Annual Computing and Communication Workshop and Conference (CCWC). pp. 0586–0591. IEEE (2022)
16. Zohaib, S.M., Sajjad, S.M., Iqbal, Z., Yousaf, M., Haseeb, M., Muhammad, Z.: Zero trust vpn (zt-vpn): A systematic literature review and cybersecurity framework for hybrid and remote work. Inf. **15**(11) (2024). https://doi.org/10.3390/info15110734, https://www.mdpi.com/2078-2489/15/11/734

Towards a Minimum Security Baseline for Cyber-Physical Systems Through Security Standards Harmonization

Henrique A. Fonseca[1]([✉]) [iD], João R. Campos[2] [iD], and Regina Moraes[1,2] [iD]

[1] School of Technology, UNICAMP, Limeira, Brazil
h236540@dac.unicamp.br, regina@ft.unicamp.br
[2] Department of Informatics Engineering, University of Coimbra, Coimbra, Portugal
{jrcampos,remoraes}@dei.uc.pt

Abstract. Cyber-Physical Systems (CPS) rely on data collection as a fundamental element to control physical devices through the internet. They are widespread in several environments, such as medical, smart cities, wearable devices, and space environments. Despite its importance, recent security incidents point to a neglect of system security in the development of CPS systems. Such neglect is largely due to the difficulty in understanding security requirements, whether those specified in requirements elicitation documents or those arising from security standards for specific systems. Many of these standards lack clarity and contain ambiguities, leading to subjective interpretations and inconsistent implementation. This study suggests a way to simplify and standardize security requirements, creating a Minimum Security Baseline (MSB) for CPS development, particularly in situations where several standards must be met. Large Language Models (LLMs) are used to process texts in natural language and find complements and intersections among the different documents in order to automate the generation of the MSB. The mission requirements of the CubeSat satellite, model CONASAT-0, created by INPE (National Institute for Space Research), are used as a case study. Using the OWASP IoT Security Verification Standard (ISVS) as the ontological foundation for security words, the MSB is produced by semantically examining the criteria of the NIST, ECSS, and CCSDS standards. The results include an MSB that can be valuable for guiding embedded system implementations, as engineers have a single document to follow that can be applied to CPSs in a variety of contexts.

Keywords: Cyber-Physical System · CPS · Minimum Security Baselines · MSB · CubeSat · Security Requirements Harmonization

1 Introduction

Currently, several computer systems are part of the human experience, interacting with the physical environment and collecting data to help people perform

L. A. Rodrigues and R. Oliveira (Eds.): LADC 2025, CCIS 2697, pp. 37–53, 2026.
https://doi.org/10.1007/978-3-032-11539-3_3

their tasks. Such systems, which are based on the interaction between cybernetics and the physical environment, are classified as Cyber-Physical Systems (CPS) and are applied in several areas, such as in the industrial environment, in the medical area, and for domestic purposes (for example, smart devices) [1]. Unlike traditional systems, CPSs have three central components: sensors, controllers, and actuators, allowing them to perceive the surrounding environment, adapt to it, and respond as events occur [24].

The connection between physical and cyber environments has become essential for the Industrial Internet of Things (IIoT). This allows smart applications and services to operate accurately and in real time, contributing to improved services and supply chain management. The adoption of CPSs in industry has resulted in a positive economic impact in many countries [5]. The space sector also heavily relies on CPSs, which play an essential role in modern society through applications such as telecommunications, global positioning, and Earth observation systems [21].

In recent years, the number of satellites in orbit doubled the number of existing satellites from 2019 to 2022 [19]. This growth has driven an increase in the production of low-cost satellites, including nanosatellites. They are called nanosatellites due to their tiny size and the usage of commercial standard components (COTS), ensuring a low manufacturing cost and covering a wide spectrum of use cases, from commercial to research and climate applications [8]. Using COTS, which are not designed with security in mind [11], and making its documentation available for public access, it is even easier to plan cyberattacks using the information provided. Therefore, for this type of development, it is more important to bring security requirements right at the beginning of development (shifting security requirements to the left), since many solutions can be facilitated with architectural decisions defined at this initial development stage.

It is well known that, in many contexts, the implementation of security standards is not just a matter of compliance, but a strategic necessity to ensure the continuity and success of critical operations [15]. Redundancy and overlap among different standards, which often address similar issues in slightly different ways, can lead to duplicate efforts, inefficient resource allocation, and even operational conflicts in the implementation of security controls. However, in complex projects involving multiple stakeholders - such as CPS - adhering to diverse security requirements proves to be a significant challenge [12]. Therefore, it is necessary to select standard requirements that fit the scope of the specific system.

This work aims to contribute to improving the security of CPSs, targeting the initial stages of development, where there is a notable difficulty in following the requirements proposed by security standards. Since in most cases it is necessary to comply with all security standards relevant to the application context, our contribution is a systematic method to condense and harmonize the security requirements for the development of CPSs based on Large Language Models (LLMs) to process the texts in natural language. The method consists of generating a Minimum Security Baseline (MSB), seeking to solve problems of overlap, intersection, and ambiguity found in the various standards being used. The MSB, as another contribution of this work, is then the minimum set of controls necessary to protect the system and achieve compliance with all standards.

The third contribution of this work is a case study, which is the embedded system in the CubeSat nanosatellite (CONASAT-0[1]) in the context of space CPSs. NIST (National Institute of Standards and Technology)[2], ECSS (European Cooperation for Space Standardization)[3], and CCSDS (Consultative Committee for Space Data Systems)[4], are commonly used as mandatory standards for compliance, and the OWASP IoT Security Verification Standard (ISVS) [14] serves as the ontological basis for security terms in this context.

The proposed method can also be used for other types of CPS systems where multiple standards apply. Furthermore, the use of LLM is discussed and analyzed, showing to be a promising approach to address this type of issue. Thus, the MSB is useful to facilitate the implementation of CPSs by embedded systems engineers. In our case, by achieving the expected results in the space context, the development life cycle for space CPSs will have a reference for the secure development of the system, the MSB.

This document is structured as follows: Sect. 2 presents the work most closely related to our proposal; Sect. 3 describes the proposed methodology; Sect. 4 details the experiments conducted to validate the methodology; Sect. 5 presents the results and discussion; finally, Sect. 6 concludes the document, addressing threats to validity and outlining directions for future work.

2 Related Work

The issue of integrating security principles in the early stages of the software development lifecycle is widely discussed, particularly in the DevOps development methodology. According to Wolf and Serpanos [22], gaps related to the concept of security can expose CPSs to attacks that compromise the physical integrity of the user and the data they manipulate. The integration of security into the DevOps pipeline (DevSecOps) and the adaptation to cyber-physical systems motivated the study by Yasar and Teplov [25]. In the space context, the work of Willbold et al. [21] proposed an opinion questionnaire to understand security knowledge and concluded that there is a lack of related practices in a large part of the community that develops space systems. This is especially true for systems focusing on smaller devices, such as CubeSats, which are often developed by small teams with limited resources, resulting in implementations with low security robustness.

According to Olifer et al. [12], organizations face increasing regulatory pressure and are often required to comply with multiple information security documents, such as international standards and regulations, which often present

---

[1] http://www.crn.inpe.br/conasat1/nanosatt.php.

[2] https://www.nist.gov.

[3] https://ecss.nl.

[4] https://public.ccsds.org/default.aspx.

overlapping or conflicting requirements. This complexity creates significant challenges for organizations, such as duplication of security controls, ineffective implementation, and increased associated costs. Currently, asset protection is largely based on the knowledge and experience of information security experts, which can lead to subjective and inefficient approaches. Given this scenario, Olifer et al. proposal [12] is based on the use of security ontologies and graph theory algorithms to map, visualize, and compare the requirements of different documents to eliminate redundancies and identify essential security requirements, giving rise to a MSB.

MSB is especially valuable for organizations that need to harmonize multiple security requirements, simplifying their implementation and reducing redundancies. Within the domains of compliance and software architecture, a security baseline refers to the essential set of security controls or criteria derived from security standards and regulatory requirements, defining the security measures that must be addressed in software design to ensure adherence to applicable regulations and standards [17]. As a way of structuring a document analysis, Pardo et al. [16] propose main operations between documents, such as intersection, union, differentiation, and complementarity. Furthermore, an ontological reference is required to resemble requirements in order to solve overlaps caused by ambiguous terms and circumstances when composing a MSB [12].

According to Parmar and Miles [15], security standards provide guidelines and practices that allow systems to be protected against cyber threats. They are structured documents that guide the design, implementation, and maintenance of secure systems, promoting the integrity, confidentiality, and availability of information. Regarding security standards for embedded systems in cyber-physical devices, one of the most widely used and well-known is NIST SP 800-53r5 - Security and Privacy Controls for Information Systems and Organizations [18]. It organizes controls into categories such as authentication and identity management, data protection, continuous monitoring, and presents a hierarchical and modular approach.

For the space environment, the recently conceived (2024) ECSS-E-ST-80C - Security in Space Systems Lifecycles [4] - stands out, proposing rigorous requirements for dependability attributes. It describes the mandatory validation procedures to ensure that systems meet mission requirements under extreme conditions, from design to mission decommissioning. In this standard, the categories cover aspects of reliability, fault protection, redundancy, and cybersecurity, which require complex analyses of fault tolerance, security, and redundancy of critical components.

Other relevant standards for the space sector are those proposed by CCSDS, an international organization that develops standards for data exchange in space missions [3]. The CCSDS standards are structured in "Books", each one with its specific objectives and levels of technical application. Blue Books represent formal and mandatory standards, required in communication protocols for the integrity of communications. Green Books serve as informational documents that explain the underlying concepts and technologies, allowing developers and engineers to better understand the practical application of Blue Books. Magenta Books, in turn, proposes experimental and recommended standards designed to evaluate new technologies before they are formally adopted as standards. In the space cyber-physical domain, ECSS-E-ST-80C and CCSDS Books are particularly relevant standards.

As detailed by Ndao et al. [10], CubeSats and other nanosatellites often operate in high-risk environments and handle confidential data, requiring standardized guidelines to ensure that communication, control, and data systems are reliable and interoperable. Standards promote consistency in an industry where improvisation cannot be accepted. However, inconsistent application of frameworks due to the amount of overlapping and ambiguous requirements increases the likelihood of failures and vulnerabilities, compromising entire missions [12,21].

Adhering to the security criteria outlined in various standard documents can be challenging. Methods such as semantic mapping and document integration are suggested to address redundancy and overlapping requirements [12]. However, even these techniques have difficulty associating controls with different terminologies and contexts, often requiring manual analysis to solve discrepancies [15]. Existing work in the literature has systematized the process of defining a security requirements baseline [2,17]. These works describe the process from the selection of applicable standards and regulations to the comparison between similar requirements, corroborating the idea that there are requirements with similar approaches in different standards. In Rouland et al. [17], this process is applied in the context of a SCADA system, also adopting NIST and other relevant standards. However, it is important to automate this systematized work instead of executing it manually, avoiding more effort and resources.

When thinking about automation in the context of text documents, LLMs are powerful allies to facilitate the work. Regarding semantic comparison between texts, Xu et al. [23] involve an experiment with medical reports, where the Generative Pre-trained Transformer (GPT) [13] model proved to be superior in capturing real semantic nuances in specialized textual comparisons to traditional lexical comparison methods such as ROUGE and BLEU. Traditional methods are criticized for focusing only on superficial lexical similarity, such as overlapping words or n-grams, and not deeply capturing the semantic meaning and clinical implications of medical texts. Despite some limitations, such as the necessity of minimal validation of the results by medical professionals ("human-in-the-loop"), the use of a GPT-type LLM seems promising and inspiring for this present investigation.

The works presented in this section address the problem of incorporating security practices into the embedded software development cycle in CPSs in different ways. The goal is to connect existing approaches found in the literature in order to define security requirements that comply with the necessary standards.

3   The Harmonization Method

Early information security concerns during system development can reduce future incident costs. However, challenges already exist in the requirements definition phase. For most CPSs, in addition to the functional and non-functional requirements of the business rule, they must adhere to security standards, such as those outlined in NIST SP 800-53r5 ([18]), as well as standards for specific types of systems. For instance, in space systems, the ECSS-E-ST-80C and CCSDS standards are commonly used and must be considered in addition to the security premises of the requirements that the mission has previously addressed. Therefore, to make it easier for the development team to implement the system, it is relevant to condense the security requirements from several sources into a single minimum set of controls (Minimum Security Baseline), solving overlaps or conflicts between the requirements [12].

The methodology presented in this section aims to generate a MSB, resulting from the harmonization of multiple documents, and the method can be applied to documents from any system context. Figure 1 presents the steps of the method.

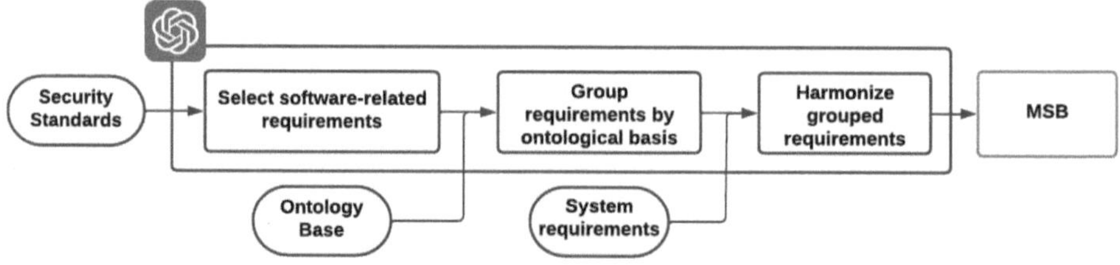

Fig. 1. Method Flow

Inspired by the work of Olifer et al. [12] and Rouland et al. [17], this work adopts an ontological reference for cybersecurity terms and approaches. For ontological and semantic comparison, the use of machine learning was explored. A GPT-type LLM was also adopted, using ChatGPT [13] as a tool to automate the process, mainly using its ability to process and generate text in natural language. The Retrieval Augmented Generation (RAG) technique was also used to minimize hallucinations. RAG allows the process to be restricted to a specific knowledge base - for example, available in PDF and DOCX formats - without the need to retrain the model [7]. To obtain more accurate and complete responses, a sequence of prompts, presented in Table 1, was defined, whose notation in the first column symbolizes the order in which each of them should be executed. This methodology has three steps, described in the following subsections.

3.1   Select Software-Related Requirements

In the first stage of the method, the security standard documents available on the proposing institutions' websites will be provided as input data. When uploading

Table 1. Prompts and their corresponding texts

Execution order	Prompt
#1	Indicate all sections of this document that relate only to software requirements
#2	Considering these security requirements in {ontology_base}, extract or create keywords that summarize the requirements of each section ({ontology_base_sections})
#3	Considering these security requirements in {Standard_Section}, relate the sections to the keywords (by sections {Ontology_base_sections}). This relationship should be 1:1
#4	Considering the {system_design_requirements} document, which of these requirements do not apply to the description of the system's operation? There are requirements that are not explicitly described in the document but the system must meet, but there are requirements that do not make sense according to the system's functionalities or that it should have
#5	Considering these sections of the {standards_name} below, are there any overlapping relationships between what is covered in the requirements of these sections? Look for similar or identical approaches. What is identical should be combined into one requirement, and what has a different approach should be kept. {standard_name_and_requirements}
#6	Considering requirements expressed in the same way (or close enough), consolidate them into a single requirement. Do this line by line. This consolidated requirement should contain excerpts from the standards indicated in a way that is sufficient to meet the requirements indicated as similar. Requirements that are in different layers or provide extra detail should be kept. Just repeat the content of the referenced sections

the documents to ChatGPT, with the assistance of RAG capability, the model's responses will refer to these documents.

This step focuses on excluding non-software-oriented requirements from the document analysis (e.g., those related to software life cycle activities). The purpose of eliminating requirements that are not relevant to the harmonization process is to improve the efficiency of the analysis [17].

By selecting the GPT-o3 model, which uses advanced reflection, it becomes possible to audit the model's reasoning, refine prompts when necessary, manually correct potential errors, and better manage uncertainties and the inherent lack of transparency in LLMs. After testing with several prompts, Prompt #1 was defined.

3.2   Group Requirements by Ontological Basis

As suggested in Olifer et al. [12], an ontological basis is used to assist in the comparison of texts that have a certain semantic similarity. In this way, the aim is to find similarities based on the concept and context in which the requirements approach is applied in the document [20]. To this end, the adoption of an ontological basis such as the HITRUST (Health Information Trust Alliance) CSF (Common Security Framework) 9.1 framework, OWASP ISVS, and CIS Controls (Center for Internet Security) v8 assists in the definition of concepts related to a context, allowing the grouping of requirements that have close concepts.

As pointed out in Xu et al. [23], LLM models deal well with labels for defining contexts, where the keywords' generation was adopted in order to abstract the concepts present in the ontological basis. Generally, these bases have several sections for each scope (e.g.: Communications and Cryptography), which can be used to group the standards' requirements by the proximity of their approaches to such keywords. To do this, Prompt #2 was used. The GPT o3 model is useful for human auditing, taking advantage of RAG's capacity to perform this task by searching in the provided ontological base document.

After obtaining the keywords for each section of the ontological document, the sections of the standard should be grouped according to the software requirements. The result of this grouping task can remain similar to what is already organized in the structure of the original standards, which this similarity indicates a good efficiency of the LLM tool due to its alignment with the kind of structure that was produced by a human.

For this grouping task, it is necessary that the keywords and the standards documents be placed in Prompt #3. In this prompt, the model is expected to establish a one-to-one relationship, where a keyword must be related to the requirement of the pattern that most abstracts its ontology. Since each keyword belongs to a section of the ontological base, it is possible to group the requirements that were related to these sections.

3.3   Harmonize Grouped Requirements

Once the software requirements from the security standards have been grouped, they can be analyzed to identify intersections among similar approaches, which can be consolidated into a single requirement [12], while those with distinct approaches should be retained in the MSB. The analysis should be performed across requirements within all the sections grouped in the previous step. The use of a LLM tool, such as ChatGPT, fits into the solution of this problem as a facilitator, aiming at the identification of these intersections. The use of this Natural Language Processing (NLP) technique offers a significant advantage in this context, as it allows for deeper semantic understanding, abstraction, and reasoning in several document structures and terminologies [9]. However, it still represents a challenge, since the way the prompt is defined significantly alters the outcome. It is also worth noting that, although they are grouped by the proximity of their approaches, they may not present intersections.

It is also necessary to verify whether the requirements apply in the context of the system that is seeking compliance with these standards. To do this, Prompt #4 was defined.

Finally, to harmonize similar requirements, a common requirement is expected to be generated, incorporating excerpts from the overlapping content found in the standards. To identify that, Prompt #5 was defined. The output of this prompt is typically a table containing sections where the requirements approaches can be merged into a single output, and sections that differ should be retained. Therefore, Prompt #6 was defined to output both the merged text and the text that should be retained separately.

Using the reasoning model, after this chain of prompts, the results will resemble Table 4 (refer to Sect. 5). The model will indicate the sections that were analyzed and a justification for why they should be harmonized or not. The next section presents some experiments and their results when these prompts were fed to the GPT o3 model.

4   The Case Study

As a proof of concept, the method was instantiated for an embedded system in the CubeSat nanosatellite, a space CPS. In this context, NIST, ECSS, and CCSDS standards are often mandatory for compliance. The next subsections present each step of the instantiated method.

4.1   Software Related Requirements

To select standards requirements that fit the scope of the specific system Prompt #1 (refer to Table 1) was submitted to GPT o3 model for execution. In this stage, the prompt was executed in a loop for each of the standard documents, using the RAG capabilities of ChatGPT. Each standard was attached per prompt, and the resulting outputs were consolidated in Table 2, which reflects the aggregated responses generated by the model.

It was observed that the model did not identify software-related requirements in the attached Green Books (350.0-G-3, 350.1-G-3, 350.4-G-2, and 350.7-G-2), with its reasoning indicating that these documents pertain to planning and application guidance within the CCSDS framework. The advantage of using this model lies precisely in its human-in-the-loop approach, which provides the means to validate the accuracy of the model's responses, since tools of this type are not intended to replace human review, but rather to support and facilitate it [6]. Furthermore, it is also evident that not all sections of the ECSS were selected, which means that the model may have understood the documents and the prompt effectively.

In parallel, beyond manually validating the LLM's output by directly reviewing the selected standards, an additional comparison was carried out against NIST SP 800-53r5 using the software-related families identified manually by Rouland et al. [17]. The result of this comparison invites further discussion,

Table 2. Sections related to software requirements identified by GPT

CCSDS Book	ECSS E-ST-80C Section
354.0-M-1 – Symmetric Key Management	5.2 Mission Security
352.0-B-2 – Cryptographic Algorithms	5.2.1 Mission Security Policy
354.0-M-1 – Symmetric Key Management	5.2.2 Mission Security Requirements
355.0-B-2 – Space Data Link Security Protocol	5.3 System Security Engineering
357.0-B-1 – Authentication Credentials	5.3.1 Introduction
	5.3.2 System Security Engineering Requirements
	5.3.3 Supply Chain Requirements
	5.3.4 System Security Engineering Plan

as the model's response included one fewer section than the one selected by the authors in their study (specifically, PL – Planning). Although the model performed with only a single discrepancy, and human review is expected, it is necessary to discuss ways to further improve this efficiency. To proceed with the method and avoid a potential cascading error from the model, the results from the related work were adopted to move forward, with suggestions for improvements and mitigations for such cases discussed in the Sect. 6.

4.2 Grouped Requirements Harmonization

In this work, we adopt OWASP ISVS [14] as an ontology reference. The ISVS is a reference guide for security controls for the lifecycle of IoT devices, from design to implementation and operation. The sections User Space Application Requirements, Software Platform Requirements, and Communication Requirements of the ISVS will be used, together with their respective requirements, so that the terms present in these sections serve as a basis for comparison with the content of the security standards addressed. Therefore, the requirements specified in the standards are grouped according to the terms proximity of the requirements defined in each section of ISVS, considering the keywords generated as proposed by Xu et al. [23].

Keywords were initially instantiated based on each selected OWASP ISVS section, according to Prompt #2. Each ISVS section had subsections, such as in User Space Application Requirements, with Identification & Authentication. Therefore, an example of the generated keywords can be seen in Fig. 2.

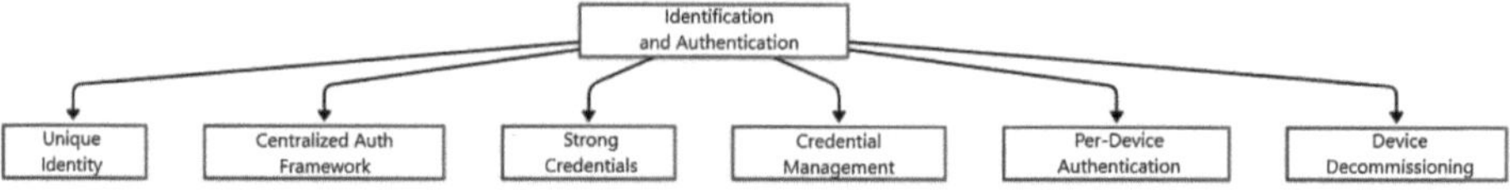

Fig. 2. Keywords generated for a section of the ontological base

After instantiating the keywords according to each ISVS section, the next step was to link them to the sections containing the security standards requirements, aiming to group them. The standards documents were then attached to ChatGPT (refer to Sect. 4.1), indicating which sections were related to the software requirements. To indicate the standards, the {Standard_Section} parameter was used, and the keywords for each ISVS section were indicated in the {Ontology_base_sections} parameter. When executing Prompt #3, with these parameters, an output similar to Table 3 was obtained.

Table 3. Mapping between standards, ISVS, and related security keywords

(Standard) Section	ISVS Section	Related Keyword
(NIST) AC-3(10)	Software Platform	Signed Kernel Modules
(ECSS) 5.2.2	Communication	Encrypted Inter-chip communication
(CCSDS 354.0-M-1) 4.3.1	Software Platform	Secure Communication Channels

Towards harmonization, it is notable that at this stage, the grouping of requirements with similar approaches is taking shape, enabling harmonization. For example, according to the output in Table 3, requirements AC-3(10) from NIST SP 800-53r5 and 4.3.1 from CCSDS Magenta can be grouped under the same section (Software Platform) and compared. However, they do not have the same related keywords, which may mean that they do not have a clear intersection. As mentioned in Sect. 3.3, not all requirements from the standards can be harmonized, and an experiment to evaluate this was conducted and described in the next subsection.

4.3 Grouped Requirements Harmonization

After grouping the requirements that supposedly have a similar approach through the ontological basis, the next step is to analyze whether these requirements can (or cannot) be harmonized into a single requirement, aiming to solve the problems of overlap and complementarity [12].

However, as proposed by Rouland et al. [17], it is also necessary to verify whether the standards' requirements apply to the system that one wishes to comply with. For that, Prompt #4 was tried. In this prompt, the CubeSat CONASAT-0 mission requirements' document and the security standards documents are attached, providing an instruction to verify which requirements are incompatible with the system. The model was shown to be unsuccessful in comprehending the system requirements as a result of this prompt, highlighting several irrelevant criteria. Using the same GPT o3 model as in the previous experiments, we can see that the reasoning highlights arguments like *"The system - in question - is not designed for interactive inputs from untrusted users or data streams; data input is limited to PCD uplinks with standard formats"*.

Thus, it would be necessary to clarify why the SI-10 (Information Input Validation) requirement of NIST SP 800-53r5 would not be applicable. The reasons for this ineffectiveness are seen as limitations of the work and discussed in the next section. Therefore, the results of this experiment (Prompt #4) were disregarded for future experiments, in order to avoid misleading assumptions that could lead to a "snowball effect" of further misinterpretations.

With the results of Sect. 4.2, we move towards harmonizing the requirements imposed by the security standards, remaining to identify and solve the overlaps and differences between their requirements, which were grouped by similarities based on the keywords of the ontology. For that, Prompt #5 (refer to Table 1) was executed. In this prompt, the use of the GPT o3 model is maintained, and the user is expected to define the security standards that he is working on as the {standards_name} parameter and use the requirements that were grouped in the output of Sect. 4.2 as the input for {standard_name_and_requirements} parameter.

Two outputs are presented in Table 4, illustrating the possible types of output. One of them exemplifies the consolidated requirements (CRs) and the other the unconsolidated requirements (URs), indicating which requirements within which sections can be harmonized (or cannot), along with the reason. All requirements provided in the input are expected to be analyzed similarly by the model. It is particularly noteworthy that the model was able to accurately identify indexes and paragraphs corresponding to specific security requirements across different standards. Moreover, within its reasoning output, the model frequently included direct references to excerpts from the original documents, demonstrating its capacity to retrieve and contextualize relevant information to support its comparisons.

As the last step of the experiment, the model is asked to generate harmonized requirements for the CRs and maintain the differences in the URs - as per Prompt #6, achieving the following output for CR_1: *"The mission shall generate (from an approved source), distribute, store, rotate, audit-log and finally destroy all master, section and certificate keys in accordance with the CCSDS key-lifecycle, using NIST-approved algorithms, so that every space-link frame and ground packet protected under ECSS 5.2.2 attains confidentiality, integrity and authenticity."*. It is notable that the model combines structural elements (e.g., verbs "generate", "distribute", "audit-log") with policy ones (e.g., "NIST-approved algorithms") and domain-specific terms (e.g., "space-link frame", "CCSDS key-lifecycle"), showing its ability to coherently integrate information from multiple sources. Further discussion is provided in the following section.

5   Results and Discussion

The experiments reported in this paper used ChatGPT and its RAG capabilities to show the potential use of this LLM tool to address overlapping software security standards requirements. Prompts were established that could lead to a possible solution to this issue. To mitigate the negative impacts that incorrect

Table 4. Consolidated (CR) and unconsolidated (UR) requirements in harmonization

Consolidated Requirement ID	Sections of each security standard	Reason for consolidation/separation according to ChatGPT
CR_1	(NIST) SC-12 (Key Establishment & Management), (NIST) SC-13 (Cryptographic Protection); (ECSS) 5.2.2 Mission Security Requirements; (CCSDS) 354.0-M-1 §4.1 Key types, §4.2 Lifecycle, §4.3.5 Key-update procedures	All three documents require strong, lifecycle-controlled keys and approved algorithms for confidentiality-and-integrity services. Wording differs, but the technical intent is identical, so a single system requirement for "approved cryptography with managed symmetric/certificate keys throughout their lifecycle" suffices
UR_1	(NIST) SC-13, (NIST) SA-9; (ECSS) 5.3.3 Supply Chain	Approaches differ: NIST frames contractual controls; ECSS mandates engineering practice and provenance analysis; CCSDS has no direct analogue. Retain distinct requirements for (a) contractual/service controls (NIST) and (b) technical supply-chain engineering controls (ECSS)

model inferences could impose on the prompt chain, GPT o3 model was chosen to be used in all experiments, allowing us to follow the tool's reasoning. It is also important to highlight that prompt engineering represents a vast area for idea exploration, where the output strongly depends on the prompt structure, which still requires further in-depth studies, as well as the evolution of this process.

The experiment that compared the model and a human-curated selection of requirements from the NIST SP 800-53r5 standard obtained in the literature and detailed in 4.1 highlights the relationship between the prompt and the output, as the model identified one fewer section compared to the selection by Rouland et al. [17].

Considering the harmonization results between CCSDS Books and ECSS E-ST-80C, a manual review confirmed the model's effectiveness in correctly excluding books 350.0-G-3, 350.1-G-3, 350.4-G-2, and 350.7-G-2, as these books are oriented towards mission planning, covering security processes relevant to software engineering but not directly related to software itself, such as threat assessment. Regarding ECSS E-ST-80C, manual document review established that the prompt effectively selected only sections pertinent to software requirements.

In choosing OWASP ISVS as an ontological basis for grouping requirements that address similar contexts through keywords, Prompt #2 showed strong effectiveness in keyword generation aimed at synthesizing the ontology of each ISVS section, a finding corroborated through manual analysis of ISVS sections. Additionally, the semantic relationship between the ontological base and the requirements' approaches was efficient, as portions of requirements either directly contained or were closely related to the meaning of the generated keywords.

However, not all outcomes demonstrated effectiveness and consequently had to be discarded in this research. Prompt #4 caused the model to overlook the necessity of certain security requirements within the system. This oversight was attributed to several reasons, including the specific formulation of the prompt and, notably, the clarity of the system requirements' descriptions. As discussed in Sect. 4.3, despite the system was not designed to receive input from unknown sources and has a standardized format, validation of all received data remains essential to prevent the injection of malicious commands or corrupted data.

When prompting the model to generate the MSB with harmonized requirements, it provided partially effective assistance, as the consolidated requirements text was not easily consumable in the everyday work of an engineering team. The text referenced the sections of the consolidated security standards rather than directly including the respective text excerpts relevant to these approaches. This issue is exemplified by the phrase "using NIST-approved algorithms" in Sect. 4.3, requiring users to directly refer to NIST SP 800-53r5 for approved algorithms, contrary to the MSB's intended goal of consolidating all harmonized requirements into a single document.

5.1   Threats to Validity

The main threat identified in this research, in terms of internal validity, is the semantic ambiguity involved in interpreting security requirements from multiple standards. Although an ontological basis (OWASP ISVS) was used to reduce this ambiguity, variations may still occur, especially when using LLMs like ChatGPT, which are sensitive to prompt formulation. Furthermore, regarding construct validity, reliability is impacted by variability in model outputs due to differences in training data, model versions, and updates to both the ontology and standard documents. Although explicit prompts and documented reasoning processes were included to enhance transparency and reproducibility, it is possible that there are variations in model results other than those presented in this research.

Notably, the dependency on prompt engineering techniques significantly influences the outcomes produced by the language models, posing a threat to the validity of the conclusion, as this sensitivity can affect reproducibility and scalability. Furthermore, difficulties were encountered in assessing the applicability of harmonized security requirements to the specific system under study, which represents a challenge to external validity, highlighting the complexity of achieving fully automated semantic comprehension. Although the proposed method produces promising results, the complexity of certain document structures can challenge ChatGPT's RAG capabilities; therefore, every output in the prompt chain should remain subject to human-in-the-loop review and auditing to ensure accuracy and completeness.

Despite these limitations, the methodology presented in this paper establishes a solid foundation for further research aimed at improving the automated harmonization of security requirements. Its potential for broader applicability across various sectors and contexts represents a meaningful step toward reinforcing the security posture of CPS in general.

6   Conclusion

This research introduces a method that employs a chain of prompts, using Chat-GPT as an LLM tool. The choice of a tool capable of interpreting and generating texts lies in the inherent complexities associated with adhering simultaneously to multiple security standards. The proposed harmonization method, which establishes a Minimum Security Baseline, effectively addresses ambiguities and redundancies found within different security standards, offering systems engineers a consolidated and simplified reference, thereby facilitating compliance and reducing implementation complexity, being applicable to any CPS.

The innovative application of LLM for automating the requirements harmonization process stands out, where the goal of this work is not to evaluate or rank LLMs, but rather to demonstrate the promise of using such models in the security requirements harmonization context. It is important to highlight that, as discussed in Sect. 5.1, the systematic validation of the accuracy of the adopted LLM remains limited, which is mitigated—although not fully resolved—by the use of the GPT with advanced reasoning (o3 model).

It is worth mentioning that prompt engineering is an area that deserves exploration due to the plurality of possible prompts and inputs, where a small change in the instruction can impact the results, as well as the chaining of prompts, which can cause the model itself to improve its responses.

The selection of the OWASP IoT Security Verification Standard as ontological proved effective for semantic analysis and grouping of security requirements, where the practical applicability of the methodology was well demonstrated through a case study in the space sector (CubeSat CONASAT-0 mission), effectively validating the proposed approach, producing an MSB as an output artifact[5].

As future work, we plan to validate the MSB by testing on a system that has implemented the harmonized requirements using the method proposed in this research, to observe whether they mitigate the most common cyberthreats in the environment where the system operates. In addition, we intend to improve the developed prompt chaining, even exploring the idea of having a prompt to check whether the reasoning is correct—similar to a "LLM reviewer". Furthermore, this "LLM reviewer" can be enhanced through role-based prompting techniques, aiming to provide the model with contextual understanding based on specific

---

[5] https://bit.ly/4kyygPQ.

expert perspectives. Additionally, the MSB will be reviewed by human domain experts to ensure completeness and applicability.

Acknowledgements. This work was financed by CAPES - Coord. de Aperfeiçoamento de Pessoal de Nível Superior - Brasil, finance code 001 and it was supported by the PPGT/FT - UNICAMP. Also, it is supported by OpConSat: Operação de Missões de Satélites Distribuídos e Constelações - SEI: 01340.007326/2024-55.

References

1. Alguliyev, R., Imamverdiyev, Y., Sukhostat, L.: Cyber-physical systems and their security issues. Comput. Ind. **100**, 212–223 (2018). https://doi.org/10.1016/j.compind.2018.04.017
2. Chen, T., Fei, J., Guo, Z., Lv, Z., Yuan, T.: Security baseline evaluation and standard research of power intelligent internet of things terminal. In: 2021 IEEE 6th International Conference on Signal and Image Processing (ICSIP), pp. 1004–1007 (2021). https://doi.org/10.1109/ICSIP52628.2021.9688732
3. CCSDS - Consultative Committee for Space Data Systems.: CCSDS Official Website. (2024). https://www.ccsds.org/
4. ECSS - European Cooperation for Space Standardization. ECSS-E-ST-80C: Space Engineering - Security in Space Systems Lifecycles (2023). https://ecss.nl/standard/ecss-e-st-80c/
5. Heng, S.: Industry 4.0: huge potential for value creation waiting to be tapped. Deutsche Bank Res. 8–10 (2014)
6. Lee, J., Lee, J., Yoo, J.J.: The role of large language models in the peer-review process: opportunities and challenges for medical journal reviewers and editors. J. Educ. Eval. Health Professions **22**, 4 (2025). https://doi.org/10.3352/jeehp.2025.22.4
7. Li, X.: Application of RAG model based on retrieval enhanced generation technique in complex query processing. Adv. Comput. Signals Syst. **8**(6), 47–53 (2024). https://doi.org/10.23977/acss.2024.080608
8. Kulu, E.: Nanosats Database (2019). https://www.nanosats.eu/. Accessed 07 Oct 2022
9. Naveed, H., et al.: A Comprehensive Overview of Large Language Models. arXiv preprint arXiv:2307.06435 (2024)
10. Ndao, M. L., Baron, C., Knudsen, E., Joao, K.: Towards a systems engineering framework for CubeSats development. In: 2024 IEEE International Systems Conference (SysCon), pp. 1–8 (2024). https://doi.org/10.1109/SysCon61195.2024.10553549
11. Nussbaum, B., Berg, G.: Cybersecurity implications of commercial off the shelf (COTS) equipment in space infrastructure. In: Space Infrastructures: From Risk to Resilience Governance, pp. 91–99 (2020)
12. Olifer, D., Goranin, N., Cenys, A., Kaceniauskas, A., Janulevicius, J.: Defining the minimum security baseline in a multiple security standards environment by graph theory techniques. Appl. Sci. **9**(4) (2019). https://doi.org/10.3390/app9040681
13. OpenAI.: Ask ChatGPT anything (2024). https://openai.com/. Accessed 10 Dec 2024

14. OWASP.: OWASP IoT Security Verification Standard (2024). https://owasp.org/www-project-iot-security-verification-standard/. Accessed 10 Dec 2024
15. Parmar, M., Miles, A.: Cyber security frameworks (CSFs): an assessment between the NIST CSF v2.0 and EU standards. In: 2024 Security for Space Systems (3S), pp. 1–7 (2024). https://doi.org/10.23919/3S60530.2024.10592293
16. Pardo, C., Pino, F., Garcia, F., Piattini, M., Baldassarre, M.: An ontology for the harmonization of multiple standards and models. Comput. Stand. Interfaces **34**, 48–59 (2012). https://doi.org/10.1016/j.csi.2011.05.005
17. Rouland, Q., Gjorcheski, S., Jaskolka, J.: Eliciting a security architecture requirements baseline from standards and regulations. In: 2023 IEEE 31st International Requirements Engineering Conference on Workshops (REW), pp. 224–229 (2023). https://doi.org/10.1109/REW57809.2023.00045
18. Ross, R., Pillitteri, V., Dempsey, K., Riddle, M., Guissanie, J.: Security and Privacy Controls for Information Systems and Organizations. NIST. 800-53(5) (2020). https://doi.org/10.6028/NIST.SP.800-53r5
19. United Nations Office for Outer Space Affairs - UNOOSA.: Online index of objects launched into outer space (2022). https://www.unoosa.org/oosa/osoindex/. Accessed 07 Aug 2024
20. Von Solms, S., Futcher, L.A.: Adaption of a secure software development methodology for secure engineering design. IEEE Access **8**, 125630–125637 (2020). https://doi.org/10.1109/ACCESS.2020.3007355
21. Willbold, J., Schloegel, M., Vögele, M., Gerhardt, M., Holz, T., Abbasi, A.: Space odyssey: an experimental software security analysis of satellites. In: 2023 IEEE Symposium on Security and Privacy, pp. 1–19 (2023). https://doi.org/10.1109/SP46215.2023.10351029
22. Wolf, M., Serpanos, D.: Safety and security in cyber-physical systems and internet-of-things systems. Proc. IEEE **106**(1), 9–20 (2018). https://doi.org/10.1109/JPROC.2017.2781198
23. Xu, S., et al.: Reasoning before comparison: LLM-enhanced semantic similarity metrics for domain specialized text analysis. arXiv preprint arXiv:2402.11398 (2024)
24. Yaacoub, J.-P., Salman, O., Noura, H., Kaaniche, N., Chehab, A., Malli, M.: Cyber-physical systems security: limitations, issues and future trends. Microprocess. Microsyst. **77**(103201), 1–33 (2020). https://doi.org/10.1016/j.micpro.2020.103201
25. Yasar, H., Teplov, S.: DevSecOps in embedded systems: an empirical study of past literature. In: Proceedings of the 17th International Conference on Availability, Reliability and Security, pp. 1–6 (2022). https://doi.org/10.1145/3538969.3544451

Towards LGPD Compliance: Analysis and Support to Prepare Your Computing Environment

Aldrey Pedrazoli[1]([✉]) [iD], Naghmeh Ivaki[2] [iD], and Regina Moraes[1,2] [iD]

[1] School of Technology, UNICAMP, Campinas, Brazil
`a150876@dac.unicamp.br`
[2] CISUC/LASI, University of Coimbra, Coimbra, Portugal
`{remoraes,naghmeh}@dei.uc.pt`

Abstract. The current business landscape has witnessed an exponential proliferation of technologies, such as big data, artificial intelligence, and the Internet of Things, which significantly impact the collection, storage, and processing of data. Innovations like mass data collection, predictive analytics, and process automation enhance companies' ability to gain valuable insights, optimize operational efficiency, and improve the customer experience. However, these technological advances also bring new responsibilities. Despite the progress, adequate data protection practices are still not consistently applied, and gaps remain in the awareness of data subjects' rights. The importance of the right to privacy and control over the use and sharing of sensitive personal data has driven the development of various solutions and regulations worldwide. In Brazil, the General Data Protection Law (LGPD), in force since 2020, emerged as a regulatory framework to guide companies' actions, encouraging the adoption of best practices in the use of technologies to protect individual rights. This work aims to present a guideline for the use of technological solutions that, if adopted by companies, can minimize their vulnerabilities related to data protection and bring them closer to compliance with the LGPD. First, compliance with the LGPD is investigated through a questionnaire conducted with Brazilian companies. Next, available technological solutions are analyzed. Finally, the two sets of results are combined to develop an interactive guideline designed to help companies assess their own compliance status and gain insights to improve their computational environment.

Keywords: Privacy · LGPD · GDPR · Compliance

1 Introduction

Technological advances and the growing volume of information collected and stored in recent decades have driven a digital revolution in several areas of society, significantly impacting the way data is collected, stored, processed, shared,

L. A. Rodrigues and R. Oliveira (Eds.): LADC 2025, CCIS 2697, pp. 54–71, 2026.
https://doi.org/10.1007/978-3-032-11539-3_4

utilized, and discarded. Today, the ability to extract knowledge from data originating from institutional systems, social networks, and public databases has become a critical competitive advantage. Despite the technological challenges involved in developing robust systems capable of efficiently extracting relevant insights, companies must continuously pursue data-driven strategies to maintain their competitiveness in the market. At the same time, to protect themselves, companies must implement complex solutions, relying on security mechanisms to safeguard data and ensure the protection of both business knowledge and the privacy of individuals associated with it. In this context, the governance and protection of sensitive data play a crucial role throughout the data lifecycle.

With the emergence of the General Data Protection Law (LGPD) [1], the importance of understanding and properly managing the data lifecycle has become even more pressing, as this legislation sets clear guidelines for the security of personal data and the protection of individual rights. Violations of this regulation can have serious consequences for a company, threatening its credibility in the market and exposing it to heavy legal penalties.

Maintaining compliance with the LGPD requires constant monitoring, internal audits, and periodic reviews. Furthermore, knowledge of supporting technologies is relevant, as the volume and diversity of information limit manual solutions. As companies continue to face several uncertainties and challenges related to the LGPD, this work aims to propose a practical guideline to support them in achieving compliance.

Several specific goals were pursued during the work's development in order to achieve such a guideline: i) identifying the challenges that companies continue to face; ii) surveying the solutions that have been used and implemented in companies; iii) surveying the technologies that can fill in the gaps that currently exist; and iv) mapping between the technologies and legal requirements while taking the complexity of the environments into consideration.

To achieve the first two objectives, we applied a questionnaire that was answered by representatives of 32 companies. The questionnaire also helped us identify the main open questions, which then guided the survey of existing technologies to support companies in implementing them. This process, in turn, provided insights for the development of the proposed practical guide.

We also conducted an analysis of the law regarding technologies that can support companies in increasing their compliance with the LGPD, along with a prioritization of actions to help companies progress from basic implementations to more complex and expensive solutions. The resulting practical guideline offers a summary of the law and requirements, presents technological solutions that can assist with LGPD compliance, and provides easier access to the law's clauses.

The rest of the paper is organized as follows: Sect. 2 presents the background on the topic as well as the works more closely related to our work; Sect. 3 presents the methodology used in this study; Sect. 4 presents the results, and finally Sect. 5 concludes the paper.

2   Background and Related Work

Brazil had already discussed data protection legislation before the regulation proposed by the European Union (EU), GDPR (General Data Protection Regulation) [2]). The *Marco Civil da Internet* [3], one of the first initiatives in this regard, did not specifically address the protection of personal data. The implementation of GDPR in May 2018 was then one of the most significant catalysts of the LGPD (*Lei Geral de Proteção de Dados*). GDPR established rigorous standards for the processing of personal data and influenced the international community to adopt similar regulations. The two regulations share significant similarities, both reflecting a global effort to protect personal data and privacy.

The LGPD addresses technological topics in several sections. The LGPD principles highlight purpose, suitability, necessity, transparency, security, prevention, and accountability. The essence of these principles reflects a concern for the appropriate and secure processing of personal data in the context of constant technological evolution. As mentioned by Muncinelli et al. [4], no single product or action guarantees LGPD compliance; instead, a clear strategy is required, including legal, technological, and management processes.

For the processing of personal data by public authorities, the LGPD establishes a legal framework that balances government responsibilities with the protection of citizens' rights and privacy. The ANPD (*Autoridade Nacional de Proteção de Dados*), as a regulatory body, has already made available guidelines on how data processing should be carried out by public authorities [5]. Accioly [6] provides a legal analysis of studies on the shared use of personal data collected by public bodies contracting SERPRO (*Serviço Federal de Processamento de Dados*), a public company, which reuses these data for paid third-party consultations without the consent or notification of the data subject.

As presented in [7], companies collected sensitive information in large quantities to conduct research on COVID-19. Paparova et al. [8] conducted an investigation on data governance, focusing on the ten-year evolution of a national digital service for personal health data in Norway. Their study highlights how the GDPR became a significant milestone in these companies.

Regarding the adoption of technological solutions, the automation of processes and systems must take these regulations into account. It is important to evaluate how data is collected, as this data serves as the foundation for any technological solution. As published by the Information Commissioner's Office [9], the United Kingdom's Data Protection Department states that data must be well documented so that it can comply with the GDPR accountability principle since all presented solutions consume this data.

Among the technologies most explicitly mentioned in the LGPD are encryption and data anonymization. Research on encryption suggests that data should be encrypted both in transit and in storage. Almeida et al. [10] highlight that selecting the appropriate encryption type is crucial, as certain technologies may become obsolete over time. They also state that data needs to be selectively encrypted, and highly sensitive data (e.g., health data) should be prioritized.

Acar et al. [11] presented a state-of-the-art on homomorphic encryption. Following the publication of Gentry [12] 's work, emphasis has shifted towards fully homomorphic encryption (FHE), which enables any operation to be performed on encrypted data. However, there are still important issues related to the computing overhead required, limiting the adoption of this technology by the industry. More recently, Fan et al. [13] investigated how to convert available computing resources into Graphics Processing Units (GPUs) to assist FHE by implementing some primitives. On the industry's part, more efficient implementation schemes have emerged, making FHE in data processing closer to achievement [14].

Regarding sensitive data, there are market solutions that can be used to perform data anonymization/pseudo-anonymization. The work by Raj and D'Souza [15] presents the efficiency of models with anonymized data and emphasizes how anonymizing data in stages increases the performance of these models. However, Bandara et al. [16] expose a risk of re-identification, that is, anonymized data still identifies a specific individual [17]. The authors evaluate four anonymization techniques to determine the risk of re-identification.

A key concern of the LGPD is informed consent. Companies must obtain permission from data owners to use their sensitive personal data. The method for collecting consent depends on the company's needs, technology, and resources. There are several tools to detect the collection of consent on websites through cookies; however, most websites offer few or no options [18]. Rhahla et al. [19] emphasize that the data subject must have the right to define their preferences regarding the frequency of collection, the granularity of the data, and the use of information that allows its disclosure to third parties. It also notes that the principle of data minimization is important, although opportunities arise from the use of large volumes of data (Big Data).

One of the LGPD's main responsibilities is the right of access, which guarantees that people can exercise their rights over how their personal data is processed. This process can be significantly aided by technological solutions. The development of a self-service portal is one technology option for this purpose, where data subjects can see what information is being gathered, ask for changes or deletions, and monitor the progress of their requests. Companies must also have effective means of communication in place so that data subjects can contact them and submit their requests in a timely and secure manner.

Access control also plays a fundamental role in the implementation of technological solutions. They can offer efficient mechanisms to control who can access, view, modify, or delete stored personal data. The work by Crockett et al. [21] presents a view of how companies can create profiles and how decisions made by such systems are expected to be GDPR compliant. The concept of an Identity Management system (IDM) is discussed in [22], in which self-sovereign identity allows users to self-manage their digital identities without depending on third-party providers to store and manage data centrally.

Cejas et al. [34] introduced *CompAi*, an AI-powered tool for analyzing companies' privacy policies against GDPR requirements. Our proposed guide complements this tool by identifying gaps in privacy policies and recommending technologies to improve compliance. Our work focuses on the LGPD clauses, offering a guideline with suggestions for technologies and tools to aid legal compliance.

3   Approach and Methodology

We first analyzed the LGPD and highlighted its clauses that could be supported by technological solutions. Next, a search was carried out in order to list an initial set of appropriate technologies and tools. To understand the position of companies in relation to the law, a questionnaire consisting of 30 questions was proposed to be answered by companies, more specifically by those responsible for cybersecurity management. The aim was to understand how companies have responded to new regulations and to identify their main challenges. The questionnaire was designed to be completed online via a virtual form. Figure 1 resumes the steps followed in this study.

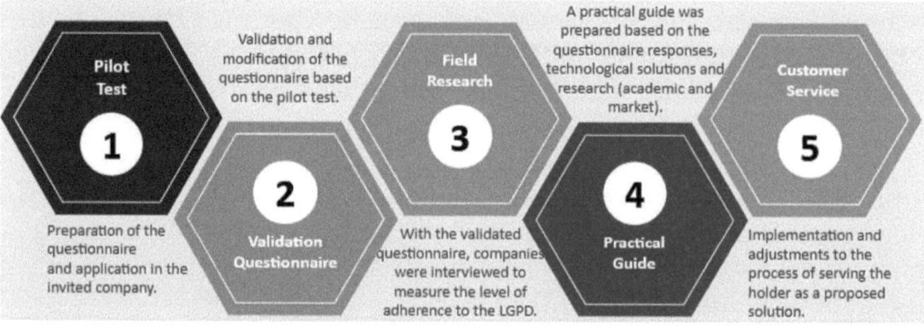

Fig. 1. The applied methodology.

Following Vieira et al. [23], the target audience was chosen to be professionals responsible for corporate security and privacy policies. Accordingly, the questionnaire's language and presentation were tailored to this audience. The questions were prepared based on the articles by Dalle Rocha and Canedo [24], Araujo et al. [25], and Machado et al. [26]. The questionnaire consists of three sections: the goal of the first section is to understand the organizational characteristics of the company (6 questions), such as size, followed by the second section, including questions (21 questions) that allow assessing knowledge of LGPD and supporting technological solutions within the company. Finally, the last section discusses the importance of this research (3 questions). The results were evaluated in most items, according to the Likert scale, with the options: completely disagree, disagree, neutral, agree, and completely agree. The questionnaire was developed based on the theoretical and practical foundations of the LGPD, ensuring that the questions address essential aspects of the legislation.

A pilot test was conducted in a guest company (see step 1 in Fig. 1) to gather example responses and collect feedback for refining the questionnaire.

To validate the questionnaire (step 2 in Fig. 1), inspired by the work of Hoss and Caten [27], the following steps were followed: content validity, exploratory factor analysis, construction validity, reliability (precision of measurement), detailed analysis of items, and descriptive statistics of factors (external validation).

In addition, an end-to-end survey of the LGPD was carried out to prepare the guide (step 3 in Fig. 1). This stage was also of great help in validating the questionnaire questions, as they were assessed to see if they would, in fact, cover the law. These validations ensure that the questions included are representative and relevant to the research objectives.

Based on the knowledge acquired about existing technological solutions through the survey carried out, as well as the responses collected by the questionnaires, a practical guide was proposed to support companies in achieving LGPD compliance (step 4 in Fig. 1). The last step of the methodology involves proposing a solution to address one of the gaps identified through the questionnaire, specifically the Customer Service (most cited), which involves guaranteeing that the customer's rights are respected (step 5 in Fig. 1). The next section presents the results and discusses our findings.

4 Results and Discussion

First, this section presents the pilot test on the questionnaire, followed by an analysis of the results of the field survey on the knowledge of companies about LGPD and the technological solutions they use. A statistical analysis is then conducted to evaluate the significance of the collected data. Drawing on these findings and LGPD documentation, a technological reference guide is introduced, outlining key topics, identified solutions, and a practical approach to accessing LGPD clauses. A recurring issue highlighted in the survey responses was the difficulty in providing effective solutions for the customer service process. To address this, a targeted proposal,developed in collaboration with one of the participating companies, is presented. Finally, the section concludes by summarizing the identified problems, challenges, and opportunities for future work.

4.1 Pilot Test

To obtain a sample of what the responses to the questions would be like and to obtain suggestions for improvements to the questionnaire, a pilot test was carried out in a guest company (see step 1 in Fig. 1). The questionnaire was sent for evaluation, and then the responses were analyzed. There were some suggestions for changes (new technological solutions according to Alex LaCasse. [28] are considered) and additions (3 new questions are added). After adding and modifying the questions suggested by the pilot test participants, the final version of the questionnaire was obtained (step 2 in Fig. 1). Similar contexts were grouped, and a statistical correlation analysis was performed on the answers obtained.

4.2   Results of the Survey

The final version of the questionnaire was sent to a list of information security experts, members of a group of companies that focus on information technology, particularly on information privacy. We have received responses from 32 companies from various sectors, including finance, retail, industry, and education. Based on the responses, 93.8% of the companies are private, and only 6% lack a designated person or department for LGPD compliance. Most of the companies are in the technology and e-commerce sectors. Most companies, around 56%, are large and have more than 1,000 employees. Furthermore, when asked about the level of sensitivity of the data processed by the company, 75% described it as high or very high sensitivity.

Another important point is to understand how these companies share information with third parties. Among 75% of companies that share information with third parties, 16.6% still do not use encryption or pseudo-anonymization methods. This supports the observation that some companies have yet to adopt a technological framework for LGPD compliance, an important subject for data holders. It is worth noting that the ANPD has already published rules for data sharing, making it clear how the processing agents should act [30].

We also realized that there are around 28% of the companies (12.5% answered "no", 12.5% "do not know" and 3% "do not want to inform") that do not address the concept of data collection minimization. This concept is crucial for legal compliance, requiring responsible data collection for specific, legitimate purposes. While large datasets benefit fields like marketing and market analysis—especially with AI support—indiscriminate data collection must be avoided.

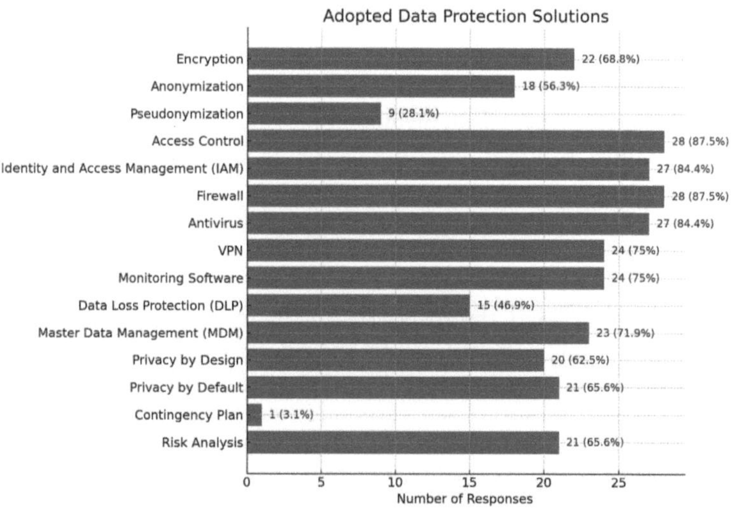

Fig. 2. Main Technological Solutions Adopted by the Companies.

Another important aspect highlighted in the law is the termination of data processing (Section IV, articles 15 and 16). Secure disposal is a critical step in the data lifecycle, especially once processing has ended and proper deletion measures must be applied. However, our survey revealed that only 75% of companies report having specific rules for this. For digital information, specialized tools can ensure irreversible deletion. In certain cases, data may be anonymized, making re-identification of subjects difficult or impossible. In these cases, data can be retained for statistical or research purposes without violating LGPD principles.

One of the questions concerns technological solutions that are used to ensure compliance with the law. Figure 2 presents these solutions and the percentage of companies adopting them. The law does not specify which technological solutions should be used. However, it is clear in Article 46 that processing agents must adopt technical and administrative security measures to protect personal data from unauthorized access and accidental or unlawful processing.

Results show that the two most widely used solutions are Access Control and Firewall. These security measures ensure protection in two pillars of information security, namely confidentiality and integrity, by controlling who can access or modify information and records. The next most commonly used solutions are Identity and Access Management (IAM), Antivirus software, and Virtual Private Networks (VPNs), which are mainly used as preventive security measures.

One technique that is required by law is data anonymization. However, only 56% of companies currently use it. A key barrier to using anonymization is the challenge of ensuring irreversibility. Despite advanced methods for anonymization, big data and AI can enable re-identification through data cross-referencing. Anonymization also reduces data accuracy and usefulness, which can limit decision-making and product development. Silva et al. [33] proposed a staged anonymization approach to balance privacy and data utilization.

Beyond legal-specific questions, the questionnaire included open-ended questions to explore company behavior. For customer service, most use electronic channels (email or online forms), though some also mentioned third parties and phone. Larger companies often use automated systems like bots and auto-replies.

When asked about Data Protection Impact Assessments (DPIAs), most respondents couldn't provide details due to business confidentiality. However, available responses indicate that DPIAs follow legal requirements: mapping processes and linking them to a legal basis. Processes based on legitimate interest are carried out by the DPIA and conducted by the privacy team together with the Data Protection Officer (DPO). Other responses include comments on business continuity plans. Article 6, Section VII of the LGPD defines security and requires measures to protect data from unauthorized access (confidentiality), accidental or unlawful destruction or loss (integrity and availability), alteration (integrity), and unauthorized communication or dissemination (confidentiality).

4.3 Analysis of the Survey's Results

The statistical software R, complemented with the TM library (text mining), was used to analyze the data collected. Text mining was necessary because most

Table 1. The Most Frequent Words in Questionnaire Answers.

Word	Frequency
Data	84
Agreement	66
Inform	62
Privacy	49
Access	48
Management	42

of the questions were discursive. TM enabled text mining by converting the collected answers into a character vector.

Dixon [29] defined four steps for text mining: problem identification, pre-processing, data mining, and post-processing. Once the text has been structured, synonyms have been grouped, and stopwords have been excluded by TM, information extraction can take place. Word frequencies are calculated based on the cleaned text. This will rank the words, showing the most used terms. Table 1 contains the most used words and the number of times each word was used.

As a result of this analysis, it is clear that the most frequent words are related to the customer service process, since they contain the words "agreement" and "inform". This information was of great importance in guiding the choice we made to implement one of the identified gaps.

Considered a crucial requirement by most companies, a partnership was established with one of them to present a solution for the customer service process (see Sect. 4.5). Two other frequently cited terms, Access and Management, relate to the access management process, highlighting concerns about unauthorized access and data leakage.

The data was also grouped to assess whether there was any pattern or trend in the responses obtained. Concentrations were identified in dominant categories, and results were then grouped by the number of employees, the level of sensitivity, and the number of technological solutions implemented by the company. It was possible to arrive at 3 clusters according to this criterion: (1) 16 large companies with high data sensitivity and a reasonable amount of implemented technological solutions (10 up to 14), composed of 50% of the companies; (2) 11 companies of varied sizes but with medium to high sensitivity, representing 34.38% of the companies; and (3) 5 medium-sized companies with low operational complexity, corresponding to 15.63% of the companies. We can see this grouping in Fig. 3. Therefore, the points in space represent the observations, while their colors indicate the clusters formed by the K-Means algorithm, which partitioned the data into these three groups based on their similarities.

These characteristics make cluster 0 strategic for actions that require greater attention to security and compliance with data protection legislation. The combination of high sensitivity and high volume of data implies the need for additional protection and segmentation measures to avoid risks associated with the process-

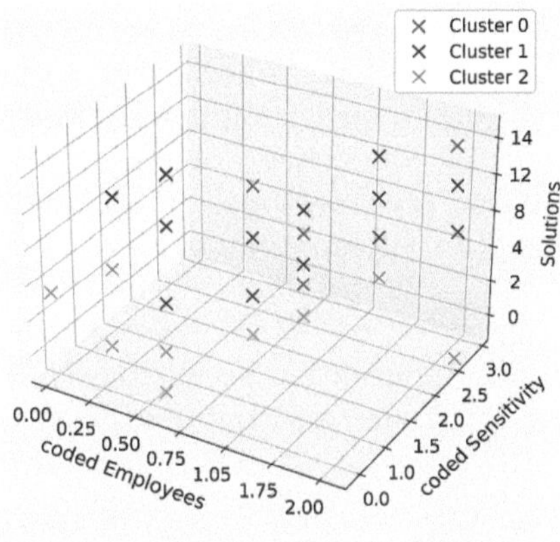

Fig. 3. Clusters of Companies.

ing of sensitive information. The other groups have predominantly lower sensitivity levels, which implies less stringent protection demands. However, there are specific cases of high sensitivity within this group, which require special attention to ensure data security. Additionally, statistical tests were applied to the data to assess normality. The Shapiro-Wilk test was applied to two variables: the company's level of knowledge about the law and the level of concern about compliance with the law when starting a new model/project. The test indicated that there is no normal distribution in both ($p = 3.581e\text{-}06$ and $1.875e\text{-}05$, respectively). The analysis was also performed considering the three clusters. The normality analysis using Shapiro-Wilker resulted in a p-value of 0.0535 for cluster 0, 0.736 for cluster 1, and 0.827 for cluster 2. Therefore, it can be concluded that clusters 1 and 2 follow a normal distribution, while for cluster 0, it is found that they are at a decision threshold and could be treated as approximately normal.

Performing a complementary analysis, we obtain the asymmetry value as −0.817, which indicates a negatively asymmetric distribution, with a greater concentration of values on the right side of the mean and a longer tail on the left. On the other hand, we have kurtosis = 3.08, and since it is close to 3, it indicates that the distribution has tails similar to those of a normal distribution. Knowing that the data follow a normal distribution helps to choose more appropriate analysis methods, simplify calculations, and make reliable predictions and inferences. Based on the results obtained, a guide was developed to help companies comply with the LGPD (see Sect. 4.4), as well as a process to solve the problem of customer services (Sect. 4.5).

4.4   Technology Reference Guide

The macro version of the proposed reference guide can be viewed in Fig. 4. The guide presents a more concise proposal for small companies and a more comprehensive proposal for medium and large companies.

For the large- and medium-sized company branches, the topics are related to specific articles of the LGPD that are subject to technological solutions (for example, items of purely legal or structural descriptions are not covered). They reflect the practical needs of compliance, ranging from support for data subjects' rights to technical and organizational data management. This guide is a tool for companies seeking to structure their practices according to legal requirements, ensuring security, privacy, and efficiency in personal data processing. The highlighted topics are Responding to Data Subject Rights (or Customer Service), Corporate Communications, Information Technology (IT) Management, Privacy, Awareness and Training Programs, and Information Security. Each of those is followed by a list of LGPD articles that discuss each of the subjects.

Customer service highlights the need for processes and tools to ensure compliance with data subject rights like access, rectification, deletion, and portability. Clear communication is key to informing data subjects, partners, and employees about data processing. IT plays a strategic role in implementing data protection measures. Privacy, a core LGPD principle, aims to protect individuals' rights and dignity. The goal of the awareness and training program is to inform and empower those involved in data processing. Information security is vital to safeguard data from unauthorized access, loss, or leaks.

Each of these branches can be expanded to include subtopics and technical solutions that can help ensure compliance with these themes. Figure 5 illustrates the expansion of customer service, including the means to comply with relevant laws and the available tools to support the company in adequately addressing customer requests. Furthermore, when the last item, "The LGPD says..." is selected, it displays the original text of the specific article of the law extracted directly from the government's official website, in its last version, thanks to the text processing provided by ChatGPT, which was configured to limit its search to the LGPD official document.

For small companies (for example, micro-enterprises and startups), the requirements are much lower and cover the essential points. The ANPD consid-

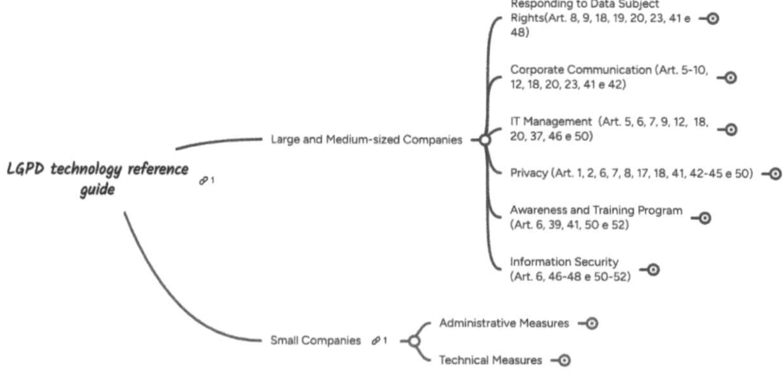

Fig. 4. Technology Reference Guide.

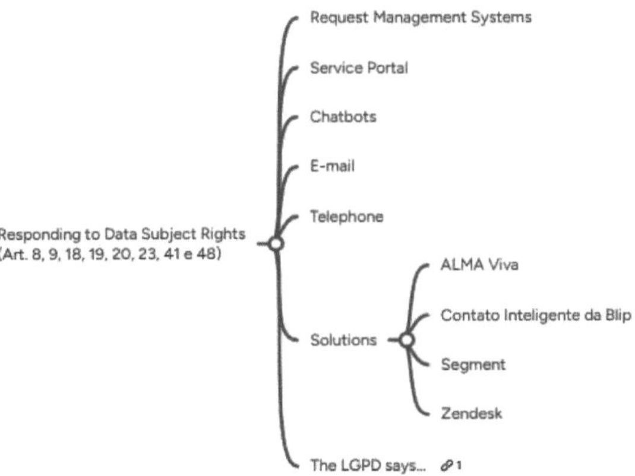

Fig. 5. Customer Service Means and Tools.

ers small businesses to be those with gross revenue in the range of R$360,000.00 to R$4,800,000.00 (*Brazilian Reais*) and establishes simplified rules, guidelines, and procedures for them, providing a checklist to help these companies adapt to the LGPD. In addition, a simplified model was created for these companies to register their personal data processing activities. The checklist entitled Information Security for Small-Scale Data Processing Agents presents two approaches: Administrative Measures and Technical Measures.

Administrative measures are related to Information Security Policy (ISP), Awareness and Training, and Contract Management. Technical measures, i.e., those that are subject to technological solutions, include Data Storage, Information Security, and Access Control. So, it is necessary to define sharing rules with clear criteria for exchanging this information between companies, ensuring that only necessary data is shared with adequate protection.

The suggested technical measures involve practices such as minimum information collection, the use of pseudonymization (e.g., encryption), and restrictions on the use of external devices. It is also recommended that backups be performed periodically in safe locations and that data be properly deleted, ensuring that it is physically destroyed when necessary. For communication security, it is essential to use encrypted connections (TLS/HTTPS) and email encryption. Firewalls should be implemented, and email services should be protected against threats. Sensitive data should only be accessible through restricted channels.

In this case, each branch can also be expanded, and the base document can be displayed on the screen with the help of ChatGPT, which accesses the document directly from the official government website where this checklist is located. At the time this work was written, there were positive reports from the companies involved, but reports from regulatory agencies on reduced complaint rates are expected soon.

4.5   Customer Service Process

To develop a solution for customer service, a partnership was established between the researchers and one of the companies that participated in the study. To support the process, the company acquired one of the tools indicated in the reference guide, the Segment tool[1]. Both parties monitored the process of acquiring and implementing the tool. The tool is a data management platform that collects, unifies, and activates customer data across systems and communication channels. It is central to the company's data strategy, offering an integrated view of customer behavior for personalized interactions. The platform supports configurable user profiles with access restrictions, ensures authenticated and encrypted communication, and anonymizes the database.

During the tool configuration, data acquisition and storage from various sources were defined, enabling personalized offers and communications for customers (see Fig. 6 [31]). Data unification reduces time and effort in managing scattered information, allowing for more effective service and reducing company vulnerability. It captures all customer actions, such as URL access or balance changes, ensuring the most up-to-date data.

Another possible configuration is the creation of audiences. This functionality allows you to create flows and customize campaigns and communications with customers, ensuring that contact is directed only to customers who have, in fact, given this explicit consent, and restricting data collection to permitted data only. It also assists in the withdrawal of consent process, allowing you to track where communications are coming from, identify data sources, and make changes to information in a more automated manner, since the tool shows all sources that retain information from a specific holder in a reverse manner.

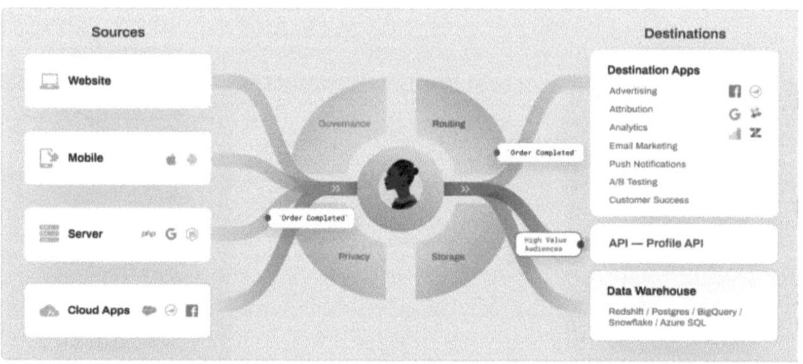

Fig. 6. Configured Connections in Segment Tool [31].

The flow depicted in Fig. 7 represents Segment's secure infrastructure, which manages data received from various customer and partner sources, processing

---

[1] https://segment.com.

and storing it securely before sending it to configured destinations. Data begins with Customer Sources (on the left side of the figure) and can be collected from websites, mobile applications (iOS and Android), or servers (using languages such as PHP, Ruby, Go, and Python). Hypertext Transfer Protocol Secure (HTTPS) requests from customers are routed to the Segment API through an Application Load Balancer, which distributes the requests to the appropriate services within the Segment infrastructure.

This infrastructure is protected with restricted access using tools such as Okta SSO and Duo MFA, while all Amazon Web Services (AWS) accounts are actively monitored by Security Incident Response Teams (SIRT). In addition, there is continuous monitoring for Server-Side Request Forgery (SSRF) attacks. The first processing point is the Tracking API, which handles events and sends them to the Event Pipeline. This pipeline ensures that data flows correctly and can be stored in Archives or sent to destinations in cloud mode. Data in archives is stored in Amazon S3 (Simple Storage Service) buckets, which are encrypted at the disk level and isolated in a separate AWS account with restricted access.

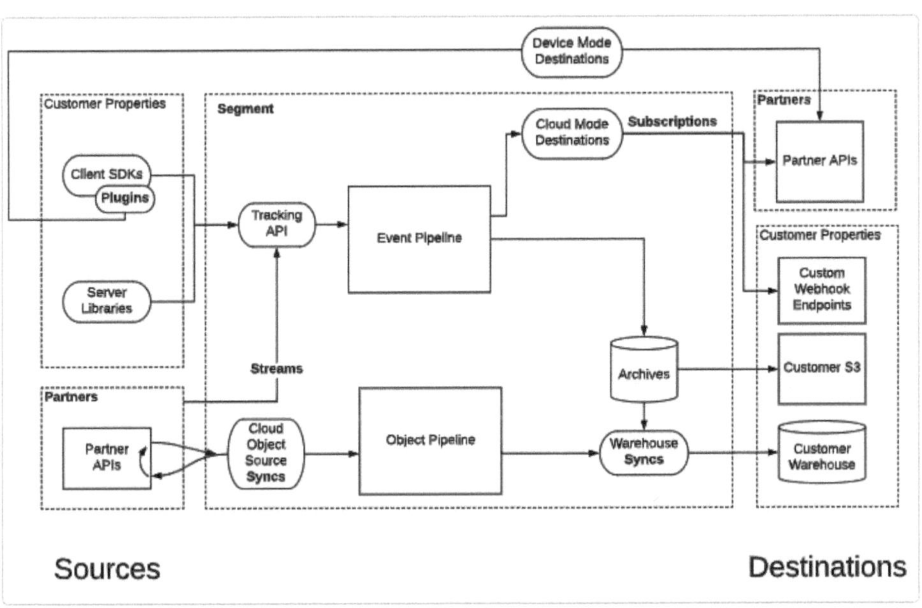

Fig. 7. Data Flow in the Segment Tool Environment. [32]

In parallel, there are Partner Sources, which represent external APIs, whose data is sent to the system via HTTPS requests, synchronizing with Cloud Objects Source Syncs and then processed by Object Pipeline, preparing it for integration with Warehouse Syncs. The finalized data can be sent to different Customer Destinations, such as custom webhooks, S3 buckets, or warehouses. The transfer is done via TLS and, in the case of S3, the AWS Assume Role

API is used for greater security, instead of using traditional API keys. This flow ensures secure, efficient data collection, processing, storage, and delivery, with multiple protection layers and flexible integration options. The tool only collects data permitted via API.

4.6   Threats to Validity

A key limitation of this guide is its generalization. Although the participating companies were from different sectors, the sample is small and may not encompass the variability of Brazilian companies. Also, based on the questionnaire, the results are dependent on the participants' perceptions or understanding of compliance and could influence their responses. As a broad reference, it may not address the specific needs of each organization, which can vary by size, sector, or data complexity. Another limitation is the ongoing evolution of legislation and technology. The LGPD may change as new data processing challenges emerge, making even up-to-date guides potentially obsolete. Continuous monitoring and adaptation are essential for compliance but can be challenging, especially for resource-limited organizations. While the guide offers tools and best practices, it doesn't cover the full complexity of cyber risks. Information security evolves rapidly, and the guide lacks details on infrastructure and security solutions needed to address new threats. Ongoing vigilance and updates are essential to mitigate these risks. Finally, while the guide supports LGPD compliance, it doesn't replace legal advice. Complex cases require interpretation by specialized lawyers. It is recommended to validate the articles of the law when consulting the guide in a few years, although in the guide itself, a topic was added with the phrase "The LGPD says..." that triggers search keys directed to ChatGPT, taking advantage of the tool's text processing capacity. Even so, it may need maintenance if the URL changes or ChatGPT has changes in the configuration that allow directing searches.

5   Conclusion and Future Work

Data protection laws like the GDPR (EU) and LGPD (Brazil) marked a major shift in global privacy and data security. This reflects the growing concern with protecting individual rights in a scenario of technological advancement. A portion of the industry remains unaware of these regulations. This study highlights the need to balance technological opportunities with the responsibility of protecting individual privacy. A questionnaire assessing LGPD adherence showed an average compliance score of 4.25 out of 5 among Brazilian companies, indicating they are generally close to a high level of commitment.

This research contributes to companies aiming for LGPD compliance. The guide developed serves as a practical tool for managers and analysts, offering guidance on interpreting and applying LGPD requirements. One company reported increased daily engagement after using the guide for two months. Each LGPD article was linked to practical actions and technological solutions, helping companies understand their obligations and implement effective data protection measures. Another key contribution was supporting the implementation of a customer service solution in partnership with a participating company. Though recently adopted, it has already improved response times and handling of data subject requests. More accurate statistics and confirmation from regulatory agencies on reduced complaint rates are expected soon. The survey results from participating companies highlight key challenges and best practices of those already compliant with the legislation. It provides valuable insights into Brazil's current compliance state, identifying gaps and opportunities for improvement.

Future research could explore several promising areas to deepen understanding of the LGPD. These include developing compliance automation tools, comparing LGPD implementation with data protection regulations like the GDPR, studying the impact of education and training on compliance, analyzing consumer perceptions, assessing the economic impact on Brazilian companies, and examining LGPD implementation in specific sectors such as healthcare, finance, and technology to identify unique challenges and solutions. As this research shows, LGPD compliance is an ongoing process that requires technical, operational, and cultural changes. Employee training, appointing data protection specialists, and creating internal audits are key to long-term compliance. The LGPD is a critical milestone, guiding companies toward more ethical and transparent data processing. By analyzing technological trends and legal compliance, this study provides practical insights to help companies adapt, fostering a data protection culture that strengthens consumer trust and market integrity.

Acknowledgements. This work was financed by CAPES - Coord. de Aperfeiçoamento de Pessoal de Nível Superior - Brasil, finance code 001 and it was supported by the PPGT/FT - UNICAMP.

References

1. LGPD. https://tinyurl.com/mtzxhc97. Accessed 14 Apr 2025
2. GDPR. https://gdpr-info.eu/. Accessed 14 Apr 2025
3. Marco civil da Internet. https://tinyurl.com/3t7kwumd. Accessed 14 Apr 2025
4. Muncinelli, G., Lima, E., Deschamps, F., Costa, S., Cestari, J: Components of the Preliminary Conceptual Model for Process Capability in LGPD (Brazilian Data Protection Regulation) Context. 12nd edn. Transdisciplinary Engineering for Complex Socio-technical Systems – Real-life App., Brazil (2020)
5. Landerdahl, C., Maiolino, I., Dias , J. Borges, L.:Tratamento de dados pessoais pelo Poder Público. Autoridade Nacional de Proteção de Dados, Brazil (2023)
6. Direito fundamental à proteção de dados pessoais no setor público: uma análise jurídica a partir do serviço federal de processamento de dados (SERPRO). https://repositorio.ufrn.br/handle/123456789/54410. Accessed 14 Apr 2025
7. Desvars-Larrive, A., et al.: A Structured Open Dataset of Government Interventions in Response to COVID-19, Sci Data (2020)

8. Paparova, D, Aanestad, M., Vassilakopoulou, P.,Bahus, M.: Data governance spaces: the case of a national digital service for personal health data. In: Proceedings of VLDB Endowment Information and Organization 2023, LNCS, vol. 33, pp. 1064–1077 (2023). https://doi.org/10.1016/j.infoandorg.2023.100451
9. Denham, E.: Update report into adtech and real time bidding, 1st edn. Information Commissioner's Office, UK (2019)
10. Almeida, J., Cunha, P., Pereira, A.: GDPR-Compliant Data Processing: Practical Considerations. 1st edn. Springer Int. Publishing, European, Mediterranean, and Middle Eastern Conference (2022)
11. Acar, A., Aksu, H., Uluagac, A., Conti, M.: A survey on homomorphic encryption schemes: theory and implementation. In: ACM 2018, New York, NY, USA, vol. 51, pp. 1–13 (2018). https://doi.org/10.1145/3214303
12. Gentry, C.: Fully homomorphic encryption using ideal lattices. In: Proceedings of 41st ACM Symposium on Theory of Computing – STOC (2009)
13. Fan, G., et al.: Towards faster fully homomorphic encryption implementation with integer and floating-point computing power of GPUs. In: 2023 IEEE International Parallel and Distributed Proceedings Symposium (IPDPS), pp. 798–808. https://doi.org/10.1109/IPDPS54959.2023.00085
14. Creeger, M.: Fully Homomorphic Encryption. https://tinyurl.com/5p4enju9. Accessed 14 Apr 2025
15. Raj, A., D'Souza, R.: Performance metrics evaluation towards the effectiveness of data anonymization. In: 2023 IEEE 8th International Conference for Convergence in Technology (I2CT), pp. 1–5 (2023). https://doi.org/10.1109/I2CT57861.2023.10126310
16. Bandara, K., Bandara, D., Fernando, S.: Evaluation of re-identification risks in data anonymization techniques based on population uniqueness. In: 2020 5th International Conference on Information Technology Research (ICITR) (2020)
17. European Commission: The working party on the protection of individuals with regard to the processing of personal data. https://tinyurl.com/mwv37dd9. Accessed 14 Apr 2025
18. Utz, C., Degeling, M., Fahl, S., Schaub, F., Holz, T.: (Un)Informed consent: studying GDPR consent notices in the field. In: Proceedings of the 2019 ACM SIGSAC Conference on Computer and Communication Security, UK (2019)
19. Rhahla, M., Allegue, S., Abdellatif, T.: Guidelines for GDPR compliance in big data systems. J. Inf. Secur. Appl. 2214–2126 (2021)
20. Teixeira, C., Vasconcelos, A., Sousa, P., Marques, M.J.: Enterprise architecture patterns for GDPR compliance. In: 23rd International Conference on Enterprise Information Systems, 2edn (ICEIS 2021) (2011)
21. Crockett, K., Goltz, S., Garratt, M.: GDPR impact on computational intelligence research. In Conferência Conjunta Internacional sobre Redes Neurais (IJCNN), pp. 1–7 (2018). https://doi.org/10.1109/IJCNN.2018.8489614
22. Naik, N., Jenkins, P.: Your identity is yours: take back control of your identity using GDPR compatible self-sovereign identity. In: 2020 7th International Conference on Behavioural and Social Computing (BESC), pp. 1–6 (2020). https://doi.org/10.1109/BESC51023.2020.9348298
23. Vieira de Melo, W., Bianchi, C: Discutindo estratégias para a construção de questionários como ferramenta de pesquisa. In: Revista Brasileira de Ensino de Ciência e Tecnologia, p. 3. Brazil Location (2015)
24. Dalle Rocha, L., Canedo, E. D.: Privacy compliance in software development: a guide to implementing the LGPD principles. In Anais Estendidos do XIX Simp. Bras. Sist. de Inf., pp. 68–70. SBC, Brazil (2023)

25. Araujo, E., Vilela, J., Silva, C., Alves, C.: Are My Business Process Models Compliant With LGPD? The LGPD4BP Method to Evaluate and to Model LGPD Aware Business Processes, 1st edn. ACM, Brazil (2021)
26. Machado, P., Vilela, J., Peixoto, M., Silva, C.: A Systematic Study on the Impact of GDPR Compliance on Organizations, 1st edn. ACM, USA (2023)
27. Hoss, M., Caten, C.: Processo de Validação Interna de um Questionário em uma Survey Research Sobre ISO 9001:2000. J. Produto e Produção(11) (2010). https://doi.org/10.22456/1983-8026.7240
28. LaCasse, A.: Privacy Tech VENDOR REPORT, 3nd edn. IAPP, Brazil (2022)
29. Dixon, M.: An Overview of Document Mining Technology. CiteSeer (1998)
30. ANPD. https://tinyurl.com/57h59wmv. Accessed 14 Apr 2025
31. Segment. https://www.ematicsolutions.com/partners/segment/. Accessed 21 May 2025
32. Segment. https://segment.com/docs/partners/conceptual-model/. Accessed 09 Apr 2025
33. Silva, H., Basso, T., Moraes, R., Elia, D., Fiore, S.: A re-identification risk-based anonymization framework for data analytics platforms. In: 2018 14th EDCC, pp. 101–106 (2018)
34. Cejas, A., Orlando, S.A., Briand, L.C.: CompAi: a tool for GDPR completeness checking of privacy policies using artificial intelligence (2024)

AI for Security and Dependability

An Empirical Study of Large Language Models as Experts in Software Trustworthiness Assessment

Saeed Javani Jananloo[1]($\boxtimes$) (iD), José D'Abruzzo Pereira[1]($\boxtimes$) (iD),
and Marco Vieira[2]($\boxtimes$) (iD)

[1] CISUC/LASI – Centre for Informatics and Systems of the University of Coimbra,
Department of Informatics Engineering, University of Coimbra, Coimbra, Portugal
`{jananloo,josep}@dei.uc.pt`
[2] University of North Carolina at Charlotte, Charlotte, USA
`marco.vieira@charlotte.edu`

Abstract. As software plays an increasingly central role in daily life, ensuring its trustworthiness is essential. Existing Software Trustworthiness Assessment (STA) techniques often lack theoretical grounding, disregard user expectations, and provide limited actionable guidance. At the same time, Large Language Models (LLMs) have shown strong capabilities in software engineering tasks, but their use for holistic and interpretable STA remains unexplored. This paper presents an exploration of using LLMs to perform context-aware STA, with a specific focus on system software functions written in C programming language. Our approach involved selecting functions from the Linux Kernel, designing tailored prompts, and executing LLM-based assessments. We report on three practical experiences, two involving expert-based assessments and one comparing results against SCOLP, a state-of-the-art automated technique. The results show that LLM-based categorizations achieve substantial agreement with most voted expert rankings, fair agreement with consensus ranking, and only slight agreement with the automated baseline. These experiences provide insight into the limitations of LLMs in supporting trustworthiness assessments in real-world systems.

Keywords: Trustworthiness Assessment · Large Language Models (LLMs) · Software Security · Software Reliability

1 Introduction

The growing reliance on software, combined with internet connectivity and weak adoption of reliable and secure development practices, has made systems increasingly vulnerable to failures and attacks [1]. For example, in 2024, the National Vulnerability Database (NVD) reported 40,003 CVEs, a 39% increase over 2023 [2], underscoring the rising challenge of ensuring software trustworthiness, which spans reliability, security, and other key properties [3]. To meet demands for faster delivery, DevOps promotes automation through Continuous Integration (CI), Continuous Delivery (CDE), and Continuous Deployment(CD) workflows [4,5], but without proper trustworthiness assessment tools, these pipelines risk pushing faults and vulnerabilities into production [6].

L. A. Rodrigues and R. Oliveira (Eds.): LADC 2025, CCIS 2697, pp. 75–93, 2026.
https://doi.org/10.1007/978-3-032-11539-3_5

To support trustworthy development, various techniques are employed throughout Software Development Life Cycle (SDLC), including both static and dynamic analysis approaches [7]. Static techniques (*e.g.*, Static Code Analysis (SCA)) examine source code without executing it, while dynamic techniques (*e.g.*, Software Penetration Testing (SPT)) assess the behavior of software during runtime [8]. Despite their widespread use, both static and dynamic methods often suffer from high rates of False Positives (FPs) and False Negatives (FNs), which reduce trust in their outputs and demand significant manual effort to verify results [9]. In contrast, state-of-the-art STA techniques, such as Security Characterization of Open-Source Functions using Logic Scoring of Preference (SCOLP) [8], perform STA by applying quality models to static features extracted from source code.

LLMs have recently emerged as powerful tools in software engineering, with many applications, including code generation [10], code review [11], bug detection [12], documentation [13], and others. In particular, they have shown promising results in software security tasks, namely Software Vulnerability Detection (SVD) and Software Vulnerability Patching (SVP) [14–16]. However, to the best of our knowledge, no work has investigated their use for STA, where multiple quality attributes such as reliability and security are jointly considered.

This paper presents an empirical study on the use of LLMs as expert agents for performing Software Trustworthiness Assessment (STA) at the code level, with an emphasis on performance, reliability, and security. This study targets C functions, given the language's low-level memory management and proneness to security vulnerabilities. Rather than aiming to detect specific bugs or vulnerabilities, we assess the overall trustworthiness of functions based on their static properties. To determine whether LLMs can effectively serve as expert proxies, we compare their assessments with those of human experts and with SCOLP [8], a state-of-the-art static analysis technique. This capability is especially valuable in large-scale code bases, where manual expert review is impractical and automated tools often lack the contextual understanding needed for meaningful prioritization tasks, such as refactoring, testing, or code review.

We pose the following Research Questions (RQs): **RQ1:** *How closely do LLMs align with human expert assessments in performing STA?*, and **RQ2:** *How closely do LLMs align with SCOLP trustworthiness assessments?* To answer such questions, we designed an approach consisting of functions extraction from a software project, prompts crafting, executing LLMs to perform STA, categorizations with experts and SCOLP, and comparing the results to understand how closely the LLM-based assessments align with those produced by experts and automated tools. Functions were categorized into five priority levels: Critical, High, Medium, Low, and Lowest [8]. This categorization reflects trustworthiness as a composite of performance, security, and reliability and can be used in CI pipelines to support decision-making during development and deployment.

We assessed three sets of C functions extracted from the Linux Kernel, a large open-source project. The selected functions varied in size, structure, complexity, and the presence or absence of known issues. To guide the reasoning of the LLMs, we employed prompt engineering techniques. We explored a wide range of prompt styles, from simple instructional formulations to more sophisticated templates designed to encourage structured reasoning and attention to software-specific properties. Some prompts emphasized known indicators of trustworthiness, such as complexity or input validation, while others introduced abstract reasoning strategies to emulate expert-level judgment. From this diverse set, we selected a subset of well-performing prompts for the final evaluation.

We included free, locally runnable models (*e.g.*, Granite3.1-Dense, Codestral, Qwen2.5-Coder, DeepSeek-R1) and proprietary commercial models (*e.g.*, ChatGPT-4o by OpenAI and Gemini2-Flash by Google). This allowed us to assess performance across a spectrum of capabilities and deployment contexts. We report on three practical evaluations where we compare LLMs trustworthiness categorization with: (1) *Most Voted Expert Ranking*, based on individual categorizations collected remotely from experts; (2) *Consensus Expert Ranking*, derived from in-person categorization poker sessions that fostered discussion and convergence; and (3) *SCOLP*, an automated approach applying logic scoring of preference over software quality models focused on input validation.

The results show that LLM-based assessments reached a substantial agreement (Weighted Kappa of 0.72) with the most-voted expert ranking, indicating strong potential for alignment with expert perception. However, agreement dropped to fair levels (Kappa of 0.32) with consensus expert rankings and with SCOLP (0.25), revealing inconsistencies when experts deliberate collectively or when compared to automated methods. These fair agreements, while outperforming SCOLP in expert alignment, suggest that while LLMs hold promise, they still fall short of consistently matching expert consensus.

This paper is organized as follows. Section 2 reviews the background and related work. Section 3 presents the approach followed in this study. Section 4 presents the results of our experiences comparing LLMs with other STAs approaches. Section 5 presents the results, which are discussed in Sect. 6. Finally, Sect. 7 concludes the paper and outlines the directions for future work.

2   Background and Related Work

Trustworthiness refers to the degree of confidence that a software system will perform as expected, encompassing attributes such as safety, security, reliability, resilience, and privacy [17]. Unlike traditional vulnerability detection tasks, STA does not aim to identify known issues, but to highlight components that may require additional review or refactoring to improve overall trustworthiness. This makes STA a broader and more nuanced activity.

Existing works on STA can be categorized into product-oriented and process-based approaches [18]. Product-oriented assessments focus on evaluating the software through static attributes or dynamic behavior, while process-based methods consider whether development practices follow trusted engineering principles. These may involve expert evaluation or analysis of development artifacts.

Attribute-based methods quantify trust-related properties, which may be pre-defined, user-specified, or derived from combinations of metrics. Such properties are then synthesized using statistical and heuristic models, including regression analysis, principal component analysis, and fuzzy logic [19,20]. Additional evidence, such as runtime data or user feedback, can be processed using frameworks like evidence theory [21], Bayesian inference [22], or weighted aggregation [23]. In contrast, behavior-based methods examine runtime traces or system calls to detect deviations from expected behavior. Techniques in this category include anomaly detection [24], finite state machine modeling [25], and bisimulation [26].

While process-based methods have been used to evaluate trustworthiness through complexity analysis and hierarchical reasoning [19,27], we focus on product-oriented assessment, particularly at the level of code functions. One representative example is SCOLP [8], a method that uses multi-criteria decision-making to categorize functions based on their likelihood of having security issues. This approach extracts static features, including software metrics, and processes them using quality models to output a trustworthiness score. Functions are then assigned to categories that reflect priority for review or refactoring.

Despite their analytical depth, traditional approaches often lack contextual understanding, struggle to scale, and rely on manually crafted rules. LLMs have demonstrated strong performance in code generation [10], review [11], documentation [13], and defect detection [12], prompting exploration into their application for software security, particularly vulnerability detection. However, their effectiveness in broader trustworthiness assessment, which encompasses reliability and security, among other properties [28], remains an open question.

Recent efforts have explored combinations of prompt engineering and structural code analysis for vulnerability detection. One such effort uses Chain of Thoughts Prompting (CoT) reasoning together with input features like Abstract Syntax Trees (ASTs) and Data Flow Graphs (DFGs) [15]. Evaluation on widely used datasets, such as Devign [29] and Reveal [30], showed improvements in accuracy using GPT models, although performance did not exceed 55%. Other works have employed multi-step prompting to better engage the model's contextual reasoning abilities. For example, an interaction strategy based on asking the model to explain code intent before querying potential vulnerabilities has achieved an accuracy of 0.74 for C and C++ functions [14].

While existing studies confirm the feasibility of using LLMs for software security, none have addressed their role in holistic trustworthiness assessment. This paper contributes to filling this gap by investigating how closely the assessments generated by LLMs align with those produced by experts and by automated methods designed for trustworthiness categorization.

3   Approach

Our approach, shown in Fig. 1, enables a systematic investigation of how effectively LLMs, acting as expert agents, perform software trustworthiness assessments compared to human experts and automated methods:

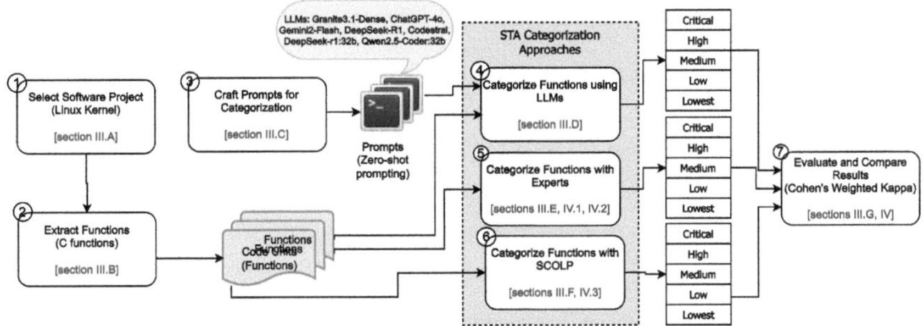

Fig. 1. Approach to do STA supported by LLMs.

1. **Select Software Project**: Choose a software system with diverse functions and a well-documented development history. In this study, we selected the Linux Kernel due to its relevance, complexity, and availability of data.
2. **Extract Functions**: Identify and extract functions from the project, including both vulnerable and patched versions, focusing on those with at least 50 lines of code to ensure meaningful analysis.
3. **Craft Prompts for Categorization**: Apply prompt engineering to design effective prompts that guide LLMs in performing the STA task. These range from simple instructions to structured, reasoning-based prompts.
4. **Categorize Functions with LLMs**: Run the selected LLMs using the crafted prompts, instructing them to assign each function a predefined trustworthiness level (*Critical, High, Medium, Low,* and *Lowest*).
5. **Categorize Functions with Experts**: Generate reference categorizations based on evaluations by human experts, following a structured process and predefined guidelines.
6. **Categorize Functions with SCOLP**: Generate reference categorizations using the automated STA technique SCOLP [8], which applies logic-based scoring over software quality models.
7. **Evaluate and Compare Results**: Assess the alignment between LLM outputs and reference categorizations by computing Cohen's Weighted Kappa agreement metrics.

3.1   Select Software Project

We selected the Linux Kernel (kernel.org) as the target software system. The Linux Kernel is a large, mature, and widely used open-source project that has been actively developed and maintained for decades. As of July 6th, 2025, it comprises approximately 36.7 million lines of code [31], making it an excellent representation of real-world, complex software.

We selected this project for several reasons: (1) it has a huge number of reported issues and corresponding fixing commits, (2) its versatility offers a diverse range of function types and complexities, (3) many of its functions have privileged access to critical system resources such as memory, and (4) its long development history provides a rich context for evaluating software trustworthiness.

Table 1. First Batch of Selected Functions

	File - Function	Commit	# Lines	Experts Most Voted	Experts Average
Vulnerable	(1) sound/core/timer.c - snd_timer_user_params	242658f	101	High	High
	(2) fs/fuse/dev.c - fuse_dev_splice_write	8fde12c	83	High	High
	(3) fs/splice.c - splice_pipe_to_pipe	8fde12c	111	High	Medium
	(4) fs/cifs/smb2pdu.c - SMB2_write	618d919	76	Medium	Medium
	(5) fs/ext4/xattr.c - ext4_xattr_set_entry	327eaf7	238	Critical	High
Non-Vulnerable	(6) fs/ext4/xattr.c - ext4_xattr_set_handle	5369a76	147	Critical	High
	(7) net/core/skbuff.c - skb_cow_data	8605330	91	Medium	Medium
	(8) fs/dcache.c - dentry_lru_isolate	946e51f	57	Low	Low
	(9) sound/usb/mixer.c - parse_audio_feature_unit	daac071	168	Medium	High
	(10) sound/usb/mixer.c - volume_control_quirks	daac071	111	Low	Medium

3.2   Extract Functions

The function extraction process was designed to capture a diverse set of functions varying in size, complexity, and characteristics relevant to trustworthiness. We selected functions with at least 50 lines of code (both vulnerable and patched versions) to ensure real-world applicability and enable comparative analysis.

Three distinct batches of functions were used in this experiment. The first batch consisted of 10 functions (5 vulnerable and 5 non-vulnerable; see Table 1), which were classified using the most voted expert ranking, as well as the SCOLP technique. The second batch included 20 functions (6 vulnerable and 14 non-vulnerable; see Table 2), later categorized through live consensus sessions by security experts and also using SCOLP. The third batch contained 40 additional ones (6 vulnerable and 34 non-vulnerable). In total, this batch included 70 unique functions from various modules of the Linux Kernel (*e.g.*, memory management, file systems, and sound drivers) to cover a wide range of real-world code patterns. The detailed list of functions is available at [32].

3.3   Craft Prompts for Categorization

In our experiments, we focused exclusively on zero-shot prompting and crafting specialized prompts that guide model behavior without training or fine-

Table 2. Second Batch of selected functions

	File - Function	Commit	Consensus Ranking
Vulnerable	(1) fs/dcache.c - __d_alloc	946e51f	Low
	(2) fs/dcache.c - __dentry_kill	946e51f	Low
	(3) fs/fuse/dev.c - fuse_dev_splice_write	15fab63	High
	(4) fs/cifs/smb2pdu.c - SMB2_write	6a3eb33	Medium
	(5) fs/splice.c - splice_pipe_to_pipe	15fab63	High
	(6) fs/cifs/smb2pdu.c - SMB2_read	088aaf1	High
Non-Vulnerable	(7) arch/x86/kvm/vmx.c - handle_cr	36ae3c0	High
	(8) sound/usb/mixer.c - get_ctl_value_v2	daac071	Medium
	(9) kernel/futex.c - futex_wait	b3eaa9f	Medium
	(10) drivers/gpu/drm/vc4/vc4_gem.c - vc4_get_bcl	0f2ff82	Critical
	(11) kernel/trace/trace.c - tracing_set_tracer	15fab63	High
	(12) fs/cifs/smb2pdu.c - smb2_readv_callback	088aaf1	Medium
	(13) mm/hugetlb.c - __vma_reservation_common	15fab63	Low
	(14) sound/core/timer.c - snd_timer_user_tselect	cec8f96	Medium
	(15) arch/x86/kvm/vmx.c - pi_pre_block	36ae3c0	Medium
	(16) arch/x86/kvm/vmx.c - vmx_set_msr	36ae3c0	Medium
	(17) kernel/trace/trace.c - instance_rmdir	15fab63	Critical
	(18) mm/gup.c - __get_user_pages_locked	15fab63	Medium
	(19) fs/cifs/smb2pdu.c - SMB2_tcon	088aaf1	High
	(20) fs/cifs/smb2pdu.c - SMB2_ioctl	088aaf1	High

Table 3. Prompts Crafted of the Experiments

Name	Explanation
$Prompt_{SMs}$	Prompt with Info about Software Metrics
$Prompt_{Reworded}$	Reworded Prompt
$Prompt_{Simple}$	Exactly the Same Prompt as for Experts
$Prompt_{Issues}$	Added main Properties of Each Group
$Prompt_{GPT}$	Prompt Reworded by ChatGPT
$Prompt_{CoT}$	Chain of Thought Prompt
$Prompt_{AutoCoT}$	Automatic Chain of Thought Prompt
$Prompt_{Self}$	Self Consistency Prompt
$Prompt_{LogiCoT}$	Logical Chain of Thought Prompting
$Prompt_{CoS}$	Chain of Symbol Prompting
$Prompt_{ToT}$	Tree of Thoughts Prompting
$Prompt_{GoT}$	Graph of Thoughts Prompting
$Prompt_{S2A}$	System 2 Attention Prompting

Table 4. LLMs used in the experiments

Name	Developed by	License	Parameter Size	Training Data	Context Window Size	Architecture	MoE
ChatGPT-4o [41]	OpenAI	Proprietary	Not Disclosed	Mixture of Text and Code	128K	Unified transformer	Yes
Gemini2-Flash [42]	Google	Proprietary	Not Disclosed	Mixture of Text, Code, Image, Audio, Video	1M	Sparse MoE transformer	Yes
DeepSeek-R1 [43]	DeepSeek	MIT	671B	2T tokens (Multilingual Text and Code)	16K	Unified transformer	No
Granite3.1-Dense [44]	IBM	Apache 2.0	8B	5T tokens (Enterprise-focused Data)	32K	Granite	No
Qwen2.5-Coder [45]	Alibaba	Free (Commercial Friendly)	32B	3T tokens (Code-centric)	128K	Qwen2	No
Codestral [46]	Mistral AI	Apache 2.0	22B	80B tokens (Code)	32K	Llama	No
Deepseek-r1 [47]	DeepSeek	Free (Commercial Friendly)	32B	2T tokens (Multilingual Text and Code)	128K	Qwen2	No

tuning. We tested a variety of prompt styles and recorded their outcomes. All the prompts are available at the following repository: https://anonymous.4open.science/r/TestedPromptsForTrustworthiness-4E73 [33].

Table 3 lists the crafted prompts available at [33]. As a starting point, we used the simplest form, the same instruction provided to human experts, resulting in $Prompt_{Simple}$. We then modified its phrasing without altering the underlying meaning, creating variants like $Prompt_{Reworded}$ and $Prompt_{GPT}$.

Then, we designed prompts that guide the LLMs through a structured reasoning process. For instance, $Prompt_{SMs}$ extends the original prompt by instructing the model to consider software metrics such as cyclomatic complexity, volume-related metrics (*e.g.*, number of statements), coupling, and cohesion (see $Prompt_{SMs}$. We also introduced $Prompt_{Issues}$, which provides characteristic traits of each trustworthiness level to help guide categorization.

Given the subjective and multi-criteria nature of trustworthiness, we crafted more advanced prompts inspired by the literature. $Prompt_{CoT}$ employs the Chain-of-Thought technique [34], breaking down decisions into intermediate reasoning steps. We extended this idea further through:

- $Prompt_{AutoCoT}$: automatic reasoning chain using "Let's think step-by-step" [35],
- $Prompt_{Self}$: improved reasoning via sampling and aggregation [36],
- $Prompt_{CoS}$: symbolic reasoning through condensed representations [37],
- $Prompt_{ToT}$: tree-structured reasoning and search [38],
- $Prompt_{GoT}$: graph-based modular reasoning with enhanced flow control [39].

These prompting strategies are known to enhance performance in tasks involving arithmetic, common sense, and symbolic reasoning. However, we observed that longer prompts tend to impair the performance of smaller LLMs due to their limited context windows and token processing capacity [40].

3.4   Categorize Functions with LLMs

LLMs are central to our evaluation, making their selection a critical step. As the development of increasingly powerful LLMs accelerates, major companies continue to invest heavily to enhance models' performance. However, if LLMs are to be trusted for STA, their effectiveness must extend beyond the largest, most resource-intensive models. Mid-range, lightweight, and cost-effective alternatives must also demonstrate sufficient capability to support broader adoption.

To explore this, we selected a diverse set of models: three widely used commercial LLMs, and four non-commercial, lightweight models that can run locally on a standard Ubuntu machine with just 32 GB of RAM. The detailed list is presented in Table 4, including authors, the type of license, training data, context window size, architecture, and whether it uses Mixture-of-Expert (MoE).

Our objective is to assess whether commercial and open-source LLMs can be effectively applied to STA. Furthermore, given the high benchmark scores of larger models such as ChatGPT-4o and Gemini2-Flash on MTEB and MMLU [48], we investigate if carefully crafted prompts can achieve good results when performing STA. The goal is to find out whether various models with different architectures, training data, and characteristics can lead to promising outcomes.

For open source LLMs, we selected four lightweight, free models that can be run locally using Meta's Ollama tool [49]. These four models (Granite3.1-Dense, Qwen2.5-coder, DeepSeek-r1, and Codestral) were used alongside the three previously selected commercial LLMs (ChatGPT-4o, Gemini2-Flash, and DeepSeek-R1) to classify functions in our dataset using all prompting strategies defined. This maintains diversity in architectural and licensing characteristics while keeping the experimental setup tractable. Results will be later compared with expert rankings (in Sects. 4.1 and 4.2) and SCOLP (in Sect. 4.3).

3.5   Categorize Functions with Human Experts

We conducted two expert-based reference experiments. The first involved 15 human experts from 7 different institutions across 4 countries who independently categorized functions into five priority groups based on their proneness to security issues. The second involved 8 experts participating in in-person categorization sessions, where consensus was reached through structured group discussion.

Most Voted Expert Ranking. For the first expert-based evaluation, 15 experts in the field of software security participated in validating the results. The participants included Ph.D. holders, working in both academia and industry, as well as current Ph.D. students, representing diverse institutions and countries. Each expert was invited via email and independently categorized a set of 10 functions (see Table 1) into five priority groups based on their perceived proneness to security issues. In addition to the individual categorizations, experts were

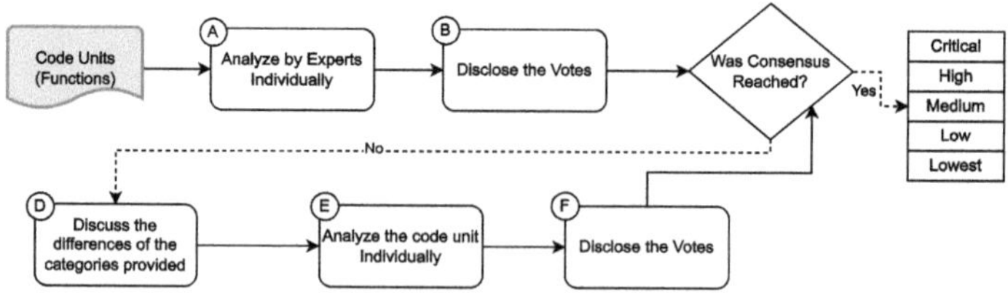

Fig. 2. The consensus expert ranking process.

also asked to perform pairwise comparisons between selected function pairs, indicating which function should be prioritized for security-focused refactoring [8]. After collecting the responses, the category receiving the highest number of expert votes for each function was selected as its *Most Voted Category*.

This approach was used to mitigate the impact of outlier opinions and ensure that the final categorization reflected a broad expert consensus. To improve consistency and minimize bias, responses showing contradictions between pairwise comparisons and individual rankings were flagged. Experts with two or more such inconsistencies were asked to review and revise their responses. The 10 functions evaluated in this phase are presented in Table 1. Comparisons between LLMs and these expert-based categorizations are presented in Sect. 3.5.

Consensus Expert Ranking. The second expert-based evaluation adopted a consensus-driven approach inspired by the Planning Poker technique [50], commonly used in agile software development. We invited eight security experts, including 5 professors and 3 Ph.D. students from our university, whose research focuses on software security. Their task was to collaboratively categorize 20 functions listed in Table 2 into predefined trustworthiness levels. Unlike the previous remote, individual assessments, this method required in-person participation to foster discussion and consensus, aiming to reduce outliers and improve judgment reliability. The consensus process unfolded as follows (see Fig. 2):

(A) Each expert independently analyzed a function and assigned it to one of the priority groups.
(B) Experts simultaneously revealed their selected priority levels using cards.
(C) If all votes were consistent, the function was assigned to the agreed-upon group.
(D) If votes differed, experts discussed their reasoning.
(E) After discussion, each expert re-evaluated the function independently.
(F) A second round of votes was revealed.
(G) If consensus is reached, the function is categorized; otherwise, steps repeat from step D or up to 5 rounds, after which the function is discarded.

The categorization took place over three in-person sessions, each involving four to five participants, and lasted six hours in total. This level of expert engagement represents a significant time investment, rarely reported in comparable studies (*e.g.*, *Michael et al.* [51] used only 7 experts and *Pavli et al.* [52] had only 11 experts, both by questionnaire and not in-person sessions). Comparisons between LLMs and these expert-based categorizations are presented in Sect. 4.2.

3.6   Categorize Functions with SCOLP

SCOLP [8] is an automated static approach designed to assess the proneness of functions to vulnerabilities. In this study, we applied SCOLP using its Input Validation Quality Model (QM), which targets potential vulnerabilities arising from improper input handling. The method extracts relevant static attributes from source code, such as the use of unsafe input functions, and memory address operations, and applies predefined weights and logical operators using Logic Scoring of Preferences (LSP). The resulting score places each function into one of five priority levels (from Lowest to Critical), guiding security reviews and refactoring without the overhead of traditional Static Analysis Tools (SATs).

Similar to our LLM-based prompting strategy, SCOLP operates without prior knowledge of a functions' overall trustworthiness. Both approaches rely solely on the function code; however, SCOLP is limited to analyzing Software Metrics (SMs) and memory-related attributes. Compared with expert evaluations, LLMs and SCOLP have access to only limited contextual information. While they emphasize different aspects of the code in their SCA, both ultimately share the same goal: prioritizing functions according to characteristics that indicate trustworthiness.

A comparison between categorizations of the third batch of functions done by SCOLP and those of LLMs is presented in Sect. 4.3. Due to the time required to evaluate all 70 functions across multiple prompts, we first identified the best-performing prompt before proceeding with the full experiment. To do this, we applied all prompt variants to the first batch of 10 functions (Table 1) and measured agreement between LLMs and experts (see Table 5, which are formulated as below:

- $f \in F$ be each function in the set of all functions F
- $LLM_{MV}(f)$: LLMs' Most Voted answer for function f
- $LLM_{Avg}(f)$: LLMs' Average answer for function f
- $Expert_{MV}(f)$: Experts' Most Voted answer for f
- $Expert_{Avg}(f)$: Experts' Average answer for function f

3.7   Evaluate and Compare Results

To compare categorizations, we used the Inter-Rater Reliability (IRR) metric known as Cohen's Weighted Kappa [53]. This metric assesses the level of agreement between two sets of labels while accounting for the severity of disagreements. Unlike unweighted Kappa [54], which treats all mismatches equally, the weighted variant penalizes greater deviations more heavily. For instance, if experts categorize a function as "Critical" while two LLMs label it as "High" and "Lowest", respectively, the unweighted Kappa assigns both errors the same penalty. In contrast, Weighted Kappa reflects the larger discrepancy of the "Lowest" classification, better capturing the quality of agreement.

We interpret Weighted Kappa scores using the Landis and Koch scale [55]: (a) less than 0: no agreement; (b) 0.00–0.20: slight agreement; (c) 0.21–0.40: fair agreement; (d) 0.41–0.60: moderate agreement; (e) 0.61–0.80: substantial agreement; (f) 0.81–1.00: almost perfect agreement.

The agreement between LLM_{Avg} and $Experts_{MV}$ has been calculated by using Weighted Kappa. As shown in Table 5, the $Prompt_{Issues}$ consistently outperformed more sophisticated reasoning-enhancement techniques, making it the best overall. Therefore, we used that for all subsequent experiments with SCOLP.

Table 5. Performance Comparison for All Prompts

Metric	Prompt	W_Kappa
LLM_{Avg} to $Experts_{MV}$	$Prompt_{Issues}$	0.72
	$Prompt_{GPT}$	0.47
	$Prompt_{Cos}$	0.41
	$Prompt_{ToT}$	0.41
	$Prompt_{Simple}$	0.39
	$Prompt_{S2A}$	0.27
	$Prompt_{CoT}$	0.21
	$Prompt_{Reworded}$	0.17
	$Prompt_{AutoCoT}$	0.13
	$Prompt_{Self}$	0.09
	$Prompt_{GoT}$	0.07
	$Prompt_{LogiCoT}$	-0.03

Table 6. Agreement of the LLMs with MV Expert Ranking ($Prompt_{Issues}$)

Metric	LLM	W_Kappa
LLM to $Experts_{MV}$	Granite3.1-Dense	0.71
	ChatGPT-4o	0.54
	Gemini2-Flash	0.51
	DeepSeek-R1	0.42
	Codestral	0.38
	deepseek-r1:32b	0.34
	Qwen2.5-Coder:32b	0.31
LLM_{Avg} to $Experts_{MV}$	(all)	0.72
LLM_{Avg} to $Experts_{Avg}$	(all)	0.63
LLM_{MV} to $Experts_{Avg}$	(all)	0.41
LLM_{MV} to $Experts_{MV}$	(all)	0.38

To determine the trustworthiness category a function belongs to based on the average rankings by the LLMs, we interpret average scores using predefined priority categories (see Sect. 3). Since the average scores fall within the range $[1,5]$ (a span of 4 units), we divide this range into 5 intervals, each with a width of 0.8. The boundaries corresponding to each category are illustrated in Fig. 3.

Group	Critical	High	Medium	Low	Lowest
Group Score	1	2	3	4	5
Average		[1-1.8)	[1.8-2.6)	[2.6-3.4)	[3.4-4.2)	[4.2-5]

Fig. 3. Scaling Average Rankings into Actual Categories.

4 Results

In this section, we compare our results with other STA approaches.

4.1 LLMs *vs* Most Voted (MV) Expert Ranking

In this section, we present the results produced by LLMs in comparison to the categorizations performed by individual human experts. As shown in Table 6, IBM's *Granite 3.1-Dense* model achieved the highest agreement with the most voted expert ranking, with a Weighted Kappa of 0.71. Following closely are *ChatGPT-4o* and *Gemini 2-Flash*, with scores of 0.54 and 0.51, respectively. IBM's *Granite 8B* is a dense, text-only model, trained on over 12 trillion tokens, with significant performance improvements over its predecessors [44]. A potential reason for its strong performance may stem from the reliance on purely textual features, supported by large-scale training data.

Table 7. Agreement of the LLMs with Experts Consensus Ranking ($Prompt_{Issues}$)

Metric	LLM	W_Kappa
LLM to $Experts_{MV}$	Granite3.1-Dense	0.40
	Codestral	0.27
	Gemini2-Flash	0.23
	ChatGPT-4o	0.20
	DeepSeek-R1	0.08
	deepseek-r1:32b	0.08
	qwen2.5-coder:32b	0.04
LLM_{Avg} to $Experts_{MV}$	(all)	0.32
LLM_{MV} to $Experts_{MV}$	(all)	0.27

Table 8. Agreement of the LLMs with SCOLP ($Prompt_{Issues}$)

Metric	LLM	W_Kappa
LLM to SCOLP	deepseek-r1:32b	0.27
	Granite3.1-Dense	0.23
	Gemini2-Flash	0.21
	ChatGPT-4o	0.18
	Codestral	0.17
	Qwen2.5-Coder:32b	0.05
	DeepSeek-R1	0.01
LLM_{Avg} to SCOLP	(all)	0.25
LLM_{MV} to SCOLP	(all)	0.30

An interesting insight from this experiment is that *with effective prompting, even smaller models can match or outperform larger commercial models.* We also calculated aggregated results for our set of LLMs (bottom part of Table 6). When comparing the average categories provided by the seven LLMs for $Prompt_{Issues}$ against the most voted expert categories, the Weighted Kappa is 0.72, indicating *substantial agreement.*

The agreement between the average LLM-assigned categories and the average expert-assigned categories yielded a Weighted Kappa of 0.63, indicating a *substantial agreement.* To compute the average category across multiple LLMs or experts, we mapped the five ordinal categories, *Lowest, Low, Medium, High,* and *Critical,* to integer values from 1 to 5, respectively. For each function, the numerical values assigned by all LLMs (or experts) were averaged and then rounded to the nearest integer. The final integer value was then mapped back to its corresponding categorical label. This approach allows us to approximate a consensus categorization over ordinal scales while preserving interpretability.

4.2 LLMs *vs* Consensus Expert Ranking

In this section, we observe the results of categorizations performed by LLMs in comparison to the consensus ranking from experts, as illustrated in Fig. 2. As shown in Table 7, the *Granite3.1-Dense* model achieved the highest agreement with the expert consensus, with a Weighted Kappa of 0.40, indicating a *fair agreement.* This is followed by *Codestral* and *Gemini2-Flash,* with Weighted Kappa scores of 0.27 and 0.23, respectively. Note that, these values are much lower than the comparison with the most voted results (previous section) potentially because our consensus expert ranking was more prone to the leader effect, when a person can influence the assessment of others.

We also calculated aggregate results for the group of LLMs. The Weighted Kappa comparing the average categories assigned by seven LLMs for $Prompt_{Issues}$ against the expert consensus ranking is 0.32, showing a *fair agreement.* Moreover, comparing the most voted categories provided by the seven LLMs to the expert consensus ranking results in a Weighted Kappa of 0.27, a fair agreement. It is important to highlight that, due to the format of the consensus ranking, only the most voted category is available, not an average ranking.

4.3   LLMs *vs* SCOLP

We compared LLM-generated categorizations with those from the state-of-the-art SCOLP approach [8]. As shown in Table 8, the Weighted Kappa between the average categories from seven LLMs and SCOLP is 0.25, indicating *fair agreement* [55]. Among individual models, deepseek-r1:32b achieved the highest alignment with SCOLP, delivering comparable performance and reinforcing its reliability.

To contextualize these results, we also measured SCOLP's agreement with expert rankings, obtaining Weighted Kappa scores of 0.30 (for most-voted) and 0.21 (for consensus). These values are close to those of the LLMs, suggesting that current LLM-based assessments perform on par with the state-of-the-art automated method. Notably, averaged LLM outputs align more closely with expert assessments than the selected SCOLP configuration. All analyses used the full set of 70 functions, ensuring broad validation across diverse code samples.

5   Discussion

After analyzing the experimental results in isolation, we now provide an overall comparison across all approaches. The first goal of this study was to explore the feasibility of using LLMs for STA in place of human experts. As presented in Table 9, the Weighted Kappa between the average categorization of the seven LLMs (LLM_{Avg}) and the most voted (MV) expert rankings ($Experts_{MV}$) is 0.72, which corresponds to a *substantial agreement* according to the Landis and Koch scale [55]. In contrast, the agreement between LLM_{Avg} and the consensus ranking derived through structured expert discussion is 0.32, indicating a *fair agreement*. These results answer **RQ1**: *How closely do LLMs align with human expert assessments in performing STA?* The findings suggest that LLMs can serve as viable substitutes for expert judgment in STA, but this also depends on how the assessment is performed by humans. For instance, some experts may be more knowledgeable about trustworthiness, C language, or even in the system/system type under assessment (*i.e.*, in our case, in Linux Kernel/Operating Systems). Moreover, this is also influenced by the method being evaluated. In our case, the MV method achieved better results than the consensus expert ranking, probably due to the leader effect when categorizing the functions (Table 10).

Beyond addressing **RQ1**, the results also yield practical insights. The *substantial agreement* of 0.72 between LLM_{Avg} and $Experts_{MV}$ offers a simple yet effective strategy: *to approximate expert-level categorization, one can submit functions to the seven LLMs and take the average of their predicted priority levels*. This ensemble-based approach not only streamlines assessment but also mitigates individual model errors.

Table 9. Weighted Kappa Total Comparison of All Configurations

	LLM_{Avg}	$Experts_{MostVoted}$	$Experts_{Consensus}$	$SCOLP$
LLM_{Avg}	1	0.72	0.32	0.25
$Experts_{Most\ Voted}$	0.72	1	–	0.30
$Experts_{Consensus}$	0.32	–	1	0.21
SCOLP	0.25	0.30	0.21	1

Further support for this conclusion comes from Table 6, which shows individual LLMs having Weighted Kappa scores ranging from 0.31 to 0.71. However, by aggregating their outputs, the average model (LLM_{Avg}) reaches a Kappa of 0.72, outperforming even the strongest individual model, *Granite3.1-Dense*. This outcome highlights how ensemble averaging can smooth out inconsistencies. For instance, if a function is mostly rated as *High* by experts, but two LLMs predict *Critical* and *Medium*, their average lands on *High*, aligning perfectly with the expert majority and yielding a higher Kappa.

This pattern mirrors how assessments are often conducted in real-world settings. Security teams typically form individual judgments before discussing and voting to reach a consensus. Our method replicates this process computationally: each LLM acts as an independent assessor, and the aggregated result functions as a consensus. This approach has proven to be not only conceptually aligned with expert evaluation practices, but also quantitatively robust, producing results that significantly correlate with expert-derived categorizations in STA.

The second goal of this work was to evaluate the viability of using LLMs for trustworthiness assessment in comparison with established automated approaches, particularly the state-of-the-art method SCOLP. As shown in Table 9, the overall agreement between the aggregated outputs of the LLMs and SCOLP yields a Weighted Kappa of 0.25, which is classified as a fair agreement [55]. While this figure alone may not offer a decisive conclusion, further comparisons provide more conclusive evidence.

For the first batch of 10 functions, the Weighted Kappa between the average LLMs categorization and the most voted expert ranking is 0.72, indicating substantial agreement. In contrast, the corresponding Kappa score between SCOLP and the expert ranking is only 0.30 (as it can be seen in Table 11), suggesting

Table 10. Separated Categorizations done by LLMs

LLM	$Experts_{MostVoted}$	$Experts_{Consensus}$	$SCOLP$
Granite3.1-Dense	0.71	0.40	0.23
Gemini2-Flash	0.51	0.23	0.21
ChatGPT-4o	0.54	0.20	0.18
Codestral	0.38	0.27	0.17
deepseek-r1:32b	0.42	0.08	0.27
DeepSeek-R1	0.42	0.08	0.01
Qwen2.5-Coder:32b	0.31	0.04	0.05

Table 11. Agreement of the SCOLP with Expert Ranking

Functions	Metric	W_Kappa
First Batch	SCOLP to $Experts_{MV}$	0.30
Categorization Poker	SCOLP to $Experts_{MV}$	0.21

a considerably weaker alignment. These results show that LLMs clearly outperform the state-of-the-art on this subset. Similarly, for the second batch of 20 functions, the Kappa between the average LLMs categorization and the expert consensus ranking is 0.32, whereas SCOLP achieves a score of just 0.21. Once again, LLMs demonstrate stronger alignment with human expert assessments than the traditional automated approach.

Based on these findings, we can now answer **RQ2**: *How closely do LLMs align with SCOLP, a state-of-the-art automated technique for STA?* The answer is that, while LLMs exhibit a fair level of agreement with SCOLP, they consistently outperform it in terms of alignment with human expert judgments. This suggests that LLMs are not only competitive with current automated techniques but may serve as more accurate and scalable alternatives for software trustworthiness assessment.

6   Threats to Validity

Internal Validity: Due to the inherent difficulty of involving human experts in large-scale studies, and the time commitment required for detailed function-level evaluation, we limited direct expert validation to 30 functions (two sets of 10 and 20). However, for the automated SCOLP approach, we expanded the dataset with 40 additional functions, to increase coverage and generalizability.

Expert assessments followed two methods: most-voted ranking and consensus ranking. The former required an extra step to prevent inconsistent categorization. The latter involved over six hours across three sessions–a level of human-in-the-loop validation that is uncommon and adds credibility. Despite participants being experienced researchers, professors, and Ph.D. students in software security, human judgment introduces variability. Consensus sessions mitigate individual bias but may suffer dominance effects, echoing challenges in real-world collaborative assessments.

External Validity: Our experiments focused on one project–the Linux Kernel. Its scale and modularity make it a strong case for system software, but the findings may not generalize to other domains (*e.g.*, smaller codebases, or web applications). It is written in C, a language known for privileged access to hardware. Thus, applicability to software in other languages (*e.g.*, Java, Python, Rust) remains an open question.

Alongside large commercial models, we evaluated lightweight locally-runnable LLMs. While these may underperform compared to proprietary models, their promising results–when paired with well-crafted prompts–suggest that constrained models remain viable. More powerful models (*e.g.*, *ChatGPT-4*, *Claude 3.5 Sonnet*) are expected to align even more closely with expert judgments, based on public benchmarks [48].

Construct Validity: Prompt engineering remains heuristic and lacks standardized best practices [56]. We tested several strategies -from Chain-of-Thought

(CoT) to Tree-of-Thought (Tree of Thoughts Prompting (ToT))– but none consistently outperformed a simpler zero-shot approach with brief category descriptions. That is because complex prompts, while potentially helpful for larger LLMs, can hinder smaller models due to context window constraints. To ensure consistency and broader applicability, we used simplified prompts across all models. While this choice may not have peak performance, it still avoids model-specific tuning biases.

7   Conclusion and Future Work

In this paper, we performed a study to understand the LLMs' ability to evaluate the trustworthiness of software functions. Our approach involved prompt engineering techniques to assign each function to a specific priority group. This categorization can inform software development teams about functions that need to be reviewed. We evaluated our method using functions from the Linux Kernel.

We validated the ability of LLMs as experts in STA against reviews by security specialists and an automatic state-of-the-art process. The results indicate that the LLM-based classification does not achieve a *strong agreement* level, especially with the security experts. For these experts, the LLMs has some level of agreement with the most voted expert ranking (0.72), followed by consensus expert ranking (0.32). The agreement level is lower when compared with SCOLP (0.25). These results show the potential to use LLMs for STA, although they are not available yet.

For future work, we plan to develop a trustworthiness assessment methodology based on LLMs, enabling source code analysis and computation of trustworthiness indicators to address existing analysis limitations. We also intend to expand the evaluation to include more software projects with different objectives.

Acknowledgment. This work is partially financed through national funds by FCT - Fundação para a Ciência e a Tecnologia, I.P., in the framework of the Project UIDB/00326/2025 and UIDP/00326/2025. This work was partially supported by "Projeto no 2024. 07660.IACDC, https://doi.org/10.54499/2024.07660.IACDC, apoiado pela medida "RE-C05-i08.M04 "Apoiar o lançamento de um programa de projetos de I&D orientado para o desenvolvimento e implementação de sistemas avançados de cibersegurança, inteligência artificial e ciência de dados na administração pública, bem como de um programa de capacitação científica", do Plano de Recuperação e Resiliência PRR, enquadrado no contrato de financiamento celebrado entre a Estrutura de Missão Recuperar Portugal (EMRP) e a Fundação para a Ciência e a Tecnologia I.P. (FCT), enquanto beneficiário intermediário."

References

1. Zhang, M., Wang, L., Jajodia, S., Singhal, A.: Network attack surface: lifting the concept of attack surface to the network level for evaluating networks' resilience against zero-day attacks. IEEE Trans. Dependable Secure Comput. **18**(1), 310–324 (2018)

2. NVD. Statistics (1999). https://nvd.nist.gov/vuln/search/statistics?form_type=Advanced&results_type=statistics&search_type=all&isCpeNameSearch=false&pub_start_date=01. Accessed 25 Mar 2025
3. Medeiros, N., Ivaki, N., Costa, P., Vieira, M.: Trustworthiness models to categorize and prioritize code for security improvement. J. Syst. Softw. **198**, 111621 (2023)
4. Ebert, C., Gallardo, G., Hernantes, J., Serrano, N.: Devops. IEEE Softw. **33**(3), 94–100 (2016)
5. Pittet, S.: Learn continuous deployment with bitbucket pipelines (2023). https://www.atlassian.com/devops/continuous-delivery-tutorials/continuous-deployment-tutorial. Accessed 25 Mar 2025
6. Prates, L., Faustino, J., Silva, M., Pereira, R.: DevSecOps metrics. In: Wrycza, S., Maślankowski, J. (eds.) SIGSAND/PLAIS 2019. LNBIP, vol. 359, pp. 77–90. Springer, Cham (2019). https://doi.org/10.1007/978-3-030-29608-7_7
7. Liu, B., Shi, L., Cai, Z., Li, M.: Software vulnerability discovery techniques: a survey. In: 2012 Fourth International Conference on Multimedia Information Networking and Security, pp. 152–156. IEEE (2012)
8. Pereira, J.D., Vieira, M.: An approach to characterize the security of open-source functions using LSP. In: 2023 IEEE 34th International Symposium on Software Reliability Engineering (ISSRE), pp. 137–147 (2023). https://doi.org/10.1109/ISSRE59848.2023.00073
9. Imtiaz, N., Rahman, A., Farhana, E., Williams, L.: Challenges with responding to static analysis tool alerts. In: 2019 IEEE/ACM 16th International Conference on Mining Software Repositories (MSR), pp. 245–249 (2019)
10. Fakhoury, S., Naik, A., Sakkas, G., Chakraborty, S., Lahiri, S.K.: LLM-based test-driven interactive code generation: user study and empirical evaluation. IEEE Trans. Softw. Eng. **50**(9), 2254–2268 (2024). https://doi.org/10.1109/TSE.2024.3428972
11. Rasheed, Z., Sami, M.A., Waseem, M., et al.: Ai-powered code review with llms: early results. arXiv preprint arXiv:2404.18496 (2024)
12. Li, H., Hao, Y., Zhai, Y., Qian, Z.: Enhancing static analysis for practical bug detection: an llm-integrated approach. Proc. ACM Program. Lang. **8**(OOPSLA1), 474–499 (2024)
13. Luo, Q., Ye, Y., Liang, S., et al.: Repoagent: an llm-powered open-source framework for repository-level code documentation generation. arXiv preprint arXiv:2402.16667 (2024)
14. Zhang, C., Liu, H., Zeng, J., Yang, K., Li, Y., Li, H.: Prompt-enhanced software vulnerability detection using chatgpt. In: Proceedings of the 2024 IEEE/ACM 46th International Conference on Software Engineering: Companion Proceedings, pp. 276–277 (2024)
15. Liu, Z., Yang, Z., Liao, Q.: Exploration on prompting llm with code-specific information for vulnerability detection. In: 2024 IEEE International Conference on Software Services Engineering (SSE), pp. 273–281. IEEE (2024)
16. Zhou, X., Zhang, T., Lo, D.: Large language model for vulnerability detection: emerging results and future directions. In: Proceedings of the 2024 ACM/IEEE 44th International Conference on Software Engineering: New Ideas and Emerging Results, pp. 47–51 (2024)
17. Medeiros, N., Ivaki, N.R., Da Costa, P.N., Vieira, M.P.A.: Towards an approach for trustworthiness assessment of software as a service. In: 2017 IEEE International Conference on Edge Computing (EDGE), pp. 220–223. IEEE (2017)
18. Tao, H., Chen, Y., Wu, H., Deng, R.: A survey of software trustworthiness measurements. Int. J. Performabil. Eng. **15**(9), 2364 (2019)

19. Shi, H., Ma, J., Zou, F.: A fuzzy comprehensive evaluation model for software dependability based on entropy weight. In: 2008 International Conference on Computer Science and Software Engineering, pp. 683–685. IEEE (2008)
20. Li, B., Cao, Y.: An improved comprehensive evaluation model of software dependability based on rough set theory. J. Softw. **4**(10), 1152–1159 (2009)
21. Amoroso, E., Taylor, C., Watson, J., Weiss, J.: A process-oriented methodology for assessing and improving software trustworthiness. In: Proceedings of the 2nd ACM Conference on Computer and Communications Security, pp. 39–50 (1994)
22. Si, G., Xu, J., Yang, J., Wen, S.: An evaluation model for dependability of internet-scale software on basis of bayesian networks and trustworthiness. J. Syst. Softw. **89**, 63–75 (2014)
23. Chen, L., Cheng, P., Liu, W.: The model and method of trustworthiness level evaluation for software product. In: 2010 Sixth International Conference on Natural Computation, vol. 2, pp. 709–715. IEEE (2010)
24. Li, P., Park, H., Gao, D., Fu, J.: Bridging the gap between data-flow and control-flow analysis for anomaly detection. In: Annual Computer Security Applications Conference (ACSAC), pp. 392–401 (2008). IEEE (2008)
25. Nami, M., Suryn, W.: From requirements to software trustworthiness using scenarios and finite state machine. In: IECON 2012-38th Annual Conference on IEEE Industrial Electronics Society, pp. 3126–3131. IEEE (2012)
26. Tian, J., Guo, Y.: Software trustworthiness evaluation model based on a behaviour trajectory matrix. Inf. Softw. Technol. **119**, 106233 (2020)
27. Zheng, Z., Ma, S., Li, W., et al.: Complexity of software trustworthiness and its dynamical statistical analysis methods. Sci. China Ser. F: Inf. Sci. **52**(9), 1651–1657 (2009)
28. Medeiros, N.P.D.S., Ivaki, N.R., Costa, P.N.D., Vieira, M.P.A.: Towards an approach for trustworthiness assessment of software as a service. In: IEEE International Conference on Edge Computing, EDGE 2017, Honolulu, HI, USA, 25–30 June 2017, pp. 220–223. IEEE Computer Society (2017). https://doi.org/10.1109/IEEE.EDGE.2017.39
29. Zhou, Y., Liu, S., Siow, J., Du, X., Liu, Y.: Devign: effective vulnerability identification by learning comprehensive program semantics via graph neural networks. Adv. Neural. Inf. Process. Syst. **32**, 1–11 (2019)
30. Chakraborty, S., Krishna, R., Ding, Y., Ray, B.: Deep learning based vulnerability detection: are we there yet? IEEE Trans. Softw. Eng. **48**(9), 3280–3296 (2021)
31. OpenHub. The platform to discover, track and compare open source (2025). https://openhub.net/p/linux/analyses/latest/languages_summary. Accessed 07 June 2025
32. FirstAuthor. Prompts (2025). https://anonymous.4open.science/r/TestedPromptsForTrustworthiness-4E73/Dataset_LinuxFunctions.csv. Accessed 07 June 2025
33. FirstAuthor. Prompts (2025). https://anonymous.4open.science/r/TestedPromptsForTrustworthiness-4E73. Accessed 07 June 2025
34. Wei, J., Wang, X., Schuurmans, D., et al.: Chain-of-thought prompting elicits reasoning in large language models. Adv. Neural. Inf. Process. Syst. **35**, 24824–24837 (2022)
35. Zhang, Z., Zhang, A., Li, M., Smola, A.: Automatic chain of thought prompting in large language models. arXiv preprint arXiv:2210.03493 (2022)
36. Wang, X., Wei, J., Schuurmans, D., et al.: Self-consistency improves chain of thought reasoning in language models. preprint arXiv:2203.11171 (2022)

37. Hu, H., Lu, H.,X Zhang, H., Song, Y.-Z., Lam, W., Zhang, Y.: Chain-of-symbol prompting elicits planning in large langauge models. arXiv preprint arXiv:2305.10276 (2023)

38. Yao, S., Yu, D., Zhao, J., et al.: Tree of thoughts: deliberate problem solving with large language models". Adv. Neural. Inf. Process. Syst. **36**, 11809–11822 (2023)

39. Yao, Y., Li, Z., Zhao, H.: Beyond chain-of-thought, effective graph-of-thought reasoning in language models. arXiv preprint arXiv:2305.16582 (2023)

40. Sahoo, P., Singh, A.K., Saha, S., Jain, V., Mondal, S., Chadha, A.: A systematic survey of prompt engineering in large language models: techniques and applications. arXiv preprint arXiv:2402.07927 (2024)

41. OpenAI. Gpt-4o: Openai's new flagship model (2024). https://openai.com/index/gpt-4o. Accessed 07 May 2025

42. DeepMind, G.: Introducing gemini 1.5 and gemini 1.5 flash (2024). https://deepmind.google/technologies/gemini/gemini-flash/. Accessed 07 May 2025

43. AI, D.: Deepseek-v2 and deepseek-r1: Advancing moe and reasoning in open llms (2025). https://deepseek.com/blog/deepseek-v2-r1.html. Accessed 07 May 2025

44. Soria, A.M.: Granite 3.1 Language Models (2023). https://huggingface.co/ibm-granite

45. Yang, A., Yang, B., Zhang, B., et al.: Qwen2. 5 technical report. arXiv preprint arXiv:2412.15115 (2024)

46. Mistral. Codestral, mistral's first-ever code model (2025). https://mistral.ai/news/codestral. Accessed 29 Apr 2025

47. Bi, X., Chen, D., Chen, G., et al.: Deepseek llm: scaling open-source language models with longtermism. arXiv preprint arXiv:2401.02954 (2024)

48. MITTRE. The platform where the machine learning community collaborates on models, datasets, and applications (2025). https://huggingface.co/. Accessed 25 Mar 2025

49. Morgan, J.: Ollama - Get up and running with large language model (2023). https://ollama.com/

50. Grenning, J.: Planning poker or how to avoid analysis paralysis while release planning. Hawthorn Woods: Renaissance Softw. Consult. **3**, 22–23 (2002)

51. Kläs, M., Nakao, H., Elberzhager, F., Münch, J.: Predicting defect content and quality assurance effectiveness by combining expert judgment and defect data-a case study. In: International Symposium on Software Reliability Engineering (ISSRE), pp. 17–26. IEEE (2008)

52. Pavlič, L., Heričko, M., Beranič, T.: An expert judgment in source code quality research domain-a comparative study between professionals and students. Appl. Sci. **10**(20), 7088 (2020)

53. Cohen, J.: Weighted kappa: nominal scale agreement provision for scaled disagreement or partial credit. Psychol. Bull. **70**(4), 213 (1968)

54. Cohen, J.: A coefficient of agreement for nominal scales. Educ. Psychol. Measur. **20**(1), 37–46 (1960)

55. Landis, J.R., Koch, G.G.: The measurement of observer agreement for categorical data. Biometrics 159–174 (1977)

56. Zhou, X., Cao, S., Sun, X., Lo, D.: Large language model for vulnerability detection and repair: Literature review and the road ahead. ACM Trans. Softw. Eng. Methodol. (2024)

FlowMon: A Workflow-Driven Visual Tool for Automated Monitoring Script Generation

Eduardo Lima[1] , Igor Vanderlei[2] , and Jean Araujo[1,2,3]

[1] Universidade Federal de Sergipe, São Cristóvão, Sergipe, Brazil
`eduardotlima@academico.ufs.br`
[2] Universidade Federal do Agreste de Pernambuco, Garanhuns, Pernambuco, Brazil
[3] Instituto de Telecomunicações, Aveiro, Portugal
`{igor.vanderlei,jean.teixeira}@ufape.edu.br`

Abstract. Computing systems are becoming increasingly complex, which makes it necessary to monitor and manage resources. However, manually creating monitoring scripts is time-consuming, error-prone, and does not scale well with system growth. This paper presents a tool that proposes the automatic generation and execution of Shell Scripts for monitoring computing resources through a workflow-based visual interface. Using an intuitive GUI (Graphical User Interface), users can drag and configure components to be evaluated within a visual flow editor. Linux monitoring commands have been transformed into high-level visual representations of computing resources, allowing users to create and execute their own scripts to monitor local or remote systems with minimal interaction or coding knowledge. To demonstrate that the application works effectively, we conducted practical tests, provided different use cases, and compared it with other tools on the market. The results demonstrated the tool's effectiveness, showcasing its ability to create and execute Shell Scripts while continuously simplifying the monitoring process and maintaining a low impact on the system.

Keywords: Monitoring · Performance Evaluation · Script Generation · Shell Scripting · Metamodels

1 Introduction

The increasing complexity of modern computational systems demands sophisticated strategies for resource monitoring and management. It is essential to assess how resources are being utilized to support critical decision-making and prevent issues such as service interruptions, resource misallocation, or financial losses [13,19]. Currently, users and system administrators rely on various types of software to perform monitoring tasks, ranging from paid and free applications to custom-built monitoring scripts [1,22].

Manually creating monitoring scripts is associated with multiple issues that compromise both the efficiency and reliability of monitoring systems [9,11]. Key

L. A. Rodrigues and R. Oliveira (Eds.): LADC 2025, CCIS 2697, pp. 94–111, 2026.
https://doi.org/10.1007/978-3-032-11539-3_6

challenges include: (i) a high likelihood of logical and syntactic errors, particularly when developed under pressure or by professionals with varying levels of expertise; (ii) difficulties in ensuring correct and continuous operation in heterogeneous environments; (iii) significant obstacles related to scalability and adaptability across different system scenarios; (iv) a lack of standardization, which hinders the maintainability and evolution of the scripts; and (v) the considerable amount of time required for development and testing, which could otherwise be invested in strategic activities [17].

Recognizing these limitations and gaps, this paper presents an approach for the automatic generation of monitoring scripts through a tool based on high-level visual modeling. The proposed solution leverages concepts from Model-Driven Development (MDD) and metamodeling to abstract the complexity of Shell script creation, enabling users with varying levels of coding expertise to design, configure, and execute effective monitoring workflows.

The proposed tool is capable of automatically generating monitoring scripts by visually composing flow structures and nodes that represent devices and their respective components. The application uses a visual representation to generate code in the Shell scripting language, without requiring prior knowledge of advanced programming. Anyone, regardless of their coding experience, can use the tool. It is a Single-Page Application (SPA) built with a client-server architecture, utilizing React.js for the frontend and Node.js for the backend. The tool, named FlowMon, is available as an open-source project, and its source code can be accessed in the GitHub repository[1]. In addition to script generation, the tool allows execution in both local and remote environments and provides real-time output through interactive visualizations.

To validate the effectiveness of the proposed approach, practical experiments were conducted to demonstrate both the functionality of the application in generating and executing scripts and its low impact on the performance of monitored systems. The results obtained indicate that the tool is capable of generating scripts that are functionally equivalent to those created manually, exhibiting correct behavior during execution and minimal impact on the performance of the monitored systems. It was observed that the use of the visual interface may promote standardization and streamline the script creation process by reducing the complexity associated with manual coding, especially for users with limited familiarity with terminal-based languages.

The remainder of this paper is organized as follows. Section 2 presents the foundational concepts. Section 3 provides a detailed overview of the tool's architecture. Section 4 describes a comprehensive case study and evaluation scenarios. Section 5 discusses related work. Finally, Sect. 6 presents final considerations, identified limitations, and directions for future work.

2   Background

This section presents the fundamental concepts necessary for understanding the paper, including topics such as Automatic Script Generation, High-Level Models, and Monitoring Scripts.

---

[1] https://github.com/eduardolima1994/flowmon/.

2.1 Automatic Script Generation

Automatic Script Generation is the process of creating scripts automatically based on predefined parameters, models, or interfaces, without requiring the user to manually write the code [8,24,32]. Key benefits of these techniques include accelerated software development, reduced errors, and the ability to produce more effective and efficient software products, significantly impacting the application development process [33]. The generated code must accurately reflect the logic and behavior defined in the original model, translating them correctly into the target language.

The software coding process can be carried out either manually or through automatic generation (see Fig. 1, adapted from [5]). In the manual approach, the developer follows a set of established rules and procedures to transform design specifications into source code. This process requires special attention to ensure requirements traceability, as well as to uphold code quality characteristics such as readability, clarity, and maintainability. Automatic code generation, on the other hand, uses formal models and templates as input, processed by tools that operate under well-defined constraints [28].

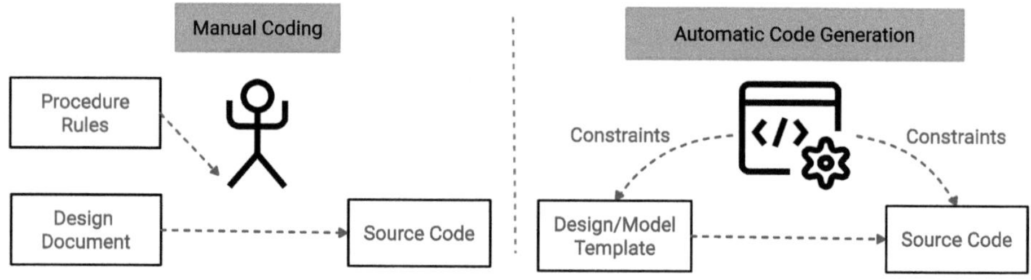

Fig. 1. Coding Processes.

Automatic code generation from system designs is a research area within MDD. The concept has versatile applications in the software industry and is based on the idea that during system implementation, the system can be modeled using standard notations such as the Unified Modeling Language (UML) [7]. During project maintenance, users can modify the system models instead of the source code and subsequently generate code from the updated system model [33]. Implementing an automatic code generation activity enables the regeneration of code that closely reflects the input model [4].

2.2 High-Level Models

Models are abstract representations of real-world systems or phenomena, used to facilitate understanding, communication, and analysis [6,16]. In Model-Driven Engineering (MDE), software engineers use them specifically to represent a system at an abstract level. The introduction of a higher abstraction technique within MDE, called metamodeling or high-level modeling, enables software engineers to describe behavior, architecture, or logic and refine their designs at an even higher level [27,30,31]. A metamodel provides an abstract syntax to distinguish between valid and invalid models; thus, a metamodel is as essential to a modeling language as grammar is to a programming language [15]. Metamodels form the foundation of MDD, whose purpose is to abstract low-level details of information systems, allowing the creation of specifications at a higher level [21,29].

Using metamodeling, code generators create unique configurations for each operator in the target code, offering an efficient and consistent alternative to manual coding [2]. A code generator reads the models and, based on defined rules, automatically produces the required code for the user, where each configuration in the model generates a different, tailored code without the need for manual writing.

A metamodel is a conceptual model of a modeling language and describes the concepts of a modeling language, their properties, and the valid connections between the language elements (see Fig. 2, adapted from [14]). In other words, metamodels are fundamental entities for model designers and tool developers because they precisely define how tools and models should work together [20].The model is an instance of the metamodel and represents, in an abstract way, a specific real-world subject. In other words, it aims to represent or simulate behaviors, structures, or relevant aspects of the actual system. In Fig. 2, the Subject refers to the real-world object or system being modeled. There is a hierarchy among the levels of abstraction: the metamodel defines the language, the language expresses models, and the models describe elements of the real world.

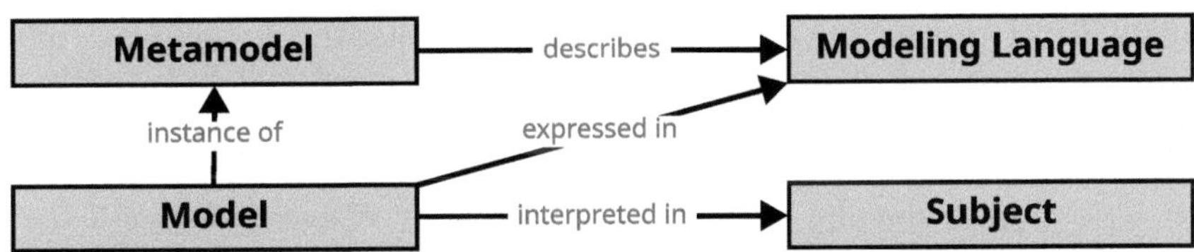

Fig. 2. Relationship Between Model, Metamodel, Language, and Subject.

2.3 Model-to-Code Transformation

Model-to-Code (M2C) transformation is a central pillar of MDE, enabling the automatic generation of software artifacts, such as source code, from abstract models [26]. The process is carried out by a transformation engine that interprets an input model, which conforms to a metamodel, and applies a set of mapping rules to produce output code in a specific programming language. M2C transformations can be classified as either visitor-based or template-based. In the visitor-based approach, the transformation logic traverses the model's tree structure, and for each node type visited, a corresponding code block is generated. In contrast, the template-based approach uses templates containing the code skeleton to be generated, with placeholders that are filled with information extracted from the model [3, 25].

The tool adopts a hybrid approach. First, a visitor-based algorithm implemented in Node.js traverses the monitoring flow graph, received as JSON from the frontend. It performs a depth-first search (DFS) starting from each device node to serialize operations and construct an intermediate representation of the monitoring logic. This representation then feeds a template-based engine that generates the final Shell script. The strategy combines the flexibility of programmatic model traversal with the clarity and maintainability of code generation templates, ensuring that the script structure faithfully reflects the logic visually defined by the user.

2.4 Monitoring Scripts

Monitoring scripts are essential components in managing computational environments, whether local, cloud-based, or hybrid. They are responsible for collecting information about the state of system resources, such as CPU utilization, memory consumption, disk usage, network latency, service availability, and the integrity of running processes. Through automated commands, it is possible to log data, generate alerts, send notifications, and trigger corrective actions, thereby mitigating operational impacts and ensuring higher service availability [34].

Manual creation of monitoring scripts poses significant challenges, as the process is often mechanical and requires deep knowledge of operating system commands, resource-specific metrics, and the logic needed to interpret the data. Manually developed scripts are prone to errors, inconsistencies, and lack of standardization, which can compromise both maintenance and scalability of the solution [9, 17]. Algorithm 1 presents an example of a system memory monitoring script.

In Linux environments, automation is primarily achieved through the creation of *.sh* (Shell Script) files, widely used to configure monitoring routines, execute sequential commands, manipulate log files, and interact efficiently with the operating system [10, 17, 18]. By automatically generating scripts from abstract models, it is possible to ensure standardization, reduce human errors, facilitate maintenance, and rapidly adapt scripts to different contexts and requirements.

3 Tool Overview

The tool was developed as a web application to ensure cross-platform portability. It was designed as a reactive SPA, capable of efficiently responding to changes in data or environment, and interacting with the user by dynamically rewriting the web page with new data—without the need to reload entire pages [12, 23, 35]. The main goal is to provide faster transitions and updates, enhancing the overall user experience.

Algorithm 1: System memory monitoring script.

```
1  Input: TOTAL_TIME, INTERVAL
2  Output: Memory usage log: total;used;free;shared;timestamp
3    #!/bin/bash
4    TOTAL_TIME=60
5    INTERVAL=2
6    initial_time=$(date +%s)
7  while true do
8      current_time=$(date +%s)
9      if (( current_time - initial_time >= TOTAL_TIME + 1 )) then
10       break
11     end if
12     date_time=$(date +"%Y-%m-%d %H:%M:%S")
13     mem=$(free | grep Mem)
14     mem_total=$(echo $mem | awk '{print $2}')
15     mem_used=$(echo $mem | awk '{print $3}')
16     mem_free=$(echo $mem | awk '{print $4}')
17     mem_shared=$(echo $mem | awk '{print $6}')
18     echo "$mem_total;$mem_used;$mem_free;$mem_shared;$date_time"
19     sleep $INTERVAL
20   end while
```

3.1 Metamodel

The application is based on a metamodel that formally defines the abstract syntax of the visual modeling language. The metamodel specifies the language concepts, properties, and valid relationships. The model created by the user in the graphical interface is an instance of the metamodel. The application's metamodel defines the following core elements:

Element. This is the base metaclass for all visual components. It contains a *name* attribute for identification.

Node. Represents the building blocks of the flow. Nodes are divided into three main categories: *Flow nodes*, which control the structure and execution of the script; *Monitoring (trigger) nodes*, which, when connected to a *Device* node, activate the collection of specific metrics; *Utility nodes*, which add information or custom logic to the flow.

Link/Edge. Defines the directed connections between nodes, establishing the execution sequence and data flow. Each Link has a *source* and a *target*, both of which are instances of Node.

The following multiplicity and relationship constraints are used to validate the model:

1. An Element must contain exactly one Start node, ensuring a unique entry point for workflow execution and the definition of global timing configurations.
2. The Start node must originate at least one Link, connecting exclusively to Device nodes to establish independent monitoring branches.
3. The workflow is only useful if it monitors at least one device. The direct connection to Device establishes independent monitoring branches.
4. Monitoring or Utility nodes must receive an incoming connection from a Device or another Monitoring node within the same branch, preventing orphan nodes and ensuring that every metric collection is associated with a specific device.
5. A Monitoring Node can have at most one outgoing Edge. Within a device branch, metric collection is modeled as a linear sequence to simplify script generation. Complex logic branches are not supported at this level to maintain model clarity and predictability of the generated script.
6. The workflow must contain at least four connected nodes.
7. Every branch initiated by a Device must end in a Finish node.
8. Monitoring properties (e.g., cpuState, memoryState) are global attributes activated by the presence of their respective Monitoring Nodes in the flow.

3.2   M2C Transformation Algorithm

The M2C transformation process represents a component of the FlowMon architecture that converts metamodel instances into executable Shell scripts. The algorithm receives the model as a JSON structure and starts a new generation process for each `Device` node, allowing parallel monitoring of multiple devices. The traversal is performed by a visitor implemented through depth-first search, which systematically explores the flow branching from each `Device` node. During the traversal, the algorithm collects and orders information from the Monitoring Nodes and Utility Nodes into an intermediate structure that preserves the dependencies and execution sequence specified in the visual model.

Code generation uses a specialized template engine that processes the intermediate structure through predefined templates. The engine dynamically fills the variable parts with data extracted from the model, containing the structural skeleton of the Shell script. The resulting script features an architecture that distinguishes fixed code from dynamically generated code. The fixed code includes invariant elements such as the shebang (`#!/bin/bash`), the `while` loop structure, the `sleep $INTERVAL` instruction, and `timestamp` capture mechanisms. The generated code represents the customized dynamic parts: declaration of temporary variables, metric collection commands (such as `cpu=$(mpstat | grep all)`), `awk` commands for extraction and formatting, and the composition of the final `echo` line with variables selected in the model.

This separation ensures that the control logic remains standardized, while the data collection logic is customized by the visual model.

3.3   Architecture

The tool's architecture is based on a client-server structure (see Fig. 3), where the frontend is responsible for the visual interface and the backend manages script generation and execution. This separation allows a clear distinction between frontend and backend responsibilities, contributing to greater system flexibility and scalability. The frontend consists of a single-page application (SPA) developed with React.js, utilizing the ReactFlow library to enable users to visually construct workflows. This layer manages the model state (including nodes, connections, and configurations) and sends the workflow structure as a JSON payload to the backend via a REST API.

The backend is implemented in Node.js using the Express.js framework and is responsible for interpreting the received model, generating the corresponding Shell scripts, and coordinating their execution. Script execution can occur locally on the server machine or remotely on target devices accessed via the Secure Shell (SSH) protocol, with the tool designed to operate in Linux-based environments.

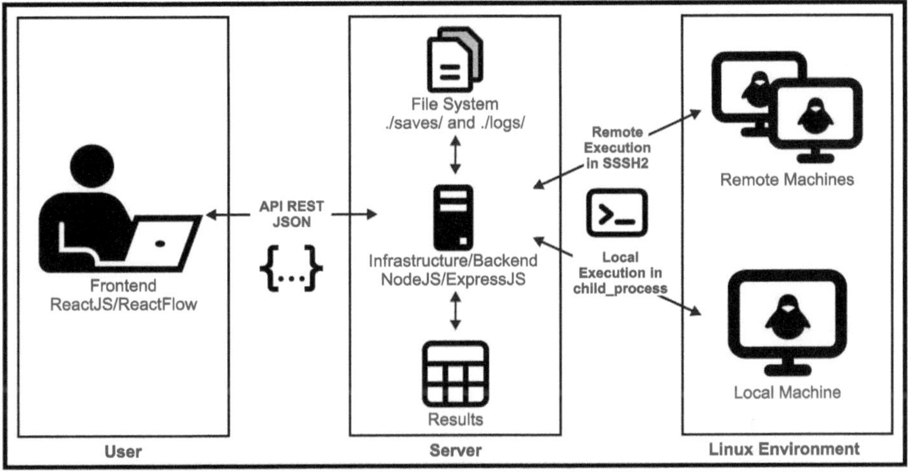

Fig. 3. Application macroarchitecture.

3.4   Main Interface and Nodes

The application's main interface is divided into a menu, modeling area, nodes panel, node configuration panel, and action panel for node operations (see Fig. 4).

Nodes. Each node is a high-level visual representation of a computational resource or a Linux system monitoring command. Nodes include advanced functionality buttons:

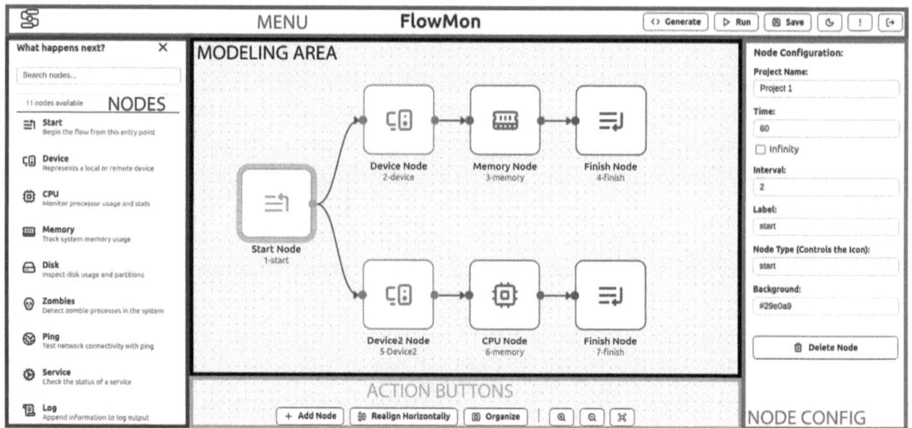

Fig. 4. Application home screen.

Device and Flow Cloning: The user interface allows cloning a device along with its associated monitoring flow. It also includes a bulk cloning feature from a *.csv* file, enabling rapid creation of multiple monitoring flows for different devices.

Flow Collapse/Expand: Users can visually collapse or expand the node flow associated with a device to simplify the view.

Node Deletion: This can be performed by clicking the floating button overlaying each node or by selecting the node and pressing the delete key.

Each node type is detailed in Table 1.

Menu. It provides eight main features: (i) generate script; (ii) generate and execute script; (iii) save project; (iv) toggle light/dark theme; (v) export model; (vi) import model; (vii) export UML diagram; and (viii) exit the application. The export feature offers a mechanism to export monitoring models to a JSON file via a button that allows saving it on the user's computer. Similarly, the import model feature provides a way to restore a previously exported model through an import button. Another export option was implemented: a button that converts the created flow model into a widely recognized format by the community, UML. The application allows users to save their workflows on the server. By clicking *Save*, each project is saved in a unique directory, where it can be restored from the saved projects list and reused at any time.

Modeling Area. This is where the user builds workflows and constructs monitoring logic by connecting different types of nodes. By sequentially connecting nodes from different categories, the user defines the behavior and logic of the script to be generated.

Table 1. Classification and description of system node types.

Name	Node Type	Description
Start	Flow	The entry point of any workflow. Defines global settings such as duration and interval, which can be inherited by subsequent nodes
Device	Flow	The central component representing the target machine (local or remote). Each *device* node generates an independent `while` loop in the final script, aggregating commands from monitoring nodes connected to it
Finish	Flow	Marks the end of a *Device* loop by inserting the `done` command and a `sleep` instruction to respect the defined collection interval
CPU	Monitoring	Uses the `mpstat` command to collect processor statistics (e.g., user, system, *iowait* usage)
Memory	Monitoring	Uses the `free` command and reads from `/proc/meminfo` to monitor memory usage (e.g., used, free, *cache*)
Disk	Monitoring	Executes the `df` command to inspect disk usage (e.g., total space, used, percentage)
Zombies	Monitoring	Uses `ps aux` together with `awk` to count zombie processes
Ping	Monitoring	Tests connectivity to a target address using the `ping` command
Service	Monitoring	Checks the status of a specific service using `pgrep` and `pidstat` to collect metrics for a particular process
Log	Utility	Inserts a user-defined text message as an extra column in the output file
Comment	Utility	Adds a comment line (#) in the generated script, serving as internal documentation

Node Addition Panel. Allows the user to insert different types of nodes available in the model, organized by category and functionality, facilitating the identification and proper use of each element. The panel features an integrated search bar that enables quickly locating a specific node using keywords.

Node Configuration Panel. Responsible for displaying and enabling the modification of the properties of the currently selected node in the modeling area. Through the panel, it is possible to adjust specific attributes for each node type, such as data collection intervals, associated monitoring commands, target addresses for remote execution via SSH, as well as other contextual configurations like metrics to be collected or service names. The interface is adaptive; the fields displayed vary according to the selected node type, ensuring that only relevant options are shown to the user. The panel also offers features to change the selected node's type and color, allowing more efficient and visually organized customization of the modeling flow.

Action Buttons. Provides specific controls that allow adding new nodes, automatically rearranging diagram elements, and aligning nodes. It includes dedicated buttons to adjust the modeling area view, including zoom-in and zoom-out functionalities, facilitating navigation and manipulation of workflows at different levels of detail.

3.5 Data Visualization and Terminal

The tool offers an integrated panel combining a text terminal with a data visualization area, providing instant feedback to the user about the monitoring process. A core feature of the panel is displaying the complete Shell code generated by the tool, allowing the user to inspect the resulting script from the visual model and edit it if necessary. The integrated terminal uses a tab system to manage output from multiple devices simultaneously, allowing the user to switch between results for each device.

The script generation process starts when the user clicks the *Generation* button in the menu, while script execution is triggered by clicking *Run*. In both cases, the frontend sends the JSON representation of the workflow to the backend, which is responsible for generating the *.sh* script file and, if requested, executing it. Script execution is handled independently depending on the target environment. For local execution, the backend uses Node.js's *child_process* module to run the script directly on the server machine. For remote execution, instead of transferring the script file, the backend uses the *ssh2* library to connect to the remote host and runs the command *bash -s*, allowing the backend to stream the generated script content directly to the remote process via SSH.

Regardless of the execution scenario—local or remote—the script's standard output (*stdout*) and error output (*stderr*) are captured in real time. The outputs are then transmitted back to the frontend, which updates the terminal interface and monitoring charts, offering instant and continuous feedback to the user. The collected data visualization in charts can be filtered by date and time range, enabling a more focused analysis of the results.

3.6 Saved Projects, Login, and Registration

In the **Saved Projects** area, it is possible to download an entire project as a *.zip* file, download independent files, delete projects, and create new projects (see Fig. 5). In the **Registration** area, new users can register, and in **Login**, users are authenticated using hashed passwords (*bcrypt*) and JSON Web Tokens (JWT) for session management.

4 Case Study and Evaluation

To validate the proposed approach, functionality tests and preliminary performance experiments were conducted, focusing on demonstrating the tool's viability and efficiency. Tests were carried out on the latest long-term support (LTS) versions of the Linux operating systems Ubuntu, Debian, and Mint to ensure compatibility, stability, and to evaluate the tool's behavior across different distributions.

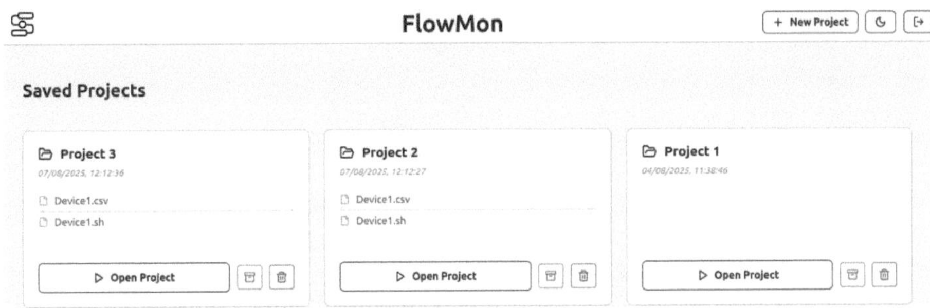

Fig. 5. Saved projects area.

4.1 Functional Validation

To validate the software tool, a test scenario was designed to verify the script generation logic of the application (see Fig. 6). Initially, a simple workflow was modeled in the interface composed of: *Start* → *Device* (configured as local) → *Memory* (configured to monitor used and free memory) → *Finish*. The monitoring interval was set to 5 s over a 1-min test period.

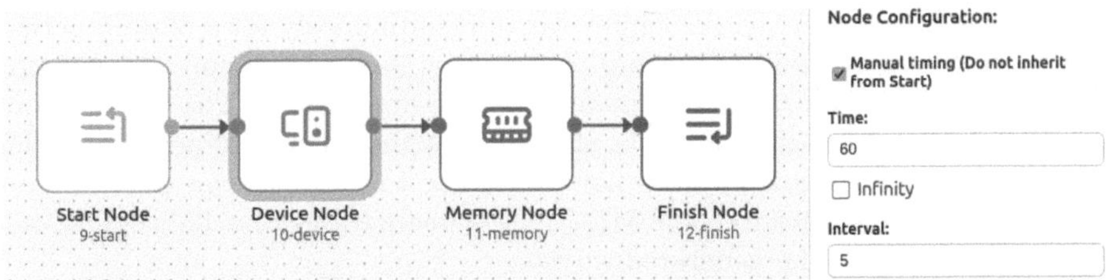

Fig. 6. Test scenario for validation.

The tool then generated a Shell script containing a *while* loop that, on each iteration, executed the *free* command, used *awk* to extract the desired values, and waited 5 s using the *sleep 5* command. The result was analyzed and confirmed that the generated script exactly matched the expected behavior and the logic defined in the visual model. The test demonstrated that the tool's core translation component, responsible for converting the JSON model into Shell script, is functioning correctly. The tool was tested by executing the generated script, and the results were satisfactory. During the test, the script was able to collect real-time memory usage data. The data were analyzed and graphically presented by the application, demonstrating the efficiency and accuracy of the process (see Fig. 7).

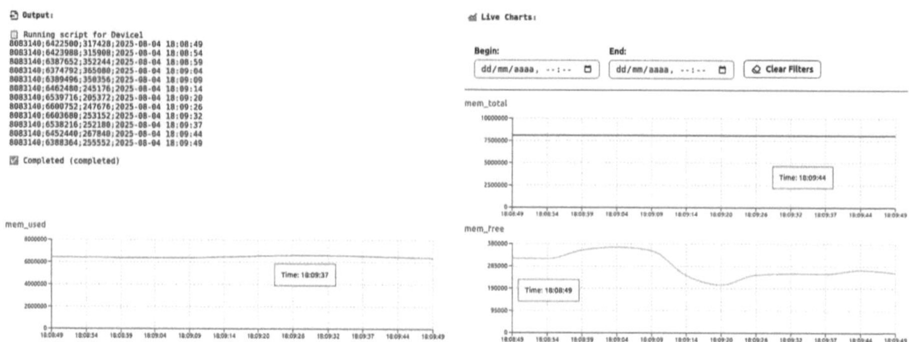

Fig. 7. Script execution result.

4.2   Performance Evaluation

Two experiments were conducted to assess the impact of the scripts generated by the application in a real environment, following a methodology similar to tool evaluation.

Experiment 1: Local Monitoring. A script generated to monitor CPU, memory, and disk usage on a local machine was run continuously for a 60-min period. Simultaneously, a second monitoring process was used to measure the resource consumption of the script itself generated by the application. The results, comparable to those of low-impact tools, showed that the script had negligible CPU utilization, with occasional spikes not exceeding 1%, and a constant, low resident memory usage around 4.3 MB. This demonstrates the lightweight and low-impact nature of the generated scripts.

Experiment 2: Remote Monitoring. In this scenario, a script was generated to monitor memory usage of a remote server. The network traffic (upload and download) generated by the application's SSH connection to execute the monitoring and receive data was measured on the local machine and run continuously for a 10-min period. The analysis showed very low and stable network usage, averaging approximately 6.26 KB/s upload and 14.61 KB/s download. The result confirms the efficiency of the remote execution mechanism, which transmits data economically without overloading the network.

4.3   Threats to Validity

An analysis of the research requires identifying potential threats that could influence the results. The threats to the validity of this work are presented below.

Internal Validity: It lies in the possibility of uncontrolled factors influencing the performance of the generated scripts. Although the experiments were conducted in controlled environments, variations in the operating system, script execution time, concurrent workload, or network configurations could affect the resource consumption metrics. To mitigate this issue, the tests were carried out on multiple Linux distributions (Ubuntu, Debian, and Mint) and during periods of low system activity, aiming to isolate the impact of the script.

Construct Validity: Translating the visual model into a functional Shell script is a critical point. A construct threat would be an inadequate mapping between the metamodel constructs and the generated Linux commands. The implementation of the M2C transformation algorithm, which traverses the node graph and applies code templates, was validated through functional tests that compared the behavior of the generated script with the logic defined visually, ensuring that the model's semantics were preserved.

Conclusion Validity: The reliability of the conclusions depends on the accuracy of the collected data. The use of standard system monitoring tools (such as `mpstat`, `free`, `df`) to assess the impact of the generated script itself minimizes the introduction of bias. However, the accuracy of these tools and the granularity of the data collection (time intervals) may limit the detection of very short consumption spikes, which represents a threat to the conclusion regarding the low impact of the tool.

5   Related Works

Several tools have been developed to facilitate the monitoring of computing systems. This section presents a relational analysis of the main existing approaches. The UNAME Tool [1] represents a solution for the automatic generation of monitoring scripts. Using a simple web interface, it allows users to select resources to be monitored and generate corresponding Shell scripts. Although effective, UNAME Tool shows limitations in terms of flexibility and the ability to model complex monitoring flows, offering less flexibility in monitoring multiple resources, does not build monitoring workflows, and does not support advanced visual modeling. The proposed application addresses these limitations by providing a more intuitive visual interface, script execution, and the capability to create complex monitoring workflows.

Another relevant work is AALFlow [8], a model-driven approach for integrating heterogeneous Internet of Things (IoT) solutions in the domain of Assisted Living Environments (AAL). Similarly, AALFlow employs a metamodel and a graphical editor to enable users to model information flows that combine multiple AAL systems. From the visual models, the tool automatically transforms them into executable code, specifically targeting Apache Beam and Apache NiFi platforms. However, the proposals differ in their application domains and output technologies; while AALFlow focuses on integrating complete AAL systems at a higher level of abstraction, our tool addresses the more fundamental task of monitoring computing resources by generating and executing Shell scripts.

Also noteworthy is the contribution in the area of metamodeling, which proposes a comprehensive metamodel for the Extended Entity-Relationship (EER) Model, with full support for Chen's notation [15]. Although the primary focus of this work is conceptual database modeling, the proposed metamodeling approach bears a strong relation to the presented tool, especially in using high-level models as a basis for automated generation of computing artifacts. While the metamodel formally defines the constructs and formation rules of the EER aiming at generating relational schemas and CASE tools, our proposal applies similar metamodeling concepts to visually represent, validate, and translate monitoring workflows into Shell scripts.

Table 2 presents a comparative analysis contrasting the functionalities implemented in FlowMon with methodologies adopted in other studies.

Table 2. Comparison of methodologies/functionalities in other studies.

Methodology/Functionality	FlowMon	UNAME Tool [1]	AALFlow [8]	EERMM [15]
Script Generation	Yes	Yes	Yes	No
Visual Interface (Workflow)	Yes	No	Yes	No
Explicit Metamodel	Yes	No	Yes	Yes
Script Execution	Yes	Yes	No	No
Remote Monitoring (SSH)	Yes	Yes	No	No
Graphical Results Display	Yes	No	No	No
Multi-Device Monitoring	Yes	No	No	No

6   Final Considerations and Future Work

This paper presented a web-based tool that addresses the challenges of manual monitoring script creation through a visual, flow-based modeling approach. By enabling automatic generation and integrated execution of scripts for Linux environments, the tool significantly reduces the complexity, time, and errors associated with this task, making computational resource monitoring more accessible and efficient for a broader audience. The evaluation demonstrated the proposal's feasibility, validating both the functional correctness of the generated scripts and their low impact on the performance of monitored systems. The results reinforce that abstraction through visual models simplifies script creation while maintaining performance in data collection, positioning the tool as a solution for environments that require uninterrupted monitoring.

As future work, we will pay special attention to application security by implementing a credential protection system and performing stricter validation of all user-provided information, thereby preventing potential attacks and malicious actions.

References

1. Araujo, J., Melo, C., Cordeiro, C.: Uname tool: automatic generation of computer resources monitoring scripts. In: 2021 16th Iberian Conference on Information Systems and Technologies (CISTI), pp. 1–7 (2021). https://doi.org/10.23919/CISTI52073.2021.9476223

2. Bhadra, M., Lopera, D.S., Kunzelmann, R., Ecker, W.: A model-driven architecture approach to accelerate software code generation. In: 2024 7th International Conference on Software and System Engineering (ICoSSE), pp. 23–30 (2024). https://doi.org/10.1109/ICoSSE62619.2024.00012

3. Bonta, E., Bernardo, M.: Padl2java: a java code generator for process algebraic architectural descriptions. In: 2009 Joint Working IEEE/IFIP Conference on Software Architecture & European Conference on Software Architecture, pp. 161–170 (2009). https://doi.org/10.1109/WICSA.2009.5290802

4. Boulanger, J.L.: 13 - tools qualification. In: Boulanger, J.L. (ed.) Certifiable Software Applications, vol. 2, pp. 171–197. Elsevier (2017). https://doi.org/10.1016/B978-1-78548-118-5.50013-2. https://www.sciencedirect.com/science/article/pii/B9781785481185500132

5. Boulanger, J.L.: 13 - software application coding. In: Boulanger, J.L. (ed.) Certifiable Software Applications, vol. 3, pp. 261–285. Elsevier (2018). https://doi.org/10.1016/B978-1-78548-119-2.50013-3. https://www.sciencedirect.com/science/article/pii/B9781785481192500133

6. Bézivin, J.: On the unification power of models. Softw. Syst. Model. **4**(2), 171–188 (2005). https://doi.org/10.1007/s10270-005-0079-0

7. Bézivin, J., Muller, P.A.: Uml: the birth and rise of a standard modeling notation. In: Bézivin, J., Muller, P.A. (eds.) The Unified Modeling Language. «UML»'98: Beyond the Notation, pp. 1–8. Springer, Heidelberg (1999)

8. Caballero-Torres, P., Cano-Crespo, M., Ortiz, G., Medina-Bulo, I.: Aalflow: a model-driven approach for the integration of internet of things heterogeneous solutions for ambient assisted living. IEEE Internet Things J. **11**(20), 33798–33810 (2024). https://doi.org/10.1109/JIOT.2024.3432617

9. Chen, Z., Zhang, N., Si, P., Chen, Q., Liu, C., Zheng, Z.: Shellfusion: an answer generator for shell programming tasks via knowledge fusion. In: 2023 IEEE/ACM 45th International Conference on Software Engineering: Companion Proceedings (ICSE-Companion), pp. 93–97 (2023). https://doi.org/10.1109/ICSE-Companion58688.2023.00032

10. Dakic, V., Redzepagic, J.: Linux Command Line and Shell Scripting Techniques: Master practical aspects of the Linux command line and then use it as a part of the shell scripting process. Packt Publishing Ltd (2022)

11. Dong, Y., Li, Z., Tian, Y., Sun, C., Godfrey, M.W., Nagappan, M.: Bash in the wild: language usage, code smells, and bugs. ACM Trans. Softw. Eng. Methodol. **32**(1) (2023). https://doi.org/10.1145/3517193. https://doi-org.ez20.periodicos.capes.gov.br/10.1145/3517193

12. Drechsler, J., Mogk, R., Salvaneschi, G., Mezini, M.: Thread-safe reactive programming. Proc. ACM Program. Lang. **2**(OOPSLA) (2018). https://doi.org/10.1145/3276477

13. Dyskin, A.V., et al.: Computational monitoring in real time: review of methods and applications. Geomech. Geophys. Geo-Energy Geo-Res. **4**(3), 235–271 (2018). https://doi.org/10.1007/s40948-018-0086-6

14. Favre, J.M., NGuyen, T.: Towards a megamodel to model software evolution through transformations. Electron. Notes Theor. Comput. Sci. **127**(3), 59–74 (2005). https://doi.org/10.1016/j.entcs.2004.08.034. https://www.sciencedirect.com/science/article/pii/S1571066105001398

15. Fidalgo, R.N., Alves, E., España, S., Castro, J., Pastor, O.: Metamodeling the enhanced entity-relationship model. J. Inf. Data Manag. **4**(3), 406–406 (2013)

16. Friedenthal, S., Moore, A., Steiner, R.: Chapter 2 - model-based systems engineering. In: Friedenthal, S., Moore, A., Steiner, R. (eds.) A Practical Guide to SysML (Second Edition), pp. 15–27. The MK/OMG Press, Morgan Kaufmann, Boston (2012). https://doi.org/10.1016/B978-0-12-385206-9.00002-8. https://www.sciencedirect.com/science/article/pii/B9780123852069000028

17. Greenberg, M., Kallas, K., Vasilakis, N.: Unix shell programming: the next 50 years. In: Proceedings of the Workshop on Hot Topics in Operating Systems, HotOS '21, pp. 104–111. Association for Computing Machinery, New York (2021). https://doi.org/10.1145/3458336.3465294

18. Herold, H.: Linux-Unix-Shells: Bourne-Shell, Korn-Shell, C-Shell, bash, tcsh. Pearson Deutschland GmbH (1999)

19. Ignarra, M., et al.: A workflow for automated testing of a safety-critical embedded subsystem. In: 2025 IEEE International Conference on Software Testing, Verification and Validation Workshops (ICSTW), pp. 149–156 (2025). https://doi.org/10.1109/ICSTW64639.2025.10962490

20. Kelly, S., Tolvanen, J.P.: Domain-Specific Modeling: Enabling Full Code Generation. John Wiley & Sons, Hoboken (2008)

21. Kleppe, A.G., Warmer, J.B., Bast, W.: MDA Explained: The Model Driven Architecture: Practice and Promise. Addison-Wesley Professional, Boston (2003)

22. Kline, K., McDowell, D., Dorsey, D., Gordon, M.: Service and Systems Monitoring, pp. 133–155. Apress, Berkeley (2022). https://doi.org/10.1007/978-1-4842-8230-4_5

23. Kowalczyk, K., Szandala, T.: Enhancing seo in single-page web applications in contrast with multi-page applications. IEEE Access **12**, 11597–11614 (2024). https://doi.org/10.1109/ACCESS.2024.3355740

24. Le, T.H.M., Chen, H., Babar, M.A.: Deep learning for source code modeling and generation: models, applications, and challenges. ACM Comput. Surv. **53**(3) (2020). https://doi.org/10.1145/3383458

25. Luhunu, L., Syriani, E.: Comparison of the expressiveness and performance of template-based code generation tools. In: Proceedings of the 10th ACM SIGPLAN International Conference on Software Language Engineering, SLE 2017, pp. 206–216. Association for Computing Machinery, New York (2017). https://doi.org/10.1145/3136014.3136021

26. Mahmood, H., Jilani, A.A.A., Rauf, A.: A lightweight framework for automated model-to-code transformation. In: 2011 IEEE 14th International Multitopic Conference, pp. 279–283 (2011). https://doi.org/10.1109/INMIC.2011.6151488

27. Osis, J., Donins, U.: Chapter 3 - adjusting unified modeling language. In: Osis, J., Donins, U. (eds.) Topological UML Modeling, pp. 83–99. Computer Science Reviews and Trends, Elsevier, Boston (2017). https://doi.org/10.1016/B978-0-12-805476-5.00003-4. https://www.sciencedirect.com/science/article/pii/B9780128054765000034

28. Pelechano, V., Pastor, O., Insfrán, E.: Automated code generation of dynamic specializations: an approach based on design patterns and formal techniques. Data Knowl. Eng. **40**(3), 315–353 (2002). https://doi.org/

10.1016/S0169-023X(02)00020-4. https://www.sciencedirect.com/science/article/pii/S0169023X02000204

29. Pleuss, A., Wollny, S., Botterweck, G.: Model-driven development and evolution of customized user interfaces. In: Proceedings of the 5th ACM SIGCHI Symposium on Engineering Interactive Computing Systems, EICS '13, pp. 13–22. Association for Computing Machinery, New York (2013). https://doi.org/10.1145/2494603.2480298

30. Rossini, A., de Lara, J., Guerra, E., Rutle, A., Wolter, U.: A formalisation of deep metamodelling. Form. Asp. Comput. **26**(6), 1115–1152 (2014). https://doi.org/10.1007/s00165-014-0307-x

31. Sprinkle, J., Rumpe, B., Vangheluwe, H., Karsai, G.: 3 metamodelling. In: Giese, H., Karsai, G., Lee, E., Rumpe, B., Schätz, B. (eds.) Model-Based Engineering of Embedded Real-Time Systems: International Dagstuhl Workshop, Dagstuhl Castle, Germany, 4–9 November 2007. Revised Selected Papers, pp. 57–76. Springer, Heidelberg (2010). https://doi.org/10.1007/978-3-642-16277-0_3

32. Sîrbu, A.G., Czibula, G.: Automatic code generation based on abstract syntax-based encoding. application on malware detection code generation based on mitre attack techniques. Expert Syst. Appl. **264**, 125821 (2025). https://doi.org/10.1016/j.eswa.2024.125821. https://www.sciencedirect.com/science/article/pii/S0957417424026885

33. Uyanik, B., Sayar, A.: Analysis and comparison of automatic code generation and transformation techniques on low-code platforms. In: Proceedings of the 2023 5th International Conference on Software Engineering and Development, ICSED '23, pp. 17–27. Association for Computing Machinery, New York (2024). https://doi.org/10.1145/3637792.3637795

34. YeboAH, F., et al.: Automated scripting for real-time responses to suspicious user actions. In: 2024 IEEE 3rd International Conference on Computing and Machine Intelligence (ICMI), pp. 1–6 (2024). https://doi.org/10.1109/ICMI60790.2024.10585642

35. Zhang, G.: Specifying and model checking workflows of single page applications with tla+. In: 2020 IEEE 20th International Conference on Software Quality, Reliability and Security Companion (QRS-C), pp. 406–410 (2020). https://doi.org/10.1109/QRS-C51114.2020.00075

Reasoning over Vulnerabilities
via LogiSec of Thoughts: A Reductio Ad Absurdum-Based LLM Framework

Claudio A. S. Lelis[1] , Cesar A. C. Marcondes[1(✉)] , and Kevin Fealey[2]

[1] Aeronautics Institute of Technology, São José dos Campos, SP 12228-900, Brazil
`claudio.lelis@ga.ita.br`, `cesar.marcondes@gp.ita.br`
[2] AppSecAI, Inc., Los Altos, CA, USA
`kevin@appsecure.ai`

Abstract. As the importance of software security escalates, identifying and addressing source code vulnerabilities becomes essential to maintaining robust and trustworthy systems. Static Application Security Testing (SAST) tools play a vital role in detecting potential weaknesses, yet their high false-positive rates often burden developers with time-consuming manual verification–risking both inefficiencies and unintended functional changes during remediation. This research introduces LogiSec of Thoughts, a novel, prompt-driven reasoning framework designed to improve the triage of vulnerabilities identified by SAST tools. Rooted in the classical Reductio ad Absurdum method, LogiSec of Thoughts guides a Large Language Model (LLM) through a structured four-step reasoning process to evaluate the plausibility of each vulnerability. By attempting to refute the existence of the vulnerability and reasoning through contradictions, the model is prompted to critically assess whether the issue is logically and contextually sound. This methodology operates independently of external expert systems and is adaptable for integration into secure development pipelines. By reducing false positives and improving the prioritization of actionable security issues, LogiSec of Thoughts offers a promising step toward intelligent, automated code security assessment.

Keywords: Static Application Security Testing (SAST) ·
Vulnerability Triage · Large Language Models (LLMs) · Source Code
Security · False Positive Reduction

1 Introduction

Static Application Security Testing (SAST) tools are widely used in software development to detect potential vulnerabilities early in the lifecycle. However, these tools often produce a large number of false positives, requiring manual triage to determine whether each flagged issue truly represents a security concern [2,8]. This verification step is labor-intensive and may divert developers' attention from critical issues. Improving the efficiency and reliability of vulnerability triage remains an open challenge in secure software engineering.

L. A. Rodrigues and R. Oliveira (Eds.): LADC 2025, CCIS 2697, pp. 112–129, 2026.
https://doi.org/10.1007/978-3-032-11539-3_7

Recent developments in Large Language Models (LLMs) have demonstrated their applicability to various software engineering tasks, including vulnerability detection, code summarization, and program repair [4,28]. These models exhibit the capacity to reason over source code and interpret natural language vulnerability descriptions. In the security domain, LLMs have been applied to tasks such as vulnerability classification and code repair [1,17,26]. Despite these advances, their application to vulnerability triage–specifically, assessing the plausibility of a vulnerability report in context–has received limited attention.

This research investigates how structured, role-based prompting (rather than model fine-tuning) can be used to assess whether a reported SAST finding corresponds to a contextually exploitable vulnerability. The central objective is to assess whether a vulnerability report corresponds to a semantically meaningful and contextually valid issue in the source code.

We investigate three prompting strategies designed to structure the reasoning process:

- **Conservative prompting**, which instructs the model to classify a reported vulnerability as `FALSE` unless it can identify clear evidence supporting the issue.
- **Reductio ad Absurdum prompting**, which frames the task as a logical refutation by assuming the code is secure and testing whether contradictions arise.
- **LogiSec of Thoughts (LSoT)**, a multi-prompt strategy that extends the reductio approach by introducing stepwise self-reflection to assess the consistency of the security assumption across distinct reasoning stages.

These methods are evaluated on a subset of the OWASP Benchmark Java dataset [16], using a variety of metrics including true positive rate (TPR), false positive rate (FPR), and F1-score. Our ablation analysis compares the effectiveness of each strategy in reducing false positives while maintaining acceptable detection rates. We emphasize multi-prompt orchestration and in-context learning so that LSoT remains pluggable across different LLM backends without requiring model retraining.

This study contributes to ongoing research on the use of LLMs in software security [22,23,25], with an emphasis on the understudied area of triage. By investigating logic-based prompting techniques tailored for post-SAST vulnerability assessment, we aim to reduce manual verification effort and improve the reliability of early-stage security analysis.

2   Background and Related Works

This section presents the foundational concepts and focused related works relevant to this research, with an emphasis on the use of Large Language Models (LLMs) in vulnerability assessment and triage.

LLMs are deep neural models trained on large-scale text corpora using self-supervised objectives. They leverage attention mechanisms [19] to model contextual relationships among tokens. Architectures such as GPT [3] and Codex

[5] have demonstrated the ability to generate and understand source code across various programming languages. Despite their utility, these models may reflect biases in training data and lack task-specific reasoning, motivating the need for targeted prompting strategies [20,24].

In software engineering (SE), LLMs have been applied to a variety of tasks, including code generation, summarization, and repair [6]. Prompt engineering has become a central method to adapt LLMs to specific SE tasks without fine-tuning. Techniques such as zero-shot and few-shot prompting [3,18], in-context learning [7,14], and structured reasoning methods like Chain of Thought (CoT) [21], Auto-CoT [27], and Logical CoT (LogiCoT) [29] have shown promise in guiding LLMs through complex tasks.

Recent studies have begun applying these prompting techniques to software vulnerability analysis. For instance, VSP [15] uses vulnerability-semantics-guided CoT prompting to improve vulnerability identification. VRpilot [10] incorporates CoT and feedback from static analyzers to guide patch generation, while other works emphasize prompt context sensitivity [11] and model fine-tuning for improved repair accuracy [9].

Despite these advances, the problem of vulnerability triage–deciding whether a reported vulnerability is plausible in context–has received limited attention. Most prior work focuses on detection or repair, often overlooking the verification of SAST outputs. The study in [22] highlights LLMs' limitations in real-world vulnerability repair for Java, further reinforcing the need for reasoning-centered strategies.

This research departs from prior remediation-focused approaches and concentrates on vulnerability triage. We introduce three prompting strategies tailored to this task: conservative prompting, a single-prompt reductio approach, and the proposed multi-step LogiSec of Thoughts method. In contrast to prior work, our focus is on logical plausibility assessment rather than patch generation, aiming to reduce false positives in static analysis workflows.

3   Solution

This section presents the proposed solution for improving vulnerability triage using Large Language Models (LLMs). The goal is to assist developers in accurately assessing the validity of security warnings generated by Static Application Security Testing (SAST) tools, with a particular focus on reducing false positives in automated analysis.

The research began by exploring strategies to simplify the post-processing of SAST reports–specifically, the triage of vulnerability alerts that may or may not represent real security issues. Initial efforts focused on empirically evaluating how LLMs respond when presented with vulnerability reports and associated source code. These experiments revealed that LLMs often accept vulnerability reports uncritically, echoing the SAST tool's conclusions without performing a rigorous contextual assessment.

In response to these findings, the scope of the research was refined to focus explicitly on improving vulnerability triage. A dedicated *Triage Module* was developed to address this need. The module is designed to evaluate the plausibility of reported vulnerabilities by reasoning about the relationship between the reported issue and the code context. Triage Module serves a dual purpose: it functions both as a Triage tool, responsible for assessing the security status of source code, and as a validation process that verifies the effectiveness of the remediation by confirming that the vulnerabilities have been properly fixed in the remediated version of the source code.

To evaluate the proposed approach, we employed the *OWASP Benchmark Dataset* [16], a widely adopted resource for assessing the performance of application security tools. The dataset was selected due to its comprehensive coverage of vulnerabilities and their established use as benchmarks in the field of software security. The dataset consists of 2,740 labeled test cases across a wide range of vulnerability types, providing a robust basis for evaluating triage accuracy. Its comprehensive coverage ensures that results generalize across common security categories.

The triage methodology was developed incrementally over three distinct phases. Each phase introduced a new prompting strategy, culminating in the proposed LogiSec of Thoughts framework:

- **Phase 1**: Introduced a conservative prompting approach to reduce false positives by defaulting to a negative classification unless strong evidence of a vulnerability is found.
- **Phase 2**: Applied a single-prompt *reductio ad absurdum* method to reason about contradictions stemming from the assumption of code security.
- **Phase 3**: Developed the **LogiSec of Thoughts** framework, a structured multi-prompt approach that integrates self-reflection at each step to enable more precise and explainable triage.

Each of these phases is described in detail in the following subsections, including their motivation, design, and evolution.

3.1 Triage Module – Phase 1: Initial Conservative Approach

Phase 1 aimed to explore whether prompt engineering alone could reduce the false positive rate (FPR) of LLM-based vulnerability assessment. Initial experiments revealed that LLMs tend to affirm the presence of vulnerabilities based on SAST tool output, even when contextual evidence is weak. To counter this, we tested two conservative prompts:

- `phase1_v0_user_prompt`: A naive baseline that presented source code and vulnerability descriptions independently, without explicitly referencing SAST. The goal was to observe whether the LLM could assess the plausibility of a vulnerability on its own. Results showed that the model still leaned toward affirming vulnerability presence, keeping FPR high.
- `phase1_v1_user_prompt`: A conservative strategy in which the LLM was instructed to output **FALSE** unless it could justify a vulnerability claim. This reversed the bias and resulted in improved FPR but introduced a potential increase in false negatives.

This phase revealed a trade-off between conservatism and recall. While the conservative prompt reduced noise, it also risked dismissing valid issues due to insufficient reasoning depth. These observations motivated a shift toward structured logic in Phase 2.

3.2 Triage Module – Phase 2: Reductio Ad Absurdum with Self-reflection

To overcome the limitations of conservative bias, Phase 2 introduced a logic-oriented reasoning strategy using reductio ad absurdum. The central idea was to test the assumption that the code is secure and assess whether this leads to contradictions.

Two prompt variants were developed:

- phase2_v0_user_prompt: This single-prompt format embedded the assumption of non-vulnerability, asked the LLM to search for contradictions, and required a conclusion. Despite its structure, the LLM often bypassed intermediate reasoning and produced shallow conclusions.
- phase2_v1_user_prompt: To address this, self-reflection was added as an explicit instruction. The model was prompted to internally verify its own reasoning before finalizing the response. This improved the consistency and reliability of its output, albeit still within the limits of single-prompt reasoning.

While Phase 2 established a more grounded reasoning process, its one-shot nature limited interpretability and flexibility. This led to the multi-prompt extension introduced in Phase 3: LogiSec of Thoughts.

3.3 LogiSec of Thoughts LSoT

Phase 3 (*Multiple-Prompt Reductio Ad Absurdum with Self-Reflection*) advances the Triage Module by introducing a structured reasoning process distributed across multiple prompts. This phase builds on insights from Phase 2 and is specifically designed to handle cases where single-prompt reasoning lacks sufficient depth.

While Phase 2 used a reductio ad absurdum strategy in a single step, it struggled to manage complex reasoning paths, often yielding inconsistent assessments. In response, Phase 3 retains the same logical foundation but decomposes the evaluation into distinct, sequential prompts. Each prompt introduces a reasoning step followed by targeted self-reflection, enhancing both precision and reliability in vulnerability assessment.

The shift from a single-prompt to a multiple-prompt framework was inspired by two key research works: the Logical of Thoughts (LoT) [30] and the methodology of self-reflection in Large Language Models [13]. These works introduced frameworks for iterative reasoning through multiple steps, allowing models to refine their conclusions and self-correct. The Logical of Thoughts method uses chain growth and a recursive process to enable a model to explore logical contradictions, while self-reflection offers a mechanism for the model to internally verify its reasoning before finalizing an output.

However, adapting these ideas directly for security vulnerability assessment presented challenges. LoT focuses on open-ended logical reasoning, such as solving mathematical problems or answering factual queries, where the scope of reasoning is more flexible. Security assessments require a more deterministic structure to ensure that the aspects of the code and its vulnerabilities are examined thoroughly and in a predictable manner. LoT's strength in dynamically expanding chains of thought becomes a limitation in this context because the reasoning process could diverge or grow excessively, leaving critical areas of the security evaluation under-examined or unresolved. This inspired the development of a multi-prompt approach, tailored to the domain of security reasoning.

The hypothesis guiding Phase 3 is that a structured, multiple-prompt approach–coupled with tailored self-reflection–can improve the accuracy of vulnerability detection in source code by systematically testing the assumption of security against possible contradictions. By dividing the process into distinct prompts and embedding self-reflection after each step, the model is better equipped to identify security violations, reducing both false positives and false negatives.

In terms of metrics, we expect:

1. Improve the model's ability to detect genuine vulnerabilities (higher True Positive Rate - TPR).
2. Reduce the rate of false positives by ensuring that each contradiction is carefully considered before concluding vulnerability (lower False Positive Rate - FPR).
3. Maintain or slightly reduce the rate of false negatives by introducing the self-reflection process at each step (False Negative Rate - FNR).

Formalization of the LogiSec of Thoughts Framework. Phase 3 is grounded in a formal adaptation of the Logical of Thoughts (LoT) framework [30], applying the principle of *reductio ad absurdum* to the domain of source code vulnerability triage. The method tests whether the assumption that code is secure can be sustained in light of potential contradictions derived from the code's logic or vulnerability interactions.

The classical LoT model begins with an assumption P and derives a contradiction $\neg Q$:

$$C = P \wedge \neg Q \tag{1}$$

This principle is extended in LoT using a growing reasoning chain:

$$C_i = P \wedge T_1 \wedge \cdots \wedge T_{i-1} \wedge \neg T_i \tag{2}$$

where each T_i represents an intermediary logical inference, and $\neg T_i$ indicates a contradiction at that step.

While LoT dynamically expands the reasoning chain, such flexibility can be problematic for vulnerability triage, where specific security conditions must be evaluated in a consistent, bounded manner. Security assessments require control over the reasoning path, with checks focused on known vulnerability types, such as input validation for SQL Injection or access control for authorization flaws.

Security-Specific Adaptation. The LogiSec of Thoughts (LSoT) adapts LoT into a fixed-sequence, prompt-driven reasoning structure. Each reasoning step is aligned with a specific prompt, forming a deterministic evaluation path. The contradiction here is not an abstract inconsistency but a domain-specific failure of a security property.

This leads to the following adapted contradiction model:

$$C = P_{\text{Code is Secure}} \land \neg Q_{\text{Contradictory Vulnerability Condition}} \tag{3}$$

Here, P is the assumption of security, and Q represents a specific behavior or pattern derived from the vulnerability class. For example, in an SQL Injection case, Q may involve unsanitized user input reaching a database call.

The general multi-step reasoning chain is adapted as:

$$C_i = P_{\text{Code is Secure}} \land T_1(\text{e.g., input validation}) \land \cdots \land T_{i-1}(\text{e.g., access control})$$
$$\land \neg T_i(\text{contradiction in logic or control flow}) \tag{4}$$

Each T_i corresponds to a specific reasoning step related to the vulnerability type under consideration.

Mapping Prompts to Reasoning Steps. The logical structure above maps directly to the prompting strategy used in Phase 3:

- **Prompt 1** assumes the code is secure and asks the model to justify this assumption (P).
- **Prompt 2** introduces vulnerability information and checks for contradiction $(\neg Q)$.
- **Prompt 3** performs a final check for absurdities in control flow or behavior $(\neg T_i)$.
- **Prompt 4** concludes the assessment based on prior steps.

To illustrate how this reasoning is implemented through prompting, the Fig. 1 present concise templates for Prompts.

These templates demonstrate how formal reasoning steps are grounded in structured interactions with the LLM.

Each system prompt encourages tailored self-reflection to ensure the model critically reviews its output before moving on to the next stage.

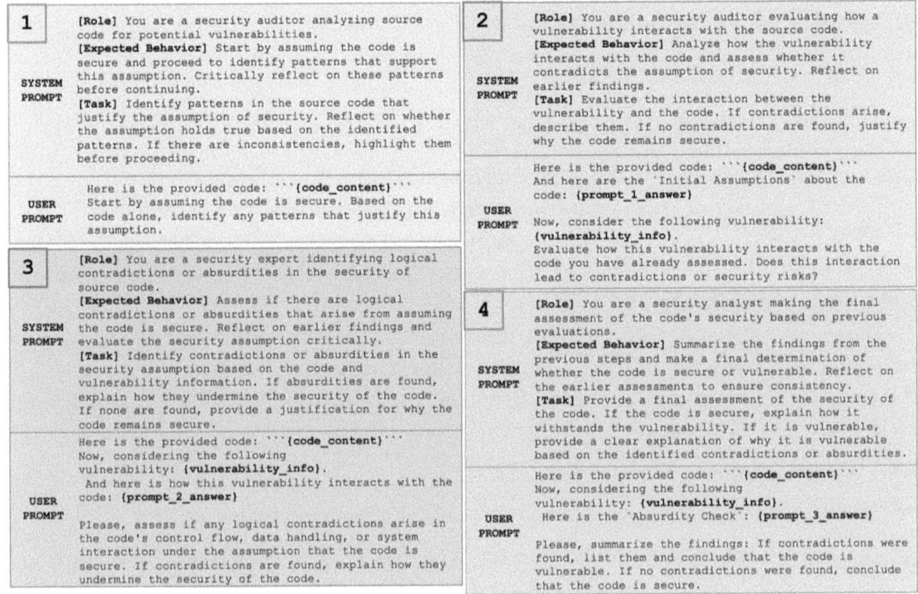

Fig. 1. The four prompt-blocks used in the LogiSec of Thoughts method. This is the example for "assuming secure" variation.

3.4 Novelty of the Approach: LogiSec of Thoughts

LogiSec of Thoughts encompasses the core idea of enabling logical reasoning while specifically tailoring it to the domain of security. By combining the structure of *Reductio Ad Absurdum* with the error-checking power of **tailored self-reflection**, this methodology foster a rigorous, step-by-step evaluation of code security.

The novelty of this approach lies in:

- **Fixed Structure**: Unlike LoT's dynamic chain growth, the multiple-prompt approach of LSoF is deterministic, making it ideal for tasks that require a fixed sequence of reasoning steps.
- **Tailored Self-Reflection**: By introducing self-reflection after each prompt, the propagation of errors and uncertainties are reduced, ensuring that each reasoning step is thoroughly vetted before moving to the next.
- **Security-Specific Adaptation**: This approach is uniquely designed for security vulnerability assessment, addressing the specific challenges posed by evaluating code and vulnerabilities, which are not present in open-ended reasoning tasks.

This phase represents a step forward from traditional reasoning models like LoT by adapting the framework specifically for security assessment. The proposed LogiSec of Thoughts approach holds promise as a robust methodology for logical security assessments, combining the best of structured reasoning with domain-specific adaptations for security analysis.

4   Experiments and Analysis

This section describes our staged experimental workflow, designed to evaluate the LogiSec of Thoughts (LSoT) method as a Decision Support System (DSS) layer for triaging SAST findings. The experiments progress from controlled ablation tests on the OWASP Benchmark metadata to real SARIF-based triage scenarios using Semgrep output.

This progressive design ensures that each experiment informs the next, aligning our goal of improving post-SAST triage through structured reasoning and LLM interpretability. Each stage is detailed for reproducibility and transparency.

4.1   Goal-Question-Metric (GQM)

Our evaluation uses a clear Goal-Question-Metric framework:

Goal: Assess whether LSoT effectively reduces false positives and improves triage precision when layered on top of a modern SAST tool, supporting developers and security practitioners.

Research Questions:

- RQ1 - Does LSoT reduce the noise inherent in raw SAST output?
- RQ2 - What trade-offs exist between false positive reduction and true positive retention under different prompt constraints?
- RQ3 - Is LSoT generalizable across different LLM backends?

Metrics Calculation. We use standard classification metrics (Precision, Recall, F1-score) to evaluate LSoT's performance. To show its practical impact as a DSS on top of raw SAST output, we highlight two intuitive complementary metrics:

- **False Positive Reduction (%):** Proportion of SAST false positives correctly discarded by LSoT. Since the baseline SAST flags every finding as vulnerable, all non-vulnerabilities in the ground truth ($GT = FALSE$) are false positives by default. LSoT's true negatives ($GT = FALSE$, $Prediction = FALSE$) represent the fraction of noise removed:

$$\text{FP Reduction (\%)} = \frac{TN_{LSoT}}{|GT = FALSE|} \times 100.$$

- **True Positive Retention (%):** Proportion of actual vulnerabilities kept by LSoT despite filtering:

$$\text{TP Retention (\%)} = \frac{TP_{LSoT}}{|GT = TRUE|} \times 100.$$

These metrics help quantify LSoT's practical trade-off: the goal is to maximize false positive reduction while retaining as many true positives as possible.

4.2   Dataset

For all experiments we used the OWASP Benchmark Java dataset, randomly selecting 300 source code cases (153 originally vulnerable, 147 originally secure) across diverse vulnerability types. The filtered metadata CSV file and the SARIF file used in the experiments are available in [12].

Annotation and Ground-Truth Procedure. In Stage 1 (ablation study), ground truth labels were derived directly from the OWASP Benchmark metadata. In Stages 2 and 3, ground-truth labels were refined by a senior cybersecurity expert, since Semgrep can detect additional vulnerabilities not covered by the OWASP Benchmark's expected results.

The procedure is described below. First, Semgrep was executed over the OWASP Benchmark Java corpus to produce SARIF findings. If a Semgrep finding was located in the same file and the same source-region (line range) indicated in the OWASP Benchmark metadata, that finding was labeled automatically, same as metadata. If a Semgrep finding occurred in the same file but with a different region (i.e., the file matched but the reported region diverged from the metadata), the senior expert assessed only the reported region: if the specific region did not contain the vulnerability described in the metadata, the finding was labeled FALSE. If Semgrep reported a finding for a file/CWE pair not present in the OWASP metadata, the senior expert evaluated the file, the CWE, and the region together; if the specific CWE vulnerability was present in the reported region, the finding was labeled TRUE, otherwise FALSE.

4.3   Reproducibility

All experiments were executed with deterministic settings when supported by the backend. Unless otherwise stated, generation temperature was set to 0.0 and we recorded model version strings and run logs.

It is worthy to mention that we did not fine-tune any LLM for this work. All results rely solely on multi-prompt orchestration and in-context learning. This design keeps LSoT pluggable and model-agnostic. The prompt templates for both LSoT variants ("assuming secure" and "assuming vulnerable") are available in [12].

4.4   Stage 1: Prompt Ablation Study

Our first stage is an ablation study that explores how prompt design and classification assumptions affect LLM-based vulnerability triage performance in a controlled setting.

To ensure reproducibility and limit variability, all LLM runs in this stage were conducted with temperature set to 0.0. The goal was to evolve from naive, single-prompt strategies to more structured reasoning, ultimately motivating the design of the multi-prompt LSoT framework.

We evaluated four single-prompt configurations:

- **phase1_v0** (Naive Baseline): Presents the source code and vulnerability description without explicit connection, letting the LLM decide independently.
- **phase1_v1** (Conservative): Instructs the LLM to assume the code is secure unless strong contradictory evidence is found. Aims to reduce false positives.
- **phase2_v0** (Reductio ad Absurdum): Embeds an initial assumption of non-vulnerability and asks the LLM to identify logical contradictions.
- **phase2_v1** (Reductio with Self-Reflection): Adds an explicit self-verification step to strengthen the model's internal reasoning.

Finally, we tested the full LSoT framework in two configurations: assuming the code is secure, and assuming the code is vulnerable. This comparison helps reveal how different classification assumptions shape triage behavior.

In this specific context of ablation test where metadata of OWASP Benchmark was used as input, each prompt was evaluated using standard classification metrics: True Positive Rate (TPR), False Positive Rate (FPR), False Negative Rate (FNR), Accuracy, and F1-score.

Table 1 summarizes the results across prompt configurations for the GPT-4o-mini LLM.

Table 1. Stage 1 Ablation Study – Prompt Configuration Comparison (GPT-4o-mini)

Prompt	TPR	FPR	FNR	Accuracy	F1-score
phase1_v0	100.00%	78.91%	0.00%	61.33%	53.67%
phase1_v1	88.89%	55.78%	11.11%	67.00%	65.04%
phase2_v0	100.00%	82.31%	0.00%	59.67%	50.86%
phase2_v1	100.00%	75.51%	0.00%	63.00%	56.36%
LSoT (assuming secure)	100.00%	100.00%	0.00%	51.00%	33.77%
LSoT (assuming vulnerable)	68.63%	39.46%	31.37%	64.67%	64.57%

Key observations from Stage 1 include:

- **Impact of Conservative Assumption:** The **phase1_v1** prompt reduced the FPR from nearly 79% (naive) to 56%, showing that explicit assumptions can meaningfully lower false alarms.
- **Reductio's Trade-off:** Reductio ad Absurdum variants achieved perfect TPR but incurred high FPRs (75–82%), highlighting that high sensitivity may come at the cost of increased noise.
- **LSoT Improvements:** When combining multiple prompts under the LSoT structure and assuming the code as vulnerable, we saw the best balance between lower FPR and competitive F1-score.

Table 2. Stage 1 Ablation Study – Best Configuration Across LLMs

LLM	TPR	FPR	FNR	Accuracy	F1-score
GPT-4o-mini	68.63%	39.46%	31.37%	64.67%	64.57%
Claude-3.5-Haiku	69.28%	37.41%	30.72%	66.00%	65.93%
LLaMA 3.2	74.51%	42.86%	25.49%	66.00%	65.66%

To check robustness, we also tested the best-performing prompt configuration (`LSoT_assuming_vulnerable`) across different LLMs: Claude-3.5 Haiku, GPT-4o-mini, and LLaMA 3.2. Table 2 shows that performance was consistent across models, motivating its selection for Stage 2.

Overall, these results demonstrate how structured prompt engineering and classification assumptions influence triage performance in a perfectly labeled dataset. However, they do not account for the noise inherent in real SAST findings. This gap motivated Stage 2.

4.5 Stage 2: SARIF-Based DSS Triage with Interventions

In Stage 2, we test LSoT's practical impact as a DSS layer on top of an actual SAST tool. We used Semgrep to scan, the same as in ablation test, OWASP Benchmark randomly selected 300 Java files, producing a SARIF file with 289 findings spanning 211 files. Unlike Stage 1, this scenario introduces realistic noise, since all findings must initially be treated as potentially vulnerable.

The selected LSoT configuration (assuming vulnerable, using the Claude-3.5 Haiku LLM) was applied to the Semgrep SARIF file in three conditions:

1. **No Intervention:** Baseline triage with original file names.
2. **Anonymization:** Anonymized source files to limit the LLM's ability to detect known dataset patterns.
3. **FLAGS Constraints:** Added explicit prompt constraints to prevent the LLM from disregarding intentionally vulnerable or educational code as "secure".

Motivation: During early runs of LSoT on the SARIF output, we observed that the LLM sometimes recognized the source code as part of a well-known educational dataset (OWASP Benchmark). In such cases, the model tended to classify code marked as intentionally vulnerable as "secure" due to its didactic context, undermining true positive retention. To mitigate this bias, we designed two interventions:

– Anonymization of source file names and project identifiers to obscure recognizable dataset cues. **Anonymization Process:** Each Java file name was replaced with a randomized identifier. Any project-specific comments or package names referencing the OWASP Benchmark were also obfuscated. No code logic was altered.

124   C. A. S. Lelis et al.

– Prompt constraints ("FLAGS") added to the system and user prompts, explicitly instructing the LLM to ignore educational context when assessing exploitability.

Our intention was that anonymization would reduce bias by removing recognizable tokens, while FLAGS constraints would provide stronger semantic guidance, resulting in improved balance between false positive reduction and true positive retention.

Table 3. Stage 2 – SARIF-Based DSS Triage with Interventions (Claude-3.5-Haiku)

Intervention	Precision	Recall	F1	FP Reduction %	TP Retention %
No	0.6992	0.4388	0.5392	60.22%	43.88%
Anonymization	0.7415	0.5561	0.6356	59.14%	55.61%
FLAGS	0.7513	0.7551	0.7532	47.31%	75.51%

Table 3 summarizes the results where the FLAGS intervention showed the best trade-off, reducing nearly 47% of Semgrep's false positives while retaining over 75% of true positives. This demonstrated that prompt constraints meaningfully improve DSS behavior when dealing with realistic SARIF input.

4.6   Stage 3: LLM Generalization for DSS Consistency

Finally, in Stage 3, we tested whether the best intervention (FLAGS) generalizes across different LLM backends. Using the same SARIF input and FLAGS constraints, we ran the triage with Claude-3.5 Haiku, GPT-4.1-nano, and LLaMA 3.2.

Table 4. Stage 3 – FLAGS Intervention Generalization Across LLMs

LLM	Precision	Recall	F1	FP Reduction %	TP Retention %
Claude-3.5-Haiku	0.7513	0.7551	0.7532	47.31%	75.51%
GPT-4.1-nano	0.7975	0.9643	0.8730	48.39%	96.43%
LLaMA 3.2	0.8159	0.8367	0.8262	60.22%	83.67%

Table 4 shows that each LLM achieved competitive performance, with GPT-4.1-nano yielding the highest true positive retention (96%) and LLaMA 3.2 delivering the highest precision and strongest false positive reduction (60%). This consistency across models reinforces the practical flexibility of deploying LSoT as a DSS layer with different LLM cost/performance profiles.

5   Results and Discussion

This section summarizes the key findings across all three experimental stages, directly addressing our research questions (RQs) and highlighting practical lessons learned.

Answer to RQ1 – Noise Reduction: Across all experiments, LSoT consistently reduced the noise inherent in raw SAST output. For example, when triaging Semgrep's OWASP Benchmark findings, the best configuration (FLAGS intervention) achieved up to 60% false positive reduction while retaining the majority of true positives. Without LSoT, developers must treat every SAST finding as equally credible, but with this DSS layer, much of that manual burden is alleviated.

Answer to RQ2 – Trade-offs: The results show that prompt structure and constraints significantly affect the balance between noise reduction and vulnerability retention. The FLAGS intervention outperformed naive anonymization: although anonymization removed slightly more false positives (59%), it also lost more true positives. In contrast, FLAGS maintained higher F1-scores by guiding the LLM to reason carefully about intentional vulnerabilities in benchmark code. Overall, depending on the LLM used, practitioners can tune this trade-off from 47–60% FP reduction and 76–96% TP retention.

Answer to RQ3 – Generalizability: LSoT's effectiveness is not tied to a single LLM backend. When we reran the FLAGS intervention with different models, LLaMA 3.2 achieved the strongest FP reduction (60%) with good TP retention (84%), while GPT-4.1-nano maximized TP retention (96%) with slightly less FP reduction (48%). This demonstrates that organizations can adapt LSoT to their operational needs without sacrificing core DSS benefits.

5.1   Insights and Lessons Learned

The staged approach highlighted several key takeaways. First, single-prompt strategies can only go so far; multi-step structured reasoning is essential to handle the complex context of intentionally vulnerable code. Second, LLMs often rely on dataset cues, making prompt constraints (like FLAGS) critical for reliable real-world triage. Third, the OWASP Benchmark's dual role (realistic yet educational) requires special care: LSoT's constraints help mitigate misclassifications caused by "it's just a benchmark" signals.

To illustrate how LSoT reasoning changes under different interventions, we analyze a representative OWASP Benchmark case (`BenchmarkTest00251.java`) flagged as vulnerable for CWE-501 (Trust Boundary Violation) across interventions which the ground truth is "Vulnerable":

- the *no-intervention* run interprets the snippet as largely secure due to superficial input filtering and partial output encoding;
- the *anonymization* run exposes additional implicit checks and reports the snippet as PARTIALLY SECURE;

- the *FLAGS* (constrained prompt) run confirms the core trust-boundary violation and returns VULNERABLE.

The contrast shows that structured prompt constraints can surface the core vulnerability while other runs emphasize contextual nuance. And, it also highlights the value of LSoT's transparent reasoning output for human triage. Notably, only the FLAGS intervention correctly confirms the Trust Boundary Violation (CWE-501), highlighting how structured prompt constraints correct misleading cues from the OWASP Benchmark's intentionally vulnerable design. A complete, per-intervention transcript and the detailed LSoT explanations for `BenchmarkTest00251.java` are provided in the artifact repository [12].

5.2   LSoT as a Decision-Support System

An important property of LSoT is that it returns a compact reasoning chain alongside each final assessment. These human-auditable rationales are intended to assist developers and security reviewers during triage, supporting prioritized manual inspection rather than replacing human judgment. The transparent explanations are central to LSoT's value as a DSS, even in cases where aggregate metrics show modest numeric differences.

Practical Applicability and DSS Profiles: Practitioners can layer LSoT on top of any modern SAST tool to streamline manual review, saving significant time otherwise spent sifting through low-confidence findings. The flexibility across LLMs lets teams choose a DSS profile that fits their risk appetite and resource constraints:

- **Max TP retention**: GPT-4.1-nano – ideal when missing any real vulnerability is unacceptable.
- **Max noise filtering**: LLaMA 3.2 – suitable when teams prefer fewer findings with stronger signals.
- **Balanced**: Claude 3.5 Haiku – offers stable middle-ground precision with good generalization.

5.3   Threats to Validity

We enumerate key threats to validity and our mitigation strategies:

- **Dataset bias:** OWASP Benchmark contains intentionally vulnerable, educational examples that may not reflect production code; we mitigate this via anonymization and prompt FLAGS aiming reproduce real-world scenarios.
- **Annotation subjectivity:** Manual labeling was performed by a senior cybersecurity expert following a structured process.
- **Model training data leakage:** Some LLMs may have been exposed to public benchmarks during pretraining; anonymization and explicit FLAGS are conservative controls but cannot guarantee full elimination of leakage.

– **Variability across model versions:** Model updates may change behavior; we recorded model versions and selected temperature parameter as 0.0, where available, to aid replication.

The whole process demonstrates that LSoT transforms noisy SAST scans into prioritized, explainable insights. This provide practical, adaptable decision support for secure development pipelines in real-world environments.

6 Conclusion

In this work, We proposed LogiSec of Thoughts (LSoT), a multi-prompt orchestration framework that relies exclusively on in-context learning (no fine-tuning) and is designed to be LLM-agnostic. LSoT can be deployed as a decision-support system (DSS) for SAST triage: it produces a final assessment together with a compact, human-auditable rationale, enabling analysts to prioritize and validate automated judgments.

Results showed that LSoT can reduce up to 60% of false positives while retaining up to 96% of true positives, depending on the chosen LLM and intervention. This tradeoff highlights that different LLMs enable flexible DSS profiles: practitioners can tune LSoT to prioritize either maximum vulnerability retention or stronger false positive reduction, according to project needs.

We also found that designing prompt constraints improve classification balance, preventing the LLM from misclassifying known test patterns as secure due to their educational context. These insights reinforce the value of combining human-aligned instructions with LLM interpretability for security tasks.

Importantly, we did not fine-tune any LLM for these experiments; all results rely on in-context learning and prompt orchestration, keeping LSoT pluggable across model backends. For transparency and reproducibility, the prompts, the SARIF input for the example case, and per-run transcripts for a representative case are available in [12].

Practical impact: By integrating LSoT as a DSS layer on top of SAST tools like Semgrep, security teams and developers can reduce the time spent reviewing irrelevant findings, focus resources on real vulnerabilities, and improve the effectiveness of automated security testing pipelines. Since the beginning, LSoT was not designed to replace SAST, it supports developers by making scanner results more trustworthy.

In summary, LSoT is a practical layer to improve SAST triage: it complements existing tools by filtering noise and, crucially, providing explanations that increase analyst confidence. Future work includes validating LSoT on larger industrial codebases, integrating retrieval/chunking to address token limits, and assessing long-term operational stability in CI pipelines.

Acknowledgment. This work was supported by the Financiadora de Estudos e Projetos (FINEP), under Contract 01.22.0615.02, and by AppSecAI, Inc.

References

1. Alrashedy, K., Aljasser, A.: Can LLMs patch security issues? arXiv preprint arXiv:2312.00024 (2023)
2. Britton, T., Jeng, L., Carver, G., Cheak, P., Katzenellenbogen, T.: Reversible debugging software. Judge Business School, University Cambridge, Cambridge, UK, Technical report, vol. 229 (2013)
3. Brown, T.B., et al.: Language models are few-shot learners. arXiv preprint arXiv:2005.14165 (2020)
4. Charalambous, Y., Tihanyi, N., Jain, R., Sun, Y., Ferrag, M.A., Cordeiro, L.C.: A new era in software security: towards self-healing software via large language models and formal verification. arXiv preprint arXiv:2305.14752 (2023)
5. Chen, M., et al.: Evaluating large language models trained on code. arXiv preprint arXiv:2107.03374 (2021)
6. Fan, A., et al.: Large language models for software engineering: survey and open problems. In: 2023 IEEE/ACM International Conference on Software Engineering: Future of Software Engineering (ICSE-FoSE), pp. 31–53. IEEE (2023)
7. Garg, S., Tsipras, D., Liang, P.S., Valiant, G.: What can transformers learn in-context? A case study of simple function classes. Adv. Neural. Inf. Process. Syst. **35**, 30583–30598 (2022)
8. Gu, Z., Barr, E.T., Hamilton, D.J., Su, Z.: Has the bug really been fixed? In: Proceedings of the 32nd ACM/IEEE International Conference on Software Engineering, vol. 1, pp. 55–64 (2010)
9. Huang, K., et al.: An empirical study on fine-tuning large language models of code for automated program repair. In: 2023 38th IEEE/ACM International Conference on Automated Software Engineering (ASE), pp. 1162–1174. IEEE (2023)
10. Kulsum, U., Zhu, H., Xu, B., d'Amorim, M.: A case study of LLM for automated vulnerability repair: assessing impact of reasoning and patch validation feedback. In: Proceedings of the 1st ACM International Conference on AI-Powered Software, pp. 103–111 (2024)
11. Le, T.K., Alimadadi, S., Ko, S.Y.: A study of vulnerability repair in Javascript programs with large language models. In: Companion Proceedings of the ACM on Web Conference 2024, pp. 666–669 (2024)
12. Lelis, C.A.S.: Logisec of thoughts: data repository (2025). https://github.com/ClaudioLelis/LogiSec-of-Thoughts. Accessed 29 Aug 2025
13. Liu, F., AlDahoul, N., Eady, G., Zaki, Y., AlShebli, B., Rahwan, T.: Self-reflection outcome is sensitive to prompt construction. arXiv preprint arXiv:2406.10400 (2024)
14. Liu, P., Yuan, W., Fu, J., Jiang, Z., Hayashi, H., Neubig, G.: Pre-train, prompt, and predict: a systematic survey of prompting methods in natural language processing. ACM Comput. Surv. **55**(9), 1–35 (2023)
15. Nong, Y., Aldeen, M., Cheng, L., Hu, H., Chen, F., Cai, H.: Chain-of-thought prompting of large language models for discovering and fixing software vulnerabilities. arXiv preprint arXiv:2402.17230 (2024)
16. OWASP Foundation: OWASP benchmark project: Benchmarkjava version 1.2 (2016). https://github.com/OWASP-Benchmark/BenchmarkJava. Accessed 13 Oct 2024
17. Pearce, H., Tan, B., Ahmad, B., Karri, R., Dolan-Gavitt, B.: Examining zero-shot vulnerability repair with large language models. In: 2023 IEEE Symposium on Security and Privacy (SP), pp. 2339–2356. IEEE (2023)

18. Radford, A., et al.: Language models are unsupervised multitask learners. OpenAI Blog **1**(8), 9 (2019)
19. Vaswani, A.: Attention is all you need. In: Advances in Neural Information Processing Systems (2017)
20. Wei, J., et al.: Emergent abilities of large language models. arXiv preprint arXiv:2206.07682 (2022)
21. Wei, J., et al.: Chain-of-thought prompting elicits reasoning in large language models. Adv. Neural. Inf. Process. Syst. **35**, 24824–24837 (2022)
22. Wu, Y., et al.: How effective are neural networks for fixing security vulnerabilities. In: Proceedings of the 32nd ACM SIGSOFT International Symposium on Software Testing and Analysis, pp. 1282–1294 (2023)
23. Xu, H., et al.: Large language models for cyber security: a systematic literature review. arXiv preprint arXiv:2405.04760 (2024)
24. Yang, J., et al.: Harnessing the power of LLMs in practice: a survey on chatgpt and beyond. ACM Trans. Knowl. Discov. Data **18**(6), 1–32 (2024)
25. Zhang, J., Bu, H., Wen, H., Chen, Y., Li, L., Zhu, H.: When LLMs meet cybersecurity: a systematic literature review. arXiv preprint arXiv:2405.03644 (2024)
26. Zhang, Q., Fang, C., Yu, B., Sun, W., Zhang, T., Chen, Z.: Pre-trained model-based automated software vulnerability repair: how far are we? IEEE Trans. Dependable Secure Comput. (2023)
27. Zhang, Z., Zhang, A., Li, M., Smola, A.: Automatic chain of thought prompting in large language models. arXiv preprint arXiv:2210.03493 (2022)
28. Zhang, Z., et al.: A survey on language models for code. arXiv preprint arXiv:2311.07989 (2023)
29. Zhao, X., et al.: Enhancing zero-shot chain-of-thought reasoning in large language models through logic. arXiv preprint arXiv:2309.13339 (2023)
30. Zhao, X., et al.: Enhancing zero-shot chain-of-thought reasoning in large language models through logic. In: Proceedings of the 2024 Joint International Conference on Computational Linguistics, Language Resources and Evaluation (LREC-COLING 2024), pp. 6144–6166 (2024)

Consensus, Cryptography, and Blockchain

A Blockchain-Based Architecture for Communication Between Spectrum Access Systems

Alan Veloso[1]([✉]), Jeffson Sousa[1,2], Diego Abreu[1], Allan Freitas[3],
and Antônio Abelém[1]

[1] Federal University of Pará (UFPA), Belém, PA, Brazil
{aveloso,abelem}@ufpa.br, diego.abreu@itec.ufpa.br
[2] Center for Research and Development in Telecommunications (CPQD),
Campinas, SP, Brazil
jcsousa@cpqd.com.br
[3] Federal Institute of Bahia (IFBA), Salvador, BA, Brazil
allan@ifba.edu.br

Abstract. This paper proposes an architecture for Spectrum Access Systems (SAS) integrated with permissioned blockchain technology to enhance security, traceability, and interoperability in the communication among different SAS instances. The approach leverages smart contracts to automate data usage agreements, device registration, and spectrum coordination, replacing traditional Representational State Transfer (REST) interfaces with a distributed and auditable infrastructure. The proposed model is validated through a practical implementation using Hyperledger Besu, demonstrating feasibility and compliance with regulatory requirements. The hybrid solution offers advantages such as data immutability, shared governance, and operational resilience.

1 Introduction

The exponential growth in demand for connectivity and high-performance mobile applications has driven the evolution of mobile networks toward Fifth Generation (5G) technologies and, in the near future, Sixth Generation (6G) [5]. These new communication paradigms require more efficient and dynamic management of the radio frequency spectrum, a scarce and essential resource for ensuring the quality and reliability of services [1]. In this scenario, the development of intelligent spectrum management infrastructures becomes crucial to meet increasing demands for mobility, low latency, high device density, and real-time reconfiguration—key characteristics of next-generation mobile networks.

The Spectrum Access System (SAS) emerges as a regulatory and technological solution to enable dynamic spectrum sharing among different classes of users, as adopted in the Citizens Broadband Radio Service (CBRS) model in the United States. However, the traditional communication model between SAS instances, based on Representational State Transfer (REST) interfaces over HyperText

L. A. Rodrigues and R. Oliveira (Eds.): LADC 2025, CCIS 2697, pp. 133–147, 2026.
https://doi.org/10.1007/978-3-032-11539-3_8

Transfer Protocol Secure (HTTPS), has limitations regarding security, traceability, interoperability, and decentralized governance—especially in heterogeneous and distributed environments such as 5G/6G networks.

Given this context, the following research question arises: *how can secure, auditable, and interoperable communication between SASs be ensured, aligned with the requirements of 5G/6G mobile networks, without compromising performance and regulatory compliance?*

The motivation for this work lies in the potential of permissioned blockchain technology, which offers native mechanisms for strong authentication, data immutability, traceability, and automation through smart contracts. These properties can directly address the functional requirements of communication between SASs, enabling more reliable, auditable, and resilient information exchange. Such characteristics are particularly important for intelligent mobile network management, where different operators and entities dynamically share spectrum resources.

The main goal of this paper is to propose a hybrid architecture for Spectrum Access Systems with blockchain integration, in which communication between SASs occurs through a permissioned blockchain network, without replacing internal operational mechanisms. The architecture aims to ensure security, transparency, interoperability, and distributed governance—essential aspects for meeting the demands of emerging mobile networks.

The main contributions of this work include:

- The proposal of a blockchain-based architecture for inter-SAS communication targeting 5G/6G mobile network scenarios;
- The analysis of blockchain technology's compliance with the functional requirements of the SAS-SAS interface;
- A detailed description of the components, operational flows, and governance aspects of the proposed architecture;
- The presentation of a practical implementation example using Hyperledger Besu;
- A critical discussion on the advantages, limitations, and potential developments of the proposed approach in the context of mobile network management.

This paper is organized as follows: Sect. 2 presents an analysis of related work; Sect. 3 introduces the fundamentals of the Spectrum Access System and its main interfaces; Sect. 4 details the functional requirements of the SAS-SAS interface; Sect. 5 discusses how blockchain technology meets these requirements; Sect. 6 presents the proposed blockchain-integrated architecture; Sect. 7 describes a practical implementation example; Sect. 8 discusses the benefits and challenges of the approach; and finally, Sect. 9 offers final remarks and directions for future work.

2   Related Work

Recent studies have investigated the use of blockchain technologies to support dynamic spectrum management, particularly in the context of the SAS and

CBRS. These proposals aim to overcome limitations related to reliability, scalability, and security inherent in traditional centralized models.

In [10], the authors propose Blockchain-based Decentralized SAS (BD-SAS), a decentralized blockchain-based architecture that introduces two layers: a global chain (G-Chain), focused on regulatory tasks and synchronization between SASs, and local chains (L-Chains), responsible for spectrum allocation in specific regions. The architecture also includes SAS server reshuffling mechanisms for fault tolerance and resistance to adaptive adversaries. This proposal is similar to the model presented in this work, particularly regarding the decentralization of decision-making and synchronization processes among SASs.

Li et al. [3] present a framework for dynamic spectrum sharing among multiple operators, supported by a consortium blockchain. The proposal includes the use of smart contracts and a Stackelberg game-based model for optimal spectrum pricing, highlighting the flexibility of operators to act as either spectrum providers or requesters according to their needs. Although the focus is on inter-operator market dynamics, the contributions regarding decentralized governance and incentive mechanisms are relevant to distributed SASs.

In [9], the authors introduce SpectrumChain, a framework for dynamic spectrum sharing targeting 6G networks. The architecture proposes the use of a hierarchical blockchain to record spectrum allocation and ensure transaction traceability, integrating cognitive sensors to support decision-making. This approach stands out for its emphasis on scalability and the support of emerging heterogeneous network applications.

The Blockchain-assisted CBRS (B-CBRS) proposal, presented in [2], uses blockchain to coordinate spectrum access by *General Authorized Access* users, delegating to *Priority Access* users the responsibility of managing allocations based on smart contracts and optimal allocation algorithms. This model reinforces the feasibility of decentralized structures even within the traditional hierarchical spectrum access model.

In addition to these specific proposals, comprehensive surveys have also been conducted. The work by Perera et al. [4] presents a detailed survey on the use of blockchain for dynamic spectrum management. The article highlights the benefits, challenges, and opportunities of applying blockchain in the context of dynamic spectrum access, classifying existing solutions in terms of architecture type, sensing behavior, and access methods. Furthermore, it identifies research gaps and discusses future directions, establishing itself as an important reference to support new architectures such as the one proposed in this work.

Despite the growing body of literature on the application of blockchain to dynamic spectrum management—including the comprehensive 2024 survey [4]—our work introduces a novel perspective by focusing specifically on the SAS–SAS interface, an area that remains underexplored. While prior proposals such as BD-SAS [10] and SpectrumChain [9] emphasize intra-SAS coordination or high-level regulatory synchronization, they do not detail mechanisms for trustable, auditable, and real-time synchronization among independent SASs. In contrast, our architecture leverages permissioned blockchain infrastructures to ensure controlled access, secure data sharing, and automatic enforcement of inter-SAS agreements using smart contracts. This focus directly addresses the interoperability challenges in decentralized spectrum access systems, offering a practical path toward integration with existing SAS frameworks.

3   Spectrum Access System (SAS)

The SAS is a centralized dynamic spectrum management platform developed to enable efficient use of the 3550–3700 MHz band within the CBRS framework in the United States. This system is responsible for coordinating spectrum access among different user tiers—including incumbent federal users, Priority Access License (PAL) holders, and General Authorized Access (GAA) users—ensuring interference protection and compliance with the Federal Communications Commission (FCC) regulations [7,8].

SAS performs several critical functions, such as:

- Authorization of spectrum use for CBRS network devices;
- Protection of incumbent users (e.g., naval radars);
- Management of protection zones (e.g., PAL areas);
- Coordination of regulatory events and interference mitigation.

To enable these functionalities, SAS communicates with CBRS network devices, known as Citizens Broadband Radio Service Devices (CBSDs), and with other SAS instances through two main standardized interfaces: the SAS-CBSD Interface and the SAS-SAS Interface, as described below.

3.1   SAS-CBSD Interface

The SAS-CBSD interface (Fig. 1) defines the communication protocol between the SAS and end devices operating in the CBRS band, the CBSDs. This interface specifies procedures such as:

- CBSD registration;
- Inquiry of available spectrum;
- Request and grant of transmission authorizations;
- Periodic heartbeats to maintain authorization;
- Relinquishment and deregistration of devices.

Messages are encoded in JavaScript Object Notation (JSON) and transported over HTTPS using mutual authentication based on X.509 certificates.

3.2   SAS-SAS Interface

The SAS-SAS interface concerns communication between different SAS implementations, enabling information exchange to ensure consistency and interoperability of the overall system. This interface enables:

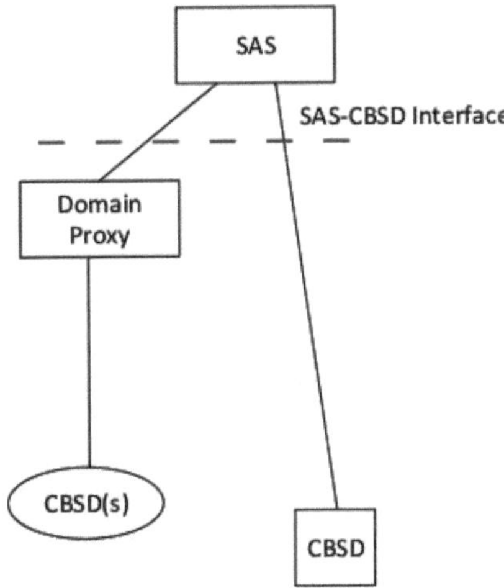

Fig. 1. SAS-CBSD Interface [8].

- Synchronization of CBSD records, geographic zones, and coordination events;
- Sharing of Environmental Sensing Capability (ESC) sensor data;
- Coordination of protection zones and regulatory actions;
- Support for both push and pull mechanisms for record transfer.

The SAS-SAS interface also employs secure protocols with Transport Layer Security (TLS) version 1.2 and mutual authentication, ensuring the integrity and confidentiality of data exchanged between SAS instances.

4   Functional Requirements of the SAS-SAS Interface

This section describes the functional requirements necessary for implementing the communication interface between automated spectrum management systems. These requirements aim to ensure security, interoperability, and consistency in the exchange of information between peer SASs.

- **Authentication and Security:** Communication between SASs must be protected by mutual authentication using TLS v1.2, with verification of digital certificates. The negotiation of secure ciphersuites is mandatory to ensure the confidentiality and integrity of transmitted data. Connections must be immediately terminated in case of authentication failures.
- **Peer SAS Discovery:** The system must support both static and dynamic mechanisms for discovering peer SASs, through services such as Domain Name System (DNS) or Dynamic Host Configuration Protocol (DHCP). Additionally, it must be possible to register and maintain the communication endpoints of the discovered SASs.

- **Data Use Agreement:** Explicit agreements must be established regarding the use restrictions of the data shared with peer SASs, in order to ensure compliance with regulatory standards and privacy policies.
- **Record Exchange:** The interface must enable the structured exchange of records related to: CBSD devices; Protected zones (PAL, PPA, exclusion zones, among others); Coordination events; ESC sensors; SAS implementations and SAS administrator information. Each record must have a unique identifier, with a hierarchy based on namespaces.
- **Data Synchronization:** The interface must support time-range requests for CBSDs, zones, and coordination events. Each request may cover up to 25 h of data, which must remain available for at least 30 d. Responses should contain only records modified within the specified time range, applying specific filters such as selecting CBSDs with active or pending grants.
- **Requests by Identifier (ID):** The retrieval of detailed information for specific records based on their unique identifiers (by-ID requests) must be supported.
- **Push-based Data Exchange:** The interface must be capable of processing push-type requests containing updated data on CBSDs, zones, and coordination events. The system must respond using appropriate HTTP status codes (e.g., 200, 422, 50x).
- **Full Record Dumps Generation:** The SAS must periodically generate, at least every seven days, a Full Record Dump containing: CBSDs with active or pending grants; Protected zones (PAL, PPA, or ad hoc); Affiliated ESC sensors. These files must remain available for at least 14 d for access by peer SASs.
- **Message Flows:** The interface must support both pull-based (on demand) and push-based (proactive) message flows. Resilience and continuity of communications must be ensured even in scenarios involving partial network failure.

5   Adherence of Blockchain Technology to Functional Requirements

Blockchain technology presents features that can significantly contribute to meeting the functional requirements defined for secure and auditable data exchange between SASs. Below, we describe how blockchain functionalities can be applied to each of the listed requirements.

Permissioned blockchain infrastructures, such as Hyperledger Fabric or Besu, support mutual authentication based on digital certificates (e.g., X.509), integrated with secure channel negotiation via TLS v1.2. The cryptographic verification of transactions and blocks ensures integrity and confidentiality, while access control policies can be applied at the communication channel level to restrict access to authorized entities only. Native support for certificate revocation and event monitoring allows for the termination of TLS connections in case of authentication failures.

Although dynamic peer discovery (via DNS/DHCP) is traditionally performed outside the scope of blockchain, endpoint registration data and SAS association records can be stored and shared immutably on the blockchain network itself. Synchronization of these records ensures traceability and reliability in the discovery and maintenance of peer connections.

Smart contracts allow for the definition and automatic enforcement of data use agreements between SASs. Contract clauses can be immutably recorded, and their automated execution ensures compliance with agreed terms, enabling transparent and non-repudiable auditing.

Blockchain can serve as a trusted repository for exchanging information on CBSDs, regulatory zones (PAL, PPA, exclusion), ESC sensors, and coordination events. The use of unique identifiers with a hierarchical structure (e.g., using namespaces) can be embedded directly in the records stored in blocks, facilitating efficient indexing and retrieval.

Blockchain's inherent traceability enables time-range queries, as each transaction and block includes timestamp records. Thus, it is possible to query records modified within specific windows, ensuring historical integrity. Furthermore, data stored on the blockchain naturally complies with retention requirements (e.g., 30 d), with filtering capabilities implemented via smart contracts.

The retrieval of specific data by unique identifier can be performed through query functions in smart contracts, ensuring access to detailed and immutable records according to the queried ID, in line with the defined hierarchical naming structure.

Proactive events (Push) can be modeled on the blockchain through transactions submitted directly by authorized peers. The confirmation of block inclusion, as well as response code verification (e.g., 200 OK, 422 Unprocessable Entity), can be associated with events in smart contracts, enabling robust and verifiable communication.

The periodic generation of dumps can be automated based on blockchain queries with predefined criteria (e.g., active CBSDs, protected zones, ESC sensors). These dumps can be stored in decentralized repositories or extracted directly via read APIs, ensuring availability for periods longer than 14 d as required.

Although blockchain itself does not define message transport, RESTful interfaces over HTTPS/TLS can be used to send/receive data in JSON format (RFC-7159), ensuring compatibility with the established protocols for message encoding and transport.

Blockchain supports both Pull flows (via record queries) and Push flows (via insertion of new transactions), offering resilience through distributed data replication. This ensures operational continuity even in the presence of node failures or temporary communication interruptions.

Thus, the adoption of blockchain technologies can enhance trust, traceability, and automation in communication between SASs, aligning with regulatory and operational requirements in cooperative environments where data integrity is paramount.

6   Proposed Architecture with Blockchain Integration

Figure 2 presents a systemic view of the proposed architecture for SAS with permissioned blockchain integration. In this approach, blockchain is used as a trust infrastructure for secure and auditable information exchange between SASs, without fully replacing internal operational components.

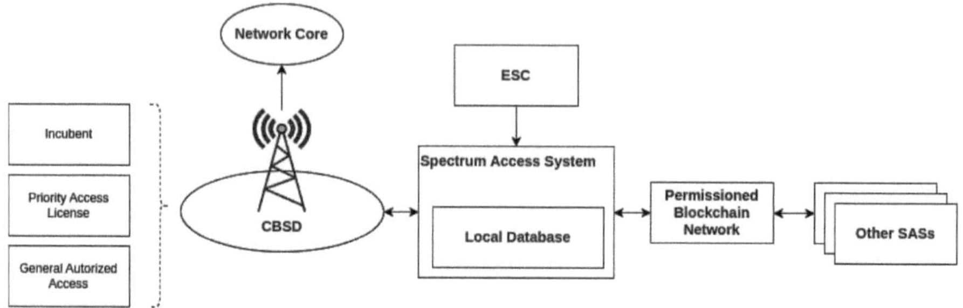

Fig. 2. SAS Architecture with Integration into a Permissioned Blockchain Network

6.1   Architectural Components

The architecture is composed of the following main elements:

- **CBSD (Citizen Broadband Radio Service Device):** Equipment responsible for operating in the dynamic spectrum. It sends information about location, power, and spectrum demands to the SAS. CBSDs include *Incumbents*, PAL, and GAA, which represent different priority levels for spectrum access, as defined by sharing rules.
- **Spectrum Access System (SAS):** Responsible for coordinating spectrum use, granting authorizations (grants), and communicating with CBSDs and other SASs. Internally, the SAS maintains a Local Database, used for rapid decision-making and temporary storage.
- **ESC (Environmental Sensing Capability):** A sensor system dedicated to detecting incumbent signals. The SAS may use ESC data to avoid causing harmful interference.
- **Permissioned Blockchain Network:** Serves as the official communication medium between SASs. Relevant information such as CBSD records, protected zones, grants, coordination events, and data agreements are published on this network, ensuring traceability, security, and transparency.
- **Other SASs:** Represent external instances with which the local SAS needs to communicate. All interaction occurs exclusively through the permissioned blockchain network.

6.2   Operational Flow

The operation of the proposed architecture follows these main steps:

1. The CBSD sends its operational information to the local SAS.
2. The SAS consults its local database to verify spectrum availability and internal policies.
3. If needed, the SAS publishes or queries information on the blockchain to check active grants, coordination events, and data on neighboring CBSDs.
4. The SAS interacts with other SASs exclusively through the permissioned blockchain, using smart contracts to record updates, query information by ID or time interval, and validate data agreements.
5. Periodic dumps and push notifications are issued as transactions on the blockchain, ensuring shared visibility and integrity.
6. ESC sensor data is considered locally and may be shared, if necessary, via blockchain.

6.3   Advantages of the Hybrid Model with Blockchain

This model preserves the classic architecture of an SAS with a local operational base for spectrum management, while adding a robust inter-SAS communication layer through blockchain. Among the benefits are:

- Transparency and traceability among SAS operators.
- Elimination of external REST channels between SASs, reducing attack surfaces.
- Immutability and native auditing of all records and message exchanges.
- Automated execution of agreements and policies via smart contracts.

The governance of the permissioned blockchain network is shared among SAS operators, who act as validating nodes. Interoperability is ensured by standardized smart contracts and common data schemas, allowing different SASs to interact transparently and securely.

7   Implementation Example: Coordinated Spectrum Management Across Multiple SASs Using Blockchain

This proposal was implemented as a module in a decentralized network infrastructure sharing solution based on blockchain [6]. This project is a partnership between the Federal University of Pará and the Center for Research and Development in Telecommunications, both from Brazil.

This implementation simulates a real-world deployment scenario in which three distinct Spectrum Access Systems (SASs), operated by different entities (e.g., commercial mobile operators or government agencies), must coordinate spectrum usage in a shared geographic region. These SASs exchange CBSD records, protected zone updates, and coordination events using the blockchain network, without relying on direct REST communication or centralized intermediaries. This multi-SAS coordination setup reflects realistic requirements in collaborative spectrum management environments, such as in dense urban areas or federated regulatory contexts.

To demonstrate the applicability of the proposed architecture, a practical implementation example is presented, based on the integration of an SAS with the Hyperledger Besu permissioned blockchain platform. The proposal considers a network of SASs coordinated by smart contracts, in which all communication between systems occurs in a distributed, secure, and auditable manner, using blockchain as the official interaction medium. The set of technologies used in this implementation is shown in Table 1.

Table 1. Technologies used in the implementation example

Component	Technology Used
Blockchain Platform	Besu (IBFT 2.0)
Smart Contracts	Solidity + Hardhat Framework
Identity Management	X.509 Certificates with TLS v1.2
SAS Local Persistence	PostgreSQL
SAS Application Service	Node.js + Express.js (Internal REST)
Monitoring and Auditing	Prometheus + Grafana
Blockchain Query Interface	Web3.js + Local REST APIs

A typical operation in this environment involves SAS-A detecting spectrum activity via ESC sensors and recording a coordination event on the blockchain. SAS-B and SAS-C, which subscribe to relevant smart contract events, receive this update and adjust their grant policies accordingly. This enables decentralized, auditable, and near real-time synchronization of decisions, even in the absence of pre-established trust among operators.

In this scenario, each SAS operates locally with its own database, responsible for managing CBSD devices, analyzing zones, monitoring ESC sensors, and making decisions regarding the granting of grants. However, instead of using direct channels such as REST or other traditional interfaces to share information with peer SASs, all relevant data—including CBSD records, protected zone updates, coordination notifications, and data usage agreements—are recorded as transactions on the permissioned blockchain based on Besu[1].

The blockchain network infrastructure uses the Istanbul Byzantine Fault Tolerance (IBFT) 2.0 consensus mechanism, suitable for permissioned environments that require fast transaction finality and Byzantine fault tolerance. Each SAS operator participates in the network as a validator node, identified by X.509 digital certificates, ensuring strong authentication and distributed access control.

---

[1] https://besu.hyperledger.org/.

Operational functions are modeled in smart contracts written in Solidity, which structure the read and write operations on the blockchain.

The SAS system is implemented using technologies widely adopted in distributed systems development. The application logic and local services are developed in Node.js using the Express.js framework[2], while local data is persisted in PostgreSQL[3]. Interactions with the blockchain are performed via the Web3.js library[4], both for submitting transactions and listening to events emitted by the smart contracts. Thus, actions such as publishing CBSD records, issuing periodic *dumps*, or responding to queries by ID are triggered directly within the blockchain environment.

To ensure continuous visibility and auditing, the architecture incorporates monitoring and analysis tools based on Prometheus[5] and Grafana[6]. These systems enable tracking of blockchain usage metrics, such as transaction volume, average block propagation time, update frequency between SASs, and average latency between recorded events.

The adoption of Besu in this architecture enables a number of benefits. Firstly, its compatibility with the Ethereum Virtual Machine (EVM) offers flexibility for smart contract development and reuse. Additionally, the use of standardized JSON-RPC APIs facilitates integration with legacy systems and monitoring tools. Finally, support for privacy mechanisms such as Tessera[7] can be incorporated in future versions, should it be necessary to maintain confidential records among subsets of network participants.

This example demonstrates that, by integrating blockchain as a native communication infrastructure between SASs, it is possible to meet regulatory requirements for security, traceability, and integrity, while building a scalable and interoperable technological foundation for dynamic spectrum management.

8   Discussion

The application of blockchain technology in communication between SASs offers important benefits, especially in terms of security, traceability, and decentralized governance. However, it also introduces technical and operational challenges. This section discusses the main advantages and limitations of adopting blockchain, considering the functional requirements addressed.

The main contribution of blockchain lies in the immutability of recorded data, enabling reliable auditing of exchanges, agreements, and updates. Native authentication mechanisms—such as digital certificates, cryptographic signatures, and TLS—enhance communication security, while the distributed nature of the network reduces single points of failure.

---

[2] https://expressjs.com/.

[3] https://www.postgresql.org/.

[4] http://web3js.org/.

[5] https://prometheus.io/.

[6] https://grafana.com/.

[7] https://docs.tessera.consensys.io/.

The ability to encode usage policies, access rules, and notifications into smart contracts provides automation and eliminates ambiguities in agreements between SASs. Data replication among nodes also contributes to fault tolerance, which is essential for critical systems like spectrum management. In permissioned networks, selective data visibility can be enforced, balancing transparency with privacy and regulatory compliance.

Nevertheless, data replication across nodes may lead to increased computational and storage requirements, especially when historical records must be retained. Transaction confirmation and block propagation can introduce latency, which may impact real-time coordination scenarios.

Adding a blockchain layer also implies architectural changes, requiring specialized expertise in smart contracts and validator node management. Defining consensus, identity, and access control policies among SAS operators—especially in multi-jurisdictional settings—adds further complexity. Even though permissioned blockchains perform better than public ones, scalability challenges may still arise with high data volumes.

Adoption should balance the benefits of security and traceability with the operational costs. In collaborative and regulated environments where trust cannot be assumed, blockchain offers a robust, auditable foundation. However, its implementation must be guided by careful performance and governance analysis to ensure long-term viability.

The proposed architecture is particularly suitable for multi-operator deployments in dense urban areas, where different SASs must coordinate shared spectrum access. Blockchain enables synchronization of records and automated enforcement of agreements, reducing interference risks. Another relevant case is cross-border spectrum sharing, where regulatory fragmentation and limited trust demand auditable coordination. Permissioned blockchains provide a tamper-resistant medium for such federated environments.

Despite its strengths, blockchain adoption introduces limitations. Permissioned platforms like Hyperledger Besu with IBFT 2.0 may incur latency ranging from hundreds of milliseconds to a few seconds, depending on block time and validator responsiveness. This can be critical in real-time applications such as emergency spectrum reallocation. Managing validator nodes and certificates, and maintaining smart contracts, requires technical resources often unavailable to smaller entities or public agencies. Furthermore, immutable records may conflict with regional data protection regulations unless privacy-preserving mechanisms are implemented.

The proposed architecture is non-intrusive and compatible with existing SAS platforms. Rather than replacing internal systems, it adds a blockchain-based communication layer interfacing via RESTful APIs and message handlers. Integration is achieved by adapter modules that convert local events (e.g., grants, zone updates) into blockchain transactions. Similarly, blockchain updates are consumed and forwarded internally. This modular design supports gradual adoption while preserving previous investments.

Blockchain adoption requires investment in validator infrastructure, certificate management, and contract development. While this adds initial complexity, the long-term benefits—such as decentralized trust, immutable logs, automation, and operational resilience—may justify the effort, particularly in collaborative or regulated contexts. Platforms like Besu offer performance optimizations and privacy tools (e.g., Tessera) that support secure and cost-effective deployment.

Although some SAS data—like protected zones and availability—are public in systems such as CBRS or Mosaic, other information may be sensitive. Real-time coordination, device usage, or operator agreements may reveal strategic infrastructure details. To address this, tools like Tessera allow private transactions among authorized nodes. Future work may explore cryptographic solutions such as Zero-Knowledge Proofs (ZKPs), which ensure correctness without exposing content, though their integration is still evolving.

Balancing transparency and confidentiality is crucial for compliance and institutional trust, especially in large-scale or cross-jurisdictional deployments. The proposed architecture can incorporate privacy-preserving techniques to enable secure and selective information sharing.

9 Final Considerations and Future Work

This paper presented a hybrid architecture proposal for SAS, integrated with permissioned blockchain technology, aiming to meet the requirements of security, traceability, interoperability, and decentralized governance in dynamic spectrum sharing environments. The proposed architecture positions blockchain as the communication infrastructure between SAS instances, while preserving established local operational mechanisms and incorporating smart contracts to automate processes and agreements among operators.

The analysis of functional requirements for the SAS-SAS interface demonstrated that the use of permissioned blockchain—especially with platforms such as Besu—robustly addresses the needs for authentication, record exchange, temporal synchronization, retrieval by identifier, periodic dumps, and proactive notifications. It also promotes regulatory compliance and operational transparency.

The proposal aligns with the emerging demands of 5G and 6G mobile networks, where dynamic and secure spectrum management becomes increasingly critical. The architecture has shown potential to provide a resilient and auditable foundation for managing spectral resources in densely distributed networks with multiple operators, as expected in advanced mobile communication scenarios.

The following directions are highlighted as future work:

- Conducting comprehensive performance evaluations in real-world scenarios with multiple SASs operating simultaneously over the blockchain network, including measurements of latency, throughput, and resource utilization;
- Detailing the experimental setup of the prototype, including software configurations, testing parameters, infrastructure characteristics, and execution environment;

- Incorporating privacy-preserving mechanisms (e.g., Tessera or zero-knowledge proofs) to protect sensitive coordination data among subsets of participants;
- Investigating the governance structures required to support decentralized decision-making in permissioned blockchain networks, including consensus rules, node onboarding policies, and conflict resolution strategies;
- Exploring interoperability frameworks for multi-jurisdictional regulatory environments, addressing cross-border legal constraints and harmonization challenges;
- Integrating the proposed architecture with advanced network management paradigms such as Network Slicing and Zero-Touch Network Management, as expected in future 5G and 6G deployments;

It is believed that advances in these directions will significantly contribute to consolidating a more secure, reliable, and scalable ecosystem for collaborative spectrum management, aligned with the demands of future mobile networks.

Acknowledgments. This work was partially funded by the National Council for Scientific and Technological Development (CNPq), through Public Call No. 068/2022; by the Coordination for the Improvement of Higher Education Personnel (CAPES); and by the São Paulo Research Foundation (FAPESP) under grants 2023/00811-0, 2023/00673-7, 2021/00199-8 (CPE SMARTNESS), 2020/04031-1, and 2018/23097-3. It also received support from the Fund for the Technological Development of Telecommunications (Funttel) and the Funding Authority for Studies and Projects (Finep)— Ministry of Science, Technology, and Innovation.

References

1. Alsaedi, W.K., et al.: Spectrum options and allocations for 6G: a regulatory and standardization review. IEEE Open J. Commun. Soc. (2023)
2. Li, Z., et al.: Blockchain-assisted dynamic spectrum sharing in the CBRS band. In: IEEE ICCC (2021)
3. Li, Z., Wang, W., Wu, Q., Wang, X.: Multi-operator dynamic spectrum sharing for wireless communications: a consortium blockchain enabled framework. IEEE Trans. Commun. (2023)
4. Perera, L., Ranaweera, P., Kusaladharma, S., Wang, S., Liyanage, M.: A survey on blockchain for dynamic spectrum sharing. IEEE Open J. Commun. Soc. **5**, 1753–1770 (2024). https://doi.org/10.1109/OJCOMS.2024.3376233
5. Salahdine, F., Han, T., Zhang, N.: 5G, 6G, and beyond: recent advances and future challenges. Ann. Telecommun. **78**(9), 525–549 (2023)
6. Sousa, J.C., Duarte, V., Pinto, M., Evaristo, B., Filho, F.J.R.: Solução descentralizada de compartilhamento de infraestrutura de redes baseada em blockchain. In: XLI Simpósio Brasileiro de Telecomunicações e Processamento de Sinais (SBrT 2024). Belém, PA, Brasil (October 2024)
7. Wireless Innovation Forum: Signaling protocols and procedures for Citizens Broadband Radio Service (CBRS): Spectrum Access System (SAS) - SAS interface technical specification. Technical report WINNF-TS-0096, Version 1.3.2, The Software Defined Radio Forum Inc. (2020)

8. Wireless Innovation Forum: Signaling protocols and procedures for citizens broadband radio service (CBRS): Spectrum access system (SAS) - citizens broadband radio service device (CBSD) interface technical specification. Technical report WINNF-TS-0016, Version 1.2.7, The Software Defined Radio Forum Inc. (2022)
9. Wu, Q.: Spectrumchain: a disruptive dynamic spectrum-sharing framework for 6G. Sci. China Inf. Sci. **66**(3), 130302 (2023). https://doi.org/10.1007/s11432-022-3692-5
10. Xiao, Y., et al.: BD-SAS: Enabling dynamic spectrum sharing in low-trust environment. IEEE Trans. (2023)

Byzantine Consensus with Secure and Intrusion-Tolerant In-Network Ordering

Gabriel Faustino Lima da Rocha[1], Eduardo A. P. Alchieri[1(✉)],
Giovanni Venâncio[2], Vinicius Fulber-Garcia[2], and Elias P. Duarte Jr.[2]

[1] Universidade de Brasília (UnB), Brasília, Distrito Federal, Brazil
`alchieri@unb.br,eduardo.hu@gmail.com`
[2] Universidade Federal do Paraná (UFPR), Curitiba, Paraná, Brazil

Abstract. Recently proposed consensus protocols make use of the network layer to ensure agreement, while the application layer is still used for termination. Those protocols employ the network layer as a sequencer that delivers ordered messages facilitating agreement. However, tolerating a malicious sequencer is a challenging task. For instance, a malicious sequencer can assign the same sequence number to different messages and send them to different replicas. To avoid this problem, the NeoBFT consensus protocol adds an additional communication step at the replicas. Although this approach mitigates the problem, it negatively impacts system performance by requiring an additional synchronization step among replicas before executing requests. This work proposes NsoBFT (Network Secure Ordered BFT), a consensus protocol that uses a secure message ordering service implemented with USIG (Unique Sequential Identifier Generator), a secure component in the network layer. Thus, no additional synchronization step is necessary for the replicas to execute requests. Experimental results comparing NsoBFT with related work show the advantage of this strategy, in particular confirming that NsoBFT outperforms NeoBFT.

Keywords: Consensus · Distributed algorithms · Intrusion tolerance

1 Introduction

Distributed consensus and agreement algorithms are the basis for solving several distributed systems problems, they have been successfully used in many different applications and contexts (e.g., [4,13,14]). In particular, consensus is basis of state machine replication [21], a comprehensive and widely used approach to build fault-tolerant systems. It has recently also received significant attention in the context of blockchains [11,18,30], and several other problems [16,25,32]. Consensus is required whenever the processes of a distributed system have to agree on a value, given an initial set of proposed values. Consensus properties can

L. A. Rodrigues and R. Oliveira (Eds.): LADC 2025, CCIS 2697, pp. 148–162, 2026.
https://doi.org/10.1007/978-3-032-11539-3_9

be classified into two categories: those that aim to guarantee agreement (*safety*), and those that ensure termination (*liveness*).

Classic consensus algorithms that assume crash faults include Paxos [15] and Raft [19], among others. Those algorithms cannot deal with arbitrary faulty behavior, often related to intrusion incidents. Intrusion-tolerant consensus algorithms are also called Byzantine Fault-Tolerant (BFT). PBFT (Practical BFT) [5,6] was the first intrusion tolerant consensus algorithm that was shown to provide feasible implementations. Since then, several variations as well as other BFT consensus algorithms have been proposed [22].

Consensus is frequently implemented in the application layer considering a message-passing distributed system composed of reliable channels. Such a channel can be implemented with a reliable transport protocol on top of a fair-loss network layer. However, the NOPaxos (Network Ordered Paxos) algorithm [17] was the first consensus solution to employ a message sequencer module implemented in the network layer to assign unique sequence numbers to messages. Thus the safety properties are guaranteed at this layer while the application layer is responsible only for termination. The main advantage of that approach is high performance. This is very relevant, as consensus algorithms are well known for being expensive. An empirical evaluation of NOPaxos shows that the algorithm presents a latency that is close to the bare network latency.

NeoBFT [23] is another consensus algorithm that employs the network layer, but it tolerates Byzantine faults and requires secure sequence numbers. The network layer in this case provides an authenticated ordering service. However, this algorithm uses an additional communication step between the replicas before executing a request. That is necessary in order to deal with the fact that a malicious sequencer can assign different sequence numbers to the same message. This extra communication step increases the overhead for running consensus, in particular due to the requirement that all messages be digitally signed, as well as the need for additional coordination between replicas at the application layer. Note that in NeoBFT both the network and application layers need to work together for ensuring the safety properties.

In the present work we propose NsoBFT (Network secure ordered BFT), a consensus algorithm that tolerates Byzantine faults while preventing a malicious sequencer from assigning different sequence numbers to the same message. NsoBFT implements a secure sequencer by using a USIG (Unique Sequential Identifier Generator) [29] which constrains the malicious actions that the sequencer can execute. Thus NsoBFT does not require additional coordination in the replicas, *i.e.*, it requires one less communication step in comparison with NeoBFT. The USIG module can be implemented in the network layer by using a co-processor coupled to a switch to perform more complex operations.

NsoBFT and other BFT consensus algorithms, such as PBFT and NeoBFT, require $3f + 1$ replicas to tolerate up to f malicious replicas, in addition to the sequencer. However we also present two variants of NsoBFT that require only $2f + 1$ replicas. The first variant is called MinNsoBFT and requires an additional communication step, while the second variant, called MinZyzNsoBFT, does not require any additional steps. In the second variant the client completes an operation when it receives the same response from all replicas. However, if this is not the case the client needs to execute additional actions to synchronize the replicas. Table 1 shows how different consensus algorithms can be compared in terms of the type of faults assumptions, number of replicas required, number of communication steps required, communication complexity, and the requirement of secure components.

Table 1. Comparison of consensus algorithms. The sequencer of the algorithms that employ the network layer to order messages (NoPaxos, NeoBFT, NsoBFT, and their variants) "intercepts" requests and includes the sequence numbers, thus requiring one less communication step.
Notes:
[1]f represents the number of tolerated faults.
[2]n represents the number of replicas in the system.

	Paxos	PBFT	NOPaxos	NeoBFT	**NsoBFT**	**MinNsoBFT**	**MinZyzNsoBFT**
Failure	crash	Byzantine	crash	Byzantine	**Byzantine**	**Byzantine**	**Byzantine**
# of replicas[1]	$2f+1$	$3f+1$	$2f+1$	$3f+1$	$3f+1$	$2f+1$	$2f+1$
Comm. steps	4	5	2	3	**2**	**3**	**2**
Comm. Comp.[2]	$O(n^2)$	$O(n^2)$	$O(n)$	$O(n^2)$	$O(n)$	$O(n^2)$	$O(n)$
Secure service	-	-	-	-	**USIG**	**USIG**	**USIG**

In addition to describing and specifying NsoBFT and variants, the algorithms were implemented and compared (NOPaxos, NeoBFT, and NsoBFT). Results show that NOPaxos presents superior performance but tolerates only crash faults, while NsoBFT outperforms NeoBFT by requiring one less communication step.

The remainder of this paper is organized as follows. Section 2 presents background and related work. Section 3 presents the NsoBFT algorithm and its variants. The experimental evaluation is presented in Sect. 4. Finally, Sect. 5 concludes the paper and discusses future work.

2   Background and Related Work: Consensus, from Paxos to NeoBFT

Consider a distributed system composed of a set of independent processes $\Pi = p_1, p_2, .., p_n$, process p_i is also refereed to as process i. The processes of Π run a *consensus* algorithm to agree on a value of a predefined set of possible values. Initially processes *propose* values, and eventually *all* correct processes *decide* on a single one of the values proposed. Thus, in order to execute a consensus instance, processes execute two primitives [12]:

- `propose(v)`: a process executes this primitive to propose value v to the set of processes in Π.

- `decide(v)`: a process executes this primitive to notify the interested party (*i.e.*, an application) that v is the decided value.

In order to ensure safety and liveness, and assuming the crash fault model, consensus must satisfy the following properties:

- **Agreement**: if a correct process decides v, then all correct processes eventually decide v.
- **Validity**: a correct process decides v only if v was previously proposed by some process.
- **Termination**: all correct processes eventually decide.

The agreement property ensures that all correct processes decide on the same value. Validity relates the decided value to the proposed values. Note that the fault model has a direct impact on validity, and changes in validity can lead to different types of consensus. The agreement and validity properties define the safety requirements of the consensus, and the termination property defines its liveness. It has been proved [10] that it is impossible to solve the consensus problem deterministically in a completely asynchronous distributed system where at least one process can fail by crashing. Therefore, most consensus solutions make some stronger synchrony assumption, e.g. the GST (Global Stabilization Time) [9] in which a system is initially asynchronous but after some unknown but finite time instant becomes synchronous respecting time limits both for process execution and message transmission.

Although several consensus algorithms have been proposed, given the nature of the algorithm introduced in the present work, we start our overview of related work with Paxos [15], which is one of the most important consensus algorithms. Paxos assumes that processes can fail by crashing. Processes assume three different roles: proposer, acceptor or learner. The algorithm consists of two phases: a preparation phase and a decision phase. Each phase requires two communication steps. As the name implies, proposers make proposals with the aim of having a majority of acceptors $(n/2+1)$ accepting a value. When that happens, a decision is taken and is never changed, this guarantees safety. In the first phase proposers send a **prepare** message with a proposal number (frequently called *ballot*) to a majority of acceptors, which can include itself. Proposer i uses increasingly larger proposal numbers, starting with i and each time incrementing with n, thus its proposal numbers are: $i, i + n, i + 2n, i + 3n, \ldots$. In this way proposal numbers from different proposers are comparable.

A Paxos acceptor only sends a positive reply to the proposer in Phase 1 if the proposal number is the largest it has received. If the proposer does not get a majority of positive replies, it sends another **prepare** message with a larger proposal number. After getting $n/2+1$ positive responses to the **prepare** message, the proposer proceeds to Phase 2 of the algorithm. In Phase 2 the proposer sends an **accept** message to the majority of acceptors, now with the value it wants to get them to accept, plus the proposal number that succeeded in the first phase. Now, an acceptor only sends a positive reply – an accepts a value – if meanwhile it has not received another message (either `prepare` or `accept`) with an even larger proposal number. In that case it returns that number to the proposer, which will try it all again with an even higher proposal number. But there is a final catch: if an acceptor has accepted a value, it must return that value to the proposer with the corresponding proposal number. The proposer now must adopt the value with the highest number as the one it will try acceptors to accept. The idea is that after a majority of acceptors accept a value, that instance of consensus has decided, nothing will change that value, and thus safety is guaranteed.

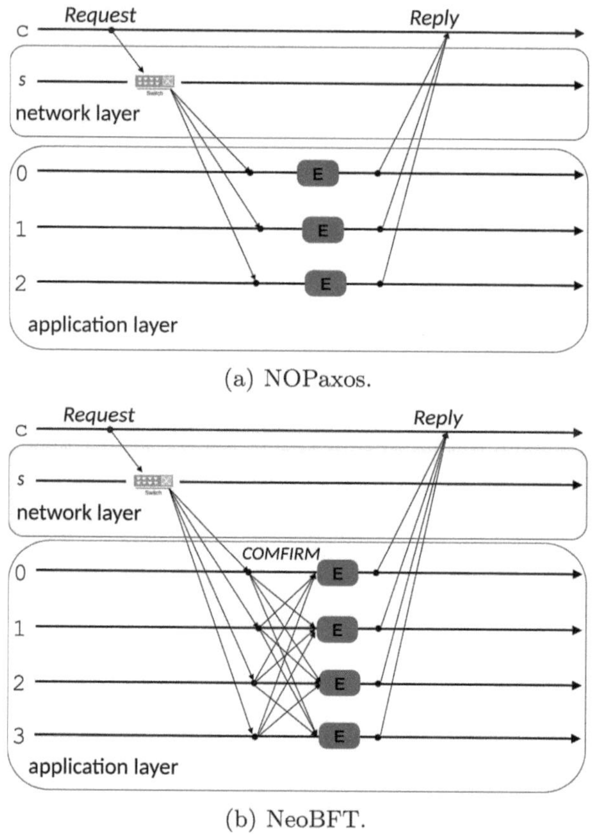

(a) NOPaxos.

(b) NeoBFT.

Fig. 1. Normal case execution for NOPaxos and NeoBFT.

Closely related to the algorithm we propose in this paper, NOPaxos (Network Ordered Paxos) [17] was the first consensus protocol to make use of the network layer to improve the performance of consensus. NOPaxos uses a sequencer at the network layer (*e.g.,* implemented in a switch) that assigns sequence numbers to requests, which are then forwarded to the replicas. The replicas deliver and execute requests in the order defined by the sequence numbers and attempt to recover any requests with missing order numbers from the other replicas. During normal execution, requests are executed in only a single round-trip time (Fig. 1a): a client broadcasts a request r to the replicas through the sequencer; the replicas add r to a log, and a leader replica also executes the operation; all replicas respond to the client with the position p at which r was added in the log, while the leader also sends the response; the client waits for $f+1$ responses with the same p, including the leader's response, and then gets the final response. The replicas also monitor and replace the sequencer and/or the leader replica in case of failures. As in other algorithms that tolerate only crashes, at least $2f+1$ replicas are needed to tolerate up to f faulty replicas. Finally, since only the leader replica executes the requests, it is unnecessary to roll back the replicas state. However, if a non-faulty leader replica is replaced due to false suspicions, its requests may not reflect the state of the new leader replica. In this case, the old leader replica updates its state from the new leader instead of performing a rollback.

NeoBFT [23] follows a similar approach to that of NOPaxos, but assumes Byzantine faults, $i.e.$, it is intrusion-tolerant. Among the Byzantine fault-tolerant consensus protocols, PBFT (Practical Byzantine Fault Tolerance) is the first to consider practical aspects [5,6]. PBFT is executed in three phases. PBFT classifies the replicas as primary (which can be seen as a leader) and backups. The primary assigns sequence numbers to proposals, and the backups use these numbers to ensure consistency. A major part of the algorithm is related to tolerating failures of the primary. The backups also monitor the primary replica to detect crashes or malicious behavior.

In order to tolerate malicious failures, in NeoBFT [23] the sequencer signs each request with its assigned sequence number, resulting in an authenticated ordering service at the network layer. This approach allows a replica to recover lost requests from other replicas by simply checking whether the corresponding signature is valid. Since a malicious sequencer can assign the same sequence number to different requests, this algorithm requires an additional communication step (as shown in Fig. 1b) to guarantee that at least $2f+1$ replicas have received the same information. When this occurs, the replicas execute the request, and the response is sent to the client, which waits for $2f+1$ identical responses to complete its operation.

Thus, NeoBFT requires $3f+1$ replicas to tolerate up to f malicious failures. Furthermore, in certain cases, it is necessary to insert a gap "request" to ensure system progress. When this occurs, or due to a sequencer change, some replicas may need to roll back their state. Finally, some alternatives for authentication at the network layer have been proposed [23], such as coupling a co-processor capable of generating signatures to the switch or using an HMAC vector implemented directly in the switch.

In terms of not very closely related works, there have been several algorithms to improve aspects of Paxos and PBFT from different perspectives. For instance, MinBFT [29] uses secure components to reduce both the number of replicas and the number of communication steps. Other algorithms have been proposed to address the coexistence of multiple replicas [20] or to consider systems in which the number of replicas is initially unknown [1]. All of these algorithms order requests by exchanging messages at the application layer.

3   The NsoBFT Consensus Protocol

This section presents the NsoBFT (Network secure ordered BFT) consensus protocol. NsoBFT is a consensus algorithm that, similar to NOPaxos and NeoBFT, employs both the network and application layers in order to provide an efficient implementation of distributed fault-tolerant consensus. Different from the other alternatives, NsoBFT uses the USIG (Unique Sequential Identifier Generator) component [29] to securely generate sequence numbers, $i.e.$, a malicious sequencer cannot assign the same sequence number to different messages. Unique sequence numbers ensure that requests are safely ordered. Consequently, NsoBFT eliminates the additional communication step required by NeoBFT and presents message exchange complexity equivalent to that of NOPaxos, which only tolerates crash failures.

3.1   System Model

NsoBFT assumes a distributed system that consists of an unbounded set of client processes and a set of n server processes, which are also called $replicas$. The Byzantine fault model is assumed, $i.e.$, processes can behave maliciously and not follow protocol specifications. A process is considered correct if it does not fail; otherwise, it is considered faulty. There are at most f faulty replicas out of $n = 3f + 1$ replicas. Processes have unique identifiers, and it is impossible to obtain additional identifiers to launch a Sybil attack [8].

The system is partially synchronous and we assume the GST model [3,9]. Thus, after an initial period of instability and from a time instant which is also called the Global Stabilization Time (GST) the system becomes and remains synchronous forever. We note that most works that solve consensus deterministically require a partially synchronous model to ensure termination.

Processes communicate by sending and receiving messages. Clients multicast their requests to replicas, which send responses back to the client over a point-to-point channel, and communicate with each other as needed. Communication channels are secure, in the sense that messages are authenticated and cannot be corrupted. Furthermore, channels are fair-loss, $i.e.$, if a message is repeatedly sent from a correct source process to a correct destination process, it will be eventually delivered. However, the network layer can lose, duplicate, or reorder messages. At least one correct sequencer is placed in the network layer ($e.g.$, in a switch) that uses the USIG to assign sequence numbers to client requests.

3.2   USIG: Unique Sequential Identifier Generator

USIG is a secure service that assigns a unique identifier and signs each message. The identifiers are: *(i)* unique (the same identifier is never assigned to two or more messages); *(ii)* monotonic (the identifier assigned to a message is never smaller than the previous one); and *(iii)* sequential (the identifier assigned to a message is always the successor of the previous one). A USIG module must be present in the switch which processes and forwards messages with the identifiers. The interface defined to access the USIG service is as follows [29]:

- `createUI(m)`: receives as parameter a message `m` and returns a UI certificate containing the unique identifier (`UI.id`) and the proof (`UI.proof`) that the identifier was created by this component and assigned to `m`. As mentioned above, the identifier is a monotonically increasing counter that increments with each call to this function. The proof is a digital signature that consists of the message hash that is encrypted with asymmetric cryptography. The private key used to generate this signature is securely stored within this component. The proof only requires the corresponding public key to be verified.
- `verifyUI(PK,UI,m)`: verifies whether the unique identifier `UI` is valid for message `m`. This function receives as a parameter the public key `PK`, associated with the respective USIG instance, to verify whether the signature contained in `UI.proof` is valid for `UI.id` and `m`.

Using the USIG component, a sequencer cannot send two different messages with the same identifier to different processes. Thus, each process only needs to store the identifier of the last message received from the sequencer in order to anticipate the expected identifier for the next message. Therefore, the actions of a malicious sequencer are limited to either sending the same message (containing any value) to all processes or sending nothing.

3.3   NsoBFT Consensus

NsoBFT is presented in two parts: the normal execution and the view changing protocol.

Normal Execution. A normal execution of BsoBFT follows the message pattern shown in Fig. 2. Note that the USIG service at the network layer is instantiated only within the sequencer. The sequencer itself could be placed at a programmable switch or as a virtual network function [28] that connects all replicas. We note that both technologies have been used to implement consensus algorithms [7,26,27].

- Initially, the client multicasts request r to the set of replicas. However, the request must pass through the sequencer before it reaches the replicas.
- The sequencer uses the USIG to add an identifier (*i.e.*, the sequence number) to r, executing `createUI(r)` to add the sequence number to the message.

- The replicas receive request r already with the sequence number UI and verify whether it (UI) is valid using function `verifyUI(PK,UI,r)`, where PK is the public key of the service, which should be widely availalbe and authenticated through a reliable and well-known CA (Certification Authority). If the sequence number passes the authentication, the replicas check if UI.id is the next number in the sequence to be delivered. Upon both conditions being met, the replicas execute r, update the log log, and send the response back to the client.
- The client waits for $2f + 1$ identical responses to complete the operation.

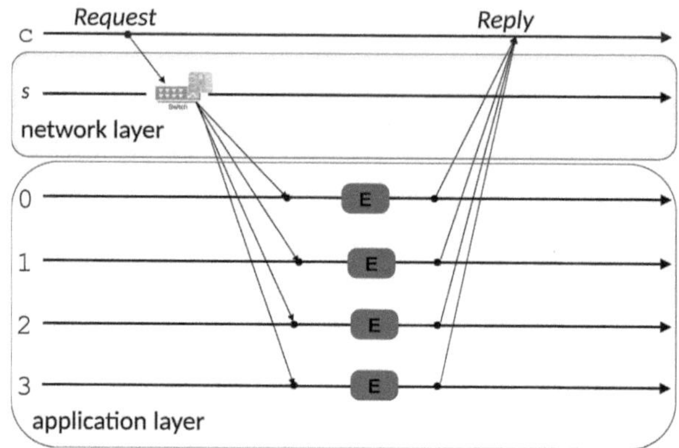

Fig. 2. NsoBFT normal case execution.

In the normal operation, if a replica does not receive a specific request, the sequence number stored in UI.id results in a gap in the delivery order. Thus, the replica must retrieve the missing request(s) from other replicas in order to continue its execution. Note that the replicas store the requests in a log. Since the UI is unique for each request, no malicious action can be performed during this procedure.

View change. If the sequencer is suspected of being faulty, a new sequencer must be chosen. To this end, it is necessary to determine up to which position in the log the requests should be maintained. The proposed view change protocol keeps in the log all requests for which at least $2f+1$ responses from the replicas have been sent to the clients (*i.e.*, those requests may have been completed successfully at the clients). On the other hand, requests removed from the log are guaranteed not to have completed at the clients.

- When a replica suspects that the sequencer is faulty, that replica sends a **VIEW-CHANGE** message to the other replicas.
- Upon receiving a **VIEW-CHANGE** message, a replica retransmits this message to the other replicas.

– When a replica receives $f + 1$ VIEW-CHANGE messages, it also sends a VIEW-CHANGE message (if it has not yet been sent). Since all correct replicas will receive those messages, the replica starts the following consensus execution to determine up to which point the log should be kept. Consequently, it also decides which log entries should be discarded:
  - A leader replica proposes its log.
  - The other replicas only accept a proposal if their own logs are not ahead of the proposed log. For this, the consensus protocol must define a predicate which is used to check whether proposals can be accepted or not [24]. This ensures that requests executed and replied from at least $2f + 1$ replicas remain in the decided log.
  - If the proposal is not accepted by at least $2f + 1$ replicas, another replica is chosen to become the leader, and the whole process is repeated.
– At the end of the consensus execution, all replicas decide on the same log l_d. After that, each replica checks its own log to executes the requests in l_d that it had missed, or rolls back the requests ahead of l_d.

Additional considerations. A malicious sequencer may choose to discard requests from specific clients. As in other implementations (*e.g.*, BFT-SMaRt [2]), to avoid such a problem, clients must also send requests to the replicas, which will wait to receive its sequence number from the sequencer. A timeout is employed as a bound to the waiting interval. If the timeout expires at some replica, that replica itself must send the request as if it were the client. A new timeout interval is triggered, and if it also expires, the replica suspects the sequencer and proposes a view change.

3.4   NsoBFT Variations: MinNsoBFT and MinZyzNsoBFT

Now we discuss two variations of NsoBFT both of which reduce the required number of replicas from $3f + 1$ to only $2f + 1$ (Table 1). Before the variations are described, it is important to recall that requests that have already completed should not be removed from the log during a view change. The variations must guarantee that this happens with f fewer replicas. The first variation is called MinNsoBFT and the second MinZyzNsoBFT:

– **MinNsoBFT**: This variant works similarly to MinBFT [29], requiring an additional communication step before executing a request. Quorums are formed with only $f + 1$ replicas. However, the additional step ensures that messages answered by at least $f + 1$ replicas will remain in the log during a view change.
– **MinZyzNsoBFT**: This variant works similarly to MinZyzzyva [29]. In this case, clients must wait for all $2f + 1$ responses to complete an operation. In executions where the network is slow (and responses do not arrive), or there are malicious replicas, an additional step is necessary: the client sends a message to all replicas and waits for the responses. These messages aim to ensure that at least $f + 1$ replicas execute all requests in order.

Note that, for both variants, the consensus protocol used for view change must tolerate Byzantine faults in a system with only $2f+1$ replicas. An example of a protocol that can be used is MinBFT [29].

4   Experimental Evaluation

This section reports the experimental evaluation of NsoBFT, with the main goal of showing the performance improvement when compared to NeoBFT. Furthermore, these protocols are also compared to NOPaxos to study the impact of Byzantine fault tolerance.

4.1   Implementation, Environment and Methodology

All three consensus algorithms that employ the network layer as a sequencer (NOPaxos, NeoBFT, and NsoBFT) were implemented in Java. Experiments were executed on the Emulab [31] testbed. We employed 6 *d430* machines (2.4 GHz E5-2630v3, with 8 cores and 2 threads per core, 64 GB of RAM) connected to a 1 Gbps switch. The NOPaxos was configured with three servers, while NeoBFT and NsoBFT were configured with four servers to tolerate up to one failure. Each server executed on a dedicated machine, while a varying number of clients were deployed on another machine. The sequencer also executed on a dedicated machine.

The software environment comprised the 64-bit Ubuntu 20 operating system and the 64-bit Java Virtual Machine (JVM) version 1.8_431. The Bouncy Castle cryptography library was also used to generate and verify 256-bit signatures. To verify the performance of the different approaches, an "empty" service was implemented, *i.e.*, nothing was processed on the replicas. The number of clients varied, and the throughput was measured on one of the replicas, while the latency was measured on one of the clients. Furthermore, the payload size varied between 0B, 100B, 1kB, and 4kB.

4.2   Experimental Results

In addition to the payload, the messages contained other information, such as the client identifiers and the sequence number. The sizes of messages without signature was the payload size plus 190 bytes. At the same time, the sizes of messages with signatures was equal to the payload size plus 536 bytes. Java serialization (*Serializable* interface) also contributed to those sizes. The average time for the sequencer to sign a packet was approximately 1.81 ms, and for the server replica to check its validity was approximately 0.22 ms, resulting in a total of 2.03 ms of processing overhead in the Byzantine fault-tolerant solutions.

Figure 3 presents the latency and throughput for the three algorithms. As expected, NOPaxos presents the highest throughput and lowest latency. This was expected, as the algorithm only tolerates crash faults and requires fewer replicas. In addition, this protocol does not employ expensive cryptographic

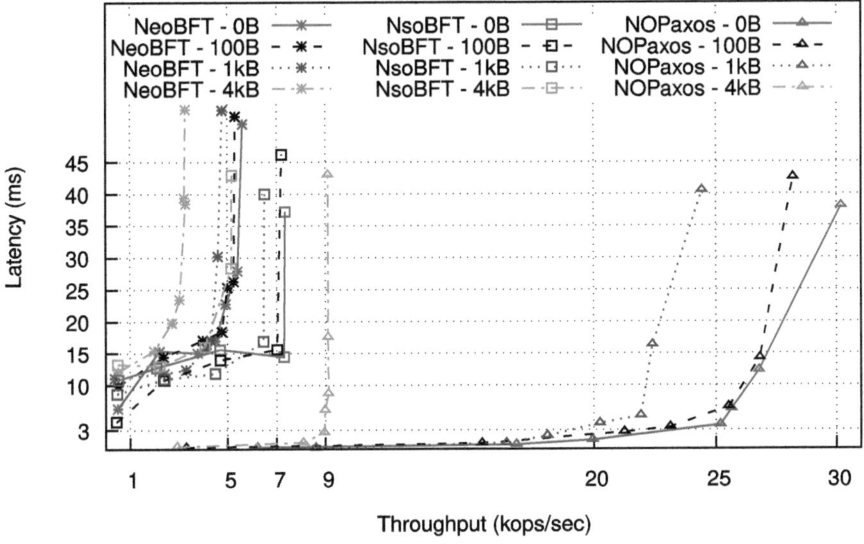

Fig. 3. Latency (95 percentile) *vs.* throughput.

primitives. NOPaxos reached a throughput of more than 25 kops/sec (a thousand operations per second) for payload sizes of 0B and 100B. For payloads of size 1kB, the throughput reached approximately 24 kops/sec. Finally, for payloads larger than 4kB, the throughput reached approximately 9 kops/sec. In all cases, the latency starts relatively low and gradually increases as the system saturates and reaches its peak throughput. From this point on, only the latency increases.

Among the protocols that tolerate Byzantine faults, NsoBFT outperformed NeoBFT because it requires one less communication step. Note that both protocols require the sequencer to sign all messages. NsoBFT presented a throughput that exceeded 7 kops/sec for payloads with 0B and 100B, while NeoBFT presented for the same payload sizes a throughput of slightly more than 5 kops/sec. For 4kB payloads, NsoBFT achieved a throughput of over 5 kops/sec, while the throughput of NeoBFT was roughly 3 kops/sec. As was the case for NOPaxos, the latency remained low up to the system saturation point. However, it is important to note that, in NeoBFT, the system saturated earlier, since this protocol requires one more communication step than NsoBFT.

Table 2 shows that the throughput varies considerably between the algorithms, especially as the number of clients increases. This confirms that the load does impact the overall system efficiency. In general, the NOPaxos algorithm tends to present higher throughputs with most combinations of clients and payloads. This is due to NOPaxos not requiring cryptography and its smaller number of replicas. Likewise, NsoBFT outperforms NeoBFT because it requires one less communication step.

Table 3 shows the latency varies according to the number of clients and the payload size. For the NOPaxos algorithm, latency remains relatively low com-

Table 2. Throughput (kops/sec) for a varying the number of clients and payload sizes.

# of clients	NOPaxos				NeoBFT				NsoBFT			
	0B	100B	1kB	4kB	0B	100B	1kB	4kB	0B	100B	1kB	4kB
1	6.22	5.30	5.60	5.93	0.49	0.51	0.37	0.51	0.51	0.43	0.46	0.48
5	16.85	15.43	16.43	8.08	2.22	2.38	2.41	2.00	2.09	1.99	1.84	1.84
10	19.96	21.25	18.11	8.95	3.77	3.98	3.30	2.72	4.69	4.70	4.49	4.07
25	25.18	23.13	20.25	8.97	4.50	4.76	4.15	3.03	7.29	7.01	6.46	4.57
50	25.63	25.52	21.90	9.12	4.93	5.00	4.32	3.28	7.35	7.20	6.51	5.18
100	26.76	26.81	22.39	9.10	5.62	5.96	4.61	3.23	7.40	7.56	6.46	5.35

Table 3. 95th percentile of the latency (ms) for a varying number of clients and payload sizes.

# of clients	NOPaxos				NeoBFT				NsoBFT			
	0B	100B	1kB	4kB	0B	100B	1kB	4kB	0B	100B	1kB	4kB
1	0.29	0.30	0.23	0.42	9.39	9.99	11.14	13.13	8.85	8.30	8.68	12.29
5	0.73	0.90	0.94	1.05	15.35	14.44	12.83	15.38	12.79	10.81	10.99	13.03
10	1.42	2.66	2.07	2.60	15.09	17.11	20.43	19.20	15.63	13.95	11.87	16.03
25	3.79	3.43	4.04	6.14	17.04	18.46	25.85	33.50	14.45	15.60	16.94	28.39
50	6.27	6.59	5.20	8.70	32.78	45.34	37.10	48.45	37.19	40.18	40.01	42.96
100	12.26	14.21	16.30	17.58	47.92	47.27	55.23	99,40	47.37	46.08	52.96	84.08

pared to the other algorithms, even with an increase in the number of clients or payload size, since the system has not yet reached its saturation point. For NeoBFT, however, latency increases considerably, especially when the number of clients is high, and the payload is larger. NsoBFT also presents high latencies under similar loads, but generally remains lower than NeoBFT.

The evaluation results confirm both that tolerating crash faults is cheaper than tolerating Byzantine faults, and make it clear that NsoBFT outperforms NeoBFT when intrusion tolerance is required since it requires one less communication step.

5   Conclusion

Consensus is a central abstraction for building reliable distributed systems, especially in environments prone to intrusions and failures. In this work we introduced the NsoBFT algorithm that employs the network layer with an USIG module to improve the performance of Byzantine consensus. Secure and unique sequence identifiers are used to mitigate the impact of malicious sequencers. The experimental evaluation provided insights into the trade-offs between performance and resilience, as crash- and intrusion-tolerant algorithms were compared. Results also confirm that NsoBFT, on the other hand, proved to be an efficient algorithm, making it an attractive option for critical applications that require high availability and data integrity.

Future work involves the implementation and evaluation of the proposed sequencer in programmable switches. Another alternative is its implementation as virtual network function. A comparison of the cost versus performance of those strategies should reveal insights not only on how efficient Byzantine consensus can be, but also on how those two different technologies (*i.e.*, programmable switches vs. network functions virtualization) compare when applied to a critical application. Other future work includes the implementation and evaluation of MinNsoBFT and MinZyzNsoBFT, the two variants of NsoBFT presented in the paper.

Acknowledgments. This work was partially supported by the Brazilian Research Council (CNPq – Conselho Nacional de Desenvolvimento Científico e Tecnológico) grant 305108/2025-5.

References

1. Alchieri, E.A.P., Bessani, A., Greve, F., Fraga, J.d.S.: Knowledge connectivity requirements for solving byzantine consensus with unknown participants. IEEE Trans. Dependable Secur. Comput. **15**(2), 246–259 (2018)
2. Bessani, A., Sousa, J., Alchieri, E.E.P.: State machine replication for the masses with BFT-SMART. In: International Conference on Dependable Systems and Networks, pp. 355–362. IEEE (2014)
3. Bravo, M., Chockler, G., Gotsman, A.: Making byzantine consensus live. Distrib. Comput. **35**(6) (2022)
4. Burrows, M.: The chubby lock service for loosely coupled distributed systems. In: The 7th Symposium on Operating Systems Design and Implementation (2006)
5. Castro, M., Liskov, B.: Practical byzantine fault tolerance. In: Symposium on Operating Systems Design and Implementation, pp. 173–186. USENIX (1999)
6. Castro, M., Liskov, B.: Practical Byzantine fault-tolerance and proactive recovery. ACM Trans. Comput. Syst. **20**(4), 398–461 (2002)
7. Dang, H.T.: P4xos: consensus as a network service. IEEE/ACM Trans. Networking **28**(4), 1726–1738 (2020)
8. Douceur, J.R.: The Sybil attack. In: International Workshop on Peer-to-Peer Systems, pp. 251–260. Springer (2002)
9. Dwork, C., Lynch, N.A., Stockmeyer, L.: Consensus in the presence of partial synchrony. J. ACM **35**(2), 288–322 (1988)
10. Fischer, M.J., Lynch, N.A., Paterson, M.S.: Impossibility of distributed consensus with one faulty process. J. ACM **32**(2), 374–382 (1985)
11. Freitas, A.E.S., Rodrigues, L.A., Duarte, E.P., Jr.: vcubechain: a scalable permissioned blockchain. Ad Hoc Netw. **158**, 103461 (2024)
12. Hadzilacos, V., Toueg, S.: A modular approach to the specification and implementation of fault-tolerant broadcasts. Department of Computer Science, Cornell University, New York - USA Technical report (1994)
13. Hunt, P., Konar, M., Junqueira, F.P., Reed, B.: {ZooKeeper}: Wait-free coordination for internet-scale systems. In: USENIX Annual Technical Conference (2010)

14. Corbett, J.C., et al.: Spanner: Google's globally distributed database. In: The 10th Symposium on Operating Systems Design and Implementation (2012)
15. Lamport, L.: The part-time parliament. ACM Trans. Comput. Syst. **16**(2), 133–169 (1998)
16. Li, C., Qiu, W., Li, X., Liu, C., Zheng, Z.: A dynamic adaptive framework for practical byzantine fault tolerance consensus protocol in the internet of things. IEEE Trans. Comput. **73**(7), 1669–1682 (2024)
17. Li, J., Michael, E., Sharma, N.K., Szekeres, A., Ports, D.R.: Just say {NO} to paxos overhead: Replacing consensus with network ordering. In: Symposium on Operating Systems Design and Implementation, pp. 467–483. USENIX (2016)
18. Liu, X., Yu, W.: A review of research on blockchain consensus mechanisms and algorithms. In: International Conference on Intelligent Informatics and Biomedical Sciences, vol. 9, pp. 1–10 (2024)
19. Ongaro, D., Ousterhout, J.: In search of an understandable consensus algorithm. In: USENIX annual technical conference (USENIX ATC 14), pp. 305–319 (2014)
20. Saramago, R.Q., Alchieri, E.A., Rezende, T.F., Camargos, L.: On the impossibility of byzantine collision-fast atomic broadcast. In: International Conference on Advanced Information Networking and Applications, pp. 414–421. IEEE (2018)
21. Schneider, F.B.: Implementing fault-tolerant services using the state machine approach: a tutorial. ACM Comput. Surv. **22**(4), 299–319 (1990)
22. Singh, A.: A survey and taxonomy of consensus protocols for blockchains. J. Syst. Architect. **127**, 102503 (2022)
23. Sun, G., Jiang, M., Khooi, X.Z., Li, Y., Li, J.: NeoBFT: accelerating byzantine fault tolerance using authenticated in-network ordering. In: ACM Special Interest Group on Data Communications Conference, pp. 239–254. ACM, New York, NY, USA (2023)
24. Vassantlal, R., Alchieri, E., Ferreira, B., Bessani, A.: Cobra: dynamic proactive secret sharing for confidential BFT services. In: Symposium on Security and Privacy, pp. 1335–1353. IEEE (2022)
25. Venâncio, G., Fulber-Garcia, V., Flauzino, J., Alchieri, E.A., Duarte, E.P.: Dependable virtual network services: an architecture for fault-and intrusion-tolerant SFCS. In: Conference on NFV and SDN, pp. 1–6. IEEE (2024)
26. Venâncio, G., Turchetti, R.C., Camargo, E.T., Duarte Jr, E.P.: Vnf-consensus: a virtual network function for maintaining a consistent distributed software-defined network control plane. Int. J. Netw. Manag. **31**(3) (2021)
27. Venâncio, G., Turchetti, R.C., Duarte, E.P.: Nfv-rbcast: enabling the network to offer reliable and ordered broadcast services. In: The 9th Latin-American Symposium on Dependable Computing, pp. 1–10. IEEE (2019)
28. Venâncio, G., Turchetti, R.C., Duarte, E.P., Jr.: NFV-coin: unleashing the power of in-network computing with virtualization technologies. J. Internet Serv. Appl. **13**(1), 46–53 (2022)
29. Veronese, G.S., Correia, M., Bessani, A.N., Lung, L.C., Verissimo, P.: Efficient byzantine fault-tolerance. IEEE Trans. Comput. **62**(1), 16–30 (2013)
30. Vukolić, M.: The quest for scalable blockchain fabric: Proof-of-work vs. BFT replication. In: IFIP WG 11.4 International Workshop Open Problems in Network Security, pp. 112–125. Springer (2015)
31. White, B., et al.: An integrated experimental environment for distributed systems and networks. ACM SIGOPS Operating Syst. Rev. **36**(SI), 255–270 (2002)
32. Zou, Y., et al.: A survey of fault tolerant consensus in wireless networks. High-Confidence Comput. **4**(2) (2024)

Thetacrypt: A Distributed Service for Threshold Cryptography

Mariarosaria Barbaraci[1(✉)] [iD], Michael Senn[1] [iD], Noah Schmid[1,2] [iD], Orestis Alpos[2] [iD], and Christian Cachin[1] [iD]

[1] Institute of Computer Science, University of Bern,
Neubrückstrasse 10, 3012 Bern, Switzerland
{mariarosaria.barbaraci,michael.senn,christian.cachin}@unibe.ch
[2] Common Prefix, Bern, Switzerland

Abstract. Threshold cryptography is a powerful and well-known technique with applications to systems relying on distributed trust. It has recently also emerged as a solution to challenges in blockchains: frontrunning prevention, managing wallet keys, and generating randomness. This work presents *Thetacrypt*, a middleware component that enables distributed applications to access a variety of threshold schemes via a unified, implementation-agnostic interface. The architecture of Thetacrypt natively supports non-interactive as well as interactive protocols, currently including six cryptographic schemes that span ciphers, signatures, and randomness generation. Additionally, it contains flexible adapters to an underlying networking layer compatible with peer-to-peer communication and a total-order broadcast channel.

Thetacrypt serves as a controlled testbed for evaluating the performance of multiple threshold-cryptographic schemes under consistent conditions, showing how the traditional microbenchmarking approach neglects the distributed nature of the protocols and their relevance when considering the performance of real deployed systems.

Keywords: Middleware · Fault Tolerance · Distributed Cryptography

1 Introduction

Distributing cryptographic capabilities within a group of nodes is a well-known technique in resilient systems that goes back to the 1990 s [15]. Based on *secret sharing*, the field of *threshold cryptography* addresses public-key cryptosystems in which only the collaboration of sufficiently many nodes may produce the cryptographic result. Private keys are protected from leaking to a minority of corrupted nodes, even if they collude. Threshold cryptography is an essential and promising technology for securing distributed systems against misbehaving, i.e. Byzantine, nodes, especially in the recent era of blockchain. This renewed interest in threshold cryptography is also reflected in an ongoing standardization effort by NIST [33].

L. A. Rodrigues and R. Oliveira (Eds.): LADC 2025, CCIS 2697, pp. 163–180, 2026.
https://doi.org/10.1007/978-3-032-11539-3_10

The tension between (static) cryptographic schemes and (dynamic) distributed algorithms makes threshold cryptography inherently complex to build. We believe that this has hampered its widespread deployment so far. Implementing cryptographic primitives is challenging because a minor mistake may compromise the security of an entire solution built on the implementation. Thus, it is common to standardize cryptographic libraries and to use them in a modular way across many applications; OpenSSL is the most prominent example. Vulnerabilities originating from custom implementations are reduced, optimizations within a common library (e.g., eliminating side-channel leakage and using hardware instructions) benefit many applications, and the scrutiny placed on a reusable codebase is amortized across many uses.

Implementing distributed cryptography poses the same technical challenges as implementing ordinary cryptosystems, but with the additional concern of handling the communication among nodes in a distributed network.

Several widely used platforms that integrate threshold cryptosystems with a distributed network have recently emerged, such as the Internet Computer [9] developed by DFINITY [16], which provides a blockchain-like public computing infrastructure, DRAND [18], a distributed randomness beacon that produces verifiable and unbiased randomness used by many secure services on the internet, or Partisia Blockchain [34], which provides private computation as a service using threshold cryptography. Distributed cryptography is also a prominent method to manage the private keys of cryptocurrency wallets in a resilient way [17,31].

However, all these solutions realize threshold cryptosystems *within* their platforms and only for their target applications. Therefore, such cryptographic implementations are specific to the needs of particular deployments and domains. They cannot easily be decoupled from the underlying communication tools, but a network transport is necessary in distributed cryptography.

To remedy this situation, this work shows how to make threshold cryptography modular and how to simplify its deployment. Our goal is to decouple distributed cryptography from particular applications, such that it can easily be composed with and integrated into diverse distributed protocols. These days, blockchain platforms offer significant communication, coordination, and synchronization capabilities, which threshold-cryptographic implementations may rely on for communication. This allows us to focus only on the implementation of the cryptographic schemes. Several research questions arise in this context:

- How does one structure a common framework that encompasses multiple types of distributed cryptosystems, such as signatures, encryption, and randomness generation?
- How can threshold cryptography be integrated with a diverse set of distributed protocols in a modular way?
- What are the precise assumptions on the communication primitives, and which are the interfaces for connecting to existing distributed platforms?

We answer these questions with *Thetacrypt*, a distributed service for threshold cryptography. It contains implementations of the most prominent distributed cryptographic schemes and organizes them into a hierarchy according to their types. Moreover, Thetacrypt's modular design allows easy integration of the threshold-cryptographic algorithms with diverse distributed applications. Since Thetacrypt does not depend on a particular networking infrastructure, it may be incorporated into existing platforms which already provide means of communication. In this way, threshold cryptography becomes a separate component in distributed applications: it improves overall security and offers higher flexibility for application developers. To our knowledge, Thetacrypt is the first system to treat threshold cryptography as a modular component that can be integrated flexibly with multiple applications.

Additionally, we use our design as a common testbed to compare implemented schemes and evaluate them under different deployment scenarios. We study how the system's performance varies with the number of nodes, network configuration, and cryptographic characteristics, providing valuable insights for protocol selection and future design. Furthermore, we introduce metrics to quantify performance imbalances among nodes and analyze their impact on the overall system. Unlike conventional microbenchmarking of individual cryptographic primitives, this broader evaluation highlights how important it is to assess threshold cryptographic protocols in realistic conditions to accurately estimate their effectiveness in practice.

We briefly mention directly relevant recent work. F3B [44] extends blockchains with threshold encryption to protect against front-running, using separate consensus and decryption committees specific to Ethereum. The Internet Computer [9] and Aptos [43] integrate threshold cryptography for secure randomness and other services, but closely couple these methods to their platforms. Other work leverages blockchains as coordination layers. Ferveo [5], for example, proposes a DKG protocol relying on BFT-based synchronization to enable threshold encryption. Finally, recent benchmarks [40] compare threshold-cryptographic libraries for BFT replication, highlighting the impact of environment and network on real-world performance.

The rest of the paper is structured as follows: Sect. 2 reviews threshold cryptography. Section 3 summarizes current approaches and describes the architecture of Thetacrypt; including details of the implemented protocols and schemes. In Sect. 4, we evaluate the performance of the service with varying numbers of nodes and different deployments. Finally, Sect. 5 concludes the paper. More details, especially on the architecture, evaluation and integration with BFT-SMaRT, appear in the full version [4].

2   Background

2.1   Fault-Tolerant Distributed Systems

Fault tolerance refers to the ability of a system to remain operational even in the presence of faulty components; it is often implemented through replication across a diverse set of *nodes* or *parties* that comprise the system. This work considers the *Byzantine* [30] fault model, where a fraction of the nodes may behave maliciously, and therefore aims at achieving *Byzantine Fault Tolerance (BFT)*.

Today BFT protocols are widely used in blockchain. The nodes maintaining a blockchain produce the chain together and must agree on the order of transactions. To do so, they run a consensus protocol for every new block, implementing total-order broadcast (TOB) [38]. The operational model varies according to the assumptions on the network delay and the fraction of Byzantine nodes, which results in different blockchain constructions [21].

2.2 Threshold Cryptography

When applied to cryptosystems, fault tolerance means that control over a cryptographic system is distributed among many parties, such that the confidentiality and integrity of the service remains intact despite failure or misbehavior of a subset of the parties. In other words, a set of n parties must collaborate and compute a cryptographic operation based on a private key together. A sufficient number or *threshold* of them, specifically $(t + 1)$ or more among the n parties, are needed to carry out an operation successfully. On the other hand, any t or fewer parties must not learn anything about the private key. Such schemes are based on *secret sharing* techniques and are known as *threshold cryptography* [15]. A threshold cryptosystem ideally produces the same cryptographic outputs or consumes the same inputs as the corresponding centralized system. Threshold cryptography is an active area of research and industrial development, and the Multi-Party Threshold Cryptography project of NIST is currently standardizing threshold-cryptographic protocols [33].

Initial distribution of the private key to the parties can be done by a centralized, trusted dealer using secret sharing or through a distributed key-generation protocol [24,35], run by the parties themselves. The latter is more secure but arguably more complex.

Communication requirements differ as well: *Non-interactive* protocols [3,7, 8,41,42] require one round of communication, allowing asynchronous execution, while *interactive* protocols [10,22,29,37] require multiple rounds, demanding a certain level of coordination.

In Thetacrypt the three most relevant kinds of threshold cryptographic schemes are implemented: *Threshold ciphers* [3,42] are public-key encryption schemes with a distributed decryption algorithm: only a group of sufficiently many parties can decrypt a ciphertext. *Threshold signatures* [7,22,23,29,41] are public-key digital signature schemes, in which the signing algorithm is distributed. Any large enough group of parties can jointly create a valid signature, while a strictly smaller group cannot. Such protocols are *robust* if they produce the correct output in spite of misbehaving parties. Finally, *distributed randomness* is obtained through threshold-random functions producing cryptographically secure *pseudorandom* values based on a shared secret held by the parties. Any group smaller than the threshold cannot distinguish such outputs from truly random values. Many schemes belong to this large category: coin-tossing schemes [8], distributed verifiable random functions (DVRFs) [19], and, more generally, distributed randomness beacons (DRBs) [10,11,14].

3 Thetacrypt

3.1 Motivation

The widespread adoption of distributed systems has renewed interest in practical deployments of threshold cryptography. As an example, e-voting systems use threshold ciphers to ensure confidentiality of the voting process, even if individual parts of the system are compromised [26,28]. Trustworthy, i.e., reliable, non-predictable, and unbiased *randomness* is a key ingredient in many distributed systems (e.g., for consensus) and applications (e.g., for games). The Internet Computer [9], for instance, uses distributed threshold-cryptographic randomness for its consensus [8]. In high-security contexts, *key management* often involves multi-factor control, sometimes managed with hardware-security modules (HSMs), as for the DNSSEC root-zone key-signing key [27]. Threshold cryptography enables this in software. Recently, commercial solutions have deployed threshold cryptography for managing cryptocurrency wallets [17,31]. Lastly, in blockchain, threshold ciphers can serve to prevent *front-running*, where advance knowledge of future transactions can otherwise be used for personal gain [13].

Developers generally want to rely on reliable and robust cryptographic libraries and, from there, develop more complex protocols. This allows to amortize the cost of writing cryptographic code across multiple client applications. Threshold cryptography introduces the additional requirement of communication between participating parties. It comes in a wide variety of forms and rely on diverse communication assumptions, leading to ad hoc implementations. Although many deployments share the common requirement that all parties obtain a consistent view of messages, the communication layers and protocols are typically specific to each platform. If common interfaces for the cryptographic schemes and modular assumptions about the communication platforms were available, a unified view on threshold cryptographic schemes could emerge, accelerating the adoption of this promising technology.

Thetacrypt provides a comprehensive solution that facilitates easy and modular implementation of threshold schemes, designed to be composable with a wide range of distributed platforms. It aims to be compatible with different network and adversarial models, depending on the guarantees offered by the underlying platform. Thetacrypt is an open-source Rust project (https://github.com/cryptobern/thetacrypt) containing circa 19000 LoC.

3.2 Model

Thetacrypt operates as a distributed service on a set of *nodes* connected via a network. The network is assumed to provide reliable communication between any two nodes, and to optionally offer access to a total-order broadcast channel. No assumptions are made on the network delay. Each node runs a stateful *Thetacrypt instance* in a dedicated process. Applications invoke the service at one node through a *remote procedure call (RPC)* in a *client-server* interaction.

The intended deployment is in conjunction with a distributed application which accesses Thetacrypt. A possible setup consists of a replicated service with as many nodes as there are Thetacrypt nodes (1:1 mapping) and with a compatible failure assumption. For instance, one service node may be grouped together with a Thetacrypt node into the same security domain or hosted on the same physical machine. In this way, n physical nodes can host a service node and a Thetacrypt node each, and up to t of the physical nodes may fail or be corrupted. Every node of the service then issues requests to its local Thetacrypt instance.

3.3   Architecture

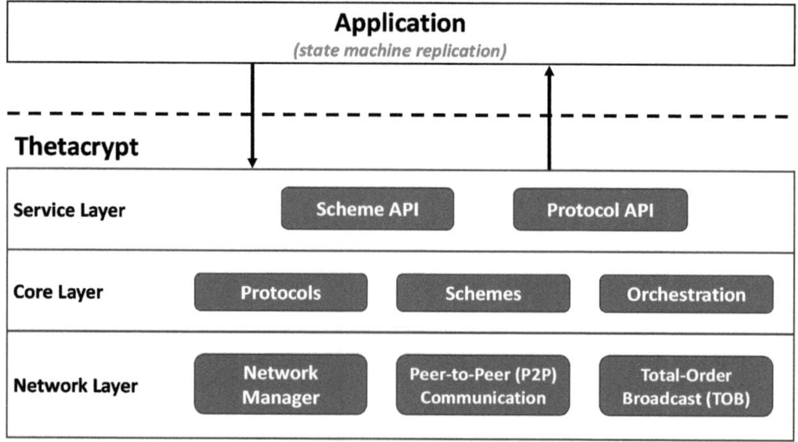

Fig. 1. Thetacrypt's layered architecture

Thetacrypt consist of three layers, as shown in Fig. 1.

Service Layer. The *service layer* exposes two RPC endpoints to an application that integrates threshold cryptographic capabilities. The *protocol API* translates between the public API and the internal protocols implemented in the core layer. The *scheme API* allows the application to access the cryptographic primitives of the *schemes module* directly, for applications that require low-level access to cryptographic operations. The service layer is implemented as a set of gRPC services [12], leveraging Protocol Buffers [25] for serialization.

Core Layer. The *core layer* connects the cryptographic primitives, protocol logic, and the management code used to handle key material and execution. This level distinguishes between local cryptographic operations and inter-node communication required by the distributed nature of threshold schemes. Of these, the *protocols module* is responsible for the overall execution and the *schemes module* is responsible for the cryptographic details. Lastly, the *orchestration module* is responsible for the concurrent execution of multiple protocol instances.

Protocols. We designed the *Threshold Round Interface (TRI)* to abstract common elements of threshold cryptographic protocols, and integrate them into a common architecture. The TRI handles the progression of round-based protocols, the finalization of the cryptographic results, local computations, and steps in response to network messages. We refer to a *round* as the local computation performed by one party in response to receiving a message, until the party produces a result or sends a message itself. We briefly present the functions of the threshold round interface.

- A function *do_round()* triggers the protocol's local computation during a round. It produces a *protocol message* which is forwarded to other parties through the network. Each message is either transported to specific parties using P2P, or broadcast to all using TOB.
- Upon receiving a message from the network, *update(message)* is called. It allows a party to update its local state, and check any conditions for termination, or progression to a future round. Based on this, the protocol either terminates, moves on to a new round, or waits for further messages.
- The function *is_ready_to_finalize()* defines the termination conditions. If satisfied, the protocol finalizes the computation.
- The function *is_ready_for_next_round()* defines the condition for progression to the next round. This may e.g. check if a certain threshold of valid messages has been received from other parties. If satisfied, the protocol advances to the next round, executing the *do_round()* function again.
- The function *finalize()* locally computes the result of the threshold operation and returns it to the management code of the orchestration module.

Each implementation of a protocol needs to provide this state-machine logic, thereby defining when to transition through phases, how to react to input from the network, and how to locally compute the final result.

Schemes. The *schemes module* performs all cryptographic calculations for the implemented threshold schemes. Implemented schemes are chosen based on their longstanding importance in literature, and their formal security proofs. Table 1 provides an overview of the implemented schemes, while a brief description of each, focusing on key characteristics and implementation details, is provided below.

SG02: A non-interactive threshold cryptosystem proposed by,Shoup and Gennaro [42]. Our implementation is based on the TDH2 [42]construction: an ElGamal-based [20] scheme with zero-knowledge proofs (ZKP) of language membership to ensure security in the threshold setting. We apply a hybrid approach [1,2] to encrypt a symmetric key under the threshold key and the actual

Table 1. Threshold schemes in Thetacrypt

Cryptographic scheme	Reference	Hardness	Verification strategy
Signature	SH00 [41]	RSA	ZKP
Signature	KG20 [29]	DL	ZKP
Signature	BLS04 [7]	DL	Pairings
Cipher	SG02 [42]	DL	ZKP
Cipher	BZ03 [3]	DL	Pairings
Randomness	CKS05 [8]	DL	ZKP

plaintext under the symmetric key. As a symmetric encryption scheme, we use ChaCha20Poly1305, a stream cipher with an integrated MAC.

BZ03: The scheme by Baek and Zheng [3] shares the properties of SG02, but is based on groups that satisfy the Gap Diffie-Hellman problem and requires pairing-friendly elliptic curves. This allows for an efficient ciphertext verification, without ZKP. The implementation uses the same hybrid approach as SG02.

SH00: The first construction of a non-interactive robust threshold signature scheme based on RSA is presented and analyzed by Shoup [41]. Signing and verification use a ZKP for correctness. Our implementation supports RSA modulus sizes between 512 and 4096 bits.

KG20: The signature scheme introduced by Komlo and Goldberg [29] (FROST) provides an optimized protocol for threshold Schnorr signatures [39]. Due to its randomized nature, the signing algorithm is an interactive protocol: the parties first jointly calculate a random nonce (first round) and then sign (second round). An optional precomputation phase allows amortization of these nonce computations over many signatures, which is optionally supported by our implementation.

Incidentally, FROST is not robust, i.e., actively deviating parties may cause the signature protocol to abort.

BLS04: The signature scheme proposed by Boneh *et al.* [7] provides short signatures compared with RSA and DSA with approximately the same level of security. The scheme uses bilinear pairings, to provide an efficient and deterministic verification algorithm.

CKS05: The coin-tossing scheme of Cachin *et al.* [8] produces pseudorandom bit strings. Essentially, the scheme is a distributed function mapping an input string to a coin value. The paper proposes two constructions, one from any distributed threshold signature scheme with unique signatures (such as the RSA-based SH00), and the other based on the Diffie-Hellman problem. Every share of a coin comes with a ZKP for validity, to ensure its correctness.

For elliptic-curve arithmetic we use MIRACL Core, a multi-language and architecturally agnostic cryptographic library [32].

Orchestration. The *orchestration module* provides an execution engine that manages multiple protocol instances, tracks related states, and schedules messages to and from the network. Its main component, the *instance manager*, initializes and keeps track of *protocol instances*. For each new instance it invokes a *protocol executor*, a state machine that manages the progress of the protocol leveraging the TRI interface as described above. The protocol executor is also responsible for providing the protocol with access to key material.

Network Layer. The *network manager module* initializes the required communication channels at startup. By default it provides peer-to-peer (P2P) communication with the option for end-to-end authentication. It can also be configured to additionally provide a total-order broadcast channel, which is needed by some multi-round schemes.

For modularity, the manager offers two interfaces: the *P2P interface* and the *TOB interface*. Specific implementations of these are either fully-fledged network modules, or proxy modules which wrap existing communication channels of a specific deployment.

In our implementation, there is a *P2P component* implementing a gossip protocol via libp2p [36]. Additionally, we develop two proxy modules, a *P2P proxy module* and a *TOB proxy module*, to integrate with communication channels of existing replicated services. Both proxy modules utilize gRPC to define their interfaces.

4   Evaluation

4.1   Experimental Configuration

System Setup. The setup contains firstly an orchestrator node, hosting a monitoring service and benchmarking client for invoking requests. This node runs on a VM with 16 GiB of RAM and 4 vCPU @ 2.2 GHz. Secondly there is a network of nodes hosting the Thetacrypt service, which we will refer to as the Θ-network, each of which runs on a virtual machine with 8 GiB of RAM and 2 vCPU @ 2.2 GHz. The benchmarking client on the orchestration node schedules requests to the Θ-network according to the experiment parameters, and collects data and monitors the state of the network. The Thetacrypt instances on the network run encapsulated in Docker containers, each limited to 1 vCPU and 6 GiB of RAM to limit interference of other services running on each node.

Parameters. To measure the performance of Thetacrypt in relevant real-world configurations, we consider the following parameters: the geographical distribution of the nodes, the number of nodes composing the Θ-network, the request rate (load), and the request payload size. We distinguish between a *local* and a *global* deployment. In the first, nodes reside in the same data center (FRA1), while in the second, they span different geographical regions (FRA1, SYD1, TOR1, SFO3) of a major cloud provider. Moreover, we choose three deployment sizes based on NIST's *threshold profiles* [33]: a *small* deployment with 7 nodes tolerating 2 faults (DO-7-L/G); a *medium* deployment using 31 nodes, with up to 10 faults (DO-31-L/G), and lastly, a *large* deployment of 127 nodes and at most 42 faults (DO-127-L/G). The value of the threshold follows from the usual BFT assumption that fewer than one-third of nodes are faulty for $(t+1)$-out-of-n schemes with $n = 3t + 1$.

Metrics. *Server-side latency* is the time taken by the Θ-network to process a request, from when a server receives the request to when it generates the final result, i.e. aggregating $t + 1$ shares, to return to the client. Consequently, it is bounded below by the network latency between nodes times the number of round trips required by the protocol. It differs from client-side latency in that it excludes one additional round-trip. We denote by $\mathcal{L}_k$ the value of the k-th percentile of the latency distribution across the requests processed by the whole Θ-network. When required, we specify the latency metric further: at the node level ($\mathcal{L}_k^{\mathrm{node}}$) and the network level ($\mathcal{L}_k^{\mathrm{net}}$).

Consequentially, we define the *threshold latency* ($\mathcal{L}_\theta^{\mathrm{net}}$) as the θ-th percentile of the latency distribution across nodes. Here, θ is calculated as $\theta = \frac{t+1}{n} \cdot 100$, where t is the threshold parameter of the scheme under test and n is the size of the network. This metric indicates how quickly the Θ-network can produce the final result. Notably, the gap between $\mathcal{L}_{95}^{\mathrm{net}}$ and $\mathcal{L}_\theta^{\mathrm{net}}$ highlights residual delays caused by slower nodes, which continue to affect overall performance even after the primary computation is completed.

As the average latency alone may not capture the full picture, we introduce additional metrics: the *Residual Delay Factor* δ_{res} and the *Latency Fairness Index* η_θ calculated as

$$\delta_{\mathrm{res}} = \frac{\mathcal{L}_{95}^{\mathrm{net}} - \mathcal{L}_\theta^{\mathrm{net}}}{\mathcal{L}_\theta^{\mathrm{net}}} \qquad \text{and} \qquad \eta_\theta = \frac{\mathcal{L}_\theta^{\mathrm{net}}}{\mathcal{L}_{95}^{\mathrm{net}}}.$$

The *Residual Delay Factor* quantifies the extent to which slow nodes influence $\mathcal{L}_{95}^{\mathrm{net}}$. Given that $\mathcal{L}_{95}^{\mathrm{net}} \geq \mathcal{L}_\theta^{\mathrm{net}}$, the value δ_{res} is in $\mathbb{R}^{\geq 0}$, therefore, the following interpretation: for values of δ_{res} approaching 1, the residual delay introduced by slow nodes has a small impact on the system's performance. In this range, the overhead remains within twice $\mathcal{L}_\theta^{\mathrm{net}}$, representing a tolerable shift equivalent to a single processing unit in the protocol's operation. Conversely, as δ_{res} gets much larger, the impact of slow nodes becomes significant, creating considerable delays and potentially degrading system responsiveness in approaching full load. The *Latency Fairness Index* evaluates how evenly the load is distributed among nodes based on their contribution to latency. The index reflects how closely the performance of the $(t + 1)$-quorum of fastest nodes lies relative to 95% of the nodes; it ranges from 0 to 1. Values of $\eta_\theta \in [0.5, 1]$ indicate a fair balance across the nodes, values close to 1 suggest that most nodes perform similarly, whereas values around 0.5 suggest an imbalance within a factor two. Values much lower than 0.5 indicate significant imbalance, where a subset of fast nodes dominates the protocol and leaves many slower nodes lagging behind. This effect may lead to bottlenecks, reduced throughput, or even vulnerabilities in protocol operation. It is worth noting that the two metrics, δ_{res} and η_θ, are inversely related. As δ_{res} increases, indicating a greater impact of slow nodes on system performance, η_θ decreases, reflecting a worsening balance between the nodes' contribution to the protocol. Conversely, a small δ_{res} suggests minimal impact of the slow nodes, and the fairness index η_θ grows accordingly, indicating a more balanced contribution from all nodes in the network.

Throughput. denotes the number of requests processed by the system per time unit and measures the system's capacity. We estimate the throughput as the ratio between the number of requests processed by the Θ-network and the elapsed time between the first and last correctly processed request. If processing extends beyond the experiment's duration, a grace period of up to 10% is considered. Conversely, when the load is high, and requests remain unprocessed, the total experiment duration is used as the time unit to ensure consistency in the metric.

Methodology. The Θ-network is restarted before each experiment to ensure a clean state. Test configurations include key lengths of 256 bit (2048 bit for RSA), communication rounds (2 rounds just for KG20) and elliptic curves, plain (Ed25519) and pairing-friendly (Bn254). We assume a setup phase with a trusted dealer distributing key material. Every evaluated threshold protocol performs both a share verification, to ensure the correctness of the shares, and a result verification upon assembly, to ensure the correctness of the final output. In ciphers, this also includes ciphertext verification of the underlying symmetric encryption scheme. Firstly, we conduct a *capacity test* of the system by increasing the request rate until the system reaches saturation, starts to degrade in latency, or exhibits failures. Every experiment lasts one minute. The goal is to identify the maximum sustainable throughput, or *usable capacity*, the system can handle without significant performance degradation. The *knee capacity* is estimated as the request rate at which the ratio of throughput to latency is maximized, marking the optimal efficiency point. The range between the knee and usable capacity defines the system's operating region, where it performs reliably under load. Here, we consider latency as the $\mathcal{L}_{95}$ value across all requests processed. Secondly, we choose the medium-scale global deployment (DO-31-G) to conduct longer experiments of five minutes, to verify that the system can handle a steady-state load over a longer period. Here, we evaluate the Θ-network performance closely, focusing on $\mathcal{L}_{50}^{\text{net}}$, $\mathcal{L}_{\theta}^{\text{net}}$, and $\mathcal{L}_{95}^{\text{net}}$, and the derived metrics ($\delta_{\text{res}}, \eta_\theta$).

4.2   Results

Capacity test. We present representative throughput-latency graphs for global deployments (Fig. 2, 3, 4), with the full analysis available in the complete version [4]. The results show that, for a given deployment size, while geographical distribution increases latency due to network delays, throughput remains largely the same, as it is governed by computational power.

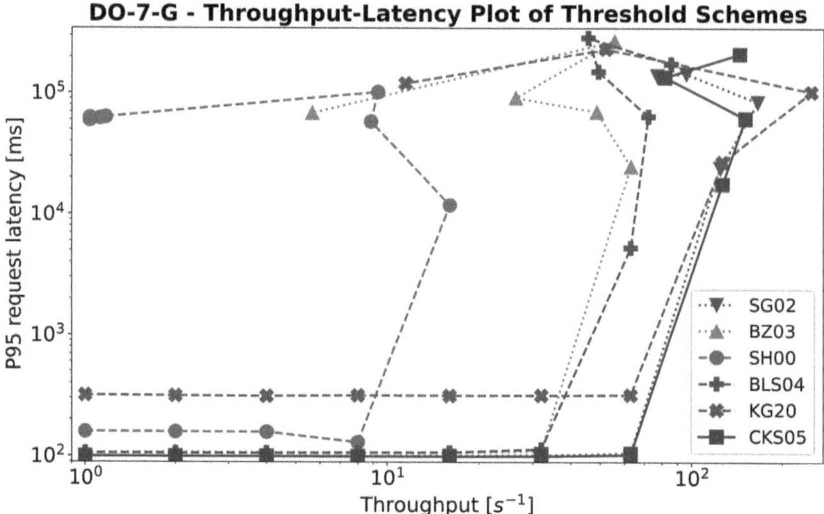

Fig. 2. Server-side Throughput-Latency graphs for DO-7-G

For each data series corresponding to a certain load and scheme, we consider $\mathcal{L}_{95}$ as function of the throughput estimated as described in Sect. 4.1. Observing the graphs, we quickly identify the *knee point* as the last point before latency increases non-linearly due to resource contention. The rightmost value of the graph, in contrast, indicates the maximum throughput that the system can handle before degrading. Latency values range from a lower bound imposed by network latency to an upper bound due to the experiment time ($\approx 60s$), as we calculate latency solely for completed requests.

The measurements show that the category of a scheme (i.e., cipher, signature, randomness) is less relevant than the underlying cryptographic assumption. Therefore, we compare schemes based on the assumptions they rely on: SG02, KG20 and CKS05 are based on the Diffie-Hellman assumption over elliptic curves (ECDH), BLS04 and BZ03 rely on pairings, finally SH00 is based on the RSA assumption. Following this grouping, we expect ECDH to be less computationally intensive than pairings, and RSA to be the most computationally intensive. The second dimension to consider is communication complexity.

We look at the crucial role of the *deployment size*. In Fig. 2, deployment DO-7-G shows pronounced differences among the schemes. Schemes relying on ECDH perform better than the those which rely on pairings. Notably, KG20, despite requiring two rounds of communication, achieves faster performance than SH00, which involves computationally heavy RSA signature operations. Thus, for small deployments, differences in local cryptographic computation are impactful, dominating even the communication overhead introduced by an additional round. Regarding knee point values, the DH-based schemes reach their knee point at 64 req/s, pairing-based at 32 req/s, and the RSA-based one at 8

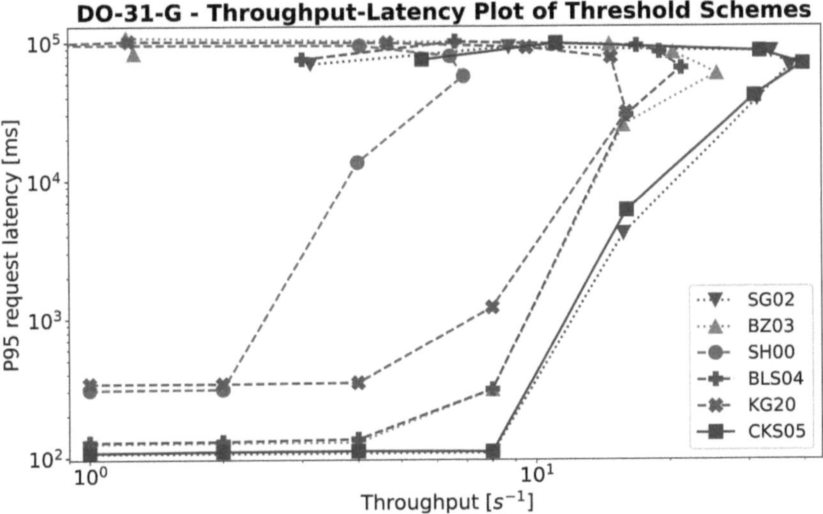

Fig. 3. Server-side Throughput-Latency graphs for DO-31-G

req/s. In DO-31-G (Fig. 3), performance differences between the schemes become less pronounced due to the increasing number of nodes, which directly affects the threshold parameter and, consequently, the overall latency. For all the non-interactive schemes except SH00, the knee point is reduced by a factor of 4 e.g., decreasing from 64 req/s to 16 req/s for SG02. SH00 here reaches the knee point at 4 req/s. As opposed to the previous case, KG20 reaches the knee point already at 8 req/s, revealing the impact of the second communication round as the deployment size scales. In DO-127-G(Fig. 4), differences between schemes are small, as system performance becomes mostly determined by the number of nodes and the network latency among them. The knee point drops further to 2 req/s for all schemes, except for SH00 and KG20, which reach it at 1 req/s.

In summary, the system performance depends on cryptographic assumptions and number of nodes. The former dominates in small deployments, while the latter does so in larger ones. The relative order of the non-interactive schemes remains consistent: ECDH-based schemes outperform pairing-based schemes, and RSA-based schemes are consistently the slowest. KG20 benefits from its mathematical assumption (ECDH) in small deployments but suffers due to its second communication round as deployment size increases.

Steady-State Analysis. We next conduct a five-minutes-long experiment in a steady state using the DO-31-G deployment, studying the latency distribution among the nodes (Fig. 5). We run this experiment under a load that corresponds to the knee capacity identified earlier. Table 2 summarizes the computed knee capacities for each scheme in DO-31-G, together with the newly introduced latency metrics. We evaluate latency differences across nodes, and the impact of the threshold parameter on the system's performance. We use $\mathcal{L}_\theta^{\mathrm{net}}$ to esti-

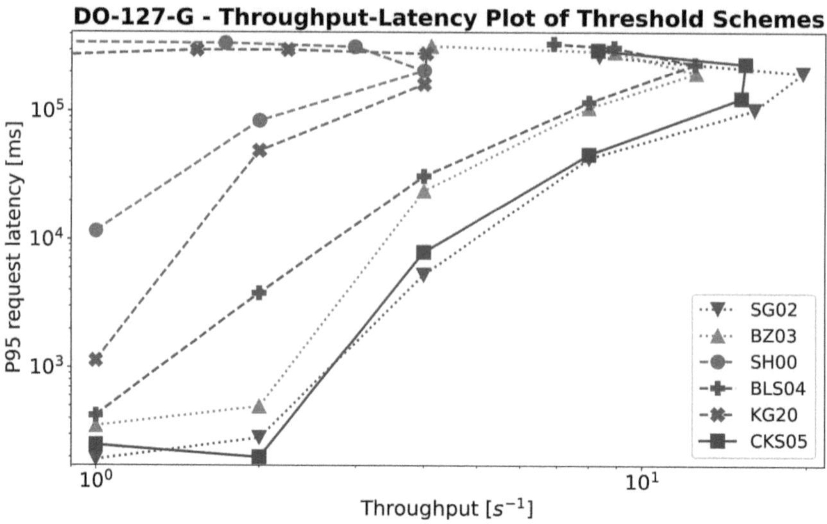

Fig. 4. Server-side Throughput-Latency graphs for DO-127-G

mate the overall request processing time, specifically when $(t+1)$-out-of-n nodes have completed the computation. As shown in Fig. 5, schemes where the local computations are more expensive exhibit higher values. The clearly visible gap increase from $\mathcal{L}_\theta^{\mathrm{net}}$ to $\mathcal{L}_{95}^{\mathrm{net}}$, on the other hand, reflects how long slow nodes continue to impact the Θ-network with residual messages from an already processed request. The numerical results in terms of δ_{res} and η_θ are shown in Table 2.

Table 2. Performance summary, using DO-31-G

Scheme	Knee Capacity	δ_{res}	η_θ
SG02	8 req/s	2.76	0.26
BZ03	4 req/s	1.07	0.48
SH00	2 req/s	0.98	0.50
BLS04	4 req/s	0.95	0.51
KG20	4 req/s	0.26	0.79
CKS05	8 req/s	3.28	0.23

This gap is highest for the non-interactive DH-based schemes and lower for pairing-based ones. If, on one side, the small $\mathcal{L}_\theta^{\mathrm{net}}$ reflect fast completion of the computation, the high δ_{res} values indicate that the network is affected by the slow nodes. The RSA-based schemes exhibit roughly the same gap as pairing-based schemes, indicating a reasonable balance between the local computation and the communication overhead. This is also reflected in their η_θ values around 0.5.

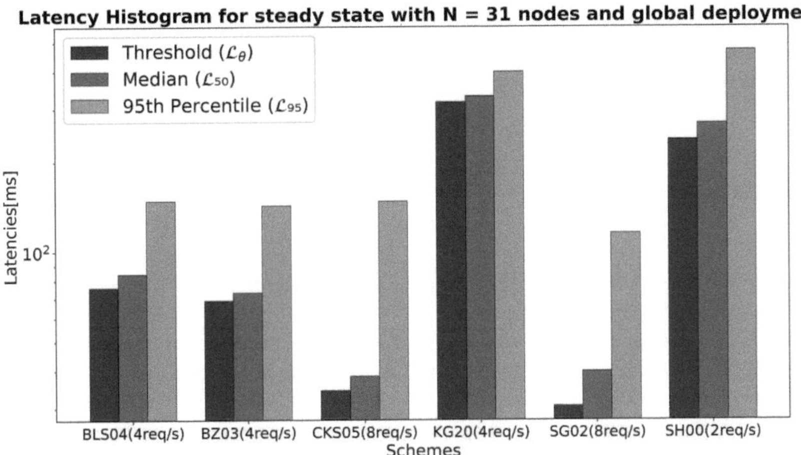

Fig. 5. Comparison of latencies($\mathcal{L}_\theta$, $\mathcal{L}_{50}$, $\mathcal{L}_{95}$)

KG20, on the other hand, presents the smallest gap ($\delta_{res} \approx 0.26$). We suspect the reason for this is the second round of communication, as well as the fixed signing group requirement, i.e., the protocol waits for the contributions of all nodes in the predefined group to complete. This is further supported by the index η_θ, which shows that the protocol is not skewed by the threshold.

4.3   Integration

We demonstrate how to integrate Thetacrypt with a replicated state-machine library, BFT-SMaRt [6], and let its applications perform threshold-cryptographic operations. Our integration has added roughly 900 new LoC to BFT-SMaRt for integrating the distributed cryptography and in total approximately 1600 LoC when also considering the code for benchmarking.

Preliminary results show that integration of threshold cryptographic operations into a replicated service can be done with a reasonable increase in latency, i.e., the added latency matches the time taken by the distributed cryptographic operations in isolation. We refer to the full version for a complete analysis.

5   Conclusion

By introducing Thetacrypt, we answer the challenge posed by the proliferation of multiple threshold-cryptographic implementations tied to proprietary communication platforms. Thetacrypt proposes a generic and modular framework for integrating distributed cryptography with replicated fault-tolerant systems, such as BFT-SMaRt. Additionally, it provides a thorough evaluation that paves the way for future research on the performance of threshold cryptography.

Acknowledgments. We thank Lukas Schacher for his contributions to the project. This work has been supported by a grant from the Interchain Foundation and by a donation from the Ripple University Blockchain Research Initiative (UBRI).

References

1. Abdalla, M., Bellare, M., Rogaway, P.: DHAES: an encryption scheme based on the diffie-hellman problem. IACR Cryptol. ePrint Arch, p. 7 (1999). http://eprint.iacr.org/1999/007

2. Abdalla, M., Bellare, M., Rogaway, P.: The oracle diffie-hellman assumptions and an analysis of DHIES. In: Naccache, D. (ed.) Topics in Cryptology - CT-RSA 2001, The Cryptographer's Track at RSA Conference 2001, San Francisco, CA, USA, April 8-12, 2001, Proceedings. Lecture Notes in Computer Science, vol. 2020, pp. 143–158. Springer (2001). https://doi.org/10.1007/3-540-45353-9_12

3. Baek, J., Zheng, Y.: Simple and efficient threshold cryptosystem from the gap diffie-hellman group. In: Proceedings of the Global Telecommunications Conference, 2003. GLOBECOM '03, San Francisco, CA, USA, 1-5 December 2003, pp. 1491–1495. IEEE (2003). https://doi.org/10.1109/GLOCOM.2003.1258486, https://doi.org/10.1109/GLOCOM.2003.1258486

4. Barbaraci, M., Schmid, N., Alpos, O., Senn, M., Cachin, C.: Thetacrypt: a distributed service for threshold cryptography (2025). https://arxiv.org/abs/2502.03247

5. Bebel, J., Ojha, D.: Ferveo: threshold decryption for mempool privacy in BFT networks. IACR Cryptol. ePrint Arch, p. 898 (2022). https://eprint.iacr.org/2022/898

6. Bessani, A.N., Sousa, J., Alchieri, E.A.P.: State machine replication for the masses with BFT-SMART. In: 44th Annual IEEE/IFIP International Conference on Dependable Systems and Networks, DSN 2014, Atlanta, GA, USA, June 23-26, 2014, pp. 355–362. IEEE Computer Society (2014). https://doi.org/10.1109/DSN.2014.43, https://doi.org/10.1109/DSN.2014.43

7. Boneh, D., Lynn, B., Shacham, H.: Short signatures from the weil pairing. J. Cryptol. **17**(4), 297–319 (2004). https://doi.org/10.1007/S00145-004-0314-9

8. Cachin, C., Kursawe, K., Shoup, V.: Random oracles in constantinople: practical asynchronous byzantine agreement using cryptography. J. Cryptol. **18**(3), 219–246 (2005). https://doi.org/10.1007/s00145-005-0318-0

9. Camenisch, J., et al.: Internet computer consensus. In: Milani, A., Woelfel, P. (eds.) PODC '22: ACM Symposium on Principles of Distributed Computing, Salerno, Italy, July 25 - 29, 2022, pp. 81–91. ACM (2022). https://doi.org/10.1145/3519270.3538430

10. Cascudo, I., David, B.: SCRAPE: scalable randomness attested by public entities. In: Gollmann, D., Miyaji, A., Kikuchi, H. (eds.) Applied Cryptography and Network Security - 15th International Conference, ACNS 2017, Kanazawa, Japan, July 10-12, 2017, Proceedings. Lecture Notes in Computer Science, vol. 10355, pp. 537–556. Springer (2017). https://doi.org/10.1007/978-3-319-61204-1_27

11. Choi, K., Manoj, A., Bonneau, J.: Sok: distributed randomness beacons. In: 44th IEEE Symposium on Security and Privacy, SP 2023, San Francisco, CA, USA, May 21-25, 2023, pp. 75–92. IEEE (2023). https://doi.org/10.1109/SP46215.2023.10179419

12. Cloud native computing foundation: GRPC: a high performance, open source universal RPC framework (2025). https://grpc.io/
13. Daian, P., et al.: Flash boys 2.0: frontrunning in decentralized exchanges, miner extractable value, and consensus instability. In: 2020 IEEE Symposium on Security and Privacy, SP 2020, San Francisco, CA, USA, May 18-21, 2020, pp. 910–927. IEEE (2020). https://doi.org/10.1109/SP40000.2020.00040, https://doi.org/10.1109/SP40000.2020.00040
14. Das, S., Krishnan, V., Isaac, I.M., Ren, L.: Spurt: scalable distributed randomness beacon with transparent setup. In: 43rd IEEE Symposium on Security and Privacy, SP 2022, San Francisco, CA, USA, May 22-26, 2022, pp. 2502–2517. IEEE (2022). https://doi.org/10.1109/SP46214.2022.9833580, https://doi.org/10.1109/SP46214.2022.9833580
15. Desmedt, Y.: Threshold cryptography. Eur. Trans. Telecommun. **5**(4), 449–458 (1994). https://doi.org/10.1002/ETT.4460050407
16. The DFINITY foundation (2025). https://dfinity.org
17. DFNS: Web3 wallets as an API (2025). https://www.dfns.co
18. DRAND: distributed randomness beacon (2025). https://drand.love
19. Galindo, D., Liu, J., Ordean, M., Wong, J.: Fully distributed verifiable random functions and their application to decentralised random beacons. In: IEEE European Symposium on Security and Privacy, EuroS&P 2021, Vienna, Austria, September 6-10, 2021, pp. 88–102. IEEE (2021). https://doi.org/10.1109/EUROSP51992.2021.00017
20. Gamal, T.E.: A public key cryptosystem and a signature scheme based on discrete logarithms. IEEE Trans. Inf. Theory **31**(4), 469–472 (1985).
21. Garay, J., Kiayias, A.: SOK: A Consensus Taxonomy in the Blockchain Era. In: Jarecki, S. (ed.) CT-RSA 2020. LNCS, vol. 12006, pp. 284–318. Springer, Cham (2020). https://doi.org/10.1007/978-3-030-40186-3_13
22. Gennaro, R., Goldfeder, S.: Fast multiparty threshold ECDSA with fast trustless setup. In: Lie, D., Mannan, M., Backes, M., Wang, X. (eds.) Proceedings of the 2018 ACM SIGSAC Conference on Computer and Communications Security, CCS 2018, Toronto, ON, Canada, October 15-19, 2018, pp. 1179–1194. ACM (2018). https://doi.org/10.1145/3243734.3243859, https://doi.org/10.1145/3243734.3243859
23. Gennaro, R., Goldfeder, S., Narayanan, A.: Threshold-Optimal DSA/ECDSA Signatures and an Application to Bitcoin Wallet Security. In: Manulis, M., Sadeghi, A.-R., Schneider, S. (eds.) ACNS 2016. LNCS, vol. 9696, pp. 156–174. Springer, Cham (2016). https://doi.org/10.1007/978-3-319-39555-5_9
24. Gennaro, R., Jarecki, S., Krawczyk, H., Rabin, T.: Secure distributed key generation for discrete-log based cryptosystems. J. Cryptol. **20**(1), 51–83 (2007). https://doi.org/10.1007/S00145-006-0347-3
25. Google: protocol buffers (2025). https://protobuf.dev/
26. Helios: helios voting (2025). https://vote.heliosvoting.org
27. Internet assigned numbers authority (IANA): DNSSEC information: root zone operator information (2025). https://www.iana.org/dnssec
28. Kho, Y., Heng, S., Chin, J.: A review of cryptographic electronic voting. Symmetry **14**(5), 858 (2022). https://doi.org/10.3390/sym14050858
29. Komlo, C., Goldberg, I.: FROST: flexible round-optimized schnorr threshold signatures. In: Dunkelman, O., Jr., M.J.J., O'Flynn, C. (eds.) Selected Areas in Cryptography - SAC 2020 - 27th International Conference, Halifax, NS, Canada (Virtual Event), October 21-23, 2020, Revised Selected Papers. Lecture Notes in Computer Science, vol. 12804, pp. 34–65. Springer (2020). https://doi.org/10.1007/978-3-030-81652-0_2

30. Lamport, L., Shostak, R.E., Pease, M.C.: The byzantine generals problem. ACM Trans. Program. Lang. Syst. **4**(3), 382–401 (1982). https://doi.org/10.1145/357172.357176
31. Lindell, Y.: Digital asset management with MPC (2023). https://www.coinbase.com/blog/digital-asset-management-with-mpc-whitepaper
32. MIRACL: MIRACL core (2024). https://github.com/miracl/core
33. National Institute of Standards and Technology (NIST): multi-party threshold cryptography (MPTC) project. https://csrc.nist.gov/Projects/Threshold-Cryptography/ (2025)
34. Partisia bockchain: prtisia: solving the blockchain trilemma (2023). https://partisiablockchain.com
35. Pedersen, T.P.: A Threshold Cryptosystem without a Trusted Party. In: Davies, D.W. (ed.) EUROCRYPT 1991. LNCS, vol. 547, pp. 522–526. Springer, Heidelberg (1991). https://doi.org/10.1007/3-540-46416-6_47
36. Protocol labs: libp2p: the peer-to-peer network (2024). https://libp2p.io/
37. Ruffing, T., Ronge, V., Jin, E., Schneider-Bensch, J., Schröder, D.: ROAST: robust asynchronous schnorr threshold signatures. In: Yin, H., Stavrou, A., Cremers, C., Shi, E. (eds.) Proceedings of the 2022 ACM SIGSAC Conference on Computer and Communications Security, CCS 2022, Los Angeles, CA, USA, November 7-11, 2022, pp. 2551–2564. ACM (2022). https://doi.org/10.1145/3548606.3560583
38. Schneider, F.B.: Implementing fault-tolerant services using the state machine approach: a tutorial. ACM Comput. Surv. **22**(4), 299–319 (1990). https://doi.org/10.1145/98163.98167
39. Schnorr, C.P.: Efficient signature generation by smart cards. J. Cryptol. **4**(3), 161–174 (1991). https://doi.org/10.1007/BF00196725
40. von Seck, R., Rezabek, F., Carle, G.: Thresh-hold: assessment of threshold cryptography in leader-based consensus. In: 2024 IEEE 49th Conference on Local Computer Networks (LCN), pp. 1–8. IEEE (2024)
41. Shoup, V.: Practical Threshold Signatures. In: Preneel, B. (ed.) EUROCRYPT 2000. LNCS, vol. 1807, pp. 207–220. Springer, Heidelberg (2000). https://doi.org/10.1007/3-540-45539-6_15
42. Shoup, V., Gennaro, R.: Securing threshold cryptosystems against chosen ciphertext attack. J. Cryptol. **15**(2), 75–96 (2002). https://doi.org/10.1007/s00145-001-0020-9
43. Xiang, Z., Das, S., Li, Z., Ma, Z., Spiegelman, A.: The latency price of threshold cryptosystem in blockchains. CoRR **abs/2407.12172** (2024). https://doi.org/10.48550/ARXIV.2407.12172
44. Zhang, H., Merino, L., Qu, Z., Bastankhah, M., Estrada-Galiñanes, V., Ford, B.: F3B: a low-overhead blockchain architecture with per-transaction front-running protection. In: Bonneau, J., Weinberg, S.M. (eds.) 5th Conference on Advances in Financial Technologies, AFT 2023, October 23-25, 2023, Princeton, NJ, USA. LIPIcs, vol. 282, pp. 3:1–3:23. Schloss Dagstuhl - Leibniz-Zentrum für Informatik (2023). https://doi.org/10.4230/LIPICS.AFT.2023.3

Modeling and Dependability Evaluation

A Practical TLA+ Library for Designing and Verifying Distributed Systems

Diogo Canut Freitas Peixoto[✉] and Odorico Machado Mendizabal

Departamento de Informática e Estatística, Universidade Federal de Santa Catarina (UFSC), Florianópolis, Brazil
`diogocanut1@gmail.com, odorico.mendizabal@ufsc.br`

Abstract. Designing distributed systems is complex, presenting challenges like concurrency and fault tolerance that extend beyond understanding business requirements and underlying technologies. Traditional testing often miss unpredictable but critical failures. Alternatively, model checking allows rigorous verification of system properties early in development. This paper aims to combine the rigor of model checking with an easy-to-use approach for the design of distributed systems, where message exchange is ever-present. To address this, we propose a modular TLA+ library for modeling communication primitives over point-to-point and broadcast abstractions. It enables designers to formally describe and verify solutions by providing these primitives as building blocks for communication subsystems. The library includes fault injection for analyzing system behavior under unreliable conditions, such as message loss, duplication, and out-of-order delivery. We formally verified classic atomic broadcast properties for the library's primitives and demonstrated its practical utility by specifying and verifying the Deferred Update Replication Protocol.

Keywords: Model checking · Reliable communication · Atomic broadcast

1 Introduction

Distributed systems serve as the foundational architecture for a wide range of modern applications, including cloud services, transactional systems, large-scale data processing, Blockchains, and the Internet of Things. As the reliance on such systems increases, so do the requirements for dependability, and reliability. However, verifying the correctness of distributed systems, characterized by concurrency, partial failures, and non-determinism, remains a fundamental challenge. Key difficulties include handling unreliable networks, maintaining consistency, achieving coordination, tolerating faults, and meeting performance constraints.

Traditional testing and debugging techniques often fall short in this domain. The highly concurrent and non-deterministic behavior of distributed systems leads to a combinatorial explosion of possible execution paths, and the difficulty of reproducing rare or timing-sensitive faults further complicates verification

L. A. Rodrigues and R. Oliveira (Eds.): LADC 2025, CCIS 2697, pp. 183–200, 2026.
https://doi.org/10.1007/978-3-032-11539-3_11

efforts [7,14]. As a result, systematic verification approaches are essential to ensure correctness beyond what conventional methods can offer.

Among such approaches, formal methods provide a means to rigorously specify and reason about system behavior. In particular, model checking enables exhaustive exploration of all possible system executions within a formally defined specification [1,4]. Unlike testing, which samples only a subset of executions, model checking systematically verifies whether a system satisfies desired properties. One widely adopted formalism in this domain is TLA+ (Temporal Logic of Actions) [12], a specification language designed for modeling and verifying concurrent and distributed systems. TLA+ allows designers to formulate and check invariants and temporal properties, facilitating the early detection of design flaws and reducing the likelihood of costly errors in later development stages.

Despite model checking expressive power and rigorous semantics, specifying and verifying complex distributed systems is far from trivial. Seminal papers on system design offer guiding principles to manage such complexity. For example, the *end-to-end argument in system design* [18] suggests that functionality critical to correctness is best implemented at the application level rather than within lower network layers, as only applications have sufficient context to enforce it effectively. Complementarily, Schneider [19] emphasizes the importance of model selection and the inherent trade-offs in abstraction. Models simplify reality by omitting irrelevant details and defining constrained behaviors, enabling analysis that would be infeasible in fully detailed systems.

To address the challenges of modeling communication in distributed systems, this paper presents a reusable TLA+ library that abstracts common communication primitives. The library aims to ease the burden on system designers by encapsulating the complexity of communication semantics and fault behavior. It includes formal models for point-to-point communication links, specifically Perfect Links, Fair-Loss Links, and Stubborn Links, allowing users to choose the desired assumptions during specification.[1] This paper extends the prior work in [17] by introducing formal abstractions for broadcast communication primitives with varying reliability guarantees. Specifically, the library includes models for Best Effort Broadcast, Reliable Broadcast, and Atomic Broadcast. Combined with the point-to-point primitives, this results in a comprehensive framework for specifying and verifying communication behaviors in distributed systems.

We also present formal property verification of the broadcast primitives, ensuring their correctness with respect to standard specifications. To demonstrate the practicality and usability of the library, we provide a case study inspired by the work in [15], which verified the Deferred Update Replication (DUR) protocol [16] using Promela and the Spin model checker. In this study, we reimplement and verify DUR in TLA+ using our communication library as the foundation. A broad set of safety and liveness properties is verified, illustrating the effectiveness and ease-of-use of our reusable approach compared to a fully customized model built from scratch.

---

[1] A preliminary version of this library, covering point-to-point primitives, was introduced in [17].

2 Related Work

The use of model checking techniques to verify the correctness of distributed systems has been widely explored in the literature, with numerous contributions advancing the state of the art in this domain. Among these techniques, TLA+ has proven to be particularly versatile, enabling the specification and verification of a wide range of distributed protocols. For example, it has been applied to verify the Pastry protocol, which implements a distributed hash table over a peer-to-peer network [13], and Tendermint, a Byzantine Fault Tolerant consensus engine used in blockchain systems [2]. TLA+ has also been employed to verify the Atomic Broadcast protocol in Zookeeper [20], validate security properties in smart contracts [11], and model the Lightning Network protocol [9].

All of these works focus on applying TLA+ to verify specific distributed protocols, requiring the full modeling of system behavior, communication semantics, and fault conditions. In contrast, our work takes a more general approach by providing a reusable TLA+ library that abstracts common communication primitives, along with configurable fault behaviors. This abstraction allows system designers to build upon predefined components instead of modeling low-level communication mechanisms from scratch. As a result, it becomes easier to prototype and verify distributed protocols, simulate faulty communication scenarios, and reason about system correctness under varying reliability guarantees.

In addition to protocol-specific applications, there is also ongoing research focused on enhancing the TLA+ ecosystem itself, including improvements to both the tool's internals and its supporting libraries. Some notable examples of community-driven modules include [10], which presents a reusable TLA+ module for modeling asynchronous message-passing systems over reliable channels using graph-based communication structures. While it emphasizes modularity, it does not extend to unreliable communication abstractions. Our work was also inspired by [5], which provides reusable TLA+ modules with guarantees such as out-of-order delivery and message duplication. However, unlike our approach, it does not provide a unified framework that includes both point-to-point communication primitives and broadcast primitives with formally defined semantics.

3 Reusable TLA+ Communication Module

In distributed systems, processes communicate through message exchange. This interaction relies on communication primitives, which provide low-level abstractions for fundamental messaging capabilities. Practical specifications of these primitives differ in terms of reliability guarantees, including message ordering, fault tolerance, and delivery integrity. This section introduces our reusable TLA+ communication library, which offers system designers a set of abstractions for both point-to-point and broadcast communication, supporting a range of reliability assumptions. Point-to-point communication is typically modeled as a link, whose behavior is characterized by two event abstractions: *Send* and *Receive*. A *Send* event represents a source process initiating the transmission of a message to a destination process. The link then governs the delivery of that message according to the guarantees it provides. Broadcast communication abstracts over the individual links connecting a group of processes, and is defined using the Broadcast and Deliver primitives. A *Broadcast* event initiates the transmission of a message to all processes in a group, while *Deliver* governs the delivery of that message to each recipient, according to the desired properties of the broadcast primitive.

The following subsections provide a brief overview of TLA+ and then present the detailed specification of the point-to-point and broadcast primitives implemented in our library.

3.1 TLA+ Overview

TLA+ (Temporal Logic of Actions) is a formal specification language designed for modeling and verifying concurrent and distributed systems [12]. It integrates set theory, first-order logic, and temporal logic to describe system behavior and properties. With support for modular specifications and parameterized modules, TLA+ facilitates the reuse of common abstractions across different model specifications.

To validate system behavior, the TLC model checker exhaustively generates the complete state space and explores all possible execution paths. This capability enables the detection of violations of *safety* and *liveness* properties, which are typically described by invariants or temporal logic formulas. TLC also supports counterexample generation and simulation-based verification, both of which are particularly effective in uncovering subtle design flaws.

However, TLA+ does not provide built-in abstractions for inter-process communication. Point-to-point communication is typically modeled using custom channel constructs, and there is no native support for broadcast primitives. Furthermore, accurately representing network behavior often requires explicitly modeling properties such as message loss, duplication, and out-of-order delivery. To address these limitations, the next sections introduce reusable TLA+ modules for both point-to-point and broadcast communication, each supporting configurable reliability guarantees. These abstractions simplify the modeling of distributed systems by encapsulating common communication behaviors and fault assumptions.

3.2 Point-to-Point Communication

The point-to-point communication primitives provided in our library include the Perfect Link, Fair-Loss Link, and Stubborn Link [3]. The *Perfect Link* ensures reliable communication by guaranteeing that messages are neither lost nor duplicated and messages are delivered only if they were sent. In contrast, the *Fair-Loss* Link permits unreliable communication by allowing message loss and providing no guarantees regarding duplication. Lastly, the *Stubborn Link* guarantees eventual delivery of messages without loss but allows message duplication. To ensure delivery ordering, we also implemented a *Perfect FIFO Link*, which extends Perfect link properties with the guarantee that if a message m_1 is sent before m_2 from process p to q, then q receives m_1 before m_2. The detailed specification of TLA+ modules for those point-to-point primitives is presented in [17], and it is omitted in this paper due to space constraints.

3.3   Broadcast Communication

For broadcast communication, our library offers abstractions for *Best-Effort Broadcast*, *Reliable Broadcast*, and *Atomic Broadcast*. Next, we describe the properties for each available broadcast abstraction based on the definitions presented in [3].

Best-Effort Broadcast. The Best-Effort Broadcast provides minimal reliability guarantees, as follows:

Property 1 (Validity). *If a correct process broadcasts a message m, then every correct process eventually delivers m.*

Property 2 (No duplication). *No message is delivered more than once.*

Property 3 (No creation). *If a process delivers a message m with sender s, then m was previously broadcast by process s.*

Reliable Broadcast. While Best-Effort Broadcast does not guarantee message delivery in the event of sender failure, Reliable Broadcast introduces the notion of agreement among correct processes, ensuring consistency in message delivery despite possible failures. Besides *Validity*, *No duplication*, and *No creation*, Reliable Broadcast adds the agreement property, as follows:

Property 4 (Agreement). *If a message m is delivered by some correct process, then m is eventually delivered by every correct process.*

Atomic Broadcast. The Atomic Broadcast, also known as Total-Order Broadcast, is a broadcast communication primitive that extends Reliable Broadcast by ensuring a global agreement not only on the set of delivered messages but also on the order in which they are delivered. This abstraction behaves as if every message broadcast were an indivisible atomic action: it is either delivered to all correct processes or to none, and when delivered, it is totally ordered with respect to all other delivered messages. Besides *Validity*, *No duplication*, *No creation*, and *Agreement*, Atomic Broadcast adds the *Total order* property, as follows:

Property 5 (Total order). *Let m_1 and m_2 be any two messages and suppose p and q are any two correct processes that deliver m_1 and m_2. If p delivers m_1 before m_2, then q delivers m_1 before m_2.*

3.4   Application Programming Interface and Specification

This section describes the API and specification details of our TLA+ communication primitives library. While the point-to-point primitives were introduced in [17], we focus here on the newly added broadcast primitives.

A high-level view of the library's abstract interface and its underlying communication modules is shown in Fig. 1. The library enables system designers to model a wide range of distributed systems, such as network protocols, consensus algorithms, or IoT applications, using a common, unified interface. The library provides four core operators: *Send* and *Receive* for point-to-point communication, and *Broadcast* and *Deliver* for broadcast communication. These operators encapsulate the reliability assumptions associated with each communication abstraction, including Perfect Links, Fair-Loss Links, Stubborn Links, as well as Best-Effort, Reliable, and Atomic Broadcasts. This modular and extensible design allows users to model diverse communication behaviors by adjusting the parameters required by each operator. In doing so, system designers can tailor communication semantics to the specific guarantees needed in their formal specifications, while benefiting from a consistent and reusable modeling interface.

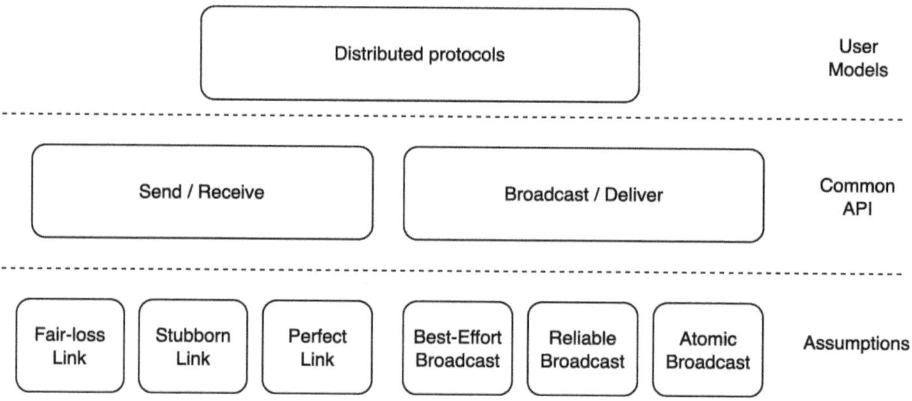

Fig. 1. Overview of the TLA+ modular communication interface.

Users can easily integrate one of our communication abstractions by extending the corresponding module instance and invoking its operators. To use a broadcast primitive, the user must first initialize the communication channel. The definition of the *Channel* operator is given below:

$$\text{Channel(groups, processes)} \triangleq$$
$$[\text{g} \in \text{groups} \mapsto [\text{p} \in \text{processes} \mapsto \langle\rangle]]$$

The *Channel* operator defines the communication structure by associating each group with a set of processes, initializing each link with an empty message queue. Once initialized, this channel is used as one of the parameters of the *Broadcast* operator, which also takes the group identifier, the sender process (wrapped inside the message for traceability), and the message to be broadcast. Next we define the *Broadcast* operator from the Atomic Broadcast module:

$$
\begin{aligned}
&\text{Broadcast(channel, group, sender, msg)} \triangleq \\
&\quad [\text{g} \in \text{DOMAIN channel} \mapsto \\
&\qquad \text{IF g} = \text{group THEN} \\
&\qquad\quad [\text{p} \in \text{DOMAIN channel[g]} \mapsto \\
&\qquad\qquad \text{AppendMessage(channel[g], sender, p, msg)} \\
&\qquad\quad] \\
&\qquad \text{ELSE} \\
&\qquad\quad \text{channel[g]} \\
&\quad]
\end{aligned}
$$

All broadcast specifications internally rely on the *AppendMessage* operator, which is responsible for inserting messages into the appropriate channels for delivery. To ensure that each message carries essential context, such as the sender's identity or a unique identifier, messages are wrapped in a structured format before being appended.

$$
\begin{aligned}
&\text{LOCAL WrapMessage(sender, receiver, msg)} \triangleq \\
&\quad [\text{sender} \mapsto \text{sender, receiver} \mapsto \text{receiver, message} \mapsto \text{msg}]
\end{aligned}
$$

$$
\begin{aligned}
&\text{LOCAL AppendMessage(groupChannel, sender, receiver, msg)} \triangleq \\
&\quad \text{Append(groupChannel[receiver], WrapMessage(sender, receiver, msg))}
\end{aligned}
$$

Among the available primitives, the Atomic Broadcast module is the most straightforward since it does not incorporate mechanisms for message loss or duplication. It assumes a reliable delivery infrastructure where all correct processes receive all messages in the same order.

In addition to the sending interface, each module defines corresponding *Deliver* and auxiliary operators. In the case of Atomic Broadcast, the auxiliary operators include *HasMessage*, *Message*, and *UnwrapMessage*. Since TLA+ is a logic-based language and does not support control-flow constructs like `await` found in procedural languages, we use *HasMessage* to check whether a message is available before proceeding. If this predicate holds, the *Message* operator retrieves the next message, and *UnwrapMessage* extracts the original message content from the metadata structure. Finally, the *Deliver* operator consumes the message, ensuring it is delivered in accordance with the semantics of the broadcast primitive. These auxiliary deliver operators for the Atomic Broadcast module are defined as follows:

$$UnwrapMessage(wrappedMessage) \triangleq wrappedMessage.message$$

$$HasMessage(channel, group, process) \triangleq$$
$$channel[group][process] \neq \langle\rangle$$

$$Message(channel, group, process) \triangleq$$
$$Head(channel[group][process])$$

$$Deliver(channel, group, process) \triangleq$$
$$[g \in \text{DOMAIN } channel \mapsto$$
$$\quad \text{IF } g = group \text{ THEN}$$
$$\quad\quad [p \in \text{DOMAIN } channel[g] \mapsto$$
$$\quad\quad\quad \text{IF } p = process \text{ THEN } Tail(channel[g][p])$$
$$\quad\quad\quad \text{ELSE } channel[g][p]$$
$$\quad\quad]$$
$$\quad \text{ELSE}$$
$$\quad\quad channel[g]$$
$$]$$

The foregoing examples show the *Broadcast/Deliver* and related operators specifically as defined in the Atomic Broadcast module. However, the internal behavior and assumptions of this operator, such as message ordering, duplication, or loss, vary depending on the broadcast primitive being used. Each broadcast module (Best Effort, Reliable, or Atomic) provides its own specification of *Broadcast*, tailored to the semantics and guarantees it aims to provide.

In our specifications, faulty behavior is inspired by the strategy outlined in [6,8]. Omission faults are modeled by allowing messages to be dropped, as it is the case of Fair-Loss Link or Best Effort Broadcast modules. The receive/delivery omission is implemented by an additional guard that, when satisfied, discards the message instead of delivering it to the recipient. To manage state space growth during verification, we introduced a configurable limit on the number of message drops in our abstraction.

In the *Channel* operator for Atomic Broadcast presented earlier, we introduce message ordering by using a sequence $\langle\rangle$, which simulates a FIFO queue. In contrast, for Best Effort and Reliable Broadcast, where there is no ordering guarantee, we represent the channel as a set, since sets in TLA+ do not impose any order. To allow multiple messages with identical content (and thus enable out-of-order delivery), each message is associated with a unique identifier. This approach can be observed in the specification of the Best Effort *Channel*, together with auxiliary local operators, as follows:

LOCAL WrapMessage(sender, receiver, msg, id) $\triangleq$
   [sender $\mapsto$ sender, receiver $\mapsto$ receiver, message $\mapsto$ msg, messageId $\mapsto$ id]

LOCAL InitChannel(groups, processes) $\triangleq$
   [g $\in$ groups $\mapsto$ [p $\in$ processes $\mapsto$ {}]]

Channel(groups, processes) $\triangleq$
   [links $\mapsto$ InitChannel(groups, processes), nextMessageId $\mapsto$ 0, totalDrops $\mapsto$ 0]

We encapsulate information about each message using the *WrapMessage* operator, while the *Channel* operator maintains the fields *nextMessageId*, which is incremented whenever a new message is sent to ensure a unique identifier, and *totalDrops*, which tracks the total number of messages dropped up to a specified limit.

4   Broadcast Properties Verification

This section provides a formal verification of our specified broadcast primitives. Properties are expressed and verified using Linear Temporal Logic (LTL). LTL allows the specification of system properties over time through temporal operators such as $\square$ (*always*) and $\lozenge$ (*eventually*), enabling statements like "a condition always holds" or "a condition eventually becomes true."

For the Atomic Broadcast primitive, we defined a verification scenario involving three processes that collectively send up to eight messages. The number of messages sent by each process and the order of execution are non-deterministic, allowing the model checker to explore all possible interleavings. This results in a comprehensive state space that captures every valid execution trace, including all possible message transmission and delivery orderings across the processes. To support this verification, we defined **sent** and **received** as mappings from each process to the set of messages it has sent and received, respectively.

Using this setup, we successfully verified that the following Atomic Broadcast properties hold. Next, we adapt each Atomic Broadcast properties to match fit to our model specification and show their representation in LTL.

Property 1 (Validity). *For every process $p \in$ Processes and message $m \in$ MessagesToSend, if m is sent by p, then p will eventually receive m:*

$$\square(m \in sent[p] \Rightarrow \lozenge(m \in received[p]))$$

Property 2 (Uniform Agreement). *For every message $m \in$ MessagesToSend and for every process $p_1 \in$ Processes, if p_1 delivers m, then eventually all other processes $p_2 \in$ Processes will also deliver m:*

$$\square(m \in received[p_1] \Rightarrow \forall p_2 \in Processes : \lozenge(m \in received[p_2]))$$

Property 3 (Uniform Integrity). *For every process $p \in Processes$ and every message $m \in MessagesToSend$, if p delivers m, then m must have been sent by some process $q \in Processes$:*

To express the Uniform Integrity, we define the predicate $Delivered(p, m)$ to indicate whether a process p has delivered a given message m. This predicate is defined using a sequence called $receivedOrdered$, which, unlike the sent and received sets, preserves the order in which messages are delivered. $Delivered(p, m)$ is true if there exists an index i such that $receivedOrdered[p][i] = m$.

$$Delivered(p, m) \triangleq \exists i \in 1..Len(receivedOrdered[p]) : receivedOrdered[p][i] = m$$

$$\Box(Delivered(p, m) \Rightarrow \exists q \in Processes : m \in sent[q])$$

Property 4 (Uniform Total Order). *For every pair of messages $m_1, m_2 \in MessagesToSend$ and every pair of processes $p_1, p_2 \in Processes$, if both m_1 and m_2 are delivered by p_1 and m_1 is delivered before m_2 by p_1, and both messages are also delivered by p_2, then p_2 must deliver m_1 before m_2:*

To express the Uniform Total Order property, we introduce two auxiliary definitions: $IndexOf$ and $DeliveredBefore$. The operator $IndexOf(seq, m)$ returns the index of the first occurrence of message m in the sequence seq. Formally, it is defined as the index i such that $seq[i] = m$, assuming m appears in the sequence. Using $IndexOf$, we then define the predicate $DeliveredBefore(p, m_1, m_2)$, which states that process p has delivered both messages m_1 and m_2, and that m_1 was delivered before m_2 in p's delivery order. This is expressed by comparing the positions of m_1 and m_2 in $receivedOrdered[p]$ using $IndexOf$.

$$IndexOf(seq, m) \triangleq \text{choose } i \in 1..Len(seq) : seq[i] = m$$

$$DeliveredBefore(p, m_1, m_2) \triangleq Delivered(p, m_1) \wedge Delivered(p, m_2)$$
$$\wedge \ IndexOf(receivedOrdered[p], m_1)$$
$$< \ IndexOf(receivedOrdered[p], m_2)$$

$$\forall m_1, m_2 \in MessagesToSend, \ \forall p_1, p_2 \in Processes : (m_1 \neq m_2) \wedge (p_1 \neq p_2) \Rightarrow$$

$$\Box(Delivered(p_1, m_1) \wedge Delivered(p_1, m_2) \wedge DeliveredBefore(p_1, m_1, m_2) \wedge$$
$$\Rightarrow \ \Diamond DeliveredBefore(p_2, m_1, m_2))$$

5   Case Study: Deferred Updated Replication Protocol

As a case study, we used our library to model and verify the Deferred Update Replication protocol. Our model is inspired by the work in [15], which presents a Promela specification of DUR, originally based on the algorithm described by Pedone and Schiper [16]. In DUR, the execution of a transaction is divided into two distinct phases: the *execution phase* and the *termination phase*.

During the *execution phase*, the transaction performs *read* and *write* operations. Write operations are executed locally and stored in a write set (ws), while read operations retrieves item's value and version from a server replica and are populated a read set (rs). The write set contains pairs of items and their new values, while the read set keeps track of items along with their values and associated version numbers. If a read targets an item that was previously written within the transaction, the value is retrieved from the write set. Otherwise, it is requested from a server replica. Communication during this phase involves only a single server replica and uses point-to-point communication over *perfect links*.

The *termination phase* begins when the transaction issues a *commit* request, which is broadcast to all server replicas using *atomic broadcast*. The message includes the transaction's *read* and *write* sets, and its identifier. Atomic Broadcast ensures that all correct replicas receive commit requests in the same total order, which is essential for maintaining consistency. Upon receiving a commit request, each replica performs a certification test to determine whether the transaction can be committed. If any item in the read set contains outdated information, indicating a conflicting concurrent update, the transaction is aborted.

5.1 DUR Specification

To model the Deferred Update Replication protocol using our TLA+ communication module, we employed our *Perfect Link FIFO* abstraction to handle point-to-point communication between the transactions and the server replicas during the *execution phase*. For the *termination phase*, we used our *Atomic Broadcast* primitives to ensure that all server replicas delivery commit requests in the same order.

Firstly, the communication modules were instantiated as follows:

$$\text{PLF} \triangleq \textsc{instance} \ \text{PerfectLinkFIFO}$$
$$\text{ABC} \triangleq \textsc{instance} \ \text{AtomicBroadcast}$$

These modules are initialized during the *Init* phase. We define both point-to-point communication links for transaction-to-server and server-to-transaction interactions, as well as create the communication channel used by the Atomic Broadcast primitive. The *Init* operator illustrated shows only the initialization of variables related to the communication primitives used in our specification.[2]

$$
\begin{aligned}
\text{Init} \ \triangleq \ & \\
& \wedge \ \text{c2s} = \text{PLF}! \text{PerfectLinkFIFO}(\text{Transactions}, \text{Servers}) \\
& \wedge \ \text{s2c} = \text{PLF}! \text{PerfectLinkFIFO}(\text{Servers}, \text{Transactions}) \\
& \wedge \ \text{abcastQueue} = \text{ABC}! \text{Channel}(\text{Groups}, \text{Servers})
\end{aligned}
$$

DUR protocol is structured into four main high-level operators:

---

[2] The complete model specification is available in https://github.com/diogocanut/tla-communication-module.

- **TransactionOperation:** Responsible for iterating over the sequence of operations within each transaction and executing the corresponding behavior based on the operation type (*read, write, commit,* or *abort*). For modularity and clarity, each operation is handled by a dedicated operator: *Transaction-Read, TransactionWrite, TransactionCommit,* and *TransactionAbort.*
- **TransactionOutcome:** Handles the reception of commit decisions from the server-to-transaction channel and updates the transaction-side outcome accordingly.
- **ServerRespondRead:** Manages the logic for responding to read requests from transactions during the *execution phase,* including validation against versioned data.
- **ServerApplyCommit:** Responsible for executing the certification test and updating the local replica state according to the received write set. Following this evaluation, the operator returns either a *commit* or an *abort* decision and notifies the transaction of the outcome.

The use of the *Broadcast* primitive occurs during the *TransactionCommit* operation, where the transaction message is propagated to all servers in the system. The use of primitives from our library is highlighted in blue.

$$
\begin{aligned}
&\text{TransactionCommit(t)} \triangleq \\
&\quad \wedge \text{LET tx} \triangleq [\\
&\qquad\qquad \text{transaction} \quad \mapsto \text{t}, \\
&\qquad\qquad \text{rs} \qquad\qquad\quad \mapsto \text{readSet[t]}, \\
&\qquad\qquad \text{ws} \qquad\qquad\quad \mapsto \text{writeSet[t]} \\
&\qquad]\text{IN} \\
&\qquad \wedge \text{abcastQueue}' = \text{ABC!Broadcast(abcastQueue, "g1", t, tx)} \\
&\qquad \wedge \text{sent}' = [\text{sent EXCEPT } ![t] = \{tx\} \cup \text{sent[t]}] \\
&\qquad \wedge \text{outcomes}' = [\text{outcomes EXCEPT } ![t] = \text{"pending"}] \\
&\qquad \wedge \text{pc}' = [\text{pc EXCEPT } ![t] = \text{pc[t]} + 1] \\
&\qquad \wedge \text{UNCHANGED } \langle \text{db, c2s, s2c, operations, writeSet, readSet, versions,} \\
&\qquad\qquad\qquad\qquad \text{pendingRead, received, decided} \rangle
\end{aligned}
$$

Subsequently, in the *ServerApplyCommit* operator, each server delivers the transaction message using the module's auxiliary operators and verifies its validity. The server then either applies the changes or aborts the transaction, sending the outcome back to the transaction via the server-to-transaction link.

$ServerApplyCommit(s) \triangleq$
 $\wedge\ ABC!HasMessage(abcastQueue, \text{``g1''}, s)$
 $\wedge\ \text{LET } tx \triangleq ABC!UnwrapMessage(ABC!Message(abcastQueue, \text{``g1''}, s)) \text{ IN}$
  $\wedge\ abcastQueue' = ABC!Deliver(abcastQueue, \text{``g1''}, s)$
  $\wedge\ received' = [received \text{ EXCEPT } ![tx.transaction] = \{tx\}$
         $\cup\ received[tx.transaction]]$
  $\wedge\ \text{IF } Valid(tx, s)$
   THEN
    $\wedge\ db' = [db \text{ EXCEPT } ![s] = ApplyWrites(db[s], tx.ws)]$
    $\wedge\ s2c' = PLF!Send(s2c, s, tx.transaction,$
      $[type \qquad \mapsto \text{``commitResponse''},$
      $outcome \mapsto \text{``committed''}])$
    $\wedge\ decided' = [decided \text{ EXCEPT } ![s][tx.transaction] = \text{``committed''}]$
   ELSE
    $\wedge\ \text{UNCHANGED } db$
    $\wedge\ s2c' = PLF!Send(s2c, s, tx.transaction,$
      $[type \qquad \mapsto \text{``commitResponse''},$
      $outcome \mapsto \text{``aborted''}])$
    $\wedge\ decided' = [decided \text{ EXCEPT } ![s][tx.transaction] = \text{``aborted''}]$
  $\wedge\ \text{UNCHANGED } \langle c2s, writeSet, readSet, versions,$
      $operations, pc, pendingRead, outcomes, sent\rangle$

To verify the correctness of the protocol, we divided the verification process into two phases. Firstly, we focused on replication properties, modeling a system with two replicated database servers and three concurrent transactions. Transactions are expressed as ordered sequences of operations, where `w(item, value)` denotes a write, `r(item)` denotes a read, and `c` represents a commit request. Transactions t_1 and t_2 enforce a specific interleaving scenario over items x and y. Specifically, t_1 writes to x, reads y, writes to y, and commits. Transaction t_2 reads both y and x, writes to x, and attempts to commit. They are designed to expose potential consistency violations and check the protocol's certification logic. A third transaction, t_3, is included with a deterministic sequence involving x and y, allowing the model checker to evaluate additional interleavings under controlled conditions. The sequences of operations for each transaction are as follows:

$$t_1 :\ w(x, 11),\ r(y),\ w(y, 21),\ c$$
$$t_2 :\ r(y),\ r(x),\ w(x, 12),\ c$$
$$t_3 :\ r(x),\ r(y),\ w(y, 22),\ c$$

The replication-level properties and respective LTL formulation considered in this phase are formally defined as follows.

Property 1 (Transaction Termination). *For all transactions $t \in$ Transactions, if a transaction has started, it must eventually reach a decision (commit or abort):*

$TransactionStarted(t) \triangleq pc[t] > 1$

$TransactionDecided(t) \triangleq outcomes[t] = \text{``committed''} \vee\ outcomes[t] = \text{``aborted''}$

$$\Box\,(TransactionStarted(t) \Rightarrow \Diamond\,TransactionDecided(t))$$

Property 2 (Uniform Total Order). *For all server replicas $s_1, s_2 \in Servers$ and all transactions $t_1, t_2 \in Transactions$:*

$$ServerFinished(s, t) \triangleq \begin{cases} decided[s][t] = \text{``committed''} \\ or \\ decided[s][t] = \text{``aborted''} \end{cases}$$

$$\Box(ServerFinished(s_1, t_1) \Rightarrow \Diamond ServerFinished(s_1, t_2))$$
$$\Rightarrow \Box(ServerFinished(s_2, t_1) \Rightarrow \Diamond ServerFinished(s_2, t_2))$$

Property 3 (DB1 - Uniform Consistency). *If a key k is updated to version $v + 1$ in one server after being at version v, then any other server that also reaches version v must eventually update it to version $v + 1$ as well:*

$$\Box(db[s_1][k].ver = v) \Rightarrow \Diamond(db[s_1][k].ver = v + 1)$$
$$\Rightarrow \Box(db[s_2][k].ver = v) \Rightarrow \Diamond(db[s_2][k].ver = v + 1)$$

Property 4 (DB2 - Value Agreement). *If two servers store the same version of a key, then they must also store the same value for that key, in all states:*

$$\Box(\forall s_1, s_2 \in Servers, \ \forall x \in Keys : db[s_1][x].ver = db[s_2][x].ver$$

$$\Rightarrow \ db[s_1][x].val = db[s_2][x].val)$$

We performed model checking of our DUR protocol specification using the TLC model checker, evaluating four core temporal properties: Transaction Termination, Uniform Total Order, Uniform Consistency, and Value Agreement. Model checking explored over 2.85 million distinct states and reached a maximum state graph depth of 32, completing in approximately 13 h. All properties were verified for all possible behaviors under the parameterized model, with no violations found.

In the second phase, we focused on conflict isolation, investigating whether the DUR protocol prevents common transactional anomalies under concurrency. We constructed scenarios involving two concurrent transactions, t_1 and t_2, each with conflicting operations and ending with either a commit or abort. Table 1 summarizes the scenarios, while Table 2 presents the verification outcomes. The LTL formula for each anomaly verification are presented, although some propositions are omitted due to space constraints.

Table 1. Operations Per Transaction

Property	t1 Operations	t2 Operations
Non-Repeatable Read	r1(x), w1(y,21), r1(x), c1	w2(x,12), r2(y), w2(y,22), c2
Lost Update	r1(x), w1(x,11), w1(y,21), c1	w2(x,12), r2(y), r2(x), c2
Dirty Read	w1(x,11), r1(y), a1	r2(y), r2(x), r2(x), c2
Write Skew	r1(x), r1(y), w1(y,21), c1	r2(x), r2(y), w2(x,12), c2

Non-repeatable Read. A non-repeatable read occurs when a transaction reads the same data item twice and, due to a concurrent modification and commit by another transaction, observes different values in each read. In the DUR protocol, however, t_1 must abort if it ever reads two different versions of x.

$$\forall t \in \textit{Transactions} : \; \Box(\textit{TwoVersionsRead}(t, \text{``x''}) \Rightarrow \Diamond \textit{TxAborted}(t))$$

Lost Update. The lost update anomaly arises when two transactions concurrently read and update the same item, but the effect of one update is overwritten and lost due to the interleaving of their operations. DUR mechanism maintains isolation by keeping uncommitted writes private to each transaction, such that each update is validated and cannot be overwritten invisibly.

$$\Box(\textit{WriteVal}(\text{``t2''}, x, 12) \Rightarrow \Diamond \textit{ReadVal}(\text{``t2''}, x, 12))$$

Dirty Read. A dirty read occurs if a transaction reads a value written by another transaction that subsequently aborts, thus exposing an uncommitted, transient state. In a problematic history, t_1 writes $x = 11$, t_2 reads x before t_1 aborts, and thus could observe a value that is rolled back. However, in DUR protocol, all updates remain invisible to other transactions until commit.

$$\Box\neg\textit{ReadVal}(\text{``t2''}, x, 11)$$

Write Skew. Write skew may occur when two transactions read overlapping items and then update disjoint items, potentially violating integrity constraints defined over the set of items. A typical problematic history involves each transaction reading both x and y, then writing to a separate item, such that a constraint could be violated if not properly synchronized. The protocol's snapshot isolation semantics, together with commit-time validation, prevent write skew.

$$\Box\neg(\exists s \in \textit{Servers} : \; \textit{TxCommitted}(\text{``t1''}) \land \textit{TxCommitted}(\text{``t2''}) \land$$
$$db[s][x].val = 12 \land db[s][y].val = 21)$$

Table 2. Summary of Model Checking Results Using TLC

Property	States Explored	Max Depth	Time (ms)	Result
Non-Repeatable Read	1,343	21	11,392	No Violations
Lost Update	919	19	5,809	No Violations
Dirty Read	476	19	3,470	No Violations
Write Skew	1,905	23	13,616	No Violations

6   Conclusion

This paper presented a modular TLA+ library that provides system designers with reusable and expressive communication abstractions for modeling distributed systems. The library includes primitives with varying reliability and ordering guarantees, enabling designers to specify systems under different assumptions about the communication infrastructure. Specifically, the library offers abstractions for point-to-point communication, including *Perfect Links*, *Fair-Loss Links*, and *Stubborn Links*, as well as broadcast communication, through *Best-Effort Broadcast*, *Reliable Broadcast*, and *Atomic Broadcast*. Each primitive encapsulates distinct communication semantics, allowing designers to precisely model failure-prone distributed systems with formal verification capabilities via the TLC model checker.

Beyond introducing these abstractions, we formally verified the broadcast primitives against standard properties such as validity, agreement, integrity, and total order, ensuring the correctness of our Atomic Broadcast specification. To demonstrate the practical utility of the library, we modeled and verified the Deferred Update Replication (DUR) protocol. The verification process was divided into two phases: first, we verified key replication-level properties, including transaction termination, uniform total order, uniform consistency, and value agreement. Then, we assessed conflict isolation by checking for anomalies such as non-repeatable reads, lost updates, dirty reads, and write skew.

This case study illustrates the practicality and reusability of our modular library for modeling and verifying complex distributed protocols. As future work, we plan to extend the framework to support additional communication abstractions and delivery guarantees, including FIFO and causal broadcast ordering. We also intend to apply the library to further case studies, reinforcing its applicability across a broader range of protocols and system designs.

References

1. Baier, C., Katoen, J.P.: Principles of Model Checking. The MIT Press (2008)
2. Braithwaite, S., et al.: Formal specification and model checking of the tendermint blockchain synchronization protocol (short paper). In: FMBC@CAV (2020). https://api.semanticscholar.org/CorpusID:228097346
3. Cachin, C., Guerraoui, R., Rodrigues, L.: Introduction to Reliable and Secure Distributed Programming, 2nd edn. Springer (2011). https://doi.org/10.1007/978-3-642-15260-3, https://infoscience.epfl.ch/handle/20.500.14299/115070
4. Clarke, E.M.: Model checking. In: Ramesh, S., Sivakumar, G. (eds.) FSTTCS 1997. LNCS, vol. 1346, pp. 54–56. Springer, Heidelberg (1997). https://doi.org/10.1007/BFb0058022
5. dmilstein: Channels: TLA+ modules for modeling message-passing with different guarantees (2019). https://github.com/dmilstein/channels. Accessed 28 Jan 2025
6. Dotti, F.L., Mendizabal, O.M., dos Santos, O.M.: Verifying fault-tolerant distributed systems using object-based graph grammars. In: Maziero, C.A., Gabriel Silva, J., Andrade, A.M.S., de Assis Silva, F.M. (eds.) LADC 2005. LNCS, vol. 3747, pp. 80–100. Springer, Heidelberg (2005). https://doi.org/10.1007/11572329_9
7. Fonseca, P., Zhang, K., Wang, X., Krishnamurthy, A.: An empirical study on the correctness of formally verified distributed systems. In: Proceedings of the Twelfth European Conference on Computer Systems, pp. 328–343 (2017)
8. Gärtner, F.C.: Fundamentals of fault-tolerant distributed computing in asynchronous environments. ACM Comput. Surv. **31**(1), 1–26 (1999). https://doi.org/10.1145/311531.311532
9. Grundmann, M., Hartenstein, H.: Towards a formal verification of the lightning network with TLA+ (2023). https://doi.org/10.48550/arXiv.2307.02342
10. House, A., Tang, P.: A TLA+ module for asynchronous message-passing systems. In: SoutheastCon 2018, pp. 1–7 (2018). https://doi.org/10.1109/SECON.2018.8479004
11. Kolb, J., Yang, J., Katz, R.H., Culler, D.E.: Quartz: a framework for engineering secure smart contracts. Technical report, UCB/EECS-2020-178, EECS Department, University of California, Berkeley (2020). http://www2.eecs.berkeley.edu/Pubs/TechRpts/2020/EECS-2020-178.html
12. Lamport, L.: The temporal logic of actions. ACM Trans. Program. Lang. Syst. **16**(3), 872–923 (1994). https://doi.org/10.1145/177492.177726
13. Lu, T., Merz, S., Weidenbach, C.: Towards verification of the pastry protocol using TLA^{âĂĽ+âĂĽ}. In: Bruni, R., Dingel, J. (eds.) FMOODS/FORTE -2011. LNCS, vol. 6722, pp. 244–258. Springer, Heidelberg (2011). https://doi.org/10.1007/978-3-642-21461-5_16
14. McDowell, C.E., Helmbold, D.P.: Debugging concurrent programs. ACM Comput. Surv. (CSUR) **21**(4), 593–622 (1989)
15. Mendizabal, O., Dotti, F.: Model checking the deferred update replication protocol, pp. 995–1008 (2013)
16. Pedone, F., Schiper, N.: Byzantine fault-tolerant deferred update replication. J. Braz. Comput. Soc. **18**(1), 3–18 (2012). https://doi.org/10.1007/s13173-012-0060-z
17. Peixoto, D., Mendizabal, O.M.: Reusable TLA+ communication primitives for modeling and verifying distributed systems. In: Proceedings of the 26th

Workshop on Testing and Fault Tolerance, pp. 113–125. SBC, Porto Alegre (2025).https://doi.org/10.5753/wtf.2025.8866, https://sol.sbc.org.br/index.php/wtf/article/view/35652
18. Saltzer, J.H., Reed, D.P., Clark, D.D.: End-to-end arguments in system design. ACM Trans. Comput. Syst. (TOCS) **2**(4), 277–288 (1984)
19. Schneider, F.B.: What good are models and what models are good? In: Distributed Systems, 2nd edn., pp. 17–26. ACM Press/Addison-Wesley Publishing Co., USA (1993)
20. Yin, J.-Q., Zhu, H.-B., Fei, Y.: Specification and verification of the Zab protocol with TLA+. J. Comput. Sci. Technol. **35**(6), 1312–1323 (2020). https://doi.org/10.1007/s11390-020-0538-7

Long-Term Experimental Evaluation of Software Aging Effects in NoSQL Database

Paulo Amaral[1,2] and Jean Araujo[1,3,4(✉)]

[1] Universidade Federal de Sergipe, São Cristóvão, Brazil
paulo.amaral@ifs.edu.br
[2] Instituto Federal de Sergipe, Aracaju, Brazil
[3] Universidade Federal do Agreste de Pernambuco, Garanhuns, Brazil
[4] Instituto de Telecomunicações, Aveiro, Portugal
jean.teixeira@ufape.edu.br

Abstract. The increasing reliance on NoSQL databases in cloud-native and data-intensive applications raises concerns about their long-term dependability. Software aging is a phenomenon that leads to performance degradation or increased failure rates in long-running systems. Although few studies have investigated the effects of aging in relational Database Management Systems (DBMSs), even less attention has been given to NoSQL systems. To address this gap, this paper presents, to the best of our knowledge, the first long-term experimental investigation of software aging in MongoDB NoSQL database. We also introduce the approach called *SW Cycles*, which accelerates aging manifestation through repeated stress-wait cycles. The experiment performed continuous read operations using 500 concurrent virtual users during 48-hour stress periods and 6 wait hours, repeating over a total span of 63.25 d. Memory usage was continuously monitored, and the collected data were analyzed using the Mann-Kendall trend test. The results indicated a statistically significant upward trend in RAM consumption, suggesting the occurrence of memory leaks and fragmentation. Using Kendall-Theil regression, we estimate system failure due to memory exhaustion, after the completion of each stress-wait cycle.

Keywords: Software Aging · NoSQL · Database Management System · DBMS · MongoDB

1 Introduction

Modern data-intensive systems rely heavily on long-running software components that must operate continuously and reliably over extended periods. As these systems evolve, a lot of evidence suggests that software can degrade over time, known as software aging phenomenon [13]. This phenomenon manifests as a gradual decline in system performance or an increased likelihood of failure due to the accumulation of internal errors, memory leaks, resource fragmentation, or state corruption during prolonged execution [10].

L. A. Rodrigues and R. Oliveira (Eds.): LADC 2025, CCIS 2697, pp. 201–217, 2026.
https://doi.org/10.1007/978-3-032-11539-3_12

In database management systems (DBMSs), software aging may impact system performance, availability, and resource efficiency, mainly in applications that require high throughput and minimal downtime. While several studies have addressed software aging in relational DBMSs [1,5,7] [8], NoSQL systems remain significantly underexplored in this regard, despite their widespread adoption in modern and cloud-native architectures. Among these, MongoDB stands out as one of the most widely used NoSQL databases [9], powering critical applications in sectors such as finance, retail, and real-time analytics.

Understanding how a NoSQL system behaves under long-term stress is essential to ensuring its dependability and resilience. However, there is currently a lack of empirical studies that investigate how these systems age, what symptoms emerge, and how performance degradation might be predicted or mitigated. This paper addresses this research gap by conducting a long-term experimental investigation of software aging in MongoDB. We introduce the method *SWCycles*, based on alternating stress and wait cycles, designed to accelerate the manifestation of aging symptoms [18]. Using a controlled environment with 500 virtual users executing continuous read operations during stress phases, we monitored memory behavior across a 63-days period. Statistical analysis using the Mann-Kendall trend test [17] revealed a consistent upward trend in RAM usage, suggesting the presence of memory leaks and fragmentation. Furthermore, regression modeling via Kendall-Theil fitting [24] was employed to project the expected time to failure due to memory exhaustion.

The remainder of this paper is organized as follows: Sect. 2 presents some related works. Section 3 covers the topics necessary for understanding this article, such as software aging and the statistical test adopted in this study. Section 4 describes the methodology that incorporates the *SWCycles* approach, illustrating the dynamics of the investigation and the details of the experimental case study. Section 5 presents the result analysis. Finally, Sect. 6 presents the conclusions and a possible future work.

2   Related Works

The concepts of software aging and rejuvenation have been consolidated and studied for over 20 years [28]. In 2002, a complex form of software aging, known as "shared memory pool lock contention" in online transaction processing (OLTP) DBMSs, was studied by [2]. The experiment lasted five months; however, the publication did not detail the environment and the OLTP server DBMS evaluated.

Ten years later, a study conducted by [1] investigated, through eight experiments, the phenomenon of aging in MySQL, caused by the activation of bugs due to concurrent operations resulting from load testing based on the TPC-E benchmark specifications. Each experiment lasted 24 h, and the trend of memory exhaustion was confirmed by the Mann-Kendall test, concluding, through statistical inference, that the estimation of a Time to Failure (TTF) depending on the workload applied, could reach a minimum of 8 d (worst case) up to approximately 500 d (best case). In the same year, Controneo & Natella [5] published an article on software aging phenomena related to integer overflow problems also in MySQL, in which an online monitoring approach was proposed to identify aging symptoms. The workload of the experiment lasted 7 d.

In 2023, a software aging analysis on PostgreSQL 14.4 was conducted and the Mann-Kendall test was also used to confirm a trend of growth and possible exhaustion of hardware resources [7]. In the following year, another study was conducted by the same author [8], involving the MySQL and MS SQL Server DBMSs. The experiments lasted 48 h, under low-load scenarios with 5, medium-load with 50, and high-load with 100 concurrent virtual users (VUs).

Table 1 shows that, among the five previous studies conducted on DBMSs in the context of software aging, few carried out long-duration experiments.

Table 1. Duration of Experiments, DBMS Investigated, and Stress Operations

Paper (Pub. Year)	Experiment Duration (days)	DBMS	Model	Mann-Kendall Test	Stress Operations
[1] (2012)	1	MySQL	Relational	Yes	Read/Write
[7] (2023)	2	PostgreSQL	Relational	Yes	Read
[8] (2024)	2	MySQL and MS SQL Server	Relational	Yes	Read
[5] (2012)	7	MySQL	Relational	Yes	Read/Write
[2] (2002)	150	Not specified	Not specified	No	Not specified
This (2025)	63.25	MongoDB	NoSQL	Yes	Read

Compared to related works, our experiment indeed adopted a continuous, long-term period ($\approx$50% of the time monitored by [2]), lasting 63.25 d (1518 h), under a concurrency of 500 VUs, in order to minimize the possibility of false positives in Mann-Kendall tests. This is a key strategy, since such detection is generally unreliable or may require long measurement periods, potentially indicating software aging even when it does not actually occur [16].

The present work, however, is likely the first investigation into the effects of software aging in a non-relational database system, specifically MongoDB, an open-source, document-oriented NoSQL database system, currently the most popular in its category according to [9]. This study also contributes with an experimental investigation methodology that incorporates the *SW Cycles* stress testing approach, complemented with graphical and statistical analysis. The experiments were conducted on the Linux Ubuntu Server operating system, using Grafana k6 as workload generation tool.

3   Background

3.1   Software Aging

Software aging is a phenomenon characterized by an increasing system failure rate and/or degradation of its performance, with its effects manifesting only after a long period of execution [6]. Its characterization is also evidenced by the progressive decline of computational system resources during its operational lifetime, eventually compromising its ability to perform tasks [10]. It is a problem that generally affects software systems that remain in operation for long periods of time [23], such as database systems, being cumulative and not causing immediate system failure. Most software aging effects are related to memory leaks and fragmentation [10], and both can cause an increase in the application's process memory usage [15].

Memory leak is a defect in the program code related to an imbalance in the routines involving memory allocation and deallocation [19]. It occurs precisely when a previously allocated memory chunk is not deallocated, usually due to the loss of reference, resulting in an orphaned chunk that can no longer be used, consequently and monotonically increasing the process size [15]. In complex programs, memory deallocation can be extremely difficult, and programmers may consciously allow leaks, considering that this extra memory usage is acceptable throughout the program execution, since attempts to fix leaks may result in even worse bugs [14]. It is important to clarify that the operating system kernel provides the infrastructure for programs to request and use memory. Therefore, the responsibility for deallocation and cleanup (whether by automatic garbage collection or manual freeing) lies with the application or the programming language runtime environment, and not with the operating system.

Memory fragmentation occurs when contiguous memory pages are required to support kernel-level services, and high-order allocation requests (contiguous memory) begin to fail [19]. Linux adopts the Buddy System to divide memory into block orders. This hierarchical division of memory is used to define the coalescence of data into larger free areas [14]. In addition, memory fragmentation also causes an increase in the process size, as the application may request new memory blocks from the operating system even if it already has enough allocated memory available (but not contiguous) [15]. External fragmentation does not measure how much memory is free, but rather how contiguous that free memory is.

3.2   Mann-Kendall Test

The Mann-Kendall trend test is a non-parametric statistical test designed to determine whether there is a trend in a time series and whether it is statistically significant, by verifying the null hypothesis, H_0, which suggests that no trend exists in the temporal data, against the alternative hypothesis, H_1, which indicates a monotonic upward or downward trend in the series data [17]. Since it is a non-parametric test, the distributions do not need to be normal; however, the data must not exhibit serial correlation [12].

Let Y be the variable or metric for which we want to determine whether a monotonic trend exists with respect to time T, that is, whether the values of Y tend to increase or decrease as T increases in the collection of monitored data pairs $((T_1, Y_1), (T_2, Y_2), \ldots, (T_n, Y_n))$. Accordingly, the hypotheses can be represented as follows:

- H_0: $\text{Prob}[Y_j > Y_i] = 0.5$, where time $T_j > T_i$.
- H_1: $\text{Prob}[Y_j > Y_i] \neq 0.5$ (two-sided test).

The objective is to determine, for any pair of recorded observations, whether the probability of the latter observation being greater than the former is different from 0.5. If the probability is greater than 0.5, it indicates a tendency for Y to increase over time; if the probability is less than 0.5, it suggests a tendency for Y to decrease over time.

On the other hand, Sen's slope [24] estimates the robust overall trend slope of the time series and corresponds to the median of all slopes calculated for all pairs of points in the time series, where $T_j > T_i$. Therefore, for a time series of Y values observed at times T, Sen's slope is the median of the set of slopes calculated for all pairs ($i < j$), defined by:

$$\text{Sen's Slope} = \text{median} \left\{ S_{ij} \mid S_{ij} = \frac{Y_j - Y_i}{T_j - T_i}, \forall i < j \right\}$$

where:

- S_{ij} represents the slope of the straight line between each pair of data points in the series;
- Y_i and Y_j represent the values of the metric of interest at times T_i and T_j;
- T_i and T_j are the observation time instants, with the condition that $T_j > T_i$, for $j > i$, at sequential and distinct time points;
- The denominator $T_j - T_i$ represents the time difference between the two observations.

The literature has widely reported the use of the Mann-Kendall test in statistical data analyses when investigating the phenomenon of software aging [1,5,7,8,16].

4   Methodology

To structure the methodological procedures employed in this work, the following subsections detail the workload approach proposed to accelerate the manifestation of software aging symptoms and the design of the experimental study, which comprises the test environment, stress parameters, monitored metrics, as well as tools used.

4.1   *SWCycles* Workload Approach

As far as the state of the art mapped by [3,4,6,25,27], has been reached, the methodology proposed and employed in this study, as shown in Fig. 1, includes the *SWCycles* procedure (or Cycles of Stress and Wait), which consists of the systematic execution of successive soak load tests, close to the software's capacity limit, interspersed with rest intervals, aiming to accelerate the emergence of aging effects. It differs from the procedure adopted by the SWARE method [20], which

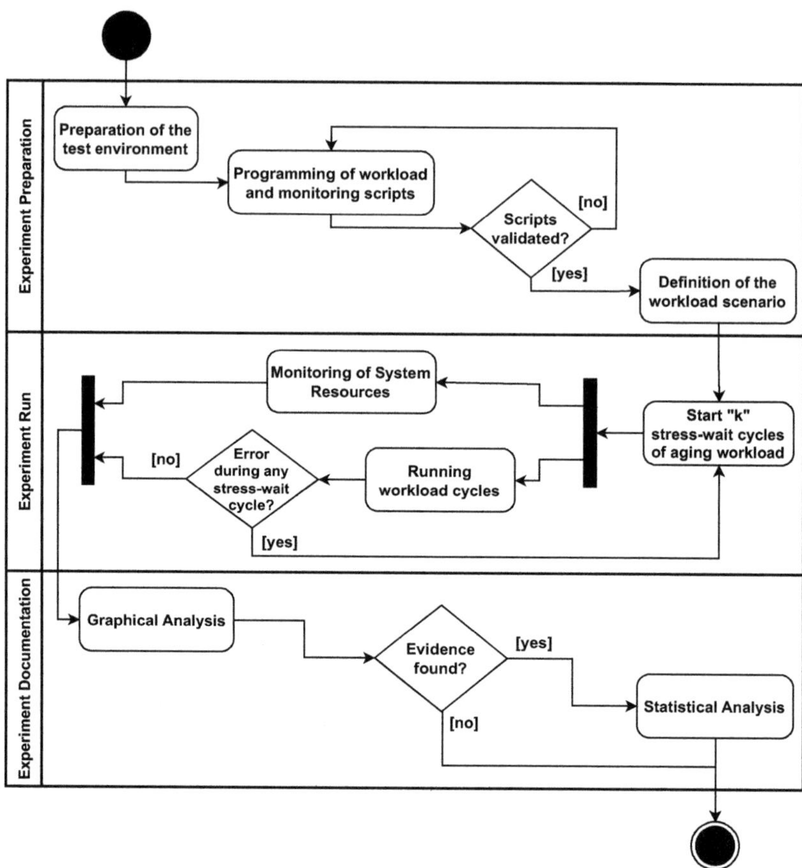

Fig. 1. Software aging investigation methodology

refers only to a single stress load submission, followed by a subsequent wait period and a possible later rejuvenation action.

The *SWCycles* does not aim to observe the effectiveness of rejuvenation actions, thereby eliminating the third stage of SWARE. In contrast, after an initial Wait phase (W_0), the Stress and Wait phases are executed k times (k_cycles of Stress-Wait), as shown in the functional paradigm Algorithm 1 and represented by Eqs. 1 and 2. In addition to accelerating the effects of aging caused by stress in a controlled experiment [18, 26], the objective of SWCycles is to favor a visual perception of software aging symptoms, through the effect of progressive growth of the "floor" of use of the monitored metric, under constant load, observing it in the waiting phases.

$$SWCycles(k, p, q) = Wait(q)_0 + \sum_{i=1}^{k} \Big(Stress(p)_i + Wait(q)_i \Big) \tag{1}$$

$$\text{where} \begin{cases} k \geq 1 \\ p = \text{number of hours for the Stress phase} \\ q = \text{number of hours for the Wait phase} \end{cases}$$

Simplifying:

$$SWCycles(k, p, q) = Wait(q)_0 + k \cdot \left(Stress(p) + Wait(q) \right) \tag{2}$$

Algorithm 1 : SWCYCLES — Stress-Wait Cycles

Require: $k\_cycles \in N^+$ {Number of cycles}
Require: $p\_hours \in N^+$ {Stress phase duration (hours)}
Require: $q\_hours \in N^+$ {Wait phase duration (hours)}

1: **Main Function:** SWCycle_k(k_cycles, p_hours, q_hours)
2: **Call** Wait(q_hours)
3: **for** $n = 1$ **to** k_cycles
4:    **Call** PerformStressPhase(p_hours)
5:    **Call** Wait(q_hours)
6: **end for**

7: **Function:** Wait(t) {Time to wait (hours)}
8: Suspend execution for t hours

9: **Function:** PerformStressPhase(t) {Time to execute load (hours)}
10: Execute stress workload continuously for t hours

However, when conducting an experiment, the duration of the wait phase must be long enough to observe whether any system metric remained in a degraded state. It should be approximately the same length as the stress load duration or last long enough to evidence the cumulative process of software aging [20]. In our study, we adopted a wait phase duration of 6 h, corresponding to 1/8 of the stress phase duration (48 h).

4.2 Experimental Study

The experiment included the execution of 28 stress-wait cycles, totaling 63.25 d, in an environment composed of two virtual machines, as described in Table 2; one acting as a client, running the workload generation software, and the other as a server hosting the NoSQL DBMS MongoDB, version 8.0.4 (Community Server) [22], both operating on an isolated internal private network with a gigabit virtual switch. The machines were virtualized with a type 1 hypervisor on a host with an Intel Xeon E5-2680 v4 processor, 2.40 GHz, 28 cores, 128 GB RAM, 2 TB NVMe M.2 SSD disk, Linux Ubuntu 22.04.5 LTS operating system, kernel 6.8.0–52-generic.

The stress loads considered only read operations on a MongoDB collection named "bp" (boarding pass), containing a total of 10 million documents,

Table 2. Virtual Machine (VM) Configuration

VM	Hardware	Softwares
Client	4 vCPUs, 2.40GHz, 16 GB RAM, 100 GB SSD Disk	Ubuntu 22.04.3 LTS (Kernel 5.15.0), Grafana k6
Server	4 vCPUs, 2.40GHz, 16 GB RAM, 100 GB SSD Disk	Ubuntu 22.04.3 LTS (Kernel 5.15.0), MongoDB Community Server, version 8.0.4

which were randomly queried with a high computational cost using the method `bp.find({_id: {"$in": [ array_with_1800_ids ]}})`, in a thematic database of booking flights. Insert, update and delete operations were not adopted for two reasons: a) Because such operations would imply changes to the database state, which would make it difficult, in some metrics, to distinguish between aging symptoms and the expected behavior in transactional operations. Massive read operations are sufficient to maximize the efforts of resource management mechanisms, such as RAM, buffer/cache, and swap, in a controlled manner, without interference or influence from data update routines; and b) Because the experiment is not a comparative performance evaluation or a software benchmark test, but is only intended to accelerate the accumulation of internal bugs, such as unfinished threads and memory leaks, which, consequently, can trigger the manifestation of aging symptoms in the main metrics, such as increased memory and CPU consumption, latency degradation, throughput, I/O rate, obtained simply from intense and massive query operations with high computational cost.

The default buffer and cache configurations of MongoDB were maintained, except for the connection limit, which was increased to support the requests generated by a single extreme workload scenario, corresponding to 500 VUs, as illustrated in Fig. 2. The intent of the method is to stress the software and provoke the manifestation of the effects of aging. The intent is not to investigate its causes or to examine the dynamics of aging for performance optimization or tuning for database deployment purposes, as this would involve optimizations at different levels, from infrastructure planning to fine-tuning various other DBMS configuration parameters.

The "$in" operator was used to allow the query to return multiple documents at once, and the value of the filtered field "_id" had to match the custom sequential *ObjectId* of each document. This operator compares each parameter against every stored document in the collection, which can lead to performance issues, and the use of hundreds of parameters or more may negatively impact query performance [21]; however, this was the objective: to overload MongoDB close to the limit of its capacity. The array size consisted of 1800 randomly generated

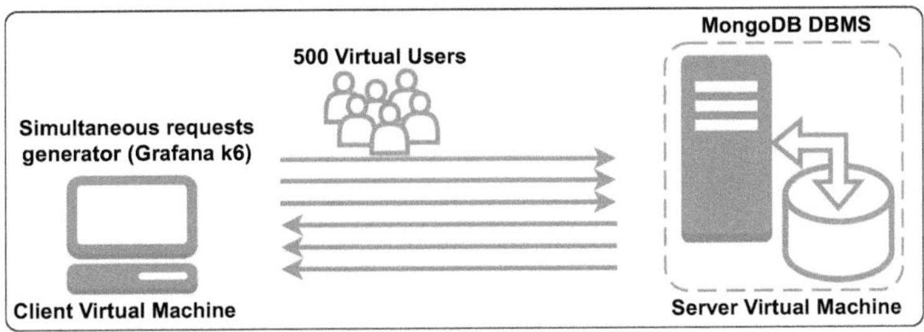

Fig. 2. Workload scheme

ids in JavaScript, within the load generation script code executed by the custom binary of Grafana k6, aiming to return ≈ 2 MB of documents, each document with ≈ 1.14 KB.

Bash scripts were developed for monitoring server resources (RAM, CPU, Network Rates, Disk I/O Rates), sending output data to a text file every 60 s. Python programs and Gnuplot were used for statistical analyses and for generating graphs based on the monitored data.

5   Result Analysis

To better understand the effects observed during the experiment, this section presents an analysis of the monitored data. The following subsections include a graphical evaluation of the main metrics, a statistical evaluation using the Mann-Kendall trend test, and an estimation of the *TTF* based on memory usage. These analyses aim to validate the occurrence of aging symptoms and estimate the system crash.

5.1   Data Analysis

Figure 3 shows the step-by-step, stair-like evolution of RAM usage, progressing from a lower to a higher state during the "wait" phases of each stress-wait cycle. At the beginning of the experiment, it can be seen that the RAM consumption starts at a low level, representing a basic allocation sufficient to keep the MongoDB service active.

After each stress-wait cycle, RAM usage exhibits a growth pattern with abrupt peaks at the beginning of each workload, and its consumption no longer returns to the level of the initial wait phase (W_0). As the cycles progress, there is a continuous and almost linear accumulation of RAM usage, even during subsequent rest phases, following an arithmetic progression at an approximate rate of 40 MB per cycle, starting from the second cycle of constant workload. This behavior suggests that MongoDB could supposedly be causing: a) memory leaks; and/or b) a progressive accumulation resulting from data not being released in temporary cache memories and transfer buffers, intended to speed up the exchange and access of information returned by queries.

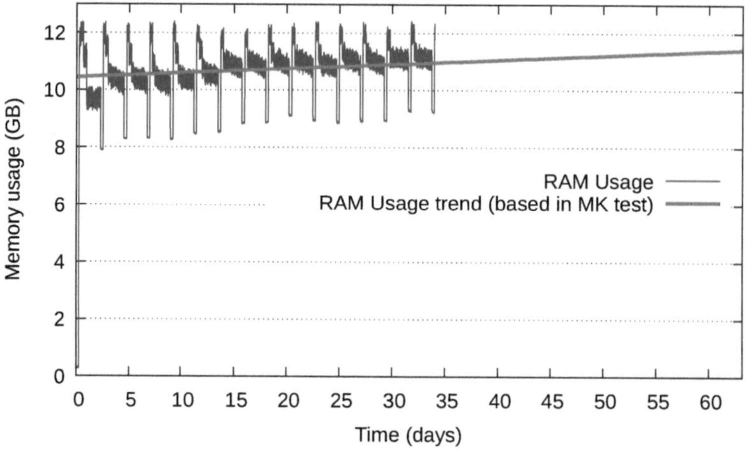

Fig. 3. Evolution of RAM usage(Color figure online)

However, the combined decreasing behaviors of the *Buff/Cache* and *Available RAM* metrics, shown in Fig. 4, denote a strong correlation with the growth of RAM usage. This growth pattern was driven solely by the possibility of memory leaks, contradicting the assumption that RAM usage growth could also result from the legitimate accumulation of data in buffers and caches, since the workload of requests was kept constant, limited to 500 VUs. Therefore, the observed downward behavior suggests that the system is releasing part of the buffer/cache, forcing moderate use of *Swap*; however, a portion of the temporary memory is not being returned to the operating system. On the contrary, total RAM usage continues to increase without any workload growth, likely due to the retention of data that has not been released.

Indeed, although it shows an apparent trend toward stabilization, the continuous upward curve of the Resident Set Size (RSS), displayed in Fig. 5, corresponding to the portion of memory occupied by the */usr/bin/mongod* process, helps to corroborate a possible suspicion of a memory leak.

Other metrics whose data exhibited relevant effects, represented in Fig. 6, were: the usage of the *Swap* memory and external memory fragmentation, on a normalized scale from 0 to 1 (0% to 100%). The data for the fragmentation calculation referred to the *Normal Zone*, collected from */proc/buddyinfo*, and the fragmentation level was calculated according to Eq. 3 [11], where the denominator represents the total number of free pages and the numerator corresponds to the size (in pages) of the largest free memory block at the time of measurement.

$$External\ Fragmentation = 1 - \frac{Largest\ Block\ Of\ Free\ Memory}{Total\ Free\ Memory} \tag{3}$$

In the aforementioned Fig. 6, therefore, a high level of memory fragmentation (red curve) can be observed, always above 98%, in addition to the increase in

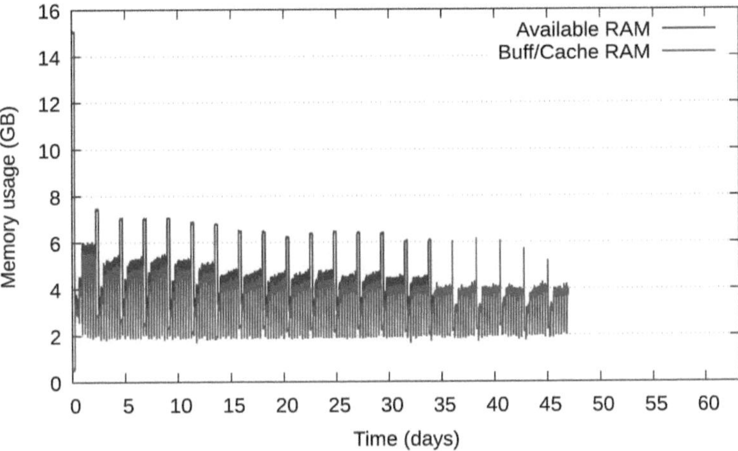

Fig. 4. Evolution of buff/cache usage and available RAM(Color figure online)

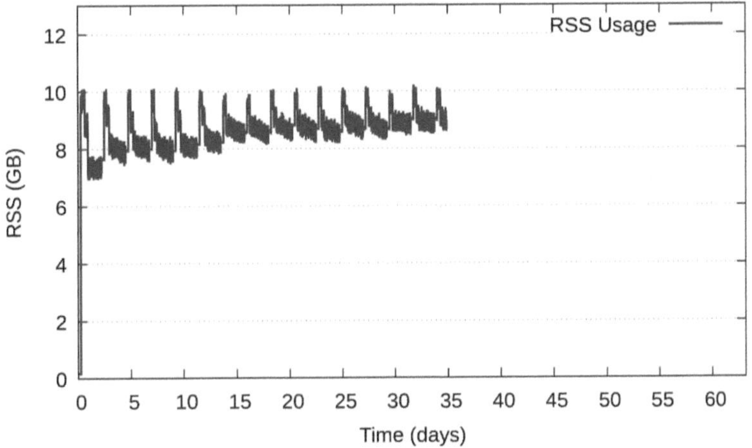

Fig. 5. Resident Set Size evolution of the *mongod* process(Color figure online)

RAM usage (blue curve), evidencing a gradual decline in available memory, typical of a progressive software aging process.

The decline in the *Swap* usage curve occurs due to the availability of free RAM. And as long as RAM is available, swap memory will be increasingly less necessary. However, if the trend of continuous RAM usage growth persists and reaches a level close to exhaustion, this scenario will result in a substantial increase in *Swap* usage, leading to slowdowns, system freezes, and ultimately causing the MongoDB service to crash due to the process known as the *Out of Memory Killer (OOM Killer)*, which, in critical situations that compromise the system, terminates processes to free memory.

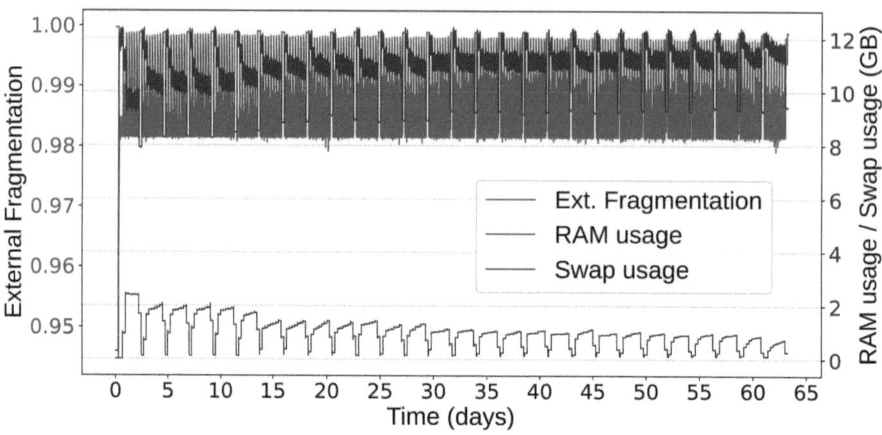

Fig. 6. RAM and Swap usage, and memory fragmentation(Color figure online)

5.2   Statistical Analysis

According to the monitored data, the average CPU usage in user mode, considering only the periods of stress loads applied to MongoDB, reached a level of 80.6%, a typical manifestation of a bottleneck due to the intense overload of operations. Similarly, the average rates of network transfer and disk read/write were, respectively, 502.4 Mbps (TX), 8.1 Mbps (RX), only 62.9 MBytes/s in disk reading, due to the high capacity for data caching, and 1.8 MBytes/s in writing, related to journaling operations of MongoDB and the operating system, in addition to buffer/cache flushing and consequent swap usage. The average latency per cycle was 17.6 s, with a median of 17.5 s. The average throughput per cycle was 28.5 requests per second, with a median of 28.4 requests per second. These values indicated symmetry in the data, suggesting a distribution close to normal.

RAM usage was the most prominent indicator metric of aging, which is why the *Mann-Kendall* test was applied to its monitored temporal data.

Table 3 presents the main parameters computed by the test.

The result describes a statistically significant increasing trend in RAM usage, due to an almost zero p-value ($p < 0.001$) and a Kendall's coefficient (τ) $\tau = 0.346$, which confirms a moderate monotonic correlation between the variables "*RAM Usage*" and "time", thus suggesting the occurrence of the software aging phenomenon. It indicates a moderate and continuous growth in RAM consumption over time, which may be associated with a memory leak combined with fragmentation.

5.3   Time to Failure Estimate

Based on the parameters returned by the *Mann-Kendall* test, an increasing trend in the RAM usage was confirmed, with a linear growth pattern estimated by Eq. 4.

Table 3. Mann-Kendall Test Results for RAM Usage

Parameter	Value
Trend	*increasing*
Hypothesis rejected (h)	True
p-value	0.000
Z statistic	110.68260395439707
Kendall's coefficient (τ)	0.3459500789512112
S statistic	358046485.0
S variance (var_S)	10464538756549.0
Estimated slope (Sen's slope)	11.386457 KB/min
Intercept	10946945.64 kB (10.4 GB)

$$RAM_{Usage}(t) = 10946945.64 + 11.386457 \times t \tag{4}$$

where $RAM_{Usage}(t)$ represents the memory usage in kilobytes (KB) at time t (in minutes) from the start of monitoring. The angular coefficient or Sen's *slope* [12], calculated over the entire time series, represents the RAM usage growth rate in KB/min.

This equation, known as the Theil-Sen estimator or Kendall-Theil robust line, is highly resistant to outliers [12]. It is possible to infer, through linear approximation, the time required, counting from the start of the experiment, for RAM usage to reach the 16 GB limit (16777216 KB), that is, to extrapolate the *TTF* by RAM exhaustion. Eqs. 5 and 6, used to predict the supposed *TTF*, are shown below:

$$RAM_{limit} = 10946945.64 + 11.386457 \times TTF \tag{5}$$

$$TTF = \frac{16777216 - 10946945.64}{11.386457} \approx 512035.5 \tag{6}$$

Considering that the data were collected every 1 min, it is estimated that the system would take approximately 512035.5 min (about 356 d) to reach the critical limit of 16 GB of memory usage. However, this inference may have its accuracy affected due to variations in the growth rate over time, depending on the analyzed temporal dataset, as demonstrated in Fig. 7. It should be noted that if the server VM were configured with a smaller amount of memory, for example, 13 GB of RAM, a *TTF* estimate due to exhaustion would be obtained much earlier than the 356 d.

Therefore, the results from the Theil-Sen estimator, based on the MK tests performed after each stress-wait cycle, indicate that a conclusion regarding software aging drawn from a short-duration experiment may be erroneous or premature, corroborating the findings of the study by [16], as shown in Table 4. It is noteworthy that the first 222 h, corresponding to the first 4 stress-wait cycles, were not sufficient, according to the Mann-Kendall test, to confirm the effects of aging, as they did not show a growth trend.

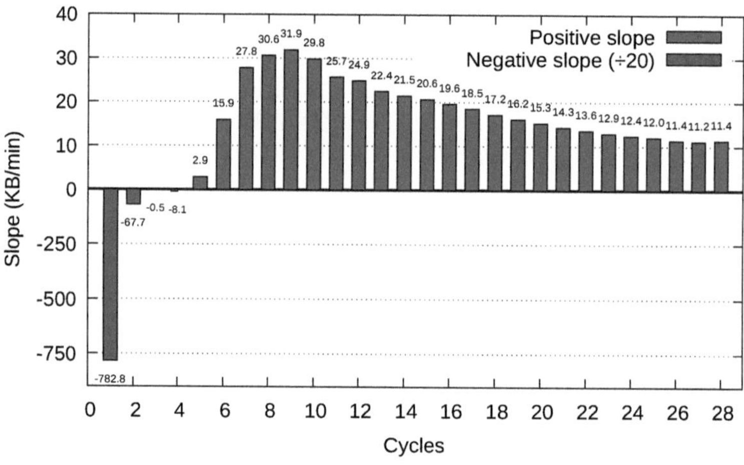

Fig. 7. RAM growth rate per cycle

Table 4. Trend Analysis and TTF Prediction After Each Stress-Wait Cycle

Cycle	Days	Slope (MB/h)	Intercept (MB)	Trend	TTF (days)
1	2.50	-45.76	11689.60	decreasing	∞*
2	4.75	-3.96	10771.84	decreasing	∞*
3	7.00	-0.03	10482.31	no trend	∞*
4	9.25	-0.48	10546.31	decreasing	∞*
5	11.50	0.17	10470.91	no trend	1461.4
6	13.75	0.93	10368.75	increasing	268.3
7	16.00	1.62	10281.76	increasing	156.1
8	18.25	1.79	10265.98	increasing	142.1
9	20.50	1.86	10258.32	increasing	136.7
10	22.75	1.74	10287.72	increasing	145.3
11	25.00	1.50	10346.26	increasing	167.0
12	27.25	1.45	10361.40	increasing	172.3
13	29.50	1.31	10404.16	increasing	189.6
14	31.75	1.25	10418.31	increasing	197.8
15	34.00	1.21	10432.71	increasing	205.0
16	36.25	1.14	10451.98	increasing	215.1
17	38.50	1.08	10478.60	increasing	226.9
18	40.75	1.00	10511.66	increasing	243.1
19	43.00	0.94	10537.62	increasing	257.2
20	45.25	0.89	10563.87	increasing	271.3
21	47.50	0.84	10591.26	increasing	287.5
22	49.75	0.80	10613.31	increasing	301.5
23	52.00	0.75	10635.21	increasing	316.6
24	54.25	0.73	10651.59	increasing	327.6
25	56.50	0.70	10665.66	increasing	337.7
26	58.75	0.67	10688.50	increasing	354.9
27	61.00	0.65	10697.29	increasing	362.0
28	63.25	0.67	10690.38	increasing	355.6

Slope $\leq$ 0 or intercept $\geq$ 16 GB: will not fail.

6   Final Remarks

The continuous growth of RAM usage, totaling an increase of approximately $\approx$1.2 GB over 63.25 d (28 stress-wait cycles), revealed a possible symptom of software aging on MongoDB, obtained through the methodological investigation approach proposed in this work, called *"SWCycles"*, which consists of a long-duration non-functional software performance test. The testbed did not notably exhibit symptoms of aging in other monitored metrics (CPU, Network Rates, Disk I/O Rates), justifiably demonstrating that the system took computational advantage of the large available RAM margin, thus reducing the intensity of degradation in these metrics. A smaller amount of memory could have caused bottlenecks due to insufficient RAM and cache to efficiently store and process data, resulting in slower processing speeds and higher latency.

Nevertheless, the *SWCycles* investigation method proved useful and effective in highlighting the trend toward RAM resource exhaustion, which was confirmed by the *Mann-Kendall* statistical test. Furthermore, the results of this study encourage that attention regarding software aging should be comparatively extended to others NoSQL DBMSs and that new and deeper investigations should be conducted to confirm or refute the conclusions presented here. Finally, we implemented a truly long-duration experiment and observed that, after a long period of stress cycles, the growth rate began to gradually decrease and exhibit a logarithmic behavior curve, leading to longer *TTF* estimates, although the trend remained monotonically increasing.

As future work, we intend to investigate and compare other non-relational database solutions.

References

1. Bovenzi, A., Cotroneo, D., Pietrantuono, R., Russo, S.: On the aging effects due to concurrency bugs: a case study on mysql. In: 2012 IEEE 23rd International Symposium on Software Reliability Engineering, pp. 211–220 (2012). https://doi.org/10.1109/ISSRE.2012.50
2. Cassidy, K., Gross, K., Malekpour, A.: Advanced pattern recognition for detection of complex software aging phenomena in online transaction processing servers. In: Proceedings International Conference on Dependable Systems and Networks, pp. 478–482 (2002). https://doi.org/10.1109/DSN.2002.1028933
3. da Costa, J.T., de S. Matos, R., de Araujo, J.C.T., Maciel, P.R.M.: Systematic mapping of literature on software aging and rejuvenation research trends. In: 2021 Annual Reliability and Maintainability Symposium (RAMS), pp. 1–6 (2021). https://doi.org/10.1109/RAMS48097.2021.9605775
4. Costa, P., Ordonez, E., Araujo, J.: A systematic mapping on software aging and rejuvenation prediction models in edge, fog and cloud architectures. In: Proceedings of the 26th International Conference on Enterprise Information Systems - Volume 1: ICEIS, pp. 933–942. INSTICC, SciTePress (2024).https://doi.org/10.5220/0012633900003690

5. Cotroneo, D., Natella, R.: Monitoring of aging software systems affected by integer overflows. In: 2012 IEEE 23rd International Symposium on Software Reliability Engineering Workshops, pp. 265–270 (2012). https://doi.org/10.1109/ISSREW.2012.91

6. Cotroneo, D., Natella, R., Pietrantuono, R., Russo, S.: A survey of software aging and rejuvenation studies. J. Emerg. Technol. Comput. Syst. **10**(1) (2014). https://doi.org/10.1145/2539117, https://doi-org.ez20.periodicos.capes.gov.br/10.1145/2539117

7. Couto, H., Andrade, E., Silva, F.A., Callou, G.: Analysis of software aging in a database environment. IEEE Lat. Am. Trans. **21**(7), 821–828 (2023). https://doi.org/10.1109/TLA.2023.10244181

8. Couto, H., Machida, F., Callou, G., Andrade, E.: A comparative analysis of software aging in relational database system environments. IEEE Transactions on Emerging Topics in Computing, pp. 1–12 (2024). https://doi.org/10.1109/TETC.2024.3471684

9. DB-Engines: DB-engines ranking of database management systems (2025). https://db-engines.com/en/ranking

10. Grottke, M., Matias, R., Trivedi, K.S.: The fundamentals of software aging. In: 2008 IEEE International Conference on Software Reliability Engineering Workshops (ISSRE Wksp), pp. 1–6 (2008). https://doi.org/10.1109/ISSREW.2008.5355512

11. Hartmann, T., Noll, A., Gross, T.: Efficient code management for dynamic multi-tiered compilation systems, pp. 51–62. PPPJ '14, Association for Computing Machinery, New York, NY, USA (2014). https://doi.org/10.1145/2647508.2647513

12. Helsel, D.R., Hirsch, R.M., Ryberg, K.R., Archfield, S.A., Gilroy, E.: Statistical methods in water resources, U.S. Geological Survey Techniques and Methods, vol. 4 (2020). https://doi.org/10.3133/tm4a3

13. Huang, Y., Kintala, C., Kolettis, N., Fulton, N.D.: Software rejuvenation: analysis, module and applications. In: Proceeding of 25th Symp. on Fault Tolerant Computing, FTCS-25, pp. 381–390. Pasadena (1995)

14. Johnstone, M.S., Wilson, P.R.: The memory fragmentation problem: Solved? ACM Sigplan Notices **34**(3), 26–36 (1998)

15. Macêdo, A., Ferreira, T.B., Matias, R.: The mechanics of memory-related software aging. In: 2010 IEEE Second International Workshop on Software Aging and Rejuvenation, pp. 1–5. Ieee (2010)

16. Machida, F., Andrzejak, A., Matias, R., Vicente, E.: On the effectiveness of mann-kendall test for detection of software aging. In: 2013 IEEE International Symposium on Software Reliability Engineering Workshops (ISSREW), pp. 269–274 (2013). https://doi.org/10.1109/ISSREW.2013.6688905

17. Mann, H.B.: Nonparametric tests against trend. Econometrica **13**(3), 245–259 (1945)

18. Matias, R., Barbetta, P.A., Trivedi, K.S., Filho, P.J.F.: Accelerated degradation tests applied to software aging experiments. IEEE Trans. Reliab. **59**(1), 102–114 (2010). https://doi.org/10.1109/TR.2009.2034292

19. Matias, R., Beicker, I., Leitão, B., Maciel, P.R.: Measuring software aging effects through OS kernel instrumentation. In: 2010 IEEE Second International Workshop on Software Aging and Rejuvenation, pp. 1–6. IEEE (2010)

20. Melo, M., Araujo, J., Umesh, I.M., Maciel, P.R.M.: Sware: an approach to support software aging and rejuvenation experiments. J. Adv. Theor. Appl. Inf. **3**(1), 31–38 (2017). https://doi.org/10.26729/jadi.v3i1.2441

21. MongoDB, Inc.: $in — mongodb query operator —(2024). https://www.mongodb.com/docs/manual/reference/operator/query/in/, Accessed on 21 Jan 2025

22. MongoDB, Inc.: MongoDB community server (2025). https://www.mongodb.com/try/download/community, the free, self-managed, and source-available version of MongoDB
23. Oliveira, F., et al.: Experimental evaluation of software aging effects in a container-based virtualization platform. In: 2020 IEEE International Conference on Systems, Man, and Cybernetics (SMC), pp. 414–419 (2020). https://doi.org/10.1109/SMC42975.2020.9283358
24. Sen, P.K.: Estimates of the regression coefficient based on kendall's tau. J. Am. Stat. Assoc. **63**(324), 1379–1389 (1968). https://doi.org/10.2307/2285891
25. de Sena, G.O., Matias, R.: A systematic mapping review of memory leak detection techniques. In: 2018 IEEE International Symposium on Software Reliability Engineering Workshops (ISSREW), pp. 264–270 (2018). https://doi.org/10.1109/ISSREW.2018.00017
26. Tang, M., Zhang, P., Sun, H., Zhang, L.: A task execution framework based on aging indicator and sarimi. In: 2020 IEEE International Conference on Parallel & Distributed Processing with Applications, Big Data & Cloud Computing, Sustainable Computing & Communications, Social Computing & Networking (ISPA/BDCloud/SocialCom/SustainCom), pp. 18–25 (2020).https://doi.org/10.1109/ISPA-BDCloud-SocialCom-SustainCom51426.2020.00029
27. Valentim, N.A., Macedo, A., Matias, R.: A systematic mapping review of the first 20 years of software aging and rejuvenation research, pp. 57 – 63 (2016). https://doi.org/10.1109/ISSREW.2016.42,https://www.scopus.com/inward/record.uri?eid=2-s2.0-85009756504&doi=10.1109%2fISSREW.2016.42&partnerID=40&md5=f3b82aea33bd8b2e4b0533c0bf5d96b4
28. Yue, J., Wu, X., Xue, Y.: Microservice aging and rejuvenation. In: 2020 World Conference on Computing and Communication Technologies (WCCCT), pp. 1–5 (2020). https://doi.org/10.1109/WCCCT49810.2020.9170005

Advances in Dependable and Secure Computing (Best Paper Candidates)

Addressing Cryptographic Overheads in Low-Latency File Systems Through Ahead-of-Time Encryption

Jorge Pires Correia$^{(\boxtimes)}$ and Wagner Machado N. Zola

Federal University of Paraná, Curitiba, Brazil
`{jpcorreia,wagner}@inf.ufpr.br`

Abstract. Historically, the high latency of storage devices masked the impact of software overheads in the storage stack. However, with the advent of microsecond-scale storage devices, the performance cost of adding new software layers has become more significant. In particular, integrating cryptographic operations into file systems that run on low-latency devices poses substantial challenges. This paper investigates the application of ahead-of-time and speculative encryption techniques to in-kernel file systems, tailored for modern storage devices. Our experimental results demonstrate that these techniques significantly improve both latency and throughput, outperforming current cryptographic file systems.

Keywords: file system architecture · cryptographic file system · ahead-of-time encryption · low-latency storage

1   Introduction

Read or write requests to a storage device can be divided into two parts: (i) the **software part** represents the time spent by the storage stack, which is implemented in the Operating System (OS) and is responsible for performing management and abstraction operations; (ii) the **hardware part** is called by the software part, which represents the time spent by the storage device to satisfy the data request. When Hard Disk Drivers (HDDs) are used, software overhead in data requests is negligible because the hardware takes almost 100% of the total latency to perform I/O operations. However, flash storage devices have evolved to the point that software overhead can represent almost 50% of the total latency of a data request [24].

Although Cryptographic File Systems (CFSs) provide privacy and confidentiality to stored data, they also increase the software overhead as they constitute an additional layer on the storage stack. This additional overhead is not significant considering the usage of a high-latency storage device like HDDs, however, optimizing it in a low-latency scenario has big potential to improve the overall performance. Conceptually, the cryptographic operations are executed in sequence with the usual file system path. On a read operation, for example, the

L. A. Rodrigues and R. Oliveira (Eds.): LADC 2025, CCIS 2697, pp. 221–237, 2026.
https://doi.org/10.1007/978-3-032-11539-3_13

file system needs to wait for the disk to bring the data to memory before starting the decryption. Similarly, on a write operation, the disk must wait for the encryption to finish before starting to store the data. A clever way to make the CFS path more flexible is made possible by Warped AES (WAES) [25]. WAES is a method to execute the Advanced Encryption Standard (AES) algorithm using Counter (CTR) mode in a manner that the heavy cryptographic computation is performed in advance (**ahead-of-time**) and in **parallel**. These two WAES characteristics fit perfectly in the file system context: the ahead-of-time processing allows the heavy cryptography computation to be performed before the data is ready in memory; the parallel characteristic allows different requests to be handled at the same time.

This idea was explored by EncFS++ [3], a user-space CFS that was able to improve the latency and throughput when compared to EncFS [5], the regular user-space CFS that was used as the base for EncFS++ implementation. Despite the optimization of the cryptographic overhead itself, it is worth mentioning that the utilization of a user-space file system implies an I/O latency degradation [18], which is inherent in the communication between the user-level file system and the kernel components that compose the storage stack. For instance, the overhead imposed by FUSE [17], a popular library used to implement a user-space file system (including EncFS and EncFS++), can degrade the total I/O latency by $2\times$ with an NVMe storage device (Sect. 5). Moreover, the faster the storage device is, the more impactful the software overhead becomes [24]. Considering a RAM storage device, the FUSE latency can make the total latency almost $9\times$ worse.

Even though there is a potential for applying ahead-of-time encryption on file systems, as shown by EncFS++, the CFS design that supports this type of encryption, considering low-latency storage restrictions, lacks research. Aiming to address the presented challenges, we make the following contributions: *(i)* demonstrate the impact of CFSs in a low-latency environment; *(ii)* identify the key components of an ahead-of-time CFS; *(iii)* propose a new ahead-of-time CFS design, highlighting how the key components can be merged in the Linux storage stack; *(iv)* experimental analysis of our proposal with different workloads.

2   Background

2.1   Linux Storage Subsystem

File management in Linux is composed of different levels of components, as shown in Fig. 1. The **Virtual File System** is a software layer that acts as an interface to both user space and file systems: in the former, the VFS defines the functions that can be called to perform requests for file systems through system calls; in the latter, the VFS defines the functions and structures that they must provide, enabling the coexistence of several file systems at the same time. **File systems** form the software layer responsible for the access policy and organization of user data on storage devices and their requests. As each device may have different policies and architectures, the **block I/O layer** provides an interface for the upper systems and hides the complex and detailed management of these resources. There are some requests made by users that are optimized by the Page Cache, a set of pages in memory (RAM) that cache disk blocks. When a read request generates a cache hit on the Page Cache, or when a write request is issued to a block present in the Page Cache, the operation can be resumed in a memory copy to/from the cache to/from the user buffer without generating access to the storage hardware.

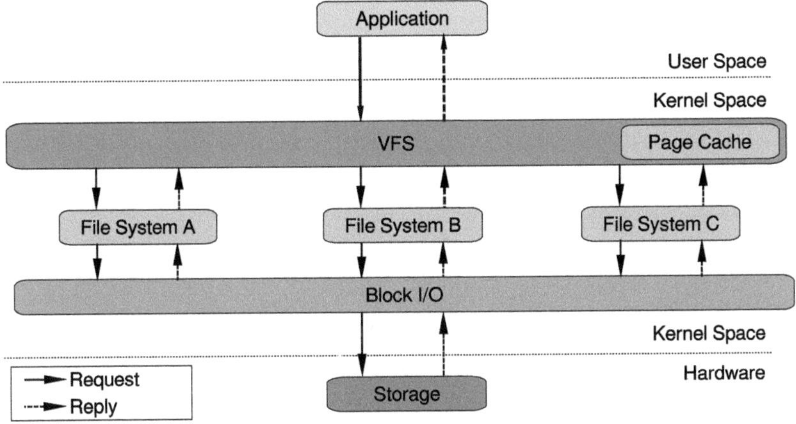

Fig. 1. Linux Storage Stack

2.2 Ahead-of-Time Encryption

Advanced Encryption Standard (AES) was standardized by NIST [2] and became the most used cryptographic specification. As a block cipher, the AES handles small data blocks of 128 bits. Since most data is bigger than the block size handled by AES, modes of operation like Cipher Block Chaining (CBC), XEX-based Tweaked-codebook mode with Ciphertext Stealing (XTS), and Counter (CTR) need to be applied to allow the usage of AES on arbitrary data size.

The CTR mode, presented in Fig. 2, processes each block individually, applying the block cipher on a per-block 128-bit counter, and the result is XORed with the plain data block. The counter can be concatenated with a random number, producing a *nonce* that is used just once with the same key. CTR can encrypt or decrypt different blocks at the same time. The security of this mode of operation has been proved, provided they are correctly applied [11], making them widely used in different scenarios. The heavy workload of cryptographic operations is performed inside the dotted area, and its parameters are the **nonce** and the **key**. As the data is not necessary in this step, it can be executed in advance, before the data is ready to be processed. This first process generates a **cryptography mask** that will be applied to the data blocks through an XOR operation, generating the encrypted or decrypted data. Such a scheme, combined with the possibility of creating masks simultaneously in different processor cores, is explored by WAES and implemented in a library called WAESlib [25].

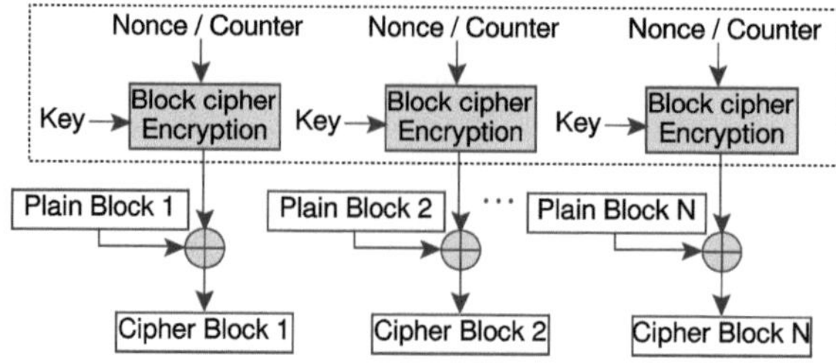

Fig. 2. CTR mode of operation

3 Viability and Potential of Ahead-of-Time Processing in a Low-Latency CFS Context

The breakdown of the execution of a typical CFS read operation is shown in Fig. 3a. Even though the CPU is free to execute some work while the underlying storage device is treating the I/O operation, all operations are executed sequentially because the data needs to be in memory to be processed. On the other hand, by applying ahead-of-time encryption, the data dependency is restricted to a minimum at the XOR step, and the previously available CPU time can be used to produce encryption masks, mostly hiding the latency of the decryption operation, as shown in Fig. 3b.

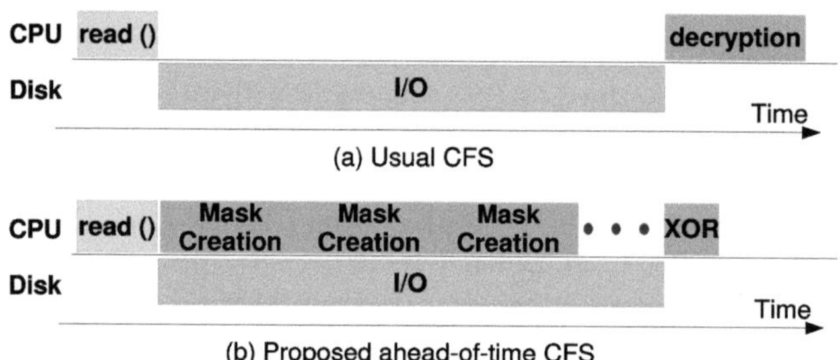

Fig. 3. Execution of usual and proposed CFS

When the read operation is called, the CFS can submit mask requests to WAESlib, and the worker threads will perform the mask creations. When both the data and the masks are ready, the actual decryption is finalized by XOR-ing the masks and the data. It is reasonable to think that the longer the I/O time is, the more masks can be created, leading to better performance. In fact, large I/O time provided by slow devices provides room to create many masks. However, using these storage devices implies a negligible impact of the cryptographic operations on the total latency of the read request. This would conceal the cryptographic optimizations.

Considering the scenario above, two questions arise: Firstly, for low-latency devices, where the cryptographic overhead is significant compared to the I/O time, would there be enough room to create masks? We can answer this question by analyzing Table 1. It shows the time of a 4kB read request, starting right after the submission to the block I/O layer until the interrupt callback. Besides, it shows the time for encrypting a 4kB data block and the time for performing an XOR between two 4kB blocks. We can notice that the NVMe device provides more room than needed, and the RAM-block device, which emulates an ideal storage device, provides less room than needed. On the other hand, we know that novel storage hardware works on a microsecond scale [23,24], which indicates that their latency is lower than our NVMe, but higher than the RAM-blocked device, as well as bigger than the mask creation time for our CPU.

This leads us to the second question: For low-latency devices where the I/O time is less than the mask creation time, it is possible to achieve good performance? The ideal scenario would be if the mask creation time is equal to the I/O time. This would allow us to hide the whole cryptographic overhead and optimize it completely. If the I/O time is bigger than necessary, it means that we are able to hide the whole cryptographic overhead and maintain the total latency really close to the vanilla file system (without cryptographic), but the bigger the unused I/O time, the less impactful the optimization will be when compared to usual CFSs. If the I/O time is shorter than the mask creation time, we will be able to use the whole I/O time to generate cryptographic masks, in other words, we will have higher optimization when compared to usual CFSs, however, the bigger the time spent after the I/O operation, the bigger will be the overhead when compared to vanilla file systems. In Sect. 5, we demonstrate how this tradeoff works in practice.

Table 1. Read times and processing times for 4096-byte operations. Hardware and software details are in Sect. 5.

Read Time	
Backed Device	Read time
RAM	557 ns
NVMe	18456 ns
Processing Time	
Operation	Time
XOR	318 ns
Mask Creation	1192 ns

If for read operations we can create masks while the I/O is being executed, masks for write operations can be created even earlier. This is possible because new blocks will have new nonces, enabling the creation of a pool of masks that will serve all write operations in the file system, as presented in Sect. 4.4.

The CTR mode of operation has the disadvantage of needing one nonce per 128-bit data block. However, WAESlib provides a way to create an abstraction of the data block size. Since file systems handle data in block granularity, it is possible to use the abstraction provided by WAESlib to store one nonce per 4096-byte data block, maintaining the space overhead below 0.4%.

To maintain the security of CTR mode [11], each nonce needs to be composed of two parts: an unpredictable number and a counter. For each write request (creation of a new block or modification of an existing one), a 64-bit unpredictable number is used with a 64-bit counter that is incremented for each data block written. WAESlib applies this restriction alongside the possibility of abstracting the mask size. At its initialization, it is possible to define a block size as a set of 128-bit blocks. With this information, the WAESlib reserves a set of bits of the 64-bit counter to use as an internal counter. A 4096-byte data block implies reserving 8 bits of the counter portion of the nonce, maintaining the usage of one nonce per 128-bit data block.

4   A Cross-Stack Ahead-of-Time Encryption File System

Throughout the idealization and implementation phase of this work, we were able to identify four key challenges that could guide our efforts: nonce storage, execution flows, WAESlib adaptation, and management of cryptographic contexts. We called our proof-of-concept implementation *ext4james*.

4.1   Nonce Storage

Since we need one 16-byte nonce for each data block, we have to handle it in a manner that its storage and retrieval do not generate significant overhead. Then, we adopted a design inspired by ext4 volume management [8] merged with the n-node introduced by EncFS++, taking advantage of the VFS storage layer and the file system layer. The first nonces of data files are stored together in a unique file called *Global File*. If necessary, each data file will have a dedicated file (referred to as *nonce files*) to store the remaining nonces. We organized the Global File as shown in Fig. 4.

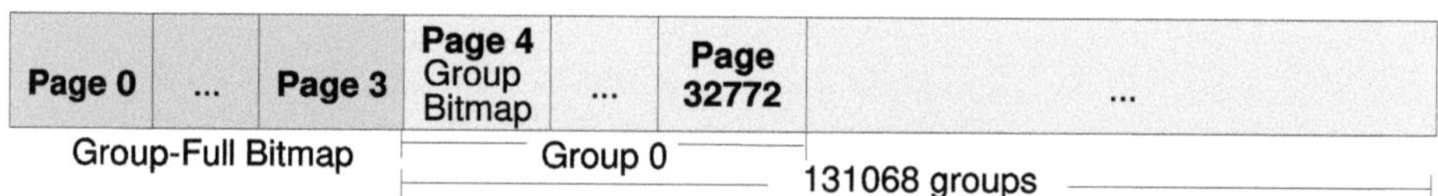

Fig. 4. Global File management

The first 256 nonces of a data file, which map its first 1MB of data, will be stored inside a page in the Global File. The Global File is divided into groups to make its management easier. Each group has $2^{15} + 1$ pages, where the first page is a bitmap that controls the usage of the other pages of this group. All the other pages in the group store the first nonces of different data files.

The first 4 pages of the Global File make up what is called Group-Full Bitmap. This bitmap indicates the groups that do not have more space to map new data files, thus composing a 2-level bitmap with the per-group bitmaps. This design provides a good use of the size of the Global File and optimized management of free pages due to the hierarchical bitmap. To address a page inside the Global File, a 32-bit integer can be used: the first 17 bits address the group, and the last 15 bits address the page inside the group.

To link the page index of the Global File (and the nonce file, if necessary) to a data file, we took advantage of the file system layer. The ext4 file system provides a mechanism called extended attributes, allowing us to store additional metadata in the inode without extra block allocations. To perform the creation, deletion, reading, and writing of the Global File and nonce files, we took advantage of the VFS layer interfaces, making these operations bypass the cryptographic operations and not impose any cryptographic overhead. To avoid the software overhead each time we access a data block, we perform nonce reading and writing in a block granularity and keep a cached block for each data file, in a way that nonce requests do not impact the CFS performance.

The nonce generation occurs on each write operation. We maintain an integer called Global Counter that is incremented by 256 (leaving 8 bits reserved for WAESlib block size abstraction) on each write request. Then, when a write operation is performed, the current Global Counter value is concatenated with an unpredictable random 64-bit value, making up the used nonce.

4.2 Execution Flows

The most important operation of an ahead-of-time CFS is the mask request. The CFS has to submit the mask creation at a moment when it is very likely that the mask will be ready when the data is also ready. If we trigger mask creations as soon as possible, right after the user performs the request at the VFS layer, we would not be able to differentiate when a request affects just the Page Cache or generates I/O operations. Then, we choose to use the interface between the file system layer and the block I/O layer, where we can ensure that an I/O request will be issued. Besides, using this interface provides information for both the file system and block I/O layer: we can access all extended attributes, and all parameters passed to the block I/O layer, which provides useful information to deal with physical addresses and helps to track this request until it is finished on the interrupt requests. The communication between the file system layer and the block I/O layer is made using a structure called `bio`, which contains information like block number and file reference. This structure is also used to keep track of the request until the storage device signals the end of the operation.

Figure 5 shows the architecture of the proposed CFS, where the dotted red arrows indicate the operations performed in write requests (encryption operations), and the dashed blue arrows represent the operations in read requests (decrypt operations). Black arrows are common for the two operation types.

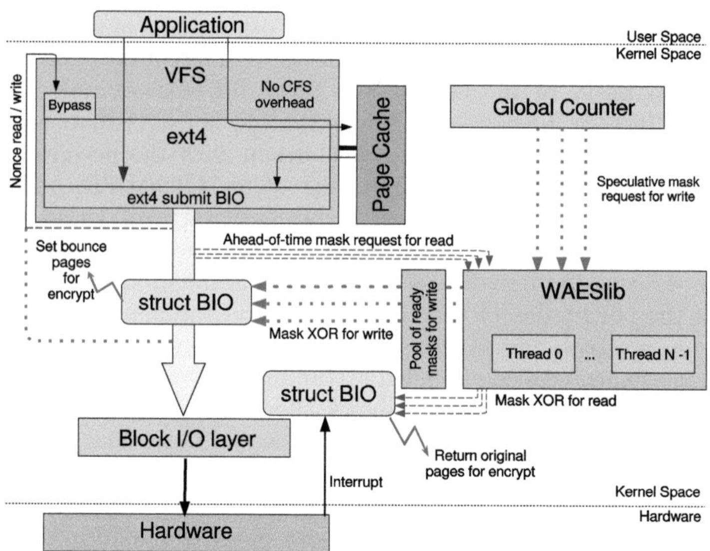

Fig. 5. ext4james architecture

Firstly, we will analyze the write operations. Write requests made by the application that just impact the Page Cache do not suffer any cryptographic overhead, as the memory is decrypted. When the kernel decides to write back some pages from the cache, or when an application performs direct write requests, ext4 creates a request to the block I/O layer by filling up and submitting a `bio` structure. As stored data needs to be encrypted, the cryptographic mask needs to be applied before the `bio` submission. It means that the mask request needs to happen even earlier. Since write operations use new nonces, the cryptographic masks for them can be created speculatively. Thus, it is possible to create a pool of masks ready to be used in any write operations, in a manner that it is very likely that a mask is ready to be applied when a request is made. After the completion of the operation, the used nonce is stored to allow the data decryption on read operations. We can not perform the encryption operation directly on the pages referenced by the `bio` because it would encrypt the Page Cache or the user memory. To avoid it, we maintain a pool of physical pages that we call *bounce pages*. The result of each encrypted page is put in a bounce page, and the `bio` references are changed to point to the used bounce pages. When the I/O operation is finished, we return the original pages to maintain the kernel management consistency.

As in the write operations, read requests that are resolved by the Page Cache do not generate cryptographic overhead. When a page needs to be brought to the Page Cache, or an application performs a direct read, ext4 builds and submits a new `bio` structure. Unlike write operations, data decryption occurs after the I/O operation. Then, the I/O time can be used to create the mask involved in the operation. When the `bio` structure is ready, right before the submission to the lower layer, the CFS already has access to the index of the blocks involved in the I/O, which is all the information needed to create masks. Then, it is possible to find the nonces referred to these blocks in the Global File or a nonce file and submit the mask creation. When the storage device generates an interrupt indicating the end of the I/O operation, the masks will likely also be ready to be applied.

4.3 WAESlib Adaption

WAESlib is responsible for providing easy-to-perform ahead-of-time encryption. Since it is a user-space library, we need to completely reimplement it to be able to use its functionalities in the kernel. Besides, the original WAESlib offloads the work to the GPU, which is not possible to do in kernel space. Then, we took advantage of AES-NI [6], a set of instructions present in contemporary CPUs that bring lower latency to encryption operations. The Crypto API [13], provided by the Linux kernel, was used to perform AES-NI-accelerated operations transparently. The XOR operation is executed through AVX instructions [12].

As mask creation requests can be handled in parallel, we create a pool of WAESlib worker threads that wake up if there is any pending request to be satisfied. The requests are queued in a binary heap, making it possible to implement a priority mechanism in the sequence of masks that are created.

4.4 Management of Cryptographic Context

A cryptographic context is a structure that represents a cryptographic operation. Each structure contains the source and destination buffer, cryptographic key, nonce, and priority. The WAESlib provides all the cryptographic contexts individually, and it is up to the CFS to manage them. As the masks for write operations are created in a different execution context than the masks for read, we manage them differently.

Firstly, we will analyze the cryptographic context management for read operations. Each read request is composed of a set of sequential blocks. Since each block needs one mask, a pool of cryptographic contexts is necessary per read operation. The ideal scenario would be to reserve the same number of contexts as the number of pages being read, which would allow the worker threads to produce the maximum number of masks they are able to. However, a set of processes performing large reading requests could acquire a large number of contexts, unbalancing the usage between other processes. Then, we set the maximum number of acquirable contexts per request. If a process is reading more pages than its context pool size, the CFS will treat the pool as a sliding window, in a manner that when a mask is applied, its context is used to create the next mask still not requested. We implemented the maximum number of contexts per request as a tunable variable that depends on the available memory and the storage device latency: a larger context pool will allocate more memory since each context needs one page to hold the mask; meanwhile, a small context pool can prevent the worker threads from producing all needed masks during I/O operation.

For write requests, we used a single fixed-size context pool. This context pool is a sliding window that will create masks given the Global Counter, starting at mount time. When a write I/O operation happens, the file system can apply a mask that was requested even before the write operation happens, and the nonce used in the operation is stored in the Global File or the dedicated nonce file. After mask utilization, the context that contained this mask can be used to create a mask that will serve further write operations.

5 Evaluation

We performed our tests using the well-known FIO [1] benchmark tool, allowing us to produce different access patterns. The described tests were executed in a Linux version 6.1.10 running on a machine equipped with an Intel(R) Core(TM) i7-10700 CPU @ 2.90GHz processor, 16GB 2933MHz DDR4 memory (RAM), and an NVMe ADATA SX6000LNP. The Linux Governor, which manages the CPU frequency scale, was set to performance mode. All operations were performed using direct I/O, and then all requests generated I/O operations.

Our evaluation seeks to achieve three main goals. The first one is to analyze the advantage of the proposed design over the existing ahead-of-time user-space stacked CFS. EncFS++ does not provide direct I/O support, which makes it difficult to measure the I/O overhead because of Page Cache optimizations. Then BBFS [14] was used to provide a baseline for user-space file systems performance. BBFS is a user-space file system implemented through the FUSE library that simply redirects every operation down to ext4. Considering that BBFS does not execute any cryptographic operation, we can enssure that EncFS++ performance is no better than BBFS.

The second objective of our evaluation is to demonstrate the advantage of the proposed system over CFSs used nowadays. For this, we ran fscrypt [9], an in-kernel Linux CFS implemented with hooks inside ext4, using XTS mode of operation through Linux Crypto API at block I/O level. We decided to compare our proposal with fscrypt because it is the default CFS present in the Linux kernel, and it runs in a very similar context to ext4james, which gives us a fair comparison of cryptographic operations and architectures. Aiming for a completely fair comparison, we also implemented and ran an ext4james version that uses CTR mode of operation without ahead-of-time encryption (default CTR), making it easy to understand when the ahead-of-time optimization is relevant. We also ran vanilla ext4 without performing cryptographic operations, to allow us to understand the overhead imposed by all CFSs. The third goal of our evaluation is to clarify the behavior of an ahead-of-time CFS, exemplifying and discussing the influences of different hardware properties on the proposed system.

Figure 6a shows the throughput of sequential read requests using the NVMe storage device. On the right y-axis, the bandwidth variation between ext4james and fscrypt is presented. Figure 6b shows the latency of the operations.

The first point to be considered by looking at the results is that just using the CTR mode does not generate performance improvements when compared to

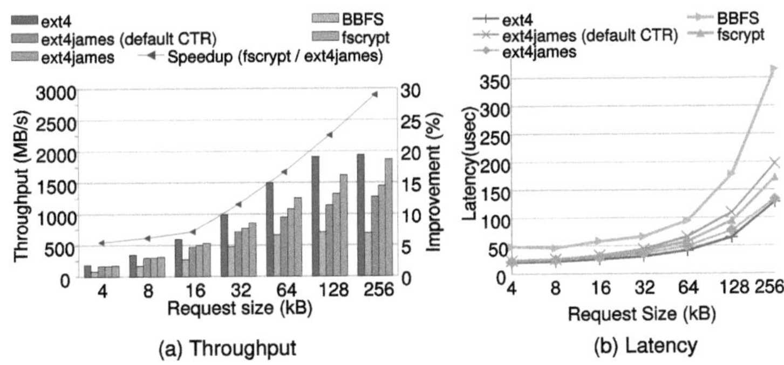

Fig. 6. Sequential read (NVMe backed)

fscrypt. The usage of XTS mode, which is optimized to be applied to storage contexts, provides better performance. However, when ahead-of-time encryption is used, the ext4james improves the throughput by up to 28% and decreases the latency by up to 22% for this scenario. Besides, even though BBFS does not perform cryptographic operations, its latency is higher than all the CFSs, demonstrating the overhead imposed by a user-space execution.

In order to help us look deeper at these results, Table 2 presents the average I/O time for different request patterns and the average time to create one mask. The I/O time starts when the file system layer submits the request to the block layer I/O and ends when the storage device generates the interrupt signaling the end of the operation. Given the request size and the average I/O time, we can calculate how much time is available to create each mask. As presented in Sect. 3, the average time to create a mask is 1192 ns. Then, for all request sizes of sequential read requests in an NVMe, there is enough room to create all masks and take total advantage of the ahead-of-time encryption, which makes the ext4james latencies very close to the vanilla ext4 latencies.

We can also verify that ext4james achieves better performance as the request size increases. There are two factors that lead to it: mask request aggregation and the impact of cryptographic operations. For a 4kB request, one mask creation is submitted at a time, while for 256kB requests, 64 mask creations are submitted at a time. If more masks are submitted together, the worker threads can handle the requests without sleep, avoiding the task switch overheads. Besides, as shown in Table 2, the storage device spends less time per block for a large request. If the I/O time is smaller, the impact of cryptographic operations on the total latency is bigger, making our proposal optimize a large portion of the whole operation.

To demonstrate that the impact of cryptographic operations is bigger for low-latency storage devices, we performed the same sequential read workload applied to a RAM block device. As shown in Fig. 7, we can verify that for a low-latency storage device, ext4james can improve the throughput by up to 77% and decrease the latency by up to 45% (compared to 28% of throughput and 22% of latency in the NVMe-backed scenario). This improvement is possible

Table 2. I/O times of sequential read (NVMe backed), sequential read (RAM backed), and random read (NVMe-backed)

I/O times of sequential read (NVMe backed)						
Request Size (kB)	4	8	16	32	64	128	256
Average I/O time (us)	18.2	20	23.5	28.6	38.3	58.4	103.5
Average us per mask	18.2	10	5.9	3.5	2.3	1.8	1.6

I/O times of sequential read (RAM backed)						
Request Size (kB)	4	8	16	32	64	128	256
Average I/O time (us)	0.4	0.7	1.3	2.5	5	9.8	19.7
Average us per mask	0.4	0.3	0.3	0.4	0.3	0.3	0.3

I/O times of random read (NVMe-backed)						
Request Size (kB)	4	8	16	32	64	128	256
Average I/O time (us)	121.8	145.6	162.1	202.7	218.2	235.1	-
Average us per mask	121.8	72.8	40.5	25.3	13.6	7.3	-

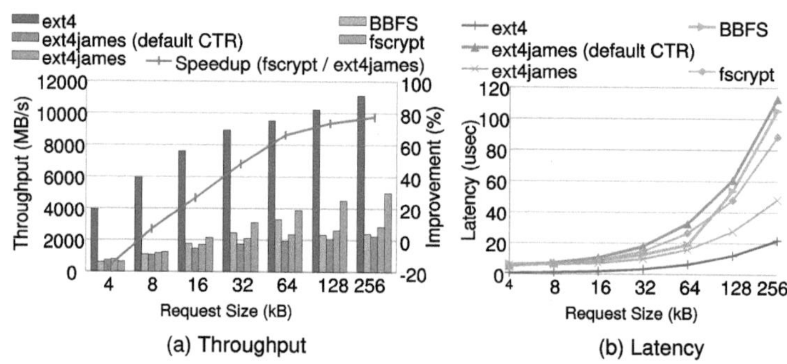

Fig. 7. Sequential read (RAM backed)

because the worker threads are able to use all the I/O time to perform mask creations that, in this case, constitute a large portion of the total operation. The high cryptographic operation overhead in this scenario also makes the CFSs latencies very close to the BBFS, even though ext4james is able to overcome BBFS latency, especially for large data requests.

Despite the increase in performance by ext4james compared to the other CFSs, the tradeoff cited in Sect. 3 arises. As the RAM block device does not provide sufficient time to create the masks given its nanosecond scale, as shown in Table 2, the distance between ext4james and the vanilla ext4 increases because of the time spent after the I/O operation to create the remaining masks.

It is worth mentioning that, for 4 KB requests, ext4james has a performance 20% worse than fscrypt. This is because the I/O operation is too fast, in a manner that the task switches to the worker threads are not worthwhile [20]. However, for this case, using CTR mode without ahead-of-time encryption has better performance, making it possible to switch between the approaches when the request size is small and the storage device is too fast.

Given the results in these two contexts, we can infer that for contemporary storage devices that work on a microsecond scale, latency improvement compared with other CFSs would be higher than the NVMe-backed scenario toward the RAM-back scenario. Furthermore, the overhead compared with the vanilla ext4 would not be as significant as shown in the RAM-backed scenario because microsecond-scale devices provide enough room to generate cryptographic masks.

Figure 8 shows the performance of random read workloads in both NVMe and RAM-backed scenarios. The results showed an improvement of the throughput by up to 9% and 78% in NVMe and RAM-backed devices, respectively, and a decrease of the latency by up to 8% and 43%, respectively. We decided not to report the 256 kB test for the NVMe-backed scenario because these results in vanilla ext4 were suffering big variations that reflected on all other file systems, precluding us from analyzing the cryptographic overheads. We believe that this behavior is a hardware characteristic, as it does not happen in the RAM-backed scenario.

We can notice that, in the NVMe-backed scenario, the gain is much smaller than in the sequential one, given that I/O time is significantly bigger, as shown in Table 2. In the 4 kB request, for example, we have room to create over 100 masks, but just have one request. The little increase in the gap between vanilla ext4 and ext4james can be attributed to the nonce I/O overhead since the cached block is invalidated across I/O requests. The RAM-backed scenario is similar to the sequential one. This shows an advantage of our proposal: the time to create masks is the same for either sequential or random patterns since they are handled in the same way.

Figure 9 presents the results generated by the sequential write workload. These results show an improvement of the throughput by up to 11% and 81% when using NVMe and RAM devices, respectively, and a decrease of the latency by up to 9% and 45%, respectively. Even though the NVMe-backed scenario showed smaller gains when compared to the sequential read, we maintain the latency close to the vanilla ext4, indicating that there is no room to increase the performance. This is confirmed by analyzing the RAM-backed scenario. There is a small improvement when compared to the sequential read, given that the masks are created before the request. The speculative mask creation also shows improvements with the 4kB request: for the read request, we have context switches from the interrupt context to the threads to apply the masks. This does not happen in write operations, then there is no case in which fscrypt has better performance. These results also show that the use of bounce pages does not impact the final performance. Figure 10 shows similar behavior in the random write workload, where our proposal improved the throughput by up to 13% and 74% in NVMe-backed and RAM-backed devices, respectively, and decreased the latency by up to 12% and 43%, respectively.

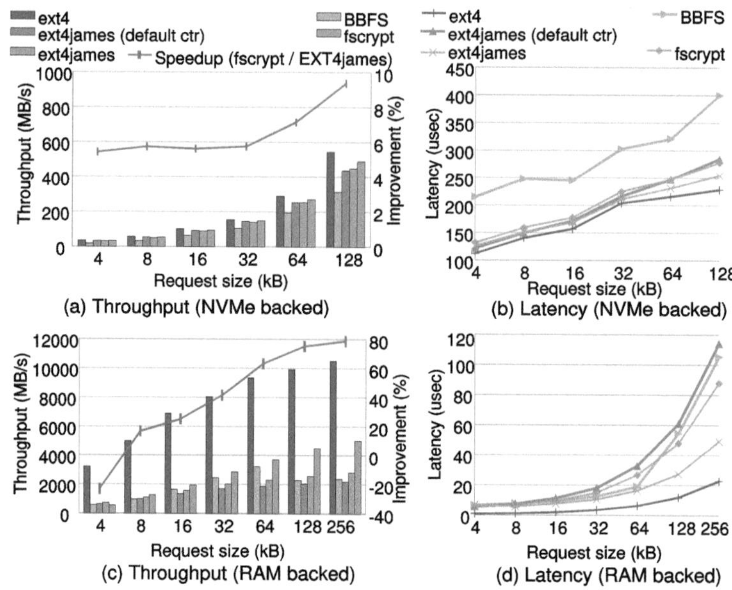

Fig. 8. Random read

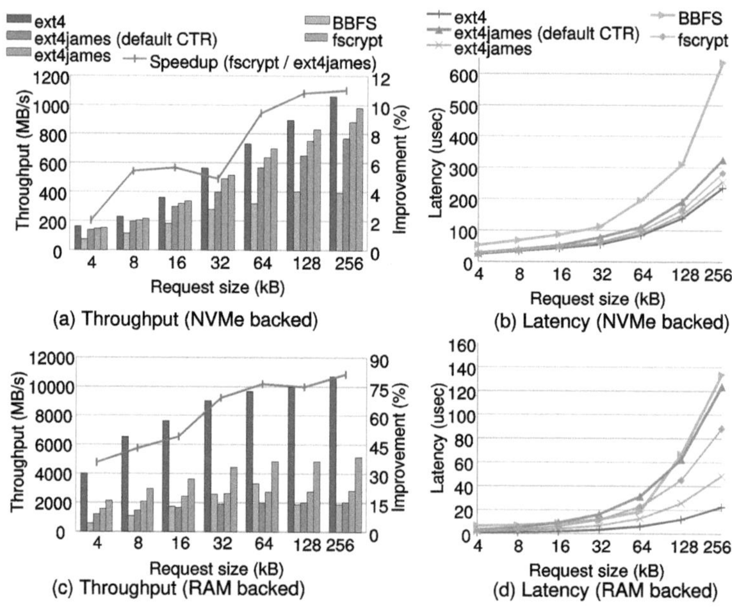

Fig. 9. Sequential write

6   Related Work

Works mostly look for performance to compensate for the cryptographic over-head, and flexibility to evict the need for change in applications. CFSs implemented in user space usually seek a specific application or flexibility. UsiFE [16] is a CFS that provides different data granularities, allowing its users to cipher specific parts of files like XMLs. SafeFS [15] tries to achieve a high level of flexibility and allows new policies like data granularity and cipher algorithms to be easily stacked and popped from the CFS. TrustFS [4] takes advantage of the SafeFS flexibility to provide support for enclaves, enabling the usage on untrusted platforms. EncFS [5] is a stacked file system that aims to provide transparent encryption, implemented using FUSE [18]. EncFS was a base CFS for some works that increment its functionalities by adding support to multi-user systems [10] or using speculative encryption using GPU [3]. CFSs implemented in kernel space usually try to achieve better performances. eCryptFS [7] is a popular stacked CFS implemented in kernel space, aiming to provide security to large-scale enterprises. eCryptFS also implements user-space daemons to take advantage of libraries available in this context. This file system was used by other works [19,21,22] which minimize the Page Cache usage by the eCryptFS, use persistent memory to create multi-layer storage, and modify the cache policy of eCryptFS dynamically.

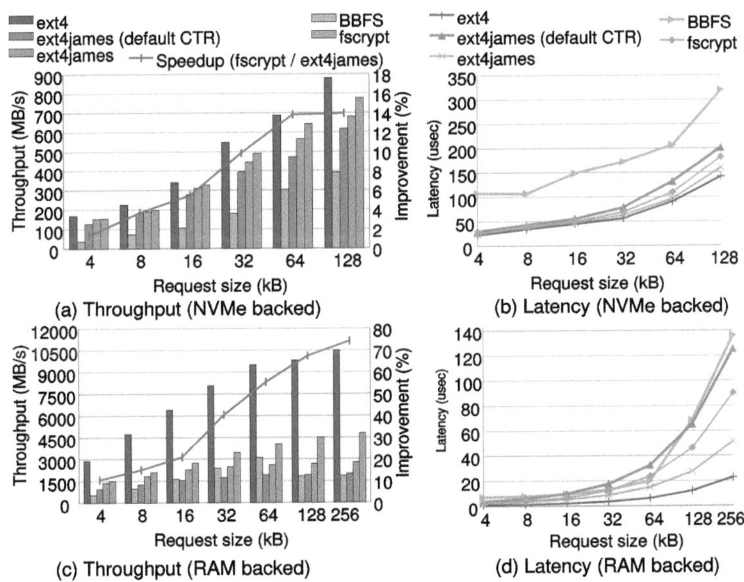

Fig. 10. Random write

7   Conclusion

This work proposed a cross-stack CFS that takes advantage of functions and information presented at each layer in the Linux storage stage to perform ahead-of-time encryption on low-latency environments. The evaluation of the proof-of-concept implementation has shown a performance improvement in different scenarios when compared to the conventional architecture, as well as provided useful discussion about the CFS behaviors. Moreover, this proposal has the potential to perform better in low-latency hardware, as the cryptographic overhead and the new file system layer compose a more significant slice of the latency of the operations. Despite we did not test our solution using contemporary hardware, we are able to understand how the CFS behaves as the I/O time decreases and understand that the optimizations of hardware allow our solution to optimize bigger portions of the total I/O latency. A more elaborate cache mechanism for nonce access and integration with key management and existing crash consistency systems are directions that can be explored in future work.

Acknowledgements. This study was financed in part by the Coordenação de Aperfeiçoamento de Pessoal de Nível Superior – Brasil (CAPES) – Finance Code 001.

References

1. Axboe, J.: Flexible io tester (fio). https://github.com/axboe/fio
2. Dworkin, M.J., et al.: Advanced Encryption Standard (AES) (2001)
3. Eduardo, V., de Bona, L.C.E., Zola, W.M.N.: Speculative encryption on GPU applied to cryptographic file systems. In: 17th USENIX Conference on File and Storage Technologies (FAST 19). pp. 93–105. USENIX Association, Boston, MA (2019). https://www.usenix.org/conference/fast19/presentation/eduardo
4. Esteves, T., et al.: TrustFS: an SGX-enabled stackable file system framework. In: 2019 38th International Symposium on Reliable Distributed Systems Workshops (SRDSW). pp. 25–30 (2019)
5. Gough, V.: EncFS: An encrypted filesystem for FUSE (2017)
6. Gueron, S.: Intel Advanced Encryption Standard (AES) New Instructions Set (2010)
7. Halcrow, M.A.: eCryptfs: An enterprise-class encrypted filesystem for Linux. In: 2005 Linux Symposium. pp. 201–218. Ottawa - Canada (2005)
8. Kernel Development Community: ext4 data structures and algorithms. https://www.kernel.org/doc/html/v6.1/filesystems/ext4/index.html (2023)
9. Kernel Development Community: Filesystem-level encryption (fscrypt). https://www.kernel.org/doc/html/v6.1/filesystems/fscrypt.html (2023)
10. Leibenger, D., Fortmann, J., Sorge, C.: EncFS goes multi-user: adding access control to an encrypted file system. In: 24th International Symposium on Research in Attacks, Intrusions and Defenses. pp. 525–533 (2016)
11. Lipmaa, H., Rogaway, P., Wagner, D.: Comments to NIST concerning AES modes of operations: CTR-mode encryption. In: First NIST Workshop on Modes of Operation. vol. 39. Citeseer. MD (2000)

12. Lomont, C.: Introduction to Intel Advanced Vector Extensions. Intel white paper **23** (2011)
13. Mueller, S., Vasut, M.: Linux kernel crypto API. https://www.kernel.org/doc/html/v6.1/crypto/index.html (2023)
14. Pfeiffer, J.J.: Writing a Fuse Filesystem: A Tutorial. https://www.cs.nmsu.edu/~pfeiffer/fuse-tutorial/ (2018)
15. Pontes, R., Burihabwa, D., et al.: SafeFS: A modular architecture for secure user-space file systems: One FUSE to rule them all. In: Proceedings of the 10th ACM International Systems and Storage Conference. pp. 1–12 (2017)
16. Sharma, R., Kallurkar, P., Kumar, S., Sarangi, S.R.: UsiFe: a user space file system with support for intra-file encryption. In: Fourth International Conference on Machine Vision (ICMV 2011): Machine Vision, Image Processing, and Pattern Analysis. pp. 321–325 (2012)
17. Szeredi, M.: Filesystem in USEr space. http://sourceforge.net/projects/avf (2003)
18. Vangoor, B.K.R., Tarasov, V., Zadok, E.: To FUSE or not to FUSE: Performance of User-Space file systems. In: 15th USENIX Conference on File and Storage Technologies (FAST 17). pp. 59–72. USENIX Association, Santa Clara, CA (2017). https://www.usenix.org/conference/fast17/technical-sessions/presentation/vangoor
19. Wang, L., Wen, Y., Kong, J., Yi, X.: Optimizing eCryptfs for better performance and security. In: Linux Symposium. p. 137. Ottawa - Canada (July 2012)
20. Wu, C.F., Chang, Y.H., Yang, M.C., Kuo, T.W.: When storage response time catches up with overall context switch overhead, what is next? IEEE Trans. Comput. Aided Des. Integr. Circuits Syst. **39**(11), 4266–4277 (2020). https://doi.org/10.1109/TCAD.2020.3012322
21. Xiao, C., Pan, Y., Xu, D., Liu, W., Sun, S., Qiu, S.: Load-aware adaptive cache management scheme for enterprise-level stackable cryptographic file system. In: 2020 IEEE 22nd International Conference on High Performance Computing and Communications; IEEE 18th International Conference on Smart City; IEEE 6th International Conference on Data Science and Systems (HPCC/SmartCity/DSS). pp. 35–43 (2020)
22. Xiao, C., Zhang, L., Liu, W., Cheng, L., Li, P., Pan, Y., Bergmann, N.: NV-ECRYPTFS: accelerating enterprise-level cryptographic file system with non-volatile memory. IEEE Trans. Comput. **68**(9), 1338–1352 (2018)
23. Yang, J., Kim, J., Hoseinzadeh, M., Izraelevitz, J., Swanson, S.: An empirical guide to the behavior and use of scalable persistent memory. In: 18th USENIX Conference on File and Storage Technologies (FAST 20). pp. 169–182. USENIX Association, Santa Clara, CA (2020). https://www.usenix.org/conference/fast20/presentation/yang
24. Zhong, Y., et al.: XRP: In-Kernel storage functions with eBPF. In: 16th USENIX Symposium on Operating Systems Design and Implementation (OSDI 22). pp. 375–393. USENIX Association, Carlsbad, CA (2022). https://www.usenix.org/conference/osdi22/presentation/zhong
25. Zola, W.M.N., De Bona, L.C.E.: Parallel speculative encryption of multiple AES contexts on GPUs. In: 2012 Innovative Parallel Computing (InPar). pp. 1–9. IEEE (2012)

Evaluating eBPF as an Alternative to Virtual Machine Introspection for High-Interaction Honeypot Implementation

Niku Waltteri Saulinpoika Nuutinen[1]([✉]) [iD], Miguel Faísco[1,2], Milan Petrusic[1], Ibéria Medeiros[2] [iD], and Hans P. Reiser[1] [iD]

[1] Reykjavik University, Reykjavik, Iceland
{niku21,miguelg,milan24,hansr}@ru.is
[2] LASIGE, DI, Faculty of Sciences, University of Lisbon, Lisbon, Portugal
ivmedeiros@fc.ul.pt

Abstract. Virtual machine introspection (VMI) has been widely used for stealthy monitoring of guest systems. However, context switching between monitoring system and monitored target introduces considerable overhead, especially for tracing common system calls, and deployment of VMI-based setups is complex. This work investigates whether extended Berkeley Packet Filter (eBPF) based tracing, a low-overhead kernel-level monitoring technique, can serve as an alternative. We compare the two paradigms in terms of performance, stealthiness, and practical applicability. Using micro-benchmarks and a prototype high-interaction SSH honeypot, we evaluate the capabilities and limitations of eBPF-based monitoring in adversarial settings. Our results highlight advantages and limitations of both, providing insights for the design of future security monitoring systems.

1 Introduction

Observing system behaviour at runtime is essential for cybersecurity applications such as intrusion detection, malware analysis, and digital forensics. Over the past decade, virtual machine introspection (VMI) has emerged as a powerful technique for security monitoring, enabling observation of guest systems from the hypervisor level while remaining hidden from the monitored guest. VMI has thus been widely adopted in security research prototypes. In parallel, recent years have seen the rise of extended Berkeley Packet Filter (eBPF) technology as an efficient kernel-level instrumentation tool. Originally designed for packet filtering, eBPF has evolved into a general-purpose tracing and observability tool, increasingly used in performance and security contexts.

This paper explores the core question: *Can eBPF-based monitoring serve as a viable alternative to VMI for cybersecurity purposes?* To address this, we focus on three key dimensions: *(a) performance impact:* is eBPF tracing significantly less

L. A. Rodrigues and R. Oliveira (Eds.): LADC 2025, CCIS 2697, pp. 238–254, 2026.
https://doi.org/10.1007/978-3-032-11539-3_14

intrusive than VMI for active monitoring tasks?, *(b) stealthiness:* how detectable is eBPF-based monitoring to an adversary and can its footprint be reduced or hidden?, and *(c) practical applicability:* how well does eBPF monitoring support real-world use cases, such as implementing a high-interaction SSH honeypot?

Our goal is not to promote eBPF as a universal replacement for VMI, but clarify their strengths and weaknesses in the context of security monitoring. The contributions of this paper are as follows:

- *Comparative analysis of tracing overhead:* VMI often incurs significant overhead due to context switches, while eBPF enables in-kernel instrumentation with potentially lower impact. We compare both approaches quantitatively using UnixBench-based micro-benchmarks.
- *Stealth techniques for eBPF monitoring:* Stealth is vital in adversarial settings such as honeypots, intrusion detection systems, and malware analysis sandboxes. VMI benefits from residing outside the monitored guest, while eBPF operates inside and is more exposed to tampering or detection. We assess their visibility and explore techniques to enhance eBPF stealthiness.
- *Practical applicability:* We evaluate the effort required to implement an exemplary security task – a high-interaction SSH honeypot – using eBPF, and compare this with an equivalent VMI-based implementation.

With these contributions, we aim to clarify when and how eBPF can serve as an effective alternative to VMI in security monitoring. This paper is structured as follows: Sect. 2 provides background on VMI and eBPF and discusses related work. Section 3 presents micro-benchmark performance evaluations. Section 4 elaborates on stealthiness, and Sect. 5 discusses an eBPF-based SSH honeypot. Finally, Sect. 6 concludes.

2   Background and Related Work

2.1   Virtual Machine Introspection

Virtual Machine Introspection (VMI) was first introduced by Garfinkel and Rosenblum [11] as a means of detecting intrusions by monitoring the internal state of virtual machines (VMs) from the outside. A core challenge in VMI is the *semantic gap* between low-level data available to the hypervisor (e.g., memory pages) and high-level abstractions inside the guest (e.g., processes, files, system calls). Bridging this gap requires detailed knowledge of guest OS internals. Despite considerable research (see surveys by Jain et al. [14] and More et al. [19]), it remains an ongoing burden of VMI, especially as OS kernels evolve.

VMI is widely used in cybersecurity research, particularly for malware analysis, memory forensics, and intrusion detection. Examples include rootkit removal in live systems [10], extracting forensic evidence from compromised VMs [12], and malware detection based on API call tracing [8]. The out-of-band nature of VMI enables tamper-resistant monitoring, although at the cost of added complexity and performance trade-offs.

Deploying VMI is difficult due to its reliance on privileged hypervisor access. Several systems have been proposed to improve deployability. CloudVMI [20] integrates remote VMI APIs in cloud platforms, CloudPhylactor [24] uses Xen security modules to deploy VMI-based monitoring software within dedicated VMs, and KVMIveggur [21] extends this approach to the KVMi. These systems provide research prototypes, with very little adoption by commercial cloud providers. The only hypervisor with out-of-the-box support for VMI is Xen.

VMI techniques fall into passive (polling) and active (event-triggered) methods [11,14]. Passive VMI observes state changes asynchronous to the control flow in the monitored system, e.g. by periodic memory snapshots. Active VMI synchronously intercepts guest operations, such as function calls or breakpoints, yielding richer, more timely information at the expense of higher overhead.

Optimising VMI performance has been a focus of prior work. For example, Lutaş et al. [17] explore techniques to reduce the number of memory-fault-related VM exits. For passive VMI, smart caching strategies have been proposed to improve performance while maintaining a consistent and up-to-date view of the monitored system [6]. Other approaches aim to reduce the impact of active VMI by offloading selected functionality into the hypervisor itself, thereby reducing guesthost context switches and overall monitoring latency [5].

2.2   Extended Berkeley Packet Filter

The extended Berkeley Packet Filter (eBPF) is a modern in-kernel execution framework that enables the execution of safe, sandboxed user code in response to kernel events, all within the kernel itself, without requiring kernel module development or recompilation. Originally designed for high-performance packet filtering, eBPF has become a general-purpose tool for tracing, observability, and security enforcement. While eBPF was initially developed for Linux, extensions for other platforms – such as eBPF for Windows [18] – have recently emerged.

eBPF programs attach to instrumentation points including kprobes (for kernel function entry/exit), uprobes (for user-space function tracing), tracepoints, and network events. They are verified for safety by the kernel before loading, ensuring that they do not crash the system or compromise its integrity. This verification model has made eBPF particularly attractive for production use, as it enables low-overhead, always-on monitoring with minimal risk. eBPF has been used to detect anomalies in system call behaviour, monitor containerised workloads, and capture forensic data in real time. Unlike VMI, eBPF runs entirely within the guest system, which simplifies deployment and integration but increases the risk of detection or tampering by adversaries with local access.

A traditional application of eBPF is network security monitoring. For instance, Dimolianis et al. [7] utilize eBPF in combination with the eXpress Data Path (XDP) to detect denial-of-service attacks. More recent approaches integrate eBPF-based monitoring with machine learning for advanced threat detection, such as SmartX Intelligent Sec [9], which performs real-time classification. These works show eBPF's effectiveness for network-layer threat detection, but our focus requires broader general-purpose monitoring across system layers.

The eBPF ecosystem has since expanded well beyond networking. For example, Syrup [15] uses eBPF to implement user-defined CPU scheduling strategies, and λ-IO [27] builds a unified I/O stack that manages both computation and storage resources across host and device. However, the authors highlight key limitations of standard eBPF, such as its static verifier, which prohibits dynamic-length loops commonly required for in-storage data processing. To overcome this, they introduce sBPF, a modified in-kernel execution model that replaces static verification with dynamic verification. While we encountered similar restrictions in our own work, our goal is to assess whether standard eBPF remains sufficient for our monitoring objectives.

Security monitoring beyond the networking domain has also seen growing interest. For example, O2C [25] combines eBPF instrumentation with machine learning to dynamically compartmentalize the OS kernel at runtime, mitigating the impact of zero-day exploits. BPFroid [2] implements eBPF-based monitoring on Android devices, tracing system calls, kernel functions, and user-level library calls to detect malware in real time. The authors explicitly emphasize stealth as a design requirement and provide a detailed analysis of the detectability of their eBPF-based tracing approach. They argue that, by operating on real systems rather than emulated environments, BPFroid avoids detection techniques commonly used by malware to evade analysis. We aim to leverage this advantage in our honeypot prototype as well, but extend the scope: While BPFroid focuses on stealth at the user level (assuming regular app permissions), we consider adversaries with root or kernel-level access and evaluate the detectability of eBPF-based monitoring in such threat models.

2.3 Performance of Monitoring Approaches

Extensive literature exists on both VMI and eBPF performance individually. For instance, Xie [26] benchmarked eBPF programs with HTTP workloads, comparing PERCPU_ARRAY and ARRAY map types. They found that PERCPU maps avoid write conflicts and scale better with CPU core count, but increase memory use and cache pressure, highlighting trade-offs in eBPF map design. In contrast, direct comparisons of VMI and eBPF remain rare.

Some works have explored the design space between purely in-guest and out-of-guest monitoring. Bushouse and Reeves [4] propose a methodology to transform in-guest monitoring agents into out-of-guest "hyperagents" that leverage hypervisor-level capabilities while retaining their original logic. This approach lowers the barrier for integrating VMI capabilities with minimal code refactoring.

Abdelraoof et al. [1] optimize VMI in Xen by adding an eBPF-inspired pre-filtering in the hypervisor. VMI often incurs high overhead from context switches, particularly when using breakpoints in the guest OS, which trigger function calls and transfer data to the hypervisor via Xen event channels. To reduce this latency, their system filters CR3 events and enables tracing only for specific guest processes, significantly reducing the overhead of system call monitoring.

Amit and Wei [3] present hyperupcalls, a mechanism that allows the hypervisor to execute verified guest-provided code with direct access to guest kernel structures. By enabling flexible and low-overhead information transfer, hyper-upcalls help mitigate the semantic gap traditionally associated with VMI.

Beyond eBPF and VMI, modern CPUs provide hardware monitoring support through performance monitoring units (PMUs), which collect low-level data such as instruction counts, branch behaviour, and memory accesses. Intel's Threat Detection Technology (TDT) repurposes PMU telemetry for security monitoring [13], achieving high performance but with a narrower scope than VMI or eBPF. As an Intel-specific, proprietary solution, TDT is promising for certain detection tasks, yet its constraints make it unsuitable for our higher-level monitoring tasks, such as extracting credentials in SSH honeypots.

3 Performance Comparison

In this work, we aim to address the lack of direct comparisons between VMI and eBPF by evaluating their strengths and limitations in comparable settings.

3.1 Methodology

Our first research question is: *Is eBPF tracing significantly less intrusive than VMI for active monitoring tasks such as system call tracing?* To assess the performance impact of system call monitoring using VMI and eBPF, we use UnixBench, a widely used suite of microbenchmarks for Unix-like systems, as our workload generator. The benchmark is executed inside a virtual machine under three different configurations: baseline (no monitoring), VMI-based monitoring (using KVMi [23] and libvmi [16]), and eBPF-based monitoring.

The monitoring task focuses on intercepting a single system call relevant to each benchmark scenario, using a subset of UnixBench. Specifically:

- The `syscall overhead (getpid)` test is used to measure pure system call monitoring overhead. It uses and traces the `getpid` system call, which is the most lightweight system call.
- The `spawn` and `execl throughput` tests are used to measure the impact of tracing two of the core system calls needed to observe high-level actions (process creation and program execution) on a system.
- The `pipe` test resembles I/O-intense workloads, where we investigate the impact of tracing all I/O operations on performance.

For each experiment, we measure the relative slowdown compared to the baseline (no monitoring) configuration.

3.2 Experimental Setup

Our experiments are conducted on two different hardware platforms: A low-end user PC (ASUS PN61, Core I7-8565U CPU, 16 GB RAM) with bare metal KVM/KVMi, and a server-class PC (Xeon Gold 6430 CPU, 512 GB RAM) with KVM (Proxmox) and a nested VM with KVMi. The monitored guest runs Linux

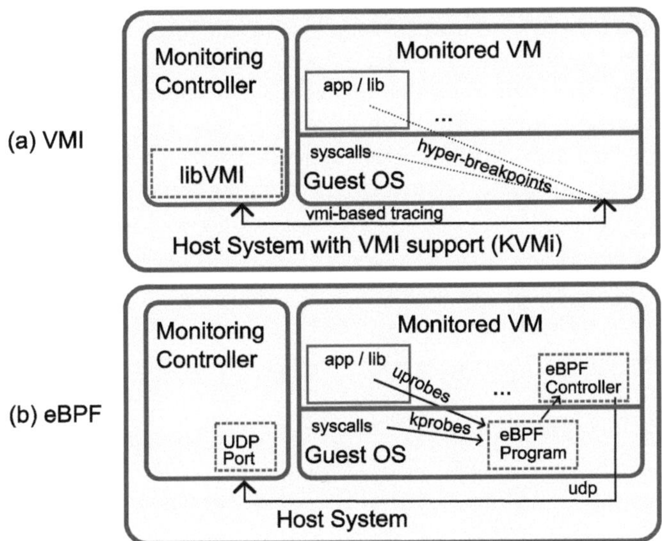

Fig. 1. VMI and eBPF deployment architecture.

6.1.0 in a VM within KVM with KVMi support enabled, and eBPF support enabled within the guest.

For the VMI version, the monitored system calls are directly recorded in a file on the KVMi host. For the eBPF version, a user-space program within the monitored guest VM retrieves the logs from the eBPF ring buffer and sends them via a network connection to the host, which then records them to a file. Figure 1 shows an overview of these architectures.

3.3   Results

The results from our benchmarking are shown in Table 1. The relative performance is shown as a percentage of the baseline performance.

When interpreting the performance measurements, the fundamental architectural difference between the two monitoring approaches must be taken into account. Concretely, VMI-based monitoring operates synchronously with the target system's execution, meaning that the monitored system is paused while handling each monitoring event (e.g., a traced system call). This synchronous design ensures that all events are reliably observed by the monitoring system, but it introduces significant overhead, particularly for frequent system calls. In contrast, eBPF executes a lightweight program synchronously within the kernel, which then emits events to a queue or ring buffer. These events are subsequently consumed asynchronously by a user-space application. While this design reduces overhead, it introduces the potential for event loss if the user-space consumer cannot keep up with the event rate.

For our benchmarks, no events were lost in the *spawn* and *execl* tests when using eBPF. In these cases, the eBPF-based approach achieved less overhead while processing the same number of events compared to VMI. However, for tests that generate a high volume of events – *getpid* and *pipe* – the VMI-based approach leads to a substantial performance degradation due to its synchronous nature. Switching to eBPF monitoring for these tests yielded a 20x to 100x improvement in performance. However, in those cases, the eBPF-based method experiences event loss as the user-space processing cannot keep pace with the kernel's event generation.

Table 1. Consolidated *UnixBench* scores with system call tracing (higher is better)

Test	Monitored Syscall	Unit	Baseline	with VMI	with eBPF
VM on simple PC					
syscall (getpid)	getpid	1k calls/s	1193561 SD=0.62%	5698 (*0.48%*)SD=4.35%	374055 (*31.34%*)SD=0.47%
spawn	clone	1k proc/s	4260SD=1.13%	2342 (*54.97%*)SD=2.63%	3945 (*92.61%*)SD=1.55%
execlthr.put	execve	calls/s	1183SD=1.13%	975 (*82.43%*)SD=0.87%	1083 (*91.53%*)SD=1.33%
pipe	write	calls/s	378727SD=0.97%	5671 (*1.50%*)SD=1.02%	134963 (*35.64%*)SD=1.15%
Nested VM on server					
syscall(getpid)	getpid	1k calls/s	2171815SD=2.02%	2171 (*0.10%*)SD=0.82%	654705 (*30.01%*) SD=4.97%
spawn	clone	1k proc/s	9865SD=3.56%	1707 (*17.41%*) SD=1.02%	9099 (*92.24%*) SD=2.05%
execlthr.put	execve	calls/s	1310SD=2.17%	760 (*5.97%*) SD=1.58%	1283 (*97.97%*) SD=1.19%
pipe	write	calls/s	652999SD=1.72%	2157 (*0.33%*)SD=0.3%	237945 (*36.44%*)SD=0.8%

In conclusion, eBPF-based monitoring tends to result in higher performance in the target. This comes at the cost of losing isolation between the target and the host, and potentially exposing the monitoring processes. The related files and processes can, however, be well hidden from commands such as `ls` and `ps aux`, even if they were to be run with elevated privileges.

4   Stealthiness Considerations

In this section, we aim to address our second research question: *How detectable is eBPF-based monitoring to an adversary and can its footprint be reduced or hidden?* We present the initial study we have been doing to try to respond to it.

4.1   Threat Model

While eBPF offers powerful monitoring capabilities, its presence can be detected by a knowledgeable adversary with sufficient privileges. Some of the methods an attacker might employ to uncover eBPF-based monitoring activities are listed next. However, we note that most of these methods to be performed require elevated privileges.

– The primary tool for examining eBPF programs on a Linux system is bpftool. With root access, an attacker can list all loaded eBPF programs (`bpftool` `prog show`). This command reveals details such as program IDs, types, attached hooks, and associated maps. By analyzing this information, an attacker can identify suspicious programs, especially those attached to syscall hooks like kprobes or tracepoints.

- eBPF programs often use maps to store and share data between kernel and user space. An attacker can list these maps with `bpftool map show`. Inspecting the contents and usage patterns of these maps can provide insights into the monitoring activities.
- If the user-space component exfiltrates data over the network, tools like `netstat` or `tcpdump` can be used to detect unusual outbound connections.
- An attacker can inspect the list of running processes to identify any unfamiliar or suspicious user-space programs related to eBPF-based monitoring.
- eBPF programs and maps are associated with file descriptors. An attacker can examine the file descriptors of processes to identify eBPF-related entries, e.g. with `ls -l /proc/<pid>/fd`. Descriptors linked to `/sys/fs/bpf/` can indicate the presence of eBPF objects.
- Loading eBPF programs can generate entries in the kernel log. An attacker can review these logs for any indications (e.g. `dmesg|grep -i bpf`)
- eBPF itself can be used to detect other eBPF programs. Tools like `Tracee` can monitor for the loading of eBPF programs, providing visibility into potential monitoring activities.

4.2   Techniques to Increase Stealth

As a takeaway, conventional eBPF-based monitoring does not reach the level of stealthiness offered by VMI-based approaches. This limitation can be a critical drawback for use cases such as malware analysis sandboxes or high-interaction honeypots, which depend on the invisibility of the monitoring infrastructure to avoid detection and evasion. To address this challenge, we explore techniques aimed at minimising the observability of ongoing eBPF monitoring, in an effort to mitigate this disadvantage.

In Linux, process enumeration – such as when running commands like `ps` – relies on the `getdents64` system call to read directory entries from the `proc` filesystem. This call returns a list of entries containing metadata, including the inode number, file type, and process ID (represented as directory names). By hooking `getdents64`, we can effectively hide specific processes by removing them from the returned list. This technique follows the approach implemented in the eBPFeXPLOIT project[1].

The same project also includes a method to prevent the monitoring process from being terminated. This is done by hooking `lsm/task_kill` call and checking the ID of the process. If the ID is in our list of protected tasks, we can return `-EPERM` instead to prevent executing the kill command. Another hook can be added to `kretprobe/sys_kill`, and by modifying the return value to `-ESRCH`,

---

[1] https://github.com/bfengj/eBPFeXPLOIT

the output will not present the process, thus indicating to the attacker that the process does not exist.

User-space tools such as `bpftool` can still be used to find the eBPF programs, so this needs another method to hide information. `bpftool` extracts information with calls such as `BPF_MAP_GET_NEXT_ID`, which we can hook and modify the return values in order to skip our program from being listed. As a result, bpftool will report an empty set, effectively hiding the presence of our eBPF components.

Finally, the mere presence of network traffic between the in-target user-space eBPF program and the outside monitoring system could raise suspicion. In future work, we aim to further obscure network communications, e.g., through covert channels or traffic shaping, and to improve the process-hiding mechanisms to be more selective and resilient against advanced detection methods. As inspiration, EvilBPF[2] includes eBPF tools for hiding files and processes, as well as a sniffer for unencrypted SSL/TLS traffic to capture downloading data, for example.

4.3 Result

In summary, while eBPF does not inherently offer the same level of stealthiness as VMI-based monitoring, prior work has demonstrated that eBPF-based monitoring can be hidden to a large extent. In our work, we adopt and extend these techniques to enhance the invisibility of our monitoring infrastructure. Although achieving this level of stealth requires additional engineering effort, we conclude that it is feasible to attain a degree of stealthiness comparable to that of VMI-based solutions using eBPF.

5 Case Study: SSH Honeypot Implementation

This section presents a concrete use case to evaluate the suitability of eBPF monitoring in adversarial settings, where attackers may attempt to detect the presence of monitoring. In particular, we aim to address our third research question: *How well does eBPF monitoring support real-world use cases, such as implementing a high-interaction SSH honeypot?*

To that end, we implement a high-interaction SSH honeypot designed to attract real attackers and observe their behaviour after initial compromise. Such systems are particularly challenging to monitor, as they must offer realistic system environments while remaining stealthy in the presence of malware or human adversaries attempting to evade analysis.

High-interaction honeypots expose a real system environment, allowing attackers to interact freely after gaining access. They contrast with low-interaction honeypots such as Cowrie[3], which rely on emulated services and are easier to detect. Sarracenia [22] exemplifies a VMI-based approach to building high-interaction SSH honeypots, using external introspection for stealthy monitoring of attacker behaviour. We follow a similar design goal but implement

---

² https://github.com/rphang/evilBPF.
³ https://github.com/cowrie/cowrie.

the honeypot using in-guest eBPF tracing. This approach significantly reduces deployment complexity and improves portability, while still enabling detailed observation of attacker actions across authentication, process activity, file access, and network behaviour.

5.1   Design Considerations

We assume attackers follow a common sequence of phases: (1) *reconnaissance:* scanning for open ports or vulnerable services; (2) *exploitation:* gaining access, typically by guessing weak passwords or explaining misconfigurations; and (3) *post-exploitation:* actions such as privilege escalation (gaining root access from a non-privileged account), establishing persistence (e.g., installing login keys or other backdoors), and launching further attacks.

Our honeypot exposes an intentionally misconfigured SSH server with weak passwords. Once an attacker has gained access, we observe a range of possible attacker behaviours, which we want to monitor and analyse in detail:

- Privilege escalation (e.g., obtaining root access from a standard user account)
- Persistence mechanisms (e.g., creating user accounts, injecting SSH authorization keys, installing cron jobs)
- Malicious activities (e.g., deploying crypto miners, conducting lateral attacks on local systems, launching outbound attacks such as denial of service (DoS) or spam)

Attacks range from simple scanning with no follow-up activity, to fully automated malware deployment, and manual exploitation by human actors. Some adversaries may try to detect whether they are interacting with a honeypot by inspecting the system environment, looking for signs of monitoring, or using some forms of honeypot fingerprinting techniques. Our aim is at being significantly more robust against such detection attempts than typical honeypot systems.

5.2   System Design

To gain insight into those attacker activities, our system design covers the following aspects:

- *Capturing login attempts.*
  We explored two complementary methods for capturing SSH login credentials. A PAM-based approach uses user-level eBPF probes on the pluggable authentication module (PAM) library to extract usernames and passwords. This method is portable and robust, as it relies on well-defined, exported symbols in the `libpam.so` shared library. An sshd-tracing method is inspired by Sarracenia and hooks internal functions of the `sshd` binary. The advantage of sshd-based tracing is that it reveals the username/password combination of all login attempts, while PAM-based method succeeds fully only for existing user accounts.

- *File system monitoring.*
  We trace kernel functions and system calls such as `open`, `write`, `close`, `chmod`, and `unlink` to detect file uploads and modifications. These allow us to reconstruct files from their write streams, detect permission changes, and record deletions. Each modified file is reconstructed and stored for analysis.
- *Network activity.*
  Rather than relying solely on external network capture, we include network-related tracing in our BPF instrumentation to link activity to specific processes. This enables accurate attribution in the presence of multiple active malware samples and allows benign background traffic (e.g., automated system updates) to be filtered out.
- *Interactive session reconstruction.*
  As in Sarracenia, we reconstruct entire interactive SSH sessions by tracing `write` system calls on the internal pipe between the shell and the `sshd`. This enables replay and detailed behavioural analysis of attacker interactions.

5.3   Attack Mitigation and System Restoration

Running a high-interaction honeypot entails risk: Once compromised, the honeypot could be used to attack other systems or propagate malware. We implemented several safeguards to mitigate this risk:

- *Network filtering:* We use strict filtering to block most outbound traffic, while allowing essential actions such as downloading second-stage payloads via HTTP(S) and resolving domain names. This allows attackers to proceed naturally while limiting abuse.
- *Connection and bandwidth limits:* Even permitted traffic is rate-limited to prevent DoS attacks or large-scale data transfer.
- *Adaptive reset policy:* The honeypot is periodically reset to a clean snapshot. The timing is dynamic: if malware lies dormant or behaves benignly, it can run for longer. High CPU usage (e.g., from crypto miners) and aggressive network behaviour will trigger earlier resets.

5.4   Implementation Details

Our system consists of two main components: a set of eBPF-based tracers running inside the honeypot VM, and an external monitoring and analysis backend. The architecture is designed to provide full visibility into attacker behaviour while maintaining low overhead and high stealth within the guest system. Figure 2 illustrates the high-level architecture of our eBPF-based high-interaction SSH honeypot. An attacker connects to the honeypot VM via SSH. This VM is instrumented with eBPF tracers and forwards monitoring data to an event listener (monitor) outside the honeypot VM (the Monitor VM in the figure). Both VMs are deployed into a Linux Debian 12.

As explained in Sect. 5.2, the sshd-tracing method, which hooks internal functions of the sshd binary, depends on symbol information. As in many production binaries, this symbol information is stripped in our installation, but our prototype mitigates this by automatically extracting symbol information from available debug symbol packages.

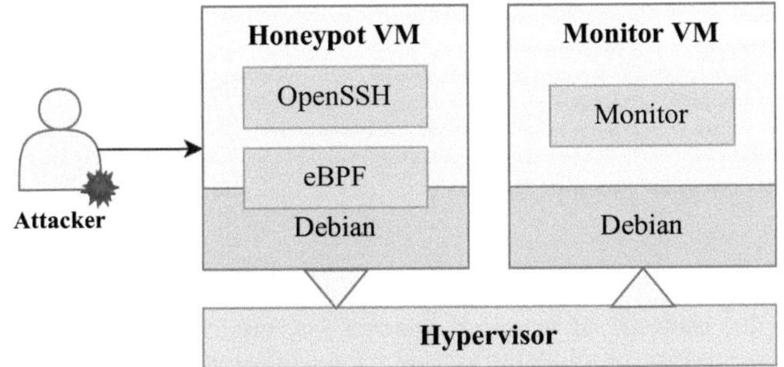

Fig. 2. eBPF-based honeypot system architecture.

An in-guest component deploys an eBPF program to trace relevant system calls, library functions, and kernel events. A minimal in-VM loader is responsible for loading the eBPF program and forwarding the resulting events to the external monitor process. Table 2 summarises the key eBPF instrumentation points used in our implementation for the actual tracing. Furthermore, our prototype leverages eBPF tracing of `getdents64` to hide the user-space eBPF loader in the proc file system for stealthiness (as previously described in Sect. 4.2).

The external monitor, implemented in Python, receives raw events, maintains internal state, reconstructs files, tracks process hierarchies and sessions, and emits structured JSON events via UDP broadcast. These events can then be consumed by local components:

- A *lifecycle manager*, which can implement the strategy to reset the honeypot VM to a clean snapshot based on activity patterns;
- An *analysis manager*, which extracts features for attack classification using both dynamic traces and static analysis of uploaded files.

5.5   eBPF Limitations

During the development of our honeypot, we observed that certain monitoring tasks are more difficult to implement with eBPF than with VMI. While VMI introduces challenges related to the semantic gap, it imposes few technical constraints on how and when data can be accessed once a relevant event is observed. In contrast, eBPF programs must pass a strict verifier, which prohibits arbitrary pointer access and disallows loops with variable iteration counts. These restrictions posed several challenges:

Table 2. eBPF tracing points used in our honeypot implementation.

Type	Trace Point	Purpose
uretprobe	`pam_get_authtok`	Capture username and password via PAM (existing users only), inspired by the `pamspy` tool[a].
uretprobe	`sshd_login`	Capture username and password by tracing `sshd` internals (all login attempts)
syscall	`sys_enter_connect`	Trace outgoing TCP connections
kretprobe	`inet_csk_accept`	Detect new incoming SSH connections
fexit	`do_sys_openat2`	Trace file openings
fentry	`filp_close`	Trace file closures; triggers file reconstruction and analysis
fentry	`chmod_common`	Detect file permission changes
LSM hook	`path_unlink`	Trace file deletions
LSM hook	`bprm_committed_creds`	Trace execution of new binaries (covers all `execv*` variants)
tracepoint	`sched_process_fork`	Track process creation and parent-child relationships
syscall	`sys_enter_write`	Monitor file modifications and session activity
tracepoint	`sched_process_exit`	Detect process termination and clean up state

[a] https://github.com/citronneur/pamspy

- For example, instead of tracing `execve` system calls directly (which would require iterating over a variably sized argument list), we opted to trace the `bprm_committed_creds` LSM hook. This provided several advantages: (1) the program arguments have already been copied into a contiguous memory region, allowing us to copy a bounded segment without looping over pointers; (2) we can access the inode of the executed binary, enabling correlation with previously uploaded files; and (3) we only need to trace a single point rather than multiple system calls (`execv`, `execve`, `execveat`).
- One notable restriction is that the `bpf_d_path` helper function, which resolves full absolute path names, is only available in certain contexts. We were able to use it successfully when tracing program execution and file closures, but not in other cases such as `unlink` or `chmod`, where access to absolute file paths would also have been useful.
- Another limitation arises when capturing data from `write` system calls in order to reconstruct file contents. eBPF ring buffer allocations must use a fixed size at compile time, whereas `write` operations produce variably sized payloads. As a workaround, we split the data into fixed-size chunks, each fitting within the buffer size limit. A variable number of such chunks can be emitted per write, as long as an upper bound is enforced. In practice, this method worked reliably for uploaded files via SFTP, downloads using tools like `wget` or `curl`, and streaming uploads over SSH (e.g., using the session piped into `tar`). As an alternative, we also support reconstructing files from VM disk snapshots. However, this is only feasible for files written to persistent storage (not `tmpfs`) and not deleted prior to snapshotting.

From a tracing perspective, our system captures the same categories of information as the VMI-based honeypot Sarracenia. The key difference lies in how the data is collected: our monitoring operates from within the guest kernel, and the resulting events must be transferred to the monitoring machine for analysis.

The in-guest monitoring processes and files are hidden from standard userspace tools such as `ls` and `ps`, making it extremely difficult for non-privileged users to detect the presence of our tracing. This form of hiding significantly increases stealthiness compared to conventional in-VM monitoring approaches.

However, a user with root privileges can perform more intrusive inspections, such as loading custom kernel modules or scanning raw memory directly. These actions can reveal traces of the honeypot infrastructure, for example, by searching for eBPF maps, loaded programs, or memory-resident buffers. At this level, achieving the same degree of isolation and transparency as VMI-based solutions like Sarracenia remains challenging.

Despite this, our system achieves a level of realism that is significantly higher than that of typical low- or medium-interaction honeypots. Moreover, any attempt to probe or fingerprint the monitoring infrastructure, whether successful or not, is observable through our tracing mechanism. As part of our future work, we plan to operate the honeypot over extended periods to collect evidence of such fingerprinting attempts, enabling us to analyse attacker behaviours that aim to detect or evade monitoring.

We have had the honeypot deployed for 6 weeks, during which we received 359066 login attempts, with 290231 successful logins as the honeypot accepts some common username and password combinations. The connections came from 3904 unique IP addresses. We keep a track of executed commands; 50297 different commands were received, and 440 malware files were analyzed, of which we found 41 unique samples. A notable point is the frequency of login attempts—for the first two weeks, the frequency was approximately equal to our Cowrie honeypot. The number of connections then suddenly multiplied, which possibly can be explained by the honeypot being listed somewhere as potentially vulnerable. On average, the eBPF-honeypot received $\approx 42\%$ more visits per IP address when compared to Cowrie.

6   Discussion and Conclusions

Our primary motivation for investigating eBPF-based monitoring solutions is the performance overhead introduced by VMI-based approaches. While VMI provides strong isolation between the monitor and the target system and thus fully stealthy observation, it also incurs higher system complexity and latency. This can degrade performance on the target machine and, in the context of honeypots, potentially signal to an attacker that monitoring is taking place. In contrast, eBPF is a native in-kernel technology that is widely supported across modern Linux distributions, including public cloud environments, making deployment significantly more practical and accessible.

In our evaluation, we compared VMI- and eBPF-based monitoring using two testbeds: a low-end user PC with a bare metal hypervisor running a virtual machine as a honeypot, and a nested virtualisation setup on a server-grade host using Proxmox with KVM and KVMi. We used micro-benchmarks based on UnixBench as stress tests that expose weaknesses in performance. The results clearly favour eBPF in terms of performance.

Although VMI has advantages in terms of stealthiness at the kernel level, our findings suggest that effective hiding of eBPF-based monitoring is achievable, especially against non-privileged attackers. Depending on what needs to be monitored, VMI could still be preferred for its isolated nature from the monitor; if the monitoring can be process-bound and filtered, the performance decrease could be mitigated enough. It is also very concealed from attackers, while eBPF requires more effort to hide.

We have implemented a prototype of our eBPF-based high-interaction SSH honeypot, which is currently deployed and active. Its design has evolved iteratively through exposure to real-world attacks as well as replayed attack traces captured using Cowrie. This process has led to a robust and flexible monitoring setup that appears well-suited to the challenges of adversarial behaviour analysis.

As future work, we aim to gain long-term operational experience with the honeypot under real attack conditions. For educational use, we plan to develop an interactive visualisation frontend to highlight attacker behaviour in a user-friendly manner. We also want to explore AI-based techniques to generate human-readable explanations of observed attacks. From a research perspective, we plan to conduct a systematic comparison of attacker behaviour and system observability across Cowrie, Sarracenia, and our eBPF-based honeypot. Finally, we intend to investigate hybrid monitoring approaches that combine the stealth benefits of VMI with the efficiency and flexibility of eBPF.

Acknowledgements. This work has been supported by the RU Research Fund and the Frostbyte cybersecurity lab, partially supported by FCT through the LASIGE Research Unit, ref. UID/408/2025, and has received co-funding from the European Unions Digital Europe programme under project NCC-IS (Grant Agreement No. 101127453).

References

1. Bilge, L., Cavallaro, L., Pellegrino, G., Neves, N. (eds.): DIMVA 2021. Detection of Intrusions and Malware, and Vulnerability Assessment. LNCS, vol. 12756. Springer, Cham (2021). https://doi.org/10.1007/978-3-030-80825-9
2. Agman, Y., Hendler, D.: BPFroid: Robust Real Time Android Malware Detection Framework (2021). https://arxiv.org/abs/2105.14344
3. Amit, N., Wei, M.: The design and implementation of hyperupcalls. In: Proceedings of the 2018 USENIX Conference on Usenix Annual Technical Conference. p. 97–111. USENIX ATC '18, USENIX Association, USA (2018)
4. Bushouse, M., Reeves, D.: Hyperagents: Migrating host agents to the hypervisor. In: Proceedings of the Eighth ACM Conference on Data and Application Security and Privacy. pp. 212–223. CODASPY '18, ACM, New York, NY, USA (2018). https://doi.org/10.1145/3176258.3176317
5. Dangl, T., Sentanoe, S., Reiser, H.P.: Retrofitting AMD x86 processors with active virtual machine introspection capabilities. In: Proceedings of the 36th International Conference on the Architecture of Computing Systems, ARCS 2023, Athens, Greece. LNCS, vol. 13949, pp. 168–182. Springer, Cham (2023). https://doi.org/10.1007/978-3-031-42785-5_12

6. Dangl, T., Sentanoe, S., Reiser, H.P.: VMIFresh: Efficient and fresh caches for virtual machine introspection. Comput. Secur. **135**, 103527 (2023). https://doi.org/10.1016/J.COSE.2023.103527

7. Dimolianis, M., Pavlidis, A., Maglaris, V.: Signature-based traffic classification and mitigation for ddos attacks using programmable network data planes. IEEE Access **9**, 113061–113076 (2021). https://doi.org/10.1109/ACCESS.2021.3104115

8. Ding, Z., Guo, Y., Xu, H., Yan, L., Cui, L., Peng, Y., Cheng, F., Hao, Z.: Seq-Trace: API call tracing based on Intel PT and VMI for malware detection. In: Algorithms and Architectures for Parallel Processing: 22nd International Conference, ICA3PP 2022, Copenhagen, Denmark, October 10–12, 2022, Proceedings. pp. 98–116. Springer-Verlag, Berlin, Heidelberg (2022). https://doi.org/10.1007/978-3-031-22677-9_6

9. Farasat, T., Kim, J., Posegga, J.: SmartX Intelligent Sec: A Security Framework Based on Machine Learning and eBPF/XDP (2024). https://arxiv.org/abs/2410.20244

10. Fraser, T., Evenson, M.R., Arbaugh, W.A.: VICI Virtual Machine Introspection for Cognitive Immunity. In: Twenty-Fourth Annual Computer Security Applications Conference, ACSAC 2008, Anaheim, California, USA, 8–12 December 2008. pp. 87–96. IEEE Computer Society (2008). https://doi.org/10.1109/ACSAC.2008.33

11. Garfinkel, T., Rosenblum, M.: A Virtual Machine Introspection Based Architecture for Intrusion Detection. In: Proceedings of the Network and Distributed System Security Symposium, NDSS 2003, San Diego, California, USA. The Internet Society (2003). https://www.ndss-symposium.org/ndss2003/virtual-machine-introspection-based-architecture-intrusion-detection/

12. Hay, B., Nance, K.: Forensics examination of volatile system data using virtual introspection. SIGOPS Oper. Syst. Rev. **42**(3), 74–82 (2008). https://doi.org/10.1145/1368506.1368517

13. Intel: Product brief: Hardware-enhanced threat detection. https://www.intel.com/content/dam/www/public/us/en/documents/product-briefs/tdt-product-brief.pdf (2021). Accessed 25 Aug 2025

14. Jain, B., Baig, M.B., Zhang, D., Porter, D.E., Sion, R.: Introspections on the semantic gap. IEEE Secur. Priv. **13**(2), 48–55 (2015). https://doi.org/10.1109/MSP.2015.35 Type: Conference Paper

15. Kaffes, K., Humphries, J.T., Mazières, D., Kozyrakis, C.: Syrup: User-defined scheduling across the stack. In: Proceedings of the ACM SIGOPS 28th Symposium on Operating Systems Principles. p. 605–620. SOSP '21, Association for Computing Machinery, New York, NY, USA (2021). https://doi.org/10.1145/3477132.3483548

16. Lengyel, T.K., et al.: LibVMI: Simplified Virtual Machine Introspection. https://github.com/libvmi/libvmi, Accessed 25 Aug 2025

17. Lutas, A., Sebestyen, G., Tosa, R., Colesa, A.: VE-VMI: High-Performance Virtual Machine Introspection Based on Virtualization Exception. In: Potolea, R., Iancu, B., Slavescu, R.R. (eds.) In: 20th International Symposium on Parallel and Distributed Computing, ISPDC 2021, Cluj-Napoca, Romania, July 28-30, 2021. pp. 73–80. IEEE (2021). https://doi.org/10.1109/ISPDC52870.2021.9521609

18. Microsoft: eBPF for Windows. https://github.com/microsoft/ebpf-for-windows, Accessed 21 Apr 2025

19. More, A., Tapaswi, S.: Virtual machine introspection: towards bridging the semantic gap. J. Cloud Comput. **3**(1), 1–14 (2014). https://doi.org/10.1186/s13677-014-0016-2

20. Qiang, W., Xu, G., Dai, W., Zou, D., Jin, H.: CloudVMI: a cloud-oriented writable virtual machine introspection. IEEE Access **5**, 21962–21976 (2017). https://doi.org/10.1109/ACCESS.2017.2758356
21. Sentanoe, S., Dangl, T., Reiser, H.P.: KVMIveggur: flexible, secure, and efficient support for self-service virtual machine introspection. Forensic Sci. Int. Digital Invest. **42** (2022). https://doi.org/10.1016/j.fsidi.2022.301397
22. Sentanoe, S., Taubmann, B., Reiser, H.P.: Sarracenia: Enhancing the performance and stealthiness of SSH honeypots using virtual machine introspection. In: Proceedings of the 23rd Nordic Conference on Secure IT Systems (2018)
23. Tarral, M.: KVMi Subsystem for KVM. https://kvm-vmi.github.io/kvm-vmi/master/kvmi.html (2020). Accessed 25 Aug 2025
24. Taubmann, B., Rakotondravony, N., Reiser, H.P.: CloudPhylactor: harnessing mandatory access control for virtual machine introspection in cloud data centers. In: 2016 IEEE Trustcom/BigDataSE/ISPA, Tianjin, China, August 23–26, 2016. pp. 957–964. IEEE (2016). https://doi.org/10.1109/TRUSTCOM.2016.0162
25. Wang, Z., Chen, T., Dai, Q., Chen, Y., Wei, H., Zeng, Q.: When ebpf Meets Machine Learning: On-the-Fly os Kernel Compartmentalization (2024). https://arxiv.org/abs/2401.05641
26. Xie, X.: Understanding the Performance of eBPF-Based Applications. https://nsg.ee.ethz.ch/files/public/theses/2024-benchmarking_ebpf_programs/thesis-1.pdf (2025). Semester Thesis
27. Yang, Z., et al.: λ-io: a unified io stack for computational storage. In: Proceedings of the 21st USENIX Conference on File and Storage Technologies. FAST'23, USENIX Association, USA (2023)

Source Code Vulnerability Detection and Interpretability with Language Models

Leonardo Silveira[(⊠)] [iD], Claudio A. S. Lelis[iD], Cesar A. C. Marcondes[iD], and Filipe A. N. Verri[iD]

Aeronautics Institute of Technology, São José dos Campos, SP 12228-900, Brazil
{leonardo.silveira,claudio.lelis}@ga.ita.br,
{cesar.marcondes,filipe.verri}@gp.ita.br

Abstract. Software vulnerability detection is crucial to prevent hostile attacks that can compromise applications and expose sensitive data. Traditional static, dynamic, and symbolic analyzers typically balance precision against computational complexity, often demanding high analytical costs or sacrificing detection accuracy. A recent alternative is the use of machine learning models, which can circumvent this trade-off by offering precise predictions with acceptable complexity. These models draw on advances in Natural Language Processing; however, most existing works focus on classification performance, with limited study of model interpretability. In this work, we fine-tuned two medium-sized language models, CodeBERT and CoTexT, for vulnerability detection in programming language code. We curated a benchmark dataset composed of vulnerable code fragments and their respective ground-truth masks, which indicates the exact tokens corresponding to vulnerabilities. We then applied the two interpretability methods—Saliency and InputXGradient, which rank the most performant interpretability techniques for text classification— to generate token-level importance heatmaps. Our evaluation shows that both methods achieve comparable precision; however, InputXGradient produces heatmaps that are substantially more interpretable. Finally, comparing the language models in terms of their ability to provide interpretation for their predictions, we observed a stark contrast, with Code-BERT providing more precise, consise and intuitive explanations for its predictions. Furthermore, our findings suggest that tokenizer design significantly influences the capacity of the model to learn code syntax and semantics, affecting both predictive performance and the clarity of generated interpretations. The results of our work underscore the critical role of interpretability and tokenizer configuration in ML-based vulnerability detection, highlighting the need to choose suitable attribution methods and tokenizer settings when employing such models.

Keywords: Deep Learning · Transformers · Vulnerability Detection · Source Code Security · Interpretability

L. A. Rodrigues and R. Oliveira (Eds.): LADC 2025, CCIS 2697, pp. 255–271, 2026.
https://doi.org/10.1007/978-3-032-11539-3_15

1   Introduction

Identifying software vulnerabilities is essential to prevent exploitation, particularly given the widespread use of open-source libraries that can propagate hidden flaws to otherwise secure applications [22]. Traditional approaches include static analysis, which applies predefined rules without executing the code [22], and dynamic or symbolic testing, which explore execution paths at runtime [30]. Structural methods, such as those based on Abstract Syntax Trees (ASTs), have also been proposed [30]. However, these techniques often suffer from high false positive rates, prohibitive runtime costs, or impractical compilation requirements—especially when only partial code is available, as in pull requests [6]. To overcome these limitations, recent work has turned to data-driven approaches, particularly deep learning, for programming language understanding tasks such as vulnerability detection.

These works have primarily leveraged techniques from the Natural Language Processing (NLP) field, using the Naturalness hypothesis [6,14], which argues that programming languages can be understood and dealt with the same tools applied to natural languages. Particularly interesting for our study is the use of pre-trained medium and large-sized Transformer language models.

The development of the Transformer architecture [27] and the self-supervised pre-training paradigm [19] significantly improved the capabilities of language models. This advancement has notably enhanced performance in free-text generation tasks for both natural and programming languages. Consequently, the primary use of these models has been for generative tasks, such as code completion and code generation, but studies have been trying to apply these models to classification tasks, such as vulnerability detection in source.

These works can be separated by the size of the models used: medium-sized language models, using architectures such as BERT and T5, with number of parameters ranging between 110 million to 220 million, and large language models, such as Llama and GPT-4, with the number of parameters going from 1 billion up to 2 trillion parameters. The difference in size makes the deployment of medium-sized language models much easier, being possible to deploy them locally. Another consequence is that the inference time of medium-sized language models is considerably smaller [8,16,20,26].

Besides the number of parameters, other differences are also important: Medium-sized language models have more varied architectures, such as encoder-only, decoder-only, or encoder-decoder configurations. Finally, these language models are usually open-source or white-boxes [2,7,10,17].

On the other hand, large language models usually are auto-regressive decoder-only, and render themselves naturally for generative tasks. Models from this family are usually closed-source or black-boxes, being accessed via third-party APIs, with notable exceptions such as Llama. Therefore, their use at scale can incur high costs and may not be feasible due to the need to share proprietary data with third-parties [16,26]. Additionally, when dealing with black-box models the user has no access to its internal parameters, hidden states or gradients.

Deploying both medium and large language models in critical areas such as vulnerability detection faces significant challenges, particularly related to robustness, trustworthiness, and interpretability. These models tend to be fragile under perturbation [11], where an imperceptible change in the input can mislead the output of the model, making them vulnerable to adversarial attacks. Additionally, [21] observed that language models tend to learn spurious features from code, such as variable names, and use them to weight their predictions. Finally, their opacity in terms of why and how they took a particular prediction is in itself a major drawback in their use [3].

In this scenario, interpretability methods can be of great help, enhancing the capacity of the models to communicate what factors from the input were the most important for their prediction. The problem interpretability methods try to solve is how to attribute the prediction of a machine learning model to its input features [24], and more informally, their purpose is to convince the user the model took the decision in the right way.

A growing number of studies argue that the hidden layers' activation values and its gradients offer insights into the model's mechanics, knowledge and confidence [1,5]. For NLP, several interpretability methods leveraging these inner properties were evaluated for the text classification task [3]. It was found that gradient-based methods, known as saliency methods, [24] perform best across model architectures. Once these techniques require access to the computation gradients, they are only applicable to white-box models. Consequently, these models can potentially provide better understanding and more transparency about their predictions and decision-making.

In this study, we aim to explore gradient-based interpretability methods applied to language models for vulnerability detection. We will use two methods from this family, Saliency and InputXGradient, in conjunction with two popular medium-sized white-box language models, CodeBERT and CoText [10,17]. Our goal is two fold:

1. Compare the Saliency and InputXgradient interpretability methods, evaluating their outputs in terms of precision, clarity and interpretability.
2. Compare the interpretability maps generated by the two language models chosen, investigating their differences and what may be causing them.

As a byproduct of our study, we curated and released a benchmark dataset for the evaluation of interpretability methods for the task of vulnerability detection. This dataset is composed of more than six thousand C/C++ vulnerable functions together with their ground-truth binary masks locating the position of the vulnerability. The goal of this dataset is to provide the community with a tool to compare and improve interpretability methods applied to models trained on this task. It should come as valuable addition, once it complements other popular datasets in the field, such as Devign [33], which are used to train models to detect vulnerabilities in code.

This study is organized as follows: Sect. 2 discusses relevant related work, Sect. 3 describes the methods used, including dataset curation, model finetuning and the workings of the interpretability methods chosen, Sect. 4 reports the results obtained and discusses the findings, and finally Sect. 5 concludes the work.

2   Related Works

This work is closely related to two research fields: vulnerability detection with language models, and interpretability of language models in the context of programming language understanding in general, and vulnerability detection in particular. We highlight the most relevant studies from these fields with relation to ours.

2.1   Vulnerability Detection with Language Models

The application of language models in programming language understanding tasks relies on the naturalness hypothesis [6,14], which argues that programming languages can be understood and dealt with using the same tools applied to natural languages.

CodeBERT [10] was the first language model pre-trained on both natural and programming languages. It is an encoder-only model inspired by BERT [8], which achieved success in NLP tasks such as text classification, that benefited from the bidirectional input attention, without requiring text generation.

Several subsequent models have been pre-trained for programming languages [2,7,12,17]. Among these, the CoTexT model [17] introduced an encoder-decoder architecture based on T5 [20]. This model combines bidirectional attention in the encoder with auto-regressive output generation, enabling its application to both classification and text generation tasks.

CodeBERT and CoTexT can be classified as open-source medium-sized language models. Therefore, the user has complete access to its parameters, hidden states and gradients. Their size makes them also suitable to local deployment.

More recently, a lot of attention has been given to large language models (LLMs), due to their impressive performance in generative or free-text generation tasks. These models usually are closed-source, or black boxes, and accessed via APIs [16], with notable exceptions existing (e.g. Llama [26]), and contrary to what is made with medium-sized language models, LLMs are usually not fine-tuned, but used with in-context learning [19].

Recent studies have tried to leverage LLMs to the task of vulnerability detection: [31] found that LLMs can struggle to provide correct, understandable, concise, consistent, and compliant responses. [25] found that LLMs can detect more vulnerabilities than traditional static testers, outperforming traditional tools in terms of recall and F1 scores. However, they are more prone to generate false positive classifications than traditional tools. This agrees with [18], who found that there is a significant performance gap between LLMs and popular static testers, primarily due to their high false positive rates. [32] found that LLMs performance relies heavily in the prompt given to the model. They found that

GPT-3.5 is competitive with medium-sized language models, such as CodeBERT, and GPT-4 achieves superior performance. However, they also highlighted the high cost of using GPT-4, and pointed that closed source models such as the GPT family requires sending data to third-party providers, which may be a restriction.

2.2 Interpretability and Explainability

The problem interpretability methods try to solve is how to attribute the prediction of a machine learning model to its input features [24], such that one may know what drove the model decision-making. More informally, its purpose is to convince the user that the model took its decision in the right way, and doing this consistently demonstrates the model is trustworthy. This is crucial for the practical use of these models in tasks that involve ethical issues or critical decisions [3, 24].

Many interpretability methods are available, but their results can vary significantly or even contradict each other [3]. This variability underscores the importance of carefully assessing these methods to select the most appropriate technique for specific model architectures and tasks.

[3] performed an extensive comparison of interpretability methods across NLP tasks using multiple model architectures, including Transformers, CNNs, and RNNs. They found gradient-based methods consistently performed best across all architectures, with InputXGradient identified as the top interpretability technique for the Transformer architecture specifically.

Studies applying interpretability methods in the field of programming language understanding, and in particular vulnerability detection, are still few when compared to NLP tasks. [23] analyzed the CodeBERT model fine-tuned for vulnerability detection by calculating the Shapley values of the input features in order to draw their importance to the predictions. [29] used the simplification-based LIME technique to find defect-prone lines in the code. [28] studied CodeBERT and GraphCodeBERT to understand their inner workings, investigating why these models worked and what features they had learned from the code.

[13] applied the Shapley and LIME, and tried to interpret attention weights using heatmaps to understand the features influencing the model predictions. They found that Shapley values sometimes produce input importances that are not intuitive, as well as observed that the model had learned spurious correlations, such as relating variable names with the output class to be predicted. For instance, they found the word "vulnerable" strongly influenced the model to predict the code as vulnerable. This is in accordance to [21], that observed that one of the challenges blocking language models from being used in critical tasks is that they are not robust under perturbation and learn non-robust features, such as variable names, that have spurious correlations with labels. [11] also pointed that language models are known to be vulnerable to adversarial attacks, where an imperceptible change to the input can mislead the output of the model.

[13, 23, 29] are similar to ours in the application of interpretability techniques to inquire about the importance of the input to the prediction. But differently from them, we compare different interpretability methods and compare the interpretability results obtained from different language models.

The studies above try to investigate the models using their inner properties, such as hidden states and gradients, which is only possible for white box or open source models. We point to more studies in the literature that argue that hidden states offer insight into the knowledge and confidence of language models [1,5]. From this perspective, these models can potentially provide a better understanding and more transparency about their predictions than black-box models.

On the other hand, studies investigating how to interpret and explain the output of black-box or closed source models need to approach the problem externally, prompting the model itself to generate an explanation for its answer, and using that output as the means for interpretability. [15] provided a framework to use language models for the tasks of vulnerability detection and explanation. The major limitation of this approach stems from the language models themselves, once they are notorious for generating false information very confidently. Even though these models have shown remarkable performance in many complex tasks involving free-text generation, they remain prone to generating the so-called hallucinations, which are produced with highly fluent language and speech confidence, making it very convincing and difficult to discern false from real information [4].

Our work is more closely related to the studies employing medium-sized and white-box language models, but differently from them, we curated a dataset for the interpretability task and provide an objective assessment of the interpretability methods. Additionally, we are interested in comparing the intepretability capability of different language models, investigating what may be the sources of the differences.

3   Methods

In this section, we first present the pre-trained models used in the study and their fine-tuning procedure, next we describe the implementation of the interpretability methods chosen, and finally, we go through the curation procedure of the benchmark dataset for interpretability, as well its evaluation metric.

3.1   Pre-trained Models and Fine-Tuning

We chose two popular medium-sized language models for our studies: CodeBERT [10], which uses an encoder-only model based on BERT, and CoTexT [17], which is a encoder-decoder based on T5. Both are pre-trained in natural language and programming languages and available in their pre-trained format.

We fine-tuned these models using the Devign dataset [33], which comprises approximately 20 thousand C/C++ functions, hand-labeled by specialists as vulnerable or not vulnerable, with balanced classes. The fine-tuning process is slightly different for both models due to the variations in their architectures.

For CodeBERT, we train a prediction head from scratch on top of the encoder model. This prediction head is simply a one-layer perceptron followed by a sigmoid activation layer. For CoTexT, in contrast, the decoder is a language model which generates tokens auto-regressively. Therefore, we fine-tune it to generate as the first token the strings the labels of our classification problem, effectively converting it to a binary classifier.

3.2 Interpretability Methods

We chose two techniques from the gradient-based family of interpretability methods: the Saliency method, which is the original method that gave origin to this group, and the variant InputXGradient, shown by [3] to be the best-performing interpretability technique for the Transformer architecture in NLP tasks.

The implementation of both methods is similar: After predicting a label for a given example, the gradients of the network are propagated back to the embedding layer. This results in one gradient vector for each token in the vocabulary, and these are filtered to leave only the tokens present in the input example. For the Saliency method, the resulting gradient matrix is the saliency matrix, holding the saliency vector for each input token. For the InputXGradient, the matrix of gradients is multiplied element-wise with the embeddings of the input tokens. The result of this operation are the saliency vectors used by the method.

The saliency vectors hold the information of how much each input token affects the output, and it is interpreted that the higher the saliency of an input is, the more important and influential that token was for the prediction. The saliency vectors are aggregated to become real numbers, called saliency scores, which represent the final importance of each input token for the prediction.

The two most common ways to aggregating saliency vectors are the mean and the Euclidean norm [3]. A possible limitation of the Euclidean norm aggregation is that it loses the information on the direction of the vector, remaining only with its magnitude. Consequently, tokens that have the same magnitude vectors, but pointing to opposite directions, will be indistinguishable. This may result in the method being unable to identify or separate tokens that are pushing the prediction of the model to different classification labels.

To test this hypothesis, we compare the InpuXGradient with Euclidean norm aggregation with the Saliency method employing mean aggregation. The mean aggregation should do better at preserving information regarding the direction of the vector, although losing the magnitude information.

For both methods, the saliency score is an unbound number. To make it suitable to represent the importance score of the input tokens and to be presented on a heatmap of saliencies, we make the following transformations:

- InputXGradient: The saliency scores aggregated by the Euclidean norm are unbounded positive numbers. We scale them to the range from 0 to 1, where 0 means the respective token does not have any importance to the prediction, and 1 means the respective token has the most importance to it.

- Saliency: The saliency score of each token is divided by the standard deviation of the saliency scores of the input sequence, resulting in values between -3 and $+3$. This choice of scaling was preferred to preserve the mean of the distribution.

3.3 Interpretability Benchmark Dataset

When using interpretability methods to understand why the model made its decision, the objective is assign importances to each input with respect to the prediction. To evaluate the interpretability methods, it is necessary ground-truth knowledge of what inputs would be most important for a human to make the correct prediction, and compare it with the interpretability output. Annotated datasets for the evaluation of interpretability methods are relatively easy to obtain for NLP tasks [3], but are lacking for programming language tasks.

To fulfill this gap, we curated a benchmark dataset for the vulnerability detection task. The dataset proposed presents the following characteristics:

- Each example in the dataset is a function written in the C/C++ programming language;
- Every function in the dataset contains at least one vulnerability;
- Each example in the dataset is accompanied by a binary mask the same length as the number of strings in the example: the mask has value 0 if that string is not part of the vulnerability, and has value 1 otherwise.

To develop this dataset, we leveraged the C/C++ vulnerability dataset named Big-Vul [9]. It contains 6,093 vulnerable functions collected from Github, and all examples have the vulnerable snippet of code together with the patch used to fix it.

From that starting point, we removed the code patches and we generated a mask locating the position of the vulnerable code snippet. An example from the dataset with the vulnerability highlighted is illustrated in Fig. 1 .

Evaluation Metric. To evaluate how well the output from the interpretability method matches the ground-truth mask, the following steps are taken:

1. Transform the saliencies scores from the interpretability method into binary values. This is done using a threshold, where saliency values above or equal to the threshold are rounded up to 1, and values below the threshold are rounded down to 0.
2. After the first step, the problem becomes a binary classification. For each example in the dataset, we calculate the precision score of how well the binary scores match the ground truth mask.
3. With the precision score of each example in the dataset, we average the results, arriving at a Mean Precision Score for the whole dataset.

```
gn ut ls _ session _ get _ data ( gn ut ls _ session _ t session , void * session _ data , size _ t * session _ data _ size ) {
        g nut ls _ dat um _ t ps ession ;
        int ret ;
        if ( session -> intern als . res um able == RES UME _ F ALSE ) return GN UT LS _ E _ IN VAL ID _ S ESSION ;
        ps ession . data = session _ data ;
        ret = _ gn ut ls _ session _ pack ( session , & ps ession );
        if ( ret < 0 ) {
                g nut ls _ assert ();
                return ret ;
        }
        * session _ data _ size = ps ession . size ;
        if ( ps ession . size > * session _ data _ size ) {
                ret = GN UT LS _ E _ SH ORT _ M EM ORY _ BU FFER ;
                goto error ;
        }
        if ( session _ data != NULL ) mem c py ( session _ data , ps ession . data , ps ession . size );
        ret = 0 ;
        error : _ gn ut ls _ free _ dat um (& ps ession );
        return ret ;
}
```

Fig. 1. Vulnerable sample from our curated dataset with the position of the vulnerability annotated. The function is tokenized using the CodeBERT tokenizer, and each of its tokens is masked with values of 0 or 1. The collection of tokens masked as 1 represents the position of the vulnerabilities in the code, and it is highlighted in red for illustration. (Color figure online)

The mean precision score is the final metric we use to evaluate how well the interpretability output matches the true binary mask. We chose to measure precision because it penalizes false positive detections, therefore benefiting models with more sensitive results, and giving low marks to models that signal too many tokens as important. For this same reason we refrain from measuring recall, which penalizes false negative detections, and could benefit models that give high importance to too many tokens.

Finally, to find the best thresholds we repeat the process for the whole range of possible values: varying the threshold from 0.1 to 0.9, with steps of 0.05, for the InputXGradient method, and from 0.1 to 2.9, with the same step-size, for the Saliency method.

4 Results

First, we apply the fine-tuned models to classify the samples of the interpretability benchmark dataset, composed uniquely of vulnerable functions. For the samples correctly predicted as vulnerable, we evaluate the resultant saliencies for the Saliency and InputXGradient against the ground-truth masks.

The results for the InputXGradient are presented in Table 1. The best results for the CodeBERT and CoTexT models were achieved with threshold values of 0.10 and 0.35, respectively. Weak results are achieved in both models, but CodeBERT presents a mean precision score more than 7 percentage points above CoTexT.

We repeat the process for the Saliency method, with results in Table 2. It can be observed that the results are similar to the previous ones, suggesting the Euclidean norm aggregation used in the InputXGradient, which loses the information on the direction of the saliency vector, is not hurting performance, or at least is as good as the mean aggregator employed by the Saliency method. Additionally, from the results, it seems that the Saliency and InputXGradient could be used interchangeably without considerable loss.

Table 1. Mean precision achieved applying the InputXGradient method to the CodeBERT and CoTexT models.

Model	Best Threshold	Mean Precision
CodeBERT	0.10	31.3%
CoTexT	0.35	24.2%

Table 2. Mean precision achieved applying the Saliency method to the CodeBERT and CoTexT models.

Model	Best Threshold	Mean Precision
CodeBERT	0.10	31.1%
CoTexT	0.35	24.2%

4.1 Comparison Between Interpretability Methods

We compare qualitatively how interpretable are the heatmaps generated by InputXGradient and the Saliency method, and how well they match the information present in the ground-truth mask. The heatmaps were generated using CodeBERT model, which achieved superior results relative to CoTexT. We show a high-level view of three representative examples in Fig. 2: each row of the figure is a vulnerable function, and horizontally we show the ground-truth annotation (left), InputXGradient result (center), and Saliency result (right).

Fig. 2. Heatmaps for three vulnerable functions, represented each in one row. The left column illustrates the ground-truth heatmaps, showing where the vulnerability is present in the code, the center column shows the InputXGradient interpretability heatmaps, and the right column shows the Saliency interpretability heatmaps.

First, we note that for the InputXGradient heatmaps (center), the red color indicates importance, with more opaque tones representing higher importance. In contrast, the Saliency heatmaps (right) use both red and blue: red, as with

InputXGradient, indicates positive importance, while blue indicates negative importance. This is because the importance scores for the Saliency method range from -3 to +3, and we interpret negative scores as evidence that a token contributes to predicting the sample as not vulnerable, whereas positive scores indicate a contribution toward predicting it as vulnerable.

When comparing the InputXGradient and Saliency heatmaps to the ground-truth tokens, the InputXGradient results provide a noticeably clearer visualization. It is easier to identify the most important code segments and to compare them with the ground-truth annotations. In contrast, the Saliency heatmaps are more difficult to interpret, as many code regions are highlighted with strong, opaque tones of both red and blue, making it challenging to distinguish which parts are considered important or not.

To further support this observation, Fig. 3 presents the same heatmaps, but with a threshold applied to display only the tokens with the highest importance scores. The InputXGradient heatmaps (center) retain very few highlighted tokens, which are frequently located at or near the positions of the vulnerabilities. The Saliency method, however, assigns high importance to a larger number of tokens, often scattered throughout the code, which complicates pinpointing the important locations for the prediction of the vulnerability.

Fig. 3. Heatmaps for three vulnerable functions. The left column shows the ground-truth, the center column the heatmaps from the InputXGradient interpretability method, and the right column for the Saliency interpretability method. The importances given by the interpretability methods to each token are filtered using a threshold.

Given that both methods achieve similar mean precision scores, and the InputXGradient results offer a more clear and concise interpretation, we focus on the InputXGradient method in the remaining work.

4.2   Comparison Between Language Models

In this section, we compare the interpretability heatmaps generated by the InputXGradient method when applied with both CodeBERT and CoTexT models, and compare their differences.

First, we plot in Fig. 4 the histograms of the saliency scores for both models. We observe that the distributions for the CodeBERT and CoTexT are similar, and that both curves show a spike in the frequency of tokens with importance close to one. One striking difference in the histograms is in their *y-axis*: the frequency. The saliency scores for CoTexT have frequencies roughly twice those of CodeBERT. Once each importance score is associated with a token appearance in the dataset, this indicates that the CoTexT tokenizer discretizes the input code in more granular pieces.

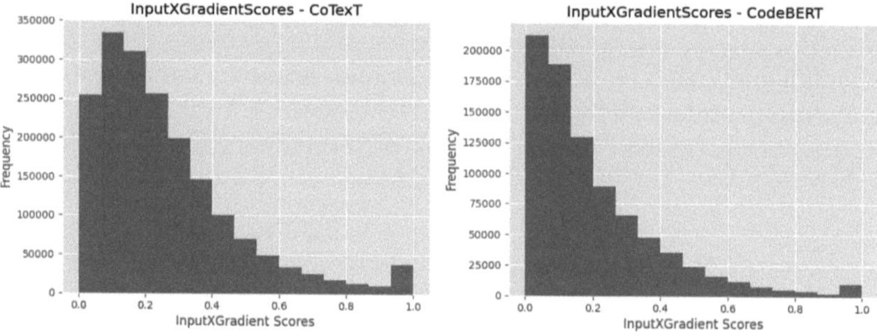

Fig. 4. Distribution of the InputXGradient importance scores for the CoTexT and CodeBERT models.

Second, we examine the interpretability heatmap generated from both models for an example input function, and we note that the observations made here generalize to the other examples we investigated in this work, but that are omitted here for brevity.

The interpretability heatmap from CodeBERT is illustrated in Fig. 5. Initially, we observe that the model attributes some importance to every token in the code. Secondly, the token * is highlighted more strongly than others. In C/C++, the * symbol denotes pointer declarations, frequently associated with memory-related vulnerabilities. This emphasis suggests the model effectively learned to recognize pointer usage as indicative of vulnerabilities due to frequent occurrences in training examples.

Moreover, the token with the highest importance in the heatmap, *alloc*, is part of the vulnerability, indicating that the model focused on a relevant element in its decision. Notably, this token appears within the *malloc* function, which allocates memory and returns a pointer to its first byte. This function frequently appears in vulnerabilities involving unsafe memory use, highlighting another aspect of the language the model has learned.

```
po pp ler _ page _ prep are _ output _ dev ( P opp ler Page * page , double scale , int rotation , g bo olean transparent ,
        Cairo Output Dev * output _ dev ;
        ca iro _ surface _ t * surface ;
        double width , height ;
        int ca iro _ width , ca iro _ height , ca iro _ row str ide , rotate ;
        unsigned char * c airo _ data ;
        rotate = rotation + page -> page -> get Rot ate ();
        if ( rot ate == 90 || rotate == 270 ) {
                height = page -> page -> get C rop Width ();
                width = page -> page -> get C rop Height ();
        }
        else {
                width = page -> page -> get C rop Width ();
                height = page -> page -> get C rop Height ();
        }
        ca iro _ width = ( int ) ce il ( width * scale );
        ca iro _ height = ( int ) ce il ( height * scale );
        output _ dev = page -> document -> output _ dev ;
        ca iro _ row str ide = ca iro _ width * 4 ;
        ca iro _ data = ( g uch ar *) g m alloc ( c airo _ height * ca iro _ row str ide );
        if ( trans parent ) mem set ( c airo _ data , 0 x 00 , ca iro _ height * ca iro _ row str ide );
        else mem set ( c airo _ data , 0 xff , ca iro _ height * ca iro _ row str ide );
        surface = ca iro _ image _ surface _ create _ for _ data ( c airo _ data , CA IRO _ FORM AT _ AR GB 32 , ca iro _ width
        output _ dev _ data -> c airo _ data = ca iro _ data ;
        output _ dev _ data -> surface = surface ;
        output _ dev _ data -> c airo = ca iro _ create ( surface );
        output _ dev -> set C airo ( output _ dev _ data -> c airo );
}
```

```
po pp ler _ page _ prep are _ output _ dev ( P opp ler Page * page , double scale , int rotation , g bo olean transparent ,
        Cairo Output Dev * output _ dev ;
        ca iro _ surface _ t * surface ;
        double width , height ;
        int ca iro _ width , ca iro _ height , ca iro _ row str ide , rotate ;
        unsigned char * c airo _ data ;
        rotate = rotation + page -> page -> get Rot ate ();
        if ( rot ate == 90 || rotate == 270 ) {
                height = page -> page -> get C rop Width ();
                width = page -> page -> get C rop Height ();
        }
        else {
                width = page -> page -> get C rop Width ();
                height = page -> page -> get C rop Height ();
        }
        ca iro _ width = ( int ) ce il ( width * scale );
        ca iro _ height = ( int ) ce il ( height * scale );
        output _ dev = page -> document -> output _ dev ;
        ca iro _ row str ide = ca iro _ width * 4 ;
        ca iro _ data = ( g uch ar *) g m alloc ( c airo _ height * ca iro _ row str ide );
        if ( trans parent ) mem set ( c airo _ data , 0 x 00 , ca iro _ height * ca iro _ row str ide );
        else mem set ( c airo _ data , 0 xff , ca iro _ height * ca iro _ row str ide );
        surface = ca iro _ image _ surface _ create _ for _ data ( c airo _ data , CA IRO _ FORM AT _ AR GB 32 , ca iro _ width
        output _ dev _ data -> c airo _ data = ca iro _ data ;
        output _ dev _ data -> surface = surface ;
        output _ dev _ data -> c airo = ca iro _ create ( surface );
        output _ dev -> set C airo ( output _ dev _ data -> c airo );
}
```

Fig. 5. Interpretability example from CodeBERT. Top: Tokenized function using the CodeBERT tokenizer, with ground-truth mask highlighting the exact position of the vulnerability. Bottom: Heatmap of the importances given by the model to each token.

Figure 6 shows the same example for the CoTexT model. The first aspect to observe is how differently the code looks after being processed by the CoTexT tokenizer, compared with the same code processed by the CodeBERT tokenizer. Notably, the CoTexT tokenizer does not contain a token for curly braces in its vocabulary, and therefore they are removed during tokenization. This detail is significant, as curly braces are structural elements of the language, and their absence may result in a loss of semantic meaning.

A second interesting point is that the CoTexT tokenizer segments words into more granular tokens compared to the CodeBERT tokenizer, as observed in Fig. 4. For instance, the word *stride* is split into three tokens: *s-tride*, while *height* and *width* are tokenized as *height* and *wid-th*, respectively. In contrast, CodeBERT tokenizes *stride* into only two tokens and keeps *height* and *width* as single tokens.

Most concerning is that the CoTexT tokenizer splits the keyword *malloc* into two tokens: *mal-loc*. This excessive granularity may hinder the model's ability to learn the semantic roles of individual language constructs, thereby reducing its capacity to make informed and interpretable predictions.

268   L. Silveira et al.

```
pop p ler _ page _ pre par e _ out put _ dev ( Pop p ler P age * page , double scale , in t rotation ,   g boo le an transparent
 c air o _ surface _ t * surface ;
double width , height ;
in t  c air o _ wid th ,  c air o _ he ight ,  c air o _ row s tri de , rotate ;
un signed  char * c air o _ data ;
rotate = rotation + page -> page -> get R o tate ( );
 if ( rot ate = = 90 | | rotate = =  270 )   height = page -> page -> get C rop W i d th ( );
width = page -> page -> get C rop He ight ( );
  else   width = page -> page -> get C rop W i d th ( );
height = page -> page -> get C rop He ight ( );
  c air o _ wid th = ( in t ) ce il ( wid th * scale );
 c air o _ he ight = ( in t ) ce il ( he ight * scale );
output _ dev = page -> document -> out put _ dev ;
 c air o _ row s tri de =  c air o _ wid th * 4 ;
 c air o _ data = ( gu char * )  g mal loc ( c air o _ he ight *  c air o _ row s tri de );
 if ( trans parent ) me m set ( c air o _ data ,  0 x 00 ,  c air o _ he ight *  c air o _ row s tri de );
else me m set ( c air o _ data ,  0 x f f ,  c air o _ he ight *  c air o _ row s tri de );
surface =  c air o _ image _ surface _ create _ for _ data ( c air o _ data , CA I RO _ FORM AT _ AR GB 32 ,  c air o _ wid th
output _ dev _ data -> c air o _ data =  c air o _ data ;
output _ dev _ data -> surface = surface ;
output _ dev _ data -> c air o =  c air o _ create (
```

```
pop p ler _ page _ pre par e _ out put _ dev ( Pop p ler P age * page , double scale , in t rotation ,   g boo le an transparent
 c air o _ surface _ t * surface ;
double width , height ;
in t  c air o _ wid th ,  c air o _ he ight ,  c air o _ row s tri de , rotate ;
un signed  char * c air o _ data ;
rotate = rotation + page -> page -> get R o tate ( );
 if ( rot ate = = 90 | | rotate = =  270 )   height = page -> page -> get C rop W i d th ( );
width = page -> page -> get C rop He ight ( );
  else   width = page -> page -> get C rop W i d th ( );
height = page -> page -> get C rop He ight ( );
  c air o _ wid th = ( in t ) ce il ( wid th * scale );
 c air o _ he ight = ( in t ) ce il ( he ight * scale );
output _ dev = page -> document -> out put _ dev ;
 c air o _ row s tri de =  c air o _ wid th * 4 ;
 c air o _ data = ( gu char * )  g mal loc ( c air o _ he ight *  c air o _ row s tri de );
 if ( trans parent ) me m set ( c air o _ data ,  0 x 00 ,  c air o _ he ight *  c air o _ row s tri de );
else me m set ( c air o _ data ,  0 x f f ,  c air o _ he ight *  c air o _ row s tri de );
surface =  c air o _ image _ surface _ create _ for _ data ( c air o _ data , CA I RO _ FORM AT _ AR GB 32 ,  c air o _ wid th
output _ dev _ data -> c air o _ data =  c air o _ data ;
output _ dev _ data -> surface = surface ;
output _ dev _ data -> c air o =  c air o _ create (
```

Fig. 6. Interpretability example from CoTexT. Top: Tokenized function using the CoTexT tokenizer, with ground-truth mask highlighting the exact position of the vulnerability. Bottom: Heatmap of the importances given by the model to each token.

These differences in the tokenizers of deep learning models are rarely discussed, yet they appear to be significant when interpreting the predictions from the model. In particular, the characteristics observed in the CoTexT tokenizer make the tokenized code harder for humans to read, lacking familiar structure, and, more importantly, may lead to the loss of crucial semantic information.

Finally, it can be observed that CoTexT, unlike CodeBERT, assigns particularly high importance to one specific token: *air*, which is part of the variable name *cairo*. This variable appears in the vulnerability region, but it is also scattered throughout the code, making it unclear whether the model is truly focusing on right things. Moreover, the tendency to assign high importance to variable names suggests the model may be learning spurious correlations. This is consistent with observations from [21], who found that language models often relied on spurious features, such as variable names, for its predictions. This behavior is undesirable, reflecting a lack of robustness, and creating opportunities for adversarial manipulation, as discussed in [11].

Our analysis shows that interpretability methods can indicate if the model is relying on spurious features to make a prediction. It also points to a possible solution: the anonymization of such features, replacing them by placeholders. The interpretability analysis can then be used to validate this anonymization, verifying if the placeholders are not receiving high importance for the predictions.

Finally, our results suggest that even when two models achieve similar performance on a task (both have accuracies in the order of $61\% - 63\%$ in the Devign test set), how they arrive at their predictions can differ significantly, and more importantly: their capacity to provide human-understandable explanations also varies considerably. This is evident in the comparison between CodeBERT and CoTexT, where the former generates interpretability heatmaps that are more coherent, human-friendly, and informative.

5   Conclusion

This work examined the interpretability of two medium-sized language models, CodeBERT and CoTexT, in the task of vulnerability detection in source code. To support this analysis, we introduced a benchmark dataset consisting of vulnerable functions annotated with ground-truth vulnerability masks, allowing for token-level comparison between model attributions and known vulnerability locations. We applied two attribution methods, InputXGradient and Saliency, to generate interpretability heatmaps for each model. The evaluation was conducted in two stages: first, by comparing the attribution methods independently based on their token-level alignment with the ground truth; and second, by comparing the output of both language models using the same interpretability method, with a focus on the impact of tokenization and model-specific behavior on the resulting attributions.

The main findings of this study are: (i) InputXGradient produces clearer, more human-aligned heatmaps than Saliency; (ii) There can be a significant difference in language models ability to provide interpretation for its prediction, as demonstrated in the comparison of CodeBERT and CoTexT; (iii) the tokenizer design significantly impacts both model understanding and interpretability capabilities; and (iv) interpretability analysis can reveal hidden model flaws not evident from accuracy alone.

As future directions, we suggest expanding the range of interpretability methods and models evaluated, improving saliency aggregation techniques, and exploring pre-/post-processing strategies as a solution for the learning of spurious features. Finally, the comparison between the ability of language models to provide interpretation for their output needs to be expanded to large language models, both white and black-boxes.

This study represents an important step toward systematically understanding model behavior in vulnerability detection tasks, with implications for improving model transparency and trustworthiness in secure software development.

Acknowledgments. This work was supported by the Financiadora de Estudos e Projetos (FINEP), contract 01.22.0615.02.

References

1. Ahdritz, G., Qin, T., Vyas, N., Barak, B., Edelman, B.L.: Distinguishing the knowable from the unknowable with language models (2024). https://arxiv.org/abs/2402.03563

2. Ahmad, W.U., Chakraborty, S., Ray, B., Chang, K.W.: Unified pre-training for program understanding and generation (2021). https://doi.org/10.48550/ARXIV.2103.06333

3. Atanasova, P., Simonsen, J.G., Lioma, C., Augenstein, I.: A diagnostic study of explainability techniques for text classification (2020). https://doi.org/10.48550/ARXIV.2009.13295

4. Augenstein, I., et al.: Factuality challenges in the era of large language models and opportunities for fact-checking (2024). https://doi.org/10.1038/s42256-024-00881-z

5. Azaria, A., Mitchell, T.: The internal state of an LLM knows when it's lying. In: Bouamor, H., Pino, J., Bali, K. (eds.) Findings of the Association for Computational Linguistics: EMNLP 2023, pp. 967–976. Association for Computational Linguistics, Singapore (2023). https://doi.org/10.18653/v1/2023.findings-emnlp.68. https://aclanthology.org/2023.findings-emnlp.68/

6. Buratti, L., et al.: Exploring software naturalness through neural language models (2020). https://doi.org/10.48550/ARXIV.2006.12641

7. Chen, M., et al.: Evaluating large language models trained on code (2021). https://doi.org/10.48550/ARXIV.2107.03374

8. Devlin, J., Chang, M.W., Lee, K., Toutanova, K.: Bert: pre-training of deep bidirectional transformers for language understanding (2018). https://doi.org/10.48550/ARXIV.1810.04805

9. Fan, J., Li, Y., Wang, S., Nguyen, T.N.: A C/C++ code vulnerability dataset with code changes and CVE summaries (2020). https://doi.org/10.1145/3379597.3387501

10. Feng, Z., et al.: Codebert: a pre-trained model for programming and natural languages (2020). https://doi.org/10.48550/ARXIV.2002.08155

11. García-Carrasco, J., Maté, A., Trujillo, J.: Detecting and understanding vulnerabilities in language models via mechanistic interpretability. In: Proceedings of the Thirty-Third International Joint Conference on Artificial Intelligence, IJCAI 2024 (2024). https://doi.org/10.24963/ijcai.2024/43

12. Hanif, H., Maffeis, S.: Vulberta: simplified source code pre-training for vulnerability detection (2022). https://doi.org/10.48550/ARXIV.2205.12424

13. Haurogné, J., Basheer, N., Islam, S.: Vulnerability detection using BERT based LLM model with transparency obligation practice towards trustworthy AI. Mach. Learn. Appl. **18**, 100598 (2024). https://doi.org/10.1016/j.mlwa.2024.100598. https://www.sciencedirect.com/science/article/pii/S2666827024000744

14. Hindle, A., Barr, E.T., Su, Z., Gabel, M., Devanbu, P.: On the naturalness of software (2012)

15. Mao, Q., Li, Z., Hu, X., Liu, K., Xia, X., Sun, J.: Towards explainable vulnerability detection with large language models (2025). https://arxiv.org/abs/2406.09701

16. OpenAI, Achiam, J., et al.: GPT-4 technical report (2024). https://arxiv.org/abs/2303.08774

17. Phan, L., et al.: Cotext: multi-task learning with code-text transformer (2021). https://doi.org/10.48550/ARXIV.2105.08645

18. Purba, M.D., Ghosh, A., Radford, B.J., Chu, B.: Software vulnerability detection using large language models. In: 2023 IEEE 34th International Symposium on Software Reliability Engineering Workshops (ISSREW), pp. 112–119 (2023). https://doi.org/10.1109/ISSREW60843.2023.00058

19. Radford, A., Narasimhan, K.: Improving language understanding by generative pre-training (2018)

20. Raffel, C., et al.: Exploring the limits of transfer learning with a unified text-to-text transformer (2019). https://doi.org/10.48550/ARXIV.1910.10683
21. Rahman, M.M., Ceka, I., Mao, C., Chakraborty, S., Ray, B., Le, W.: Towards causal deep learning for vulnerability detection. In: Proceedings of the IEEE/ACM 46th International Conference on Software Engineering, ICSE 2024. Association for Computing Machinery, New York (2024). https://doi.org/10.1145/3597503.3639170
22. Russell, R.L., et al.: Automated vulnerability detection in source code using deep representation learning (2018). https://doi.org/10.48550/ARXIV.1807.04320
23. Sotgiu, A., Pintor, M., Biggio, B.: Explainability-based debugging of machine learning for vulnerability discovery (2022). https://doi.org/10.1145/3538969.3543809
24. Sundararajan, M., Taly, A., Yan, Q.: Axiomatic attribution for deep networks (2017). https://doi.org/10.48550/ARXIV.1703.01365
25. Tamberg, K., Bahsi, H.: Harnessing large language models for software vulnerability detection: a comprehensive benchmarking study. IEEE Access **13**, 29698–29717 (2025). https://doi.org/10.1109/ACCESS.2025.3541146
26. Touvron, H., et al.: Llama: open and efficient foundation language models (2023). https://arxiv.org/abs/2302.13971
27. Vaswani, A., et al.: Attention is all you need (2017). https://doi.org/10.48550/ARXIV.1706.03762
28. Wan, Y., Zhao, W., Zhang, H., Sui, Y., Xu, G., Jin, H.: What do they capture? A structural analysis of pre-trained language models for source code (2022). https://doi.org/10.1145/3510003.3510050
29. Wattanakriengkrai, S., Thongtanunam, P., Tantithamthavorn, C., Hata, H., Matsumoto, K.: Predicting defective lines using a model-agnostic technique. IEEE Trans. Softw. Eng. **48**(5), 1480–1496 (2022)
30. Yamaguchi, F., Golde, N., Arp, D., Rieck, K.: Modeling and discovering vulnerabilities with code property graphs (2014). https://doi.org/10.1109/SP.2014.44
31. Yu, J., et al.: An insight into security code review with LLMs: capabilities, obstacles and influential factors (2024). https://arxiv.org/abs/2401.16310
32. Zhou, X., Zhang, T., Lo, D.: Large language model for vulnerability detection: emerging results and future directions. In: Proceedings of the 2024 ACM/IEEE 44th International Conference on Software Engineering: New Ideas and Emerging Results, ICSE-NIER 2024, pp. 47–51. Association for Computing Machinery, New York (2024). https://doi.org/10.1145/3639476.3639762
33. Zhou, Y., Liu, S., Siow, J., Du, X., Liu, Y.: Devign: effective vulnerability identification by learning comprehensive program semantics via graph neural networks (2019). https://doi.org/10.48550/ARXIV.1909.03496

Monitoring and Critical Infrastructures

Impact of Image Resolution on Drone Surveillance System Availability: A Stochastic Petri Net Approach

Ivson Borges[1]([✉]) [iD], Luan Lins[1] [iD], Gustavo Callou[2] [iD], and Paulo Maciel[1] [iD]

[1] Universidade Federal de Pernambuco, Recife, Brazil
`{igb,lcsl2,prmm}@cin.ufpe.br`
[2] Universidade Federal Rural de Pernambuco, Recife, Brazil
`gustavo.callou@ufrpe.br`

Abstract. Ensuring the availability and energy autonomy of drone-based surveillance systems is critical as these technologies become increasingly vital for security, disaster response, and public safety operations. The effectiveness of such systems depends not only on the reliability of their components but also on the trade-off between energy consumption and the performance of onboard artificial intelligence (AI) algorithms, which are highly sensitive to image resolution. This paper presents a stochastic modeling approach to analyze how different image resolution settings impact the operational availability of UAV-based surveillance systems. Stochastic Petri Net (SPN) models are proposed to evaluate the effects of drone and battery redundancy strategies on system availability. The model incorporates mission-critical parameters such as drone failure and repair rates, battery discharge and recharge cycles, and energy consumption as a function of image resolution. We examine the metrics under evaluation assuming Full HD, 2K, and 4K image resolutions. The results show that battery redundancy significantly improves UAV system availability, while adding a backup drone yields marginal gains, offering valuable design insights to balance energy efficiency, resolution, and operational reliability.

Keywords: Drone Surveillance System · Availability · Stochastic Petri Net

1 Introduction

Identifying objects and individuals using AI techniques has become increasingly prominent in security, public safety, and infrastructure monitoring applications. A critical factor affecting the accuracy of these AI-based systems is the quality of the input images, particularly their resolution. High-resolution images preserve fine-grained features, such as textures and contours, enabling more accurate inference. However, higher image resolution also demands greater processing power and storage capacity [5], which can lead to increased energy consumption and reduced operational autonomy in embedded systems such as drones.

L. A. Rodrigues and R. Oliveira (Eds.): LADC 2025, CCIS 2697, pp. 275–290, 2026.
https://doi.org/10.1007/978-3-032-11539-3_16

Unmanned aerial vehicles (UAVs) have emerged as versatile platforms for collecting high-resolution images across large areas [3,8]. Their mobility and flexibility make them ideal for surveillance applications in dynamic or hard-to-reach environments. However, energy constraints—primarily due to battery limitations—pose significant challenges. When operating with high-resolution image capture, drones experience faster battery depletion, which may reduce mission duration and affect the continuity of monitoring tasks.

The growing use of drones for inspection and surveillance has spurred research into their operational efficiency and reliability. For instance, some studies have developed methodologies using Colored Petri Nets to model and evaluate drone-based inspection systems, estimating metrics like monitoring frequency and flight time while accounting for stochastic influences [7]. Similarly, research employing Stochastic Petri Nets (SPNs) has explored the reliability of drone surveillance [12]. Furthermore, performance models for systems integrating drones and edge computing have been proposed to estimate metrics such as response time and resource utilization in various scenarios [16]. A significant gap persists in the literature regarding a quantitative analysis of how different image resolutions affect a drone's battery autonomy and its corresponding operational impact.

This study proposes a stochastic modeling approach to evaluate the availability and autonomy of UAV surveillance systems under varying image resolution settings. Using a Stochastic Petri Net (SPN) model, we assess two redundancy strategies: (i) adding spare batteries and (ii) adding both spare batteries and spare drones. We aim to determine how image resolution impacts system availability and quantify the trade-offs between redundancy and operational efficiency. Therefore, this paper provides system designers with insights to support the development of energy-aware and resilient surveillance system architectures. The main contributions of this paper are:

- A stochastic approach using SPN to analyze how image resolution settings impact the operational availability of UAV-based surveillance systems;
- A model validation procedure that compares the model's results against a real testbed system to increase trust in the findings;
- A comparative analysis of redundancy strategies, evaluating the impact on system availability across video resolutions when adding spare batteries versus adding both spare batteries and a spare drone;
- An analysis of the trade-offs between image resolution, energy efficiency, and operational availability provides valuable design insights for balancing these factors.

This paper is structured as follows. Section 2 describes recent related work. Section 3 outlines the concepts of evaluating availability and Stochastic Petri Nets. Section 4 describes the methodology used. Section 5 details the adopted SPN model for availability evaluation. Section 6 presents three case studies that analyze the impact of redundancy in drones and batteries on system availability. Furthermore, Sect. 7 discusses the limitations of this work. Finally, Sect. 8 presents the conclusion and discusses possible directions for future work.

2   Related Work

This section presents related work from the literature on drone availability. For instance, the authors in [6] propose models in SPN to evaluate the reliability of an architecture that uses drones to offload data from IoT devices to remote servers, such as edge or cloud computing. The analysis focuses on the availability and reliability of the system, identifying critical points and suggesting improvements to the architecture.

The study [7] presents a methodology that uses Colored Petri Nets to model and evaluate distribution network inspection systems using drones. The model enables the estimation of monitoring frequency, determination of the most suitable drone configuration, monitoring schemes, flight time, and maintenance periods, while accounting for stochastic influences such as failures and maintenance needs. However, it does not assess availability regarding autonomy or image acquisition.

Li et al. [11] address energy efficiency in the continuous execution of drone missions, proposing a conscious energy-use replacement strategy complemented by two approaches to monitor battery level. These approaches aim to minimize unnecessary consumption during travel, ensuring that drones remain operational for longer periods. However, the relationship between battery autonomy and the quality of service provided still requires more detailed modeling.

In [12], the authors propose models to represent the availability and reliability of drone surveillance systems using SPNs and consider redundancy mechanisms. However, their work did not focus on analyzing the impact of image resolution on energy consumption and system availability. In contrast, our work focuses on quantifying the effect of different image resolutions on battery autonomy and correspondent availability. By integrating quality-of-service (QoS) parameters with dependability modeling, we provide a more comprehensive evaluation that addresses a gap not explored in this study.

The study [16] proposes a model based on SPN to evaluate the performance of a forest fire prevention system that integrates drones, cameras, and edge computing. The SPN model enables the estimation of performance metrics, including average response time, resource utilization, disposal rates, and throughput, which can be analyzed in various scenarios with different resource configurations. The authors did not aim to evaluate the availability or the impact of autonomy on drone availability.

Our work proposes investigating the relationship between the quality of images captured by UAV-based surveillance systems and the resulting energy consumption, which can impact the system's availability. Unlike the related studies available, we notice that the focus is narrowly on isolated factors (e.g., availability or performance); our approach evaluates the relationship between camera resolution (Full HD, 2K, 4K) and battery performance while also modeling the impact of an availability system. The analysis conducted in this work supports designers in making decisions based on real-world operational metrics, offering a more resilient alternative to existing solutions.

Table 1 presents a comparative analysis of recent studies on drone-based systems, focusing on modeling techniques, availability, image resolution, and energy consumption. As shown, several works employ Stochastic Petri Nets [6,12,16] or Colored Petri Nets [7] to represent various aspects of UAV operations. However, only a few of them explicitly address availability [6,12], and even those do not evaluate performance indicators in an integrated manner. For example, [11] and [16] concentrate on energy efficiency but do not incorporate availability into their models. Moreover, none of the related studies consider image resolution, which is a critical factor for surveillance applications. In contrast, the approach proposed in this work combines availability analysis, image resolution, and energy consumption within a single modeling framework based on Stochastic Petri Nets. This integrated perspective provides a more realistic and reliable evaluation of drone-based surveillance systems and addresses key limitations observed in previous research.

Table 1. Comparison of related work on drone availability

Work	Modeling Technique	Availability	Image Resolution	Energy Consumption
[6]	SPN	Yes	No	No
[7]	Colored Petri Nets	No	No	Partially
[11]	Energy-aware strategies	No	No	Yes
[12]	SPN	Yes	No	Partially
[16]	SPN	No	No	Yes
This work	SPN	Yes	Yes	Yes

3   Background

A key element of system dependability is steady-state availability, which measures a system's capability to maintain operations despite failures and repairs [19]. Closely related is autonomy, defined here as a system's capacity to maintain functionality over time under specific operational conditions, such as limited energy supply. Autonomy depends on factors such as energy efficiency, operational load, and environmental constraints, which directly impact the duration of uptime.

Availability is typically calculated using Mean Time to Failure (MTTF) and Mean Time to Repair (MTTR), as shown in Eq. 1:

$$A = \frac{MTTF}{MTTF + MTTR} \tag{1}$$

When Time to Failure (TTF) and Time to Repair (TTR) follow exponential distributions with λ and μ as their respective rates, the relationship between these variables' availability simplifies, as shown in Eq. 2:

$$A = \frac{\mu}{\lambda + \mu} \tag{2}$$

Autonomy, in contrast, focuses on energy sustainability. It is measured by metrics like battery capacity, energy discharge rates, and operational lifespan under dynamic workloads. Integrating autonomy into availability models requires analyzing energy consumption patterns in conjunction with failure and repair rates. For instance, battery depletion can be modeled as a "failure" mode, where the MTTR depends on the recharge time or energy harvesting capabilities.

SPNs are a formalism that extends classical Petri nets by associating timing behavior with transitions. First introduced independently by Symons, Natkin, and Molloy [18], SPNs allow for the modeling of concurrent and stochastic systems, capturing both functional and performance aspects. These foundational efforts evolved into more expressive variants such as Generalized Stochastic Petri Nets (GSPNs) [2], Deterministic and Stochastic Petri Nets (DSPNs) [1], and extended forms such as eDSPNs [20] and Stochastic Reward Nets (SRNs) [14].

4   Methodology

This section presents the methodology adopted to assess the availability of UAV systems. The steps of the methodology are represented in Fig. 1. The first step of the methodology involves investigating the behavior of the system's components, with a focus on their availability.

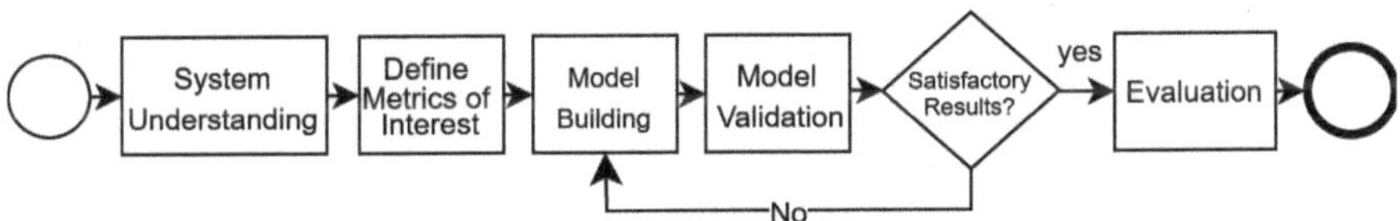

Fig. 1. Methodology.

In the Second Step, a Baseline System Architecture is created with the essential minimum values needed for optimal functioning, and system operations are monitored to identify key metrics of interest, such as availability and autonomy. In the third step, Model Building, we develop and evaluate the model based on the baseline system definitions and metrics of interest. Then, the following step is the model validation phase (fourth step), where we examine whether the model's behavior aligns with that of the real system. During this stage, we use a commercial drone and batteries to compare their autonomy and performance with respect to the resolution of images captured by the drone's camera. If the proposed model does not accurately reflect the behavior of the real system, we return to the development phase to implement the necessary adjustments.

Once the model is validated, it becomes feasible to utilize it for evaluating various system configurations. Consequently, the fifth step facilitates the investigation of a system's behavior under specific parameterizations of its components. Furthermore, it enables an assessment of the requisite number of spare batteries to maintain a predefined level of availability. During this stage, adjustments to the parameters of the components, such as failure rates, recovery times, and autonomy, can be implemented to measure their impact on system availability.

5   Architecture and Proposed Model

This section presents a proposed SPN model to evaluate steady-state availability during missions that involve image capture at different resolutions, and incorporates spare batteries and aircraft to assess their impact on system availability.

5.1   Base Architecture

Figure 2 illustrates the base architecture of a small drone surveillance system, which includes an operator and a battery charger. Traditional designs typically utilize a single drone for monitoring. However, service failures in mission-critical scenarios can risk site security, making restoration time crucial during intrusions or fire detection. To mitigate these risks, we propose a surveillance system that incorporates redundancy in drones and their batteries, thereby enhancing operational availability.

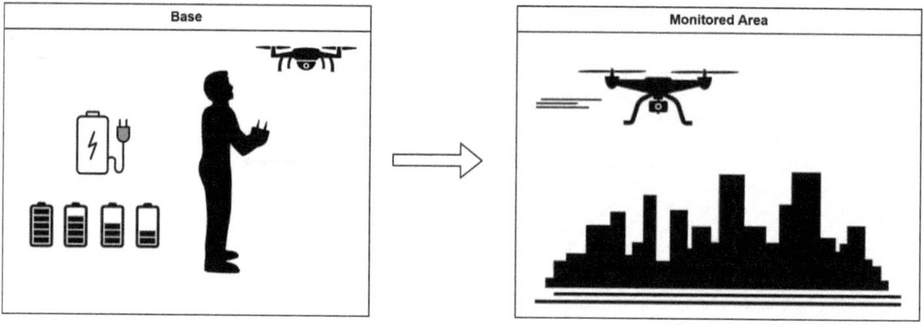

Fig. 2. Base architecture.

Additionally, the impact of image resolution on the system's autonomy and availability must be considered. Higher-resolution images require more processing power and increased battery usage, which can reduce operational time and potentially lead to more frequent battery replacements. Conversely, lower-resolution images may prolong drone operation but could compromise data quality.

Therefore, balancing image resolution with operational efficiency is essential to optimize autonomy and availability. By integrating redundancy and addressing the implications of image resolution, the proposed system aims to ensure continuous monitoring and rapid response, thereby improving overall site security.

5.2   Base Architecture Availability Model

Figure 3 shows the baseline SPN model to estimate both instantaneous and steady-state availability for the base scenario presented in Fig. 2. In addition to availability, this model evaluation allows critical metrics such as downtime and uptime to be quantified.

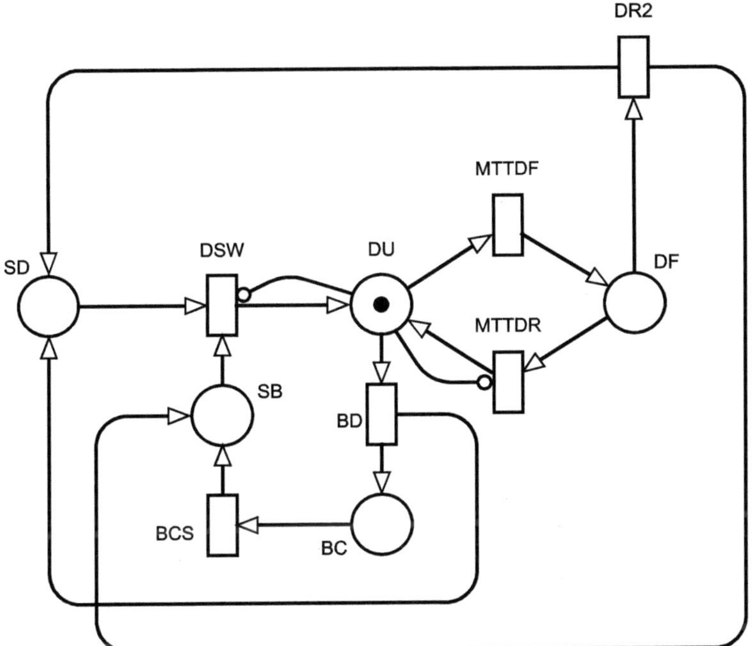

Fig. 3. Proposed SPN Model.

In the proposed SPN model the places *SB*, *SD*, *BC*, *DU*, and *DF* represent distinct states of the system. *SB* indicates the availability of spare batteries, *SD* indicates the spare drones, *BC* represents the battery charging state, *DU* signifies the operational state in which a battery-powered drone actively performs surveillance, and *DF* denotes a system failure state resulting from a drone malfunction. In addition, we have six exponential (timed) transitions: *DSW*, *MTTDF*, *MTTDR*, *DR2*, *BCS*, and *BD*; and their respective arcs. The timed transitions depend on the specified activation delay. *DSW* represents the mean time for a drone or battery swap, while *MTTDF* and *MTTDR* represent Mean Time to Drone Failure and Mean Time to Drone Repair metrics, respectively, which are important for assessing system availability aspects. The *BD* transition represents the battery discharge time, indicating the operational status of the drone battery. The *BCS* represents the battery charge time.

Table 2 summarizes the attributes of these transitions. All transitions are assigned a priority level of one. Each transition is independently marked and follows Single Server Semantics (SSS), except for *BCS*, which operates under Infinite Server Semantics (ISS). SSS defines timed transitions as only being enabled and fired by processing one token at a time from each input place, without any parallel token processing. The time counting restarts after each transition firing. In contrast, the ISS transitions simultaneously process all tokens available in their input places.

Table 2. Parameters Associated with Transitions

Transitions	Parameter	Priority	Guard Expression
MTTDF	MTTDF	1	
MTTDR	MTTDR	1	
DR2	MTTDR	1	*#DU>0*
BD	MTTBD	1	
BCS	MTTBC	1	
DSW	MTTDS	1	*#DF=0*

To ensure that only one Unmanned Aerial Vehicle (UAV) can be operational at any given time, the model incorporates two inhibitor arcs between the transitions *DSW* and *MTTDR* and the place *DU*. These arcs also determine whether a spare or recovered UAV can assume the operational role if the necessary conditions are met. Following the assigned delay, the transitions *MTTDR* and *DR2* are activated immediately upon the completion of drone repairs.

The availability can be computed by knowing the probability of place *DU* having one token, which is represented by the expression $P\{\#DU > 0\}$, using Mercury notation [17].

The UAV is characterized by specific time metrics, including Mean Time to Drone Failure (MTTDF), Mean Time to Drone Repair (MTTDR), Mean Time to Replacement Battery (MTTRB), Mean Time to Battery Charge (MTTBC), Mean Time To Drone Swap (MTTDS), and Mean Time to Battery Discharge (MTTBD), all represented by exponential distributions. The use of exponential distributions in availability models is primarily justified by their memoryless property, which implies that the probability of a future event is independent of the time that has already elapsed. This characteristic ensures temporal independence and constant failure rates, effectively reflecting the behavior of many real systems [13]. In this paper, we focus on the mean system behavior, and therefore, we assume exponentially distributed times. This modeling choice not only simplifies calculations and improves mathematical tractability but also makes the model efficient and suitable for simulating unpredictable failures. Although exponential distributions are effective in representing certain phenomena, more complex system behaviors may require the use of phase-type distributions. In such cases, alternative distributions can be incorporated into the model using the Mercury Tool [17] through Stochastic Petri Net (SPN) modeling, allowing for a more realistic and flexible representation of time-dependent processes.

6   Cases Studies

This section presents three case studies showcasing the applicability of the proposed methodology. The first study validates the adopted SPN model for the base architecture. The second study analyzes how variations in image resolution and battery redundancy affect the drone system's availability. Finally, the third study assesses the impact of changing the number of spare batteries and drones on availability.

Table 3. Parameter's values applied to cases studies

Parameter	Values(hours)
MTTFD	5034.0
MTTD	2.0
MTTBD	0.5 (Full HD)
	0.45 (2K)
	0.40 (4K)
MTTBC	0.628
MTTDS	0.016

The Mean Time To Battery Charge (MTTBC) is computed using the equation: Time (hours) $= \frac{\text{Battery capacity (mAh)}}{\text{Charger current (mA)}}$. Considering a 2830 mAh battery and a 4500 mA charging current, the charging time is 0.628 h (37.73 min), assuming 100% charging efficiency and no energy loss.

To compute the Mean Time To Battery Discharge (MTTBD), we conducted a series of controlled experiments using a commercial DJI Mavic Pro Platinum drone. In each trial, the drone was fully charged and operated continuously while recording video at different resolutions until the battery was fully depleted. Tests were repeated for each resolution setting—Full HD (1080p), 2K (1440p), and 4K (2160p)—to ensure consistency. The MTTBD was then measured for each resolution. It is important to note that the MTTBD corresponds to the total flight time available for a complete round trip, including both outbound and return legs between the drone and the base. As a result, the following mean times were obtained: Full HD (1080p) âĂŞ 29.96 min, 2K (1440p) âĂŞ 27.02 min, and 4K (2160p) âĂŞ 25.08 min, as shown in Table 3.

6.1   Case Study I Validation of Availability

This study demonstrates the procedures adopted to validate the availability obtained from the proposed SPN model (see Fig. 3). It is important to implement validation techniques that verify the consistency between this model and a real testbed system to enhance trust in the results obtained from the proposed model. These validation techniques aim to validate key aspects of the model, including assumptions and the generated output values [9].

It is important to note that once the model has been validated, we can increase our confidence in its results. This allows us to evaluate varied scenarios by improving the model without conducting experiments in the real system. The primary goal of adopting this formalism with validation is to enhance the quality of the results produced by the proposed models, which enables us to adopt the model and evaluate extensions that represent different scenarios.

A common approach for validating dependability models is to compare the results of measurements collected in a real environment with the values generated by the model [10]. This comparison verifies whether the model results conform with the behavior observed in the real system [4,15].

Validation is an important step in model building, as it ensures that models are accurate and reliable representations of the real system. It is important to remember that models are simplifications and may only capture some details and nuances. However, a well-executed validation process can improve the accuracy and reliability of models, making them suitable for making predictions and informed decisions based on the results generated.

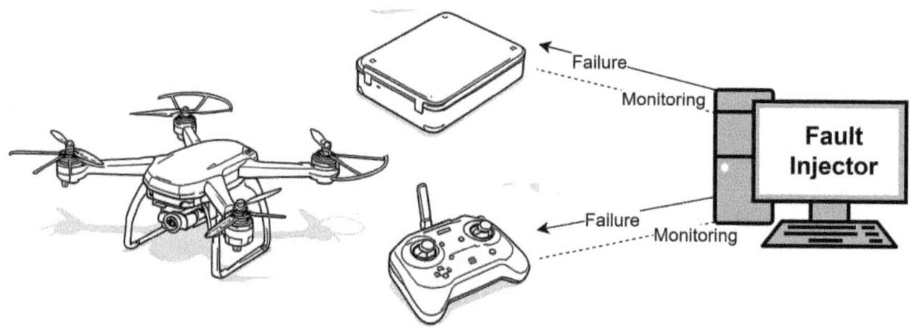

Fig. 4. Base environment.

To conduct this validation, a base environment was considered to carry out the experiments, consisting of a drone (aircraft and controller) and a battery, as shown in Figs. 4. The MTTDF, MTTDR, MTTBD, and MTTBC used for the base architecture components were obtained from [12]. We assume that the mean failure and repair times are exponentially distributed, and thus, the failure and repair rates are the inverse of MTTDF and MTTDR. Table 4 shows the values adopted for validation in hours.

To validate the proposed SPN model, the system was stressed by applying an acceleration factor of 1000, which reduces the components' failure times proportionally, effectively accelerating their MTTF. The fault injector creates a thread for each component in the system, which is responsible for injecting faults. This injector was executed on a microcomputer equipped with a 3.2 GHz AMD CPU, 16 GB of RAM, and 500 GB of storage.

The fault injector uses dedicated threads to inject failures and monitor devices in the analyzed system [4, 15]. Each thread generates random failure/repair times for devices, while another monitors system status (logging "UP" or "DOWN" every 10 s for rapid event detection). The 10-second monitoring interval struck a balance between granularity and efficiency, ensuring the timely capture of critical events. During an experiment, "UP" (operational) and "DOWN" (inactive) intervals were recorded. These intervals, multiplied by 10 s, provided MTTF and MTTR values for calculating system availability.

Since the data did not follow a clear theoretical distribution, a non-parametric bootstrap method was applied to generate 1,000 resamples from the original dataset. The mean availability from each resample was computed and ordered, with the 25th and 975th values defining the 95% confidence interval (CI). This implies that, in 95% of repeated experiments, the system availability would fall within this interval.

A comparison between the SPN model results and the empirical measurements from the testbed shows strong alignment. The SPN model estimated an availability of 0.436987, while the real system exhibited an availability of 0.4296771. The 95% confidence interval for the real system's availability was calculated as [0.421449; 0.443861]. Since the model's estimate falls within this interval, it supports the validity of the UAV surveillance system model. Thus, the model can be confidently used to compute availability and to support the design of strategies aimed at improving system performance under various operational scenarios.

Table 4. Parameter's values applied to validation

Parameter	Values(hours)
MTTDF	5034.0
MTTDR	2.0
MTTBD	0.5
MTTBC	0.628

6.2 Case Study II

This study considers the SPN model, as previously shown in Fig. 3, to evaluate system availability. In this study, variations in the battery discharge time parameters are explored to investigate their impact on system availability. The model is evaluated using stationary analysis. Stationary analysis in Petri Nets enables the evaluation of whether the network attains a stable state, where the distribution of tokens remains unchanged. Assessing the system's stability and predictability is essential.

Table 5 presents the summary results achieved, taking into account variations on MTTBD and its effects on downtime and availability metrics. The results reveal a linear correlation between MTTBD and these metrics. As MTTBD increases, a clear trend emerges, with availability levels ranging from 38.3% for 4K images to 43.7% for Full HD images. These findings suggest that optimizing MTTBD can significantly reduce downtime and improve availability, highlighting the critical role of effective energy management in maintaining high image quality captured by the drone.

Table 5. Comparison between MTTBD vs. Downtime and Availability

MTTBD (hours)	Downtime (hours)	Availability (%)
0.40	3979.38	38.31
0.45	4226.77	41.13
0.50	4449.82	43.70

Figure 5 illustrates the availability results obtained for the system, considering various numbers of spare batteries. In addition, this Figure also shows the availability assuming three different video resolutions (Full HD, 2K, and 4K). The number of batteries ranges from 1 to 10, representing the available spare batteries in the system.

It is evident that once the number of batteries reaches six, availability levels across all three resolutions begin to converge. This indicates that beyond a certain threshold, adding more batteries yields diminishing returns in terms of improved availability. For instance, while the increase in availability from five to six batteries is significant, subsequent increases from six to ten batteries provide only marginal benefits. This convergence suggests that after reaching a critical level of redundancy, the system attains a stability point where high availability is maintained, regardless of the image resolution used.

The differences in availability percentages between resolutions are more pronounced when fewer batteries are available. With only one or two batteries, Full HD resolution achieves significantly higher availability than 2K and 4K resolutions, indicating that higher resolutions require more power, thereby impacting system availability. As the number of batteries increases to three or four, availability for 2K and 4K resolutions improves, suggesting enhanced system robustness with added redundancy. However, a noticeable performance gap remains until the system reaches six batteries, beyond which availability stabilizes across all resolutions.

This suggests that while adding spare batteries improves availability, the rate of improvement depends on the initial battery count and image resolution. The convergence of availability in six batteries highlights the importance of adequate redundancy in system design, particularly for high-demand applications where maintaining high availability is crucial.

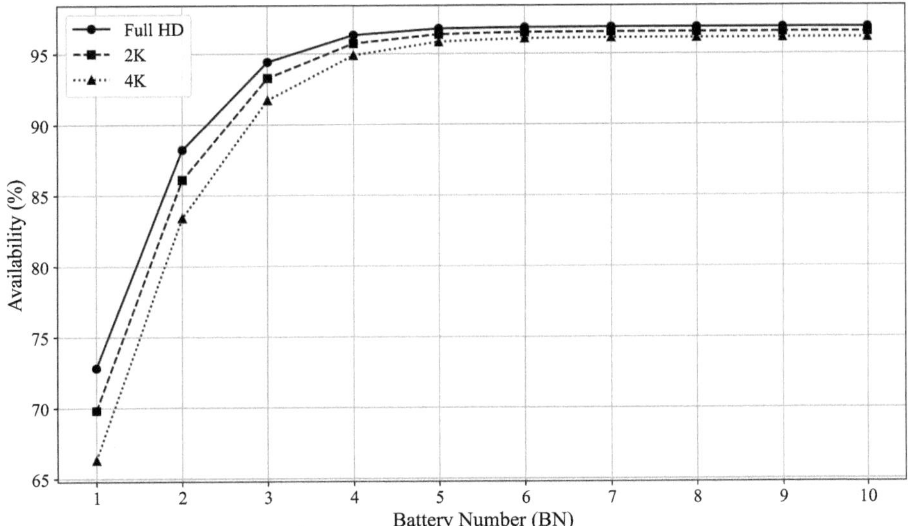

Fig. 5. Availability (%) and discharge time vs. number of spare batteries.

6.3   Case Study III

Unlike the previous study, the primary objective here is to analyze the impact of spare drones on system availability. To this end, one drone is kept active without any spare batteries but is considered redundant. Additionally, an alternative scenario is explored where a spare drone is maintained, and the number of spare batteries ranges up to ten units.

Table 6 presents the availability results comparing two configurations: (i) spare batteries and a spare drone are included, and (ii) only spare batteries are considered. Both configurations were evaluated across Full HD, 2K, and 4K video resolutions.

As expected, availability increases with the number of batteries in both setups since more batteries provide greater capacity and better performance. The percentage difference in availability between the two setups is small but consistent, indicating that adding a spare drone positively impacts.

Assuming Full HD resolution, the availability difference ranges from 0.01% to 0.04%, with the spare batteries and one spare drone strategy showing slightly

Table 6. Comparison of performance according to the number of batteries

Batteries	Spare Bat. and One Spare Drone			Only Spare Battery		
	Full HD	2K	4K	Full HD	2K	4K
1	72.83%	69.83%	66.32%	72.82%	69.82%	66.31%
2	88.24%	86.12%	83.43%	88.21%	86.09%	83.41%
3	94.45%	93.31%	91.75%	94.41%	93.28%	91.72%
4	96.34%	95.75%	94.92%	96.31%	95.72%	94.89%
5	96.80%	96.40%	95.87%	96.76%	96.36%	95.83%
6	96.88%	96.54%	96.10%	96.85%	96.50%	96.06%
7	96.90%	96.56%	96.14%	96.86%	96.53%	96.11%
8	96.90%	96.57%	96.15%	96.86%	96.53%	96.12%
9	96.90%	96.57%	96.15%	96.86%	96.53%	96.12%
10	96.90%	96.57%	96.15%	96.86%	96.53%	96.12%

better performance. For example, with one battery, the difference is 0.01% (72.83% vs. 72.82%), and with two batteries, it is 0.03% (88.24% vs. 88.21%). This trend continues across other configurations, confirming that the spare drone strategy offers a slight availability increase.

In 2K resolution, the differences are similar, varying from 0.01% to 0.03% in favor of the spare drone strategy, such as a 0.04% difference with five batteries (96.40% vs. 96.36%). In 4K resolution, differences are more evident in some setups, but generally remain around 0.01% to 0.03%.

The strategy of using spare batteries and an additional spare drone is important because it consistently boosts availability across all resolutions. This is especially vital in real-time applications, where even a small improvement can make a big difference. Moreover, having a spare drone provides security and flexibility, ensuring that operations can continue smoothly in case of a drone malfunction. The slight increase in availability with a spare drone can also justify the additional expense, particularly in scenarios where video quality and reliability are essential.

7   Limitations

This study provides valuable insights into the relationship between battery redundancy and the availability of drone systems across various video resolutions. However, the proposed model has some limitations. First, it does not account for communication failures, which can affect system availability in real-world drone operations. Additionally, the mission planning logic was simplified, excluding aspects such as route optimization, task prioritization, and environmental constraints. Despite these simplifications, the model remains an effective tool for system designers, especially in relation to the study's primary objective:

understanding how image resolution impacts drone autonomy and, consequently, overall system availability.

Another limitation of the study is the simplified treatment of battery degradation. We did not consider factors such as temperature variations, battery aging, or the number of charge-discharge cycles. Furthermore, the model assumes a static scenario in which the drone is launched and kept in a fixed position. This approach excludes flight path dynamics and does not reflect the energy consumption patterns of long-range missions. These abstractions were intentionally made to isolate and emphasize the main research goal, which is to quantify the effects of image resolution on energy consumption and evaluate its impact on drone availability. While the model abstracts several real-world complexities, it effectively highlights the trade-offs between video quality and mission endurance in drone-based systems.

8   Conclusions

This paper examines the relationship between spare batteries and drone system availability across Full HD, 2K, and 4K resolutions. The primary contribution of this study lies in quantifying the improvement in availability achieved by battery redundancy and in analyzing the trade-offs with image resolution. The results not only reveal a positive correlation between the number of batteries and availability but also highlight the diminishing returns beyond certain redundancy thresholds, underscoring the importance of balancing redundancy and resolution in system design. These findings highlight the necessity of incorporating battery redundancy into system design, particularly for high-resolution applications, and suggest several avenues for future research. However, the proposed model has certain limitations that warrant consideration. Firstly, the potential for communication failures was not considered. Additionally, the mission planning logic was abstracted. The simplified approach to battery degradation is another limitation, as it does not account for variables such as temperature and degradation. These limitations suggest opportunities for future work, including the incorporation of more realistic mission profiles, detailed battery behavior, and communication reliability into the model.

References

1. Marsan, M. A., et al.: Generalized stochastic petri nets revisited: Random switches and priorities. In: PNPM'87, pp. 44–53. IEEE Computer Society Press (1987)
2. Marsan, M. A., et al.: Modelling with generalized stochastic petri nets (1995)
3. Aposporis, P.: Object detection methods for improving UAV autonomy and remote sensing applications. In: 2020 IEEE/ACM International Conference on Advances in Social Networks Analysis and Mining (ASONAM), pp. 845–853. IEEE (2020)
4. Borges, I., Andrade, E., Silva, F.A., Callou, G.: Availability evaluation of a video surveillance system with distributed storage. Clust. Comput. **28**(4), 273 (2025)

5. Borges, I., Callou, G., Silva, F.A.: Performance evaluation and energy consumption of a video surveillance system with distributed storage. In: 2023 18th Iberian Conference on Information Systems and Technologies (CISTI), pp. 1–6. IEEE (2023)

6. Brito, C., et al.: Offloading data through unmanned aerial vehicles: a dependability evaluation. Electronics **10**(16), 1916 (2021)

7. Fedorova, A., Beliautsou, V., Zimmermann, A.: Colored petri net modelling and evaluation of drone inspection methods for distribution networks. Sensors **22**(9), 3418 (2022)

8. Hildmann, H., Kovacs, E.: Using unmanned aerial vehicles (UAVS) as mobile sensing platforms (MSPS) for disaster response, civil security and public safety. Drones **3**(3), 59 (2019)

9. Jain, R.: The art of computer systems performance analysis. john wiley & sons (1990)

10. Lavenberg, S.: Computer performance modeling handbook. Elsevier (1983)

11. Li, Y., et al.: Energy efficient strategy for uninterrupted mission execution via automatic drone replacement. In: 2020 IEEE International Systems Conference (SysCon), pp. 1–7. IEEE (2020)

12. Lins, L., Nascimento, E., Dantas, J., Araujo, J., Maciel, P.: Stochastic petri nets for drone surveillance: modeling availability and reliability. In: Proceedings of the 13th Latin-American Symposium on Dependable and Secure Computing, pp. 65–74 (2024)

13. Maciel, P.R.M.: Performance, reliability, and availability evaluation of computational systems, Volume 2: reliability, availability modeling, measuring, and data analysis. Chapman and Hall/CRC (2023). https://doi.org/10.1201/9781003306030

14. Muppala, J., Ciardo, G., Trivedi, K.S.: Stochastic reward nets for reliability prediction. Commun. Reliab. Maintainability Serv. **1**(2), 9–20 (1994)

15. Pereira, P., et al.: Availability model for edge-fog-cloud continuum: an evaluation of an end-to-end infrastructure of intelligent traffic management service. J. Supercomputing, 1–28 (2022)

16. Sabino, A., et al.: Forest fire monitoring system supported by unmanned aerial vehicles and edge computing: a performance evaluation using petri nets. Clust. Comput. **27**(7), 9735–9755 (2024)

17. Silva, B., et al.: Mercury: an integrated environment for performance and dependability evaluation of general systems. In: Proceedings of industrial track at 45th dependable systems and networks conference, DSN, pp. 1–4 (2015)

18. Symons, F.J.W.: Modelling and analysis of communication protocols using numerical petri nets. (1989)

19. Trivedi, K.S.: Probability & statistics with reliability, queuing and computer Science applications. PHI Learning Pvt, Limited (2011)

20. Zimmermann, A., Freiheit, J., German, R., Hommel, G.: Petri Net Modelling and Performability Evaluation with TimeNET 3.0. In: Haverkort, B.R., Bohnenkamp, H.C., Smith, C.U. (eds.) TOOLS 2000. LNCS, vol. 1786, pp. 188–202. Springer, Heidelberg (2000). https://doi.org/10.1007/3-540-46429-8_14

Quantitative Availability Analysis of Fog-Edge Monitoring Architectures in Bus Rapid Transit Station

Raquel F. Trajano[1]([✉]), Carlos Melo[2], and Jamilson Ramalho[1]

[1] Universidade Federal de Pernambuco, Recife, Pernambuco, Brazil
`{rft,jrd}@cin.ufpe.br`
[2] Universidade de Pernambuco, Garanhuns, Pernambuco, Brazil

Abstract. Improving the quality and reliability of public transportation services is a key requirement for addressing mobility challenges in large urban centers. Bus Rapid Transit (BRT) systems play a significant role in achieving this goal. However, their effectiveness relies on the combination of several elements, among them the monitoring of stations, which is essential for managing passenger flow and ensuring safety. Evaluating the availability of such monitoring systems at scale across an entire corridor with multiple station types is a complex challenge, as individual station analyses fail to capture the systemic risks associated with the network's topology. To address this issue, this paper proposes a hierarchical approach for modeling and evaluating the availability of monitoring systems in BRT corridors. The proposed solution employs a Fog-Edge architecture, where Fog units are placed at critical integration stations that act as hubs connecting different transit lines, and Edge units are deployed at regular stations. Availability analysis is conducted through Reliability Block Diagrams (RBDs) to represent the corridor topology and incorporate different operational requirements, such as defining the minimum number of stations that must be active for the corridor to be considered functional. We apply the proposed models to the East/West Corridor in the city of Recife, Brazil, as a set of case studies. Results show that even under a permissive operational scenario, where only the integration stations are required to function, the corridor's availability is limited to a ceiling of 91.3%. This value translates to more than 30 days of expected annual downtime, indicating that to enhance corridor resilience, investments should focus on improving the individual availability of integration stations. The series' dependency on these nodes is the dominant factor governing the reliability of the entire monitoring system. The proposed models serve as a quantitative decision-support tool for planners and stakeholders in the design and development of more reliable public transportation systems.

Keywords: System Availability · BRT Corridor · Fog-Edge Architecture · Hierarchical Modeling · Reliability Block Diagram

1   Introduction

The rapid expansion of urban centers places increasing pressure on existing infrastructure, resulting in chronic traffic congestion, deteriorating air quality, and a growing demand for more efficient and sustainable transportation solutions. High-capacity public transportation systems, such as Bus Rapid Transit (BRT), have been adopted to address these challenges. However, their effectiveness depends not only on physical infrastructure but also on the continuous operation of the systems that support them, such as monitoring systems, which help to ensure service safety and operational management [1,8,16,28].

The monitoring infrastructure in BRT corridors operates as a distributed system comprising Internet of Things (IoT) devices installed at various types of stations, each with distinct levels of criticality. Common stations are contrasted with integration stations, which act as hubs for connecting multiple transit lines or modes of transportation. Failures at critical nodes in this network can compromise the overall system operation, affecting both safety and service continuity [19,29,31].

To manage this complexity, hierarchical architectures combining Edge and Fog Computing offer promising technological solutions. In this approach, data processing occurs as close as possible to the source: Edge Computing is deployed at common stations for fast, local responses, while Fog Computing nodes positioned at integration stations aggregate and process larger segments of corridor data, acting as intermediaries between the edge and potential cloud services [27].

In this paper, we develop and evaluate a hierarchical availability model for monitoring systems in BRT corridors, based on Reliability Block Diagrams (RBD). Specifically, this work seeks to answer the following research questions:

- **RQ1:** What is the steady-state availability of a monitoring service deployed in a BRT station, considering failure and repair requirements of its hardware and communication components?
- **RQ2:** How does the corridor topology impacts the end-to-end availability under different scenarios?

Therefore, the main contributions of this paper are: (i) a hierarchical model for availability evaluation of BRT corridors, considering Fog-Edge architectures; (ii) availability evaluation for different station types and for the entire corridor, revealing bottlenecks; and (iii) a scenario-based evaluation that provides a quantitative analysis for decision-making in public transportation infrastructures.

This paper is organized as follows: Sect. 2 presents the related works. Section 3 provides the background, contextualizing the key concepts required to understand this paper. Section 4 details the evaluated environment and proposed models. Section 5 presents the case studies that demonstrate the feasibility of the proposed models. Finally, Sect. 6 presents final remarks, limitations, and future research directions.

2   Related Works

This section positions this paper's contributions by analyzing the dependability literature, with emphasis on system architectures and availability modeling methodologies within the context of transportation systems and smart city infrastructures.

In the BRT domain, Mohamed et al. [20] use traffic microsimulation to evaluate the impact of resolving physical conflicts on travel time in an overcrowded corridor. While essential for infrastructure planning, this line of research assumes fully functional technological systems, which is unrealistic in practical deployments.

Concerning technological architectures, Zakutynskyi and Rabodzei [30] propose cloud-based IoT platforms for data collection and analysis in public transportation systems. However, such centralized architectures struggle with latency and congestion in large-scale IoT deployments. Das et al. [9] highlight these limitations and advocate for decentralized approaches, such as the Fog-Edge architecture adopted by this paper, as a resilient alternative by enabling data processing closer to the source.

A complementary line of research focuses on quantitative availability evaluation through formal modeling. Araújo et al. [2] and Oliveira et al. [21] apply hierarchical models to assess the dependability of complex IoT environments. Borges et al. [4] reinforce this methodological approach by using RBD-based hierarchical modeling to evaluate the availability of distributed video surveillance systems. Although methodologically aligned with our work, these studies target different domains and topologies.

Specifically within BRT systems, availability modeling is often limited to transport service availability. Dantas et al. [7,8], for example, assess the impact of vehicle flow and passenger waiting times but do not address the availability of the underlying monitoring and control infrastructure.

In summary, the literature provides insights into BRT operational performance, IoT-based system architectures, and availability modeling in other domains. A clear gap persists at the intersection of these areas. This work addresses that gap by proposing a hierarchical availability model based on Reliability Block Diagrams (RBDs) that quantifies the end-to-end availability of the monitoring infrastructure in a BRT corridor, thereby complementing traditional performance analyses. Table 1 resumes the main differences between this paper and the current state of the art on smart cities and transportation systems, **Av. Eva.** stands for Availability Evaluation and **Corr.** for Corridor Topology.

3   Background

This section presents the fundamental concepts required to understand this paper. It explains the structure of the Bus Rapid Transit (BRT) system, the technologies used in the station monitoring infrastructure, and an overview of availability modeling and evaluation.

Table 1. Comparative analysis of related works

Work	Technique	Domain	Av. Eva.	Corr.
This Paper	RBD	Monitoring BRT Infrastructure	✓	✓
Araújo et al. (2019) [2]	CTMC	Dependability of Smart Systems	✓	✗
Oliveira et al. (2023) [21]	RBD + CTMC	Smart Farming Environments	✓	✗
Borges et al. (2025) [4]	RBD	Distributed Video Surveillance	✓	✗
Dantas et al. (2019) [8]	SPN	BRT Flow and Waiting Time	✗	✗
Dantas et al. (2021) [7]	SPN	BRT Operational Performance	✗	✗
Zakutynskyi (2023) [30]	Empirical	Public Transport Monitoring	✗	✗
Das et al. (2023) [9]	Review	Fog and Edge for IoT	✗	✗
Mohamed et al. (2022) [20]	Microsimulation	Performance of BRT Corridors	✗	✗

3.1 Bus Rapid Transit (BRT)

Bus Rapid Transit (BRT) is a high-capacity public transportation system based on bus operations. It is designed to improve mobility in large urban centers by providing a fast, comfortable, and cost-effective service. BRT systems can achieve passenger throughput similar to that of metro or Light Rail Transit (LRT) systems but offer significant advantages in terms of lower investment requirements and greater operational flexibility, as their implementation costs are considerably lower than those of rail-based alternatives [14]. According to international BRT standards, the system is defined by five essential elements:

1. **Dedicated Lanes:** Exclusive lanes physically separated from mixed traffic, allowing buses to operate without interference from congestion.
2. **Center-Aligned Stations with Off-Board Fare Collection:** Stations located in the center of the roadway, with fare collection systems that operate before boarding.
3. **Level Boarding:** Station platforms aligned with the floor height of the buses, enabling fast, accessible boarding and alighting.
4. **Intersection Priority:** Signal systems that give priority to buses at intersections, reducing stops and optimizing travel time.
5. **Advanced Operational Management:** Use of technologies for real-time fleet control and monitoring.

BRT systems have global relevance, operating in hundreds of cities and transporting millions of passengers daily. Latin America has the highest adoption rates, with Brazil standing out as the country with the largest deployment and usage of BRT systems [12]. In this work, we use the East/West Corridor of the Via Livre system in Recife, Brazil, as our case study, as it represents a critical mobility axis in the region [26].

3.2 IoT, Edge, and Fog Computing in Urban Environments

The Internet of Things (IoT) refers to a global network of interconnected objects and devices that can uniquely identify themselves and communicate through standardized protocols [13]. In urban environments, a wide range of IoT sensors is employed for real-time data collection, supporting applications in mobility, safety (e.g., presence and smoke detection), and environmental comfort (e.g., temperature, humidity, and lighting) [22].

A typical IoT architecture is organized into layers. The perception layer comprises the physical sensors and devices responsible for data collection. In contrast, the network layer handles the transmission of this information to platforms that process and analyze it [31]. The data generated by these sensors are stored in databases and used to support intelligent decision-making systems, particularly in domains such as smart cities, public health, safety, and sustainability.

Edge computing complements the IoT ecosystem by enabling data processing closer to the source through edge servers and smart devices. This approach reduces latency, supports real-time responsiveness, and increases local autonomy. Implementation strategies, such as cloudlets and fog computing, are commonly adopted to meet the performance and resilience demands of distributed systems in intelligent urban infrastructure [15,27].

Fog computing, in particular, introduces an intermediate processing layer between the edge and the cloud. Composed of fog nodes with enhanced computational capabilities, this layer aggregates data from multiple devices, performs local analysis, and forwards only relevant information to the cloud as needed [9]. This architecture enhances both system resilience and privacy, making it a strategic choice for innovative urban applications [5,11].

In the context of Bus Rapid Transit (BRT) stations, the integration of IoT, edge, and fog computing solutions plays a key role in planning and efficient facility management. These technologies support decentralized monitoring, enable faster responses (e.g., triggering safety alerts), and contribute to user comfort, well-being, and safety.

3.3   Availability Modeling

Stationary Availability is defined as the probability that a system is operational at a given point in time and is classically expressed as a function of the Mean Time To Failure (MTTF) and the Mean Time To Repair (MTTR): $\frac{MTTF}{MTTF+MTTR}$ [3].

To calculate the availability of a complete system, it is necessary to model the interrelationships between its components. The Reliability Block Diagram (RBD) is a widely used tool for this purpose, providing a visual representation of the system's success or failure logic. The structure of an RBD can include `series` configurations (indicating that all components must be functional), `parallel` configurations (where only one component needs to be operational), or more complex combinations [18] and `K-out-of-N` (KooN) configurations, which is a modeling approach in RBD that applies to redundant systems, in which the operation is ensured if at least K out of N components are active. The availability of a `K-out-of-N` system can be computed using the binomial distribution and is commonly employed to analyze the resilience of critical infrastructures [17].

$$A = \sum_{i=k}^{N} \binom{N}{i} A_c^i \times (1 - A_c)^{N-i} \tag{1}$$

$$A = \sum_{i=k}^{N} \binom{N}{i} A_c(t)^i \times (1 - A_c(t))^{N-i} \tag{2}$$

4 Proposed Architecture and Methodology

This section describes the system architecture and the approach for sizing and availability evaluation of a distributed monitoring intelligent system designed to operate at stations along a BRT public transportation corridor. The methodology is structured in two main stages: (i) system architecture specification (SAS) and (ii) hierarchical availability modeling.

4.1 System Architecture Specification (SAS)

The proposed architecture is a distributed and hierarchical system composed of two layers; the first layer has different types of computational nodes (Edge or Fog), while the second layer is composed mainly of field devices (sensors and cameras). The system is designed based on two station models that serve as building blocks for the corridor analysis: the Common Station and the Integration Station. Figure 1 presents a high-level view of a Common Station. The main difference between a Common Station and an Integration Station, aside from their size, lies in the application stack that represents the Edge or Fog unit, as shown at the bottom right and top middle of the figure, which is described as follows.

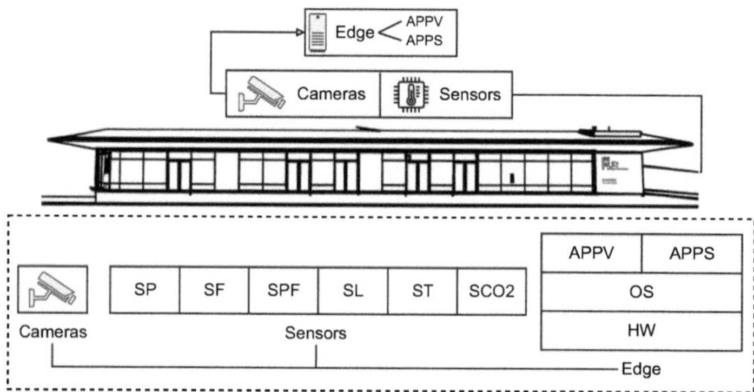

Fig. 1. High Level View of a Common Station.

- **Edge Layer (at Common Stations):** Common stations are equipped with Edge Computing units. These units serve as the local operational core, featuring storage capacity and the ability to perform inference on data collected from sensors and cameras.
- **Fog Layer (at Integration Stations):** Integration stations, such as the Caxangá Integrated Terminal, are more complex environments with upper floors and semi-open physical spaces. In these stations, the infrastructure is centralized in a Fog Computing unit. The Fog node has expanded responsibilities: In addition to processing information from its station, it is responsible for storing data (Storage) for the Edge units from neighboring common stations.
- **Sensoring and Surveillance Layer:** The sensing layer includes a heterogeneous set of sensors responsible for monitoring critical variables, including presence sensors, fine particulate matter sensors, light sensors, smoke detectors, temperature/pressure/humidity sensors, and carbon dioxide sensors. The surveillance subsystem is composed of video cameras with different focal lengths, capable of performing high-level tasks such as flow analysis and object detection [10].

Table 2 presents the sensors used by the proposed architecture and specifies their role for the evaluated environments.

Table 2. Sensor types and monitored variables.

ID	Sensor	Monitored Variable / Purpose
SP	SE-10 PIR	Detects human presence in restricted areas or crowds; supports passenger counting.
SPf	PMS5003	Measures fine particulate matter (PM 2.5).
SL	OPT3001	Measures visible light intensity; supports environmental control and passenger comfort.
SF	Smoke Detector	Detects smoke; supports fire safety.
ST	BME280	Measures temperature, pressure, and humidity.
SCO2	MG811	Detects carbon dioxide (CO_2) concentration.

4.2 Sizing and Availability Approach

The approach to analyzing the proposed architecture combines the station's physical size while hierarchically modeling its availability.

Sizing and Optimization Due to the complexity of the stations, especially the integration ones, the sizing strategy is multifaceted and based on functional zones.

1. **Zonal Planning:** The station is divided into zones (platforms, access areas, lobby, etc.). Sensor allocation is customized to meet the specific needs of each zone. For example, in the boarding zone, where buses remain stationary with their engines running, a set of air quality sensors is placed to capture data more accurately in that specific environment [24].

2. **Camera Optimization**: Within the zones, surveillance coverage is optimized using the approach proposed by Erdem and Sclaroff [10]. This model employs a formulation based on the Set Cover Problem (SCP), solved through Integer Linear Programming (ILP), to calculate the minimum number and optimal placement of cameras.

3. **Sensor Quantification**: Once the zones and technical requirements are defined, the number of sensors for each zone is determined using a computational heuristic developed for this purpose. The algorithm takes as input the properties of each zone (area, layout, and function) and, based on predefined rules (coverage area for presence sensors, density per square meter for environmental sensors, and technical standards for smoke detectors), automates the sizing process.

Hierarchical Availability Modeling (RBD). For this analysis, the proposed architecture availability is modeled using Reliability Block Diagrams (RBDs), following a hierarchical modeling approach.

1. **Availability of an Individual Component**: Each device (a sensor, camera, Edge, or Fog unit) is modeled as a series system. The failure of any component results in the system's failure. The availability of an Edge unit (A_{Edge}) is the product of the availabilities of its components:

$$A_{\text{Edge}} = A_{\text{HW}} \times A_{\text{OS}} \times A_{\text{APPV}} \times A_{\text{APPS}} \tag{3}$$

the availability of a Fog unit (A_{Fog}) is modeled in the same way:

$$A_{\text{Fog}} = A_{\text{HW}} \times A_{\text{OS}} \times A_{\text{Storage}} \times A_{\text{Database}} \times A_{\text{APPV}} \times A_{\text{APPS}} \tag{4}$$

2. **Availability of a Monitoring Zone**: For the baseline analysis, the availability of a zone is modeled as a series system of all individual devices allocated to it. In this configuration, the failure of any single sensor or camera in the zone leads to the failure of the monitoring function for that zone. The availability of the zone (A_{Zone}) is the product of all M devices that compose it:

$$A_{\text{Zone}} = \prod_{j=1}^{M} A_{\text{Device}_j} \tag{5}$$

5 Case Studies

This section presents a multi-level availability assessment for a distributed monitoring system in a Bus Rapid Transit (BRT) public transportation corridor, considering a hierarchical Fog-Edge modeling approach. Environments of this nature require high continuity of monitoring services to ensure user safety, comfort, and well-being—factors that increase trust in the service and support operational decision-making.

To apply and assess the feasibility of the proposed approach, this paper utilizes the East-West Corridor of the BRT Via Livre system, situated in the Metropolitan Region of Recife. The 12.5 km East-West corridor connects Camaragibe city to downtown Recife city, crossing major avenues such as Avenida Caxangá, and includes five integration stations and eleven common stations [26]. Designed to serve 140,000 passengers per day, this corridor plays a vital role in urban mobility for the residents of the Metropolitan Region of Recife, a city known for having one of the most congested traffic systems in Brazil—second only to São Paulo [25]. We propose three case studies organized as follows:

1. Availability Assessment of a Common Station: a baseline scenario with the minimum requirements (1 component of each) to determine the modeling approach viability.
2. Availability Assessment an Integration Station: a more complex environment requiring zonal modeling and a Fog-based infrastructure that requires a set of each kind of sensor and cameras for each zone.
3. Generalization of the model to the BRT corridor: using the previous case studies' results to analyze large-scale system availability.

In order to evaluate the proposed models, it is required to feed our models; the values to perform this task are presented in Table 3 that shows the reference MTTF and MTTR values used and extracted from literature review: [2, 4, 6, 21].

Table 3. Input Parameters

Component	MTTF (h)	MTTR (h)
Presence Sensor	300,000	1.0
Smoke Sensor	300,000	1.0
Fine Particles Sensor	13,140	2.0
Light Sensor	13,140	2.0
Temperature Sensor	13,140	2.0
CO2 Sensor	13,140	2.0
Cameras	8,760	1.67
Operating System	2,880	1.0
Hardware	8,760	1.67
Storage	43,800	24
Database	1,440	0.33
Video Application	217.8	0.46
Sensor Application	8,000	0.1

5.1   Case Study I: Availability Assessment of a Common Station

In this first case study, the availability of a common station was evaluated. The baseline architecture considered is intentionally simplified to represent a minimal functional scenario consisting of one of each sensor type, one surveillance camera, and one Edge unit (See Eq. 3). The analysis was conducted using the Mercury tool [23], which enables the modeling and evaluation of availability. Table 4 presents the results obtained for this configuration.

Table 4. Availability Values for a Common Station

Parameter	Value
MTTF (h)	178.47
MTTR (h)	0.61
Availability (%)	99.65
Annual Uptime (h)	8735.48
Annual Downtime (h)	30.33

The availability found for our common station was 99.65%, which translates into approximately 30.33 h of annual downtime. To contextualize the operational impact, this value is equivalent to an average of 35 min per week of system unavailability. As the primary purpose of this system is to ensure passenger safety, where continuity is essential, we may lack some critical information and events during unavailability periods, such as fire detection, monitoring, recording malicious actions, or managing dangerous overcrowding.

Therefore, while the availability of 99.65% represents a functional starting point, the associated downtime highlights the need to explore and invest in redundancy and resilience mechanisms to raise the availability to levels more suitable for the system's intended safety-critical applications. However, it is important to note that this is only a single common station; what about Integration Stations, which are dozens of times larger than common stations? What about the entire corridor, which is composed of a set of common and integration stations? How do we ensure passenger safety across such a wide environmental range and achieve acceptable availability values for a critical system?

5.2   Case Study II: Availability Assessment of an Integration Station

For the second case study, the availability of an Integration Station is evaluated. Using the Caxangá Integrated Terminal as a reference, this scenario introduces increased complexity due to its large area and semi-open physical environment. The objective is to quantify the impact of this scale, along with the associated Fog architecture, on system availability in an initial configuration. For this analysis, we applied the zonal dimensioning approach described in Sect. 4. Table 5 presents the results of the dimensioning process.

Table 5. Number of Sensors per Zone Generated by the Sizing Algorithm

Zone	SCO2	SF	SL	SPF	SP	ST
Boarding/Alighting Platform	2	5	4	2	18	2
Access Area and Turnstiles	1	3	3	-	8	1
Main Circulation Hall	6	19	12	-	54	5
Queue Formation Area	1	1	1	-	4	1
Administrative/Technical Area	-	1	2	-	2	1
Ticket Office Area	-	2	2	-	6	1
Restrooms	-	1	3	-	4	-

The availability of each zone was modeled as a series system composed of all sensors and cameras allocated to that zone (See Eq. 5). In this initial configuration, the failure of any individual component leads to the failure of that monitoring function within the zone. Then, the total availability of the station is computed as the product of the availability of all its zones and the availability of the Fog unit. The availability of the Fog unit was calculated similarly to that of the Edge unit, with the addition of storage and database components arranged in series (See Eq. 4). Table 6 presents the obtained results for the Integration Station.

Table 6. Availability Values for an Integration Station

Parameter	Value
Availability (%)	98.18
Annual Uptime (h)	8606.84
Annual Downtime (h)	158.96

The availability obtained was 98.18%. This value corresponds to an annual downtime of approximately 159 h, or nearly seven days. The lower availability compared to the common station (99.65%) is due to the fact that the integration station system is significantly larger, containing a much greater number of components. In the series model adopted for this analysis, the failure of any single component leads to the failure of a monitoring or surveillance service operation, thereby increasing the overall probability of system failure.

This result reveals a critical vulnerability: the mere addition of components to cover a larger area leads to an even bigger annual downtime. This result highlights the need to investigate the impact of redundancy strategies on the provided services by public administrators. Adding a surveillance and monitoring system to public transportation stations is a huge step, but not providing these systems with the means to be available nearly 100% of the time may lead to a waste of time and financial resources.

5.3 Case Study III: From East to West

The previous case studies focused on evaluating the availability of individual stations. However, a transportation system such as BRT does not operate as a set of isolated islands; it functions as an integrated network where the value for the passenger lies in the ability to travel safely, efficiently, and predictably from one end of the corridor to the other.

The failure of the monitoring system at a critical station, such as an integration station, can trigger a cascading impact throughout the entire line. Security management failures erode user confidence in the service as a whole. From a managerial perspective, monitoring system failures impairs decision-making capabilities, as an ineffective system overview prevents timely correction of operational issues.

Therefore, this case study evaluates the systemic availability of the complete BRT corridor. The goal is to understand how the individual availabilities of stations combine based on the corridor topology to determine the network's large-scale resilience and identify the key factors that govern its reliability.

East-West Corridor. To perform this analysis the corridor availability (A_{Corridor}) is modeled as a series system of its macro components: the integration stations (IS) and the segments (Seg) of common stations. The general equation used is:

$$A_{\text{Corridor}} = \left(A_{\text{Integration}}\right)^{N_{\text{IS}}} \times \prod_{j=1}^{N_{\text{Seg}}} A_{\text{CommonSeg}_j} \tag{6}$$

where the parameters $(N_{\text{IS}}, N_{\text{Seg}}, N_j)$ are defined by the topology of the East-West Corridor, and the functional requirement (K_j) is varied to create different operational scenarios.

Operational Scenarios. We evaluated three operational scenarios to understand the range of the corridor availability:

Scenario 1: Essential Operation (Only Critical Stations)

- **Scenario Definition:** This scenario aims to understand the corridor's availability when the requirement is that only the five integration stations must be operational. In this case, the monitoring system is considered operational as long as the components on these stations are functioning.
- **Model Implication:** Here, the segments of common stations have a functional requirement of K = 0 (none are mandatory). Therefore, the corridor availability is solely the product of the availabilities of the critical stations.
- **Availability Calculation:**

$$A_{\text{Corridor}} = (A_{\text{IS}})^5 \tag{7}$$

Table 7. Required stations (K) vs. total stations (N) per segment.

Segment	K (Required Stations)	N (Total Stations)
Segment$_1$	1	1
Segment$_2$	3	5
Segment$_3$	2	4
Segment$_4$	1	2

– **Scenario Definition:** This scenario represents a more realistic requirement. It demands that all five integration stations be operational, and that at least 50% of the common stations in each segment are also functional.
– **Model Implication:** The integration stations remain in series. The common station segments are modeled as K-out-of-N subsystems, where K = $\theta(0.5 *$ N), as we can see in Table 7.
– **Availability Calculation:**

$$A_{\text{Corridor}} = A_{\text{IS}}^5 \cdot A_{1\text{-of-}1}^{(\text{Seg}_1)} \cdot A_{3\text{-of-}5}^{(\text{Seg}_2)} \cdot A_{2\text{-of-}4}^{(\text{Seg}_3)} \cdot A_{1\text{-of-}2}^{(\text{Seg}_4)} \tag{8}$$

Scenario 3: Full Operational

– **Scenario Definition:** This is the most stringent and ideal scenario for any system, which defines corridor availability as the state in which all stations, without exception, are operational. This means that all stations must be functioning simultaneously.
– **Model Implication:** Here, we have a series RBD with sixteen components (5 integration stations + 11 common stations). The failure of any individual component leads to the failure of the entire corridor system. The availability is the product of the availability of all stations.
– **Availability Calculation:**

$$A_{\text{Corridor}} = (A_{\text{IS}})^5 \times (A_{\text{Common}})^{11} \tag{9}$$

Results Analysis. Figure 2a presents the availability results found for the three evaluated scenarios, while Fig. 2b presents the annual downtime in days at each evaluated scenario.

The analysis of the operational scenarios for the BRT corridor reveals that Scenario 1 (Essential Operation) defines the upper limit of availability inherent to the corridor's topology. When operating only with the critical stations, the resulting availability of 91.29% becomes the structural availability ceiling. This availability demonstrates that even if the common stations were perfect (100% available), the system as a whole would still fail for more than one month per year.

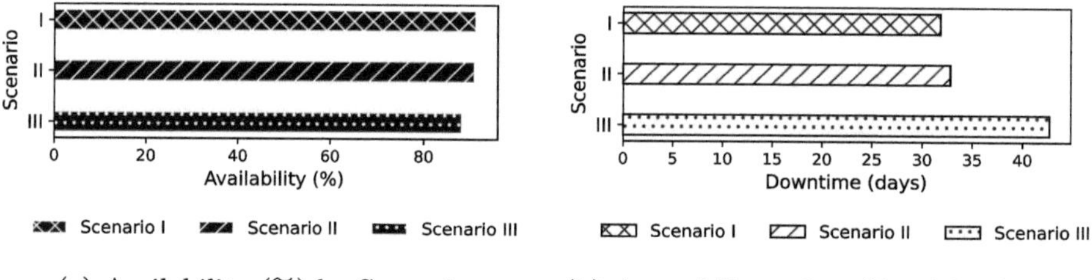

(a) Availability (%) by Scenario   (b) Annual Downtime (days) by Scenario

Fig. 2. Comparative availability and downtime analysis for evaluated scenarios.

For Scenario 2 (Resilient Operation), with the introduction of a functional requirement that 50% of the common stations in each segment be operational, availability decreases slightly to 91.02%. This result suggests that although strategies exist to make common stations more resilient, they are not the dominant factors in corridor availability.

The contrast is notable in Scenario 3 (Full Operation). By requiring all eleven common stations and all five integration stations to be operational, availability drops to 88.31%, increasing the system downtime by ten days, which is operationally unfeasible for any monitoring system.

Given the understanding of the evaluation of these scenarios, it is essential to contextualize them within the security threats inherent to major public transportation hubs, as reports and studies in the field of transport security identify stations and terminals as vulnerable points. Thus, prolonged periods of system downtime lead to severe losses in the capacity for prevention, detection, and response to incidents, increasing the risk of crimes against passengers and public property. Functional safety and immediate emergency response are also affected.

In other words, the availability figures are not merely numbers; they represent a systemic vulnerability that exposes passengers to risk. This confirms that the monitoring system is a mission-critical infrastructure, and the analysis shows that the corridor's serial topology is the main factor contributing to this high level of risk. Therefore, efforts to mitigate it should focus on strengthening the individual availability of each integration station.

6   Conclusion and Future Works

This paper presented and evaluated a hierarchical methodology to quantify the end-to-end availability of monitoring systems in BRT public transportation corridors. The main objective was to develop a generalizable model, based on a Fog-Edge architecture, capable of analyzing different operational scenarios and identifying the most effective strategies to enhance system resilience.

In response to the first research question (RQ1), which investigated the availability of monitoring services at the station level, the proposed hierarchical modeling approach demonstrated its effectiveness in quantifying the steady-state availability of both common and integration stations. While a minimum configuration for a common station achieved an availability of 99.65% (about 30 h of downtime per year), more complex integration stations showed reduced availability 98.18%, or almost 159 h of annual downtime. These results highlight how infrastructure complexity and the number of components directly impact the availability of monitoring systems in critical locations.

Regarding the second research question (RQ2), which examined the influence of corridor topology on overall system availability, the scenario-based analysis revealed that the serial interdependence of integration stations constitutes a structural bottleneck. Even in scenarios where only integration stations were required to operate, the maximum achievable corridor availability was limited to 91.29%. More stringent operating conditions, such as requiring full functionality of all common and integration stations, further reduced availability to 88.31%. These findings provide clear and quantitative answers to RQ2, confirming that improving systemic availability requires topology-based strategies rather than uniform redundancy.

Overall, the analysis confirms that improving the individual availability of integration stations is the most effective strategy for increasing corridor resilience. Redundancy efforts should be applied selectively where they provide the greatest marginal benefit rather than evenly distributed across all station types.

Thus, the results reinforce the importance of considering systemic interdependencies and operational heterogeneity when designing and evaluating monitoring architectures for public transport systems. The proposed model addresses a methodological gap in the literature and supports data-driven decision-making for the deployment of robust and efficient monitoring infrastructures, aligned with smart city principles. Ultimately, ensuring the high availability of such technological infrastructures is a critical requirement for improving the safety, reliability, and overall performance of public transportation systems. By reducing service interruptions and enhancing situational awareness, increased availability directly supports efforts to make urban mobility more efficient and resilient in the face of growing metropolitan challenges.

Based on the findings and limitations of the study, future research directions include incorporating cost-benefit analyses to estimate the return on investment in availability improvements, modeling correlated failures to assess the impact of common-cause events, and assessing security threats by simulating targeted attacks on Fog nodes and their effects on corridor-level availability.

References

1. Albertsen, N., Diken, B.: Mobility, justification, and the city. NA **14**(1) (2013)
2. Araujo, E., Dantas, J., Matos, R., Pereira, P., Maciel, P.: Dependability evaluation of an iot system: A hierarchical modelling approach. In: 2019 IEEE International Conference on Systems, Man and Cybernetics (SMC). pp. 2121–2126. IEEE (2019)
3. Avizienis, A., Laprie, J.C., Randell, B., Landwehr, C.: Basic concepts and taxonomy of dependable and secure computing. IEEE Trans. Depend. Secur. Comput. **1**(1), 11–33 (2004)

4. Borges, I., Andrade, E., Silva, F.A., Callou, G.: Availability evaluation of a video surveillance system with distributed storage. Clust. Comput. **28**(4), 273 (2025)

5. Bukhsh, M., Abdullah, S., Bajwa, I.S.: A decentralized edge computing latency-aware task management method with high availability for iot applications. IEEE Access **9**, 138994–139008 (2021)

6. Correia, L.F., Dantas, J.R., Silva, F.A.: Blockchain as a service environment: a dependability evaluation. J. Supercomput. **79**(16), 17919–17943 (2023)

7. Dantas, R., Dantas, J., Melo, C., Maciel, P.: Performance evaluation in brt systems: an analysis to predict the brt systems planning. Case Stud, Trans. Policy **9**(3), 1141–1150 (2021)

8. Dantas, R., Dantas, J., Melo, C., Oliveira, D., Maciel, P.: Sensitivity analysis in a brt system. In: 2019 IEEE International Systems Conference (SysCon). pp. 1–8. IEEE (2019)

9. Das, R., Inuwa, M.M.: A review on fog computing: Issues, characteristics, challenges, and potential applications. Telematics Inform. Rep. **10**, 100049 (2023)

10. Erdem, U.M., Sclaroff, S.: Automated camera layout to satisfy task-specific and floor plan-specific coverage requirements. Comput. Vis. Image Underst. **103**(3), 156–169 (2006)

11. Erregui, H., Aouaqi, A.E.: The Role of Internet of Things and Fog Computing in Smart Cities. Available at SSRN 5046206 (2024)

12. Global BRT Data: SOBRE O BRTDATA (2025). https://brtdata.org/, Último acesso em 23 de junho de 2025

13. Gubbi, J., Buyya, R., Marusic, S., Palaniswami, M.: Internet of things (iot): A vision, architectural elements, and future directions. Futur. Gener. Comput. Syst. **29**(7), 1645–1660 (2013)

14. ITDP: The online brt planning guide (s/d). https://brtguide.itdp.org/branch/master/guide/, acessado em 23 de junho de 2025

15. Khan, L.U., Yaqoob, I., Tran, N.H., Kazmi, S.A., Dang, T.N., Hong, C.S.: Edge-computing-enabled smart cities: a comprehensive survey. IEEE Internet Things J. **7**(10), 10200–10232 (2020)

16. Kondepudi, S., et al.: Smart sustainable cities analysis of definitions. The ITU-T Focus Group for Smart Sustainable Cities (2014)

17. Kuo, W., Zuo, M.J.: Optimal Reliability Modeling: Principles and Applications. John Wiley & Sons (2003)

18. Maciel, P.R.M.: Performance, reliability, and availability evaluation of computational systems, Volume 2: Reliability, availability modeling, measuring, and data analysis. Chapman and Hall/CRC (2023)

19. Maciel, P.R.M.: Performance, reliability, and availability evaluation of computational systems, volume I: performance and background. Chapman and Hall/CRC (2023)

20. Mohamed, M., Elmitiny, N., Talaat, H.: A simulation-based evaluation of brt systems in over-crowded travel corridors: a case study of cairo, egypt. J. Eng. Appl. Sci. **69**(1), 36 (2022)

21. Oliveira, F., Pereira, P., Dantas, J., Araujo, J., Maciel, P.: Dependability evaluation of a smart poultry house: Addressing availability issues through the edge, fog, and cloud computing. IEEE Trans. Industr. Inf. **20**(2), 1304–1312 (2023)

22. Perera, C., Zaslavsky, A., Christen, P., Georgakopoulos, D.: Context aware computing for the internet of things: a survey. IEEE Commun. Sur. tutorials **16**(1), 414–454 (2013)

23. Pinheiro, T., et al.: The mercury environment: a modeling tool for performance and dependability evaluation. In: Intelligent Environments 2021, pp. 16–25. IOS Press (2021)
24. Sharma, P.K., Mondal, T., Mondal, A., Ray, A., Mondal, S., Nandi, S., De, T., Saha, S.: Optimal placement strategy for indoor environment monitoring using portable cost-effective devices. J. Indian Chem. Soc. **97**(10b), 1861–1866 (2020)
25. TomTom: Tomtom traffic index – ranking 2024. https://www.tomtom.com/traffic-index/ranking/ (2025). acessado em 23 de junho de 2025
26. de Transporte, G.R.C.: Brt – via livre. https://www.granderecife.pe.gov.br/transporte/brt-via-livre/ (2025). acessado em 23 de junho de 2025
27. Trigka, M., Dritsas, E.: Edge and cloud computing in smart cities. Future Internet **17**(3), 118 (2025)
28. Trindade, E.P., Hinnig, M.P.F., da Costa, E.M., Marques, J.S., Bastos, R.C., Yigitcanlar, T.: Sustainable development of smart cities: a systematic review of the literature. J. Open Innovation: Tech. Mark. Complexity **3**(3), 1–14 (2017)
29. Valencia-Arias, A., Ramírez Dávila, J., Londoño-Celis, W., Palacios-Moya, L., Hernández, J.L., Agudelo-Ceballos, E., Uribe-Bedoya, H.: Research trends in the use of the internet of things in sustainability practices: A systematic review. Sustainability **16**(7), 2663 (2024)
30. Zakutynskyi, I., Rabodzei, I.: Iot system architecture for monitoring and analyzing public transport data. Multidisc. Sci. J. **5** (2023)
31. Zeng, F., Pang, C., Tang, H.: Sensors on internet of things systems for the sustainable development of smart cities: a systematic literature review. Sens. **24**(7), 2074 (2024)

Industry Track

Malware Detection in Windows Operating Systems Using AI and In-Memory Process Analysis

Jessica C. C. Patricio, Carlos H. Paiva, Renan L. Rodrigues$^{(\boxtimes)}$,
Vanessa C. Lima, and Rafael L. Gomes

Universidade Estadual do Ceará (UECE), Fortaleza, Ceará, Brazil
{jessica.cacau,henrique.paiva,renann.rodrigues,
vane.carvalho}@aluno.uece.br, rafa.lopes@uece.br

Abstract. Currently, there is a noticeable increase in concern regarding the cybersecurity of corporate and personal data due to the rise of malicious software (Malware). In this context, this work presents a solution for intelligent malware detection in Windows Operating Systems by applying Artificial Intelligence (AI) techniques to memory process data. The solution aims to detect malware with minimal impact on the user's device and network infrastructure, achieving scalability and appropriate response times through data compression and segmentation of functionalities by environment. The results demonstrate the feasibility of the solution, with the compression approach achieving approximately 60% reduction in data communication, while detection efficiency reaches around 99% within a few milliseconds.

Keywords: Malware · Artificial Intelligence · Windows · Cybersecurity

1 Introduction

Internet access has expanded in the last few years, where users and devices are connected all the time, but are susceptible to threats [7,8,11]. The occurrence of malware in Windows operating systems continues to be one of the main concerns for companies and institutions, as this system dominates corporate and domestic environments [10]. Malware (such as Spyware, Trojans, and Ransomware) responsible for attacks is frequently distributed online, targeting companies, influential figures, and government entities [4,6]. Thus, it becomes essential to develop and adopt security solutions focused on the Windows environment, making it an indispensable measure to reduce risks, mitigate the impacts of cyber incidents, and strengthen the resilience of organizations and users against the constant malvance of digital threats [9].

In this context, we propose a solution based on Artificial Intelligence and process analysis, which aims to detect malware through the inspection of the main

L. A. Rodrigues and R. Oliveira (Eds.): LADC 2025, CCIS 2697, pp. 311–319, 2026.
https://doi.org/10.1007/978-3-032-11539-3_18

memory content of devices with the Windows operating system. The solution architecture was designed to be portable, scalable, and have minimal impact on monitored devices.

The operation is based on the periodic execution of a script on the monitored device, responsible for extracting RAM memory dumps. The extracted content is compressed and sent to a remote analysis environment, where process characteristics are extracted. This data is then submitted to a previously trained AI model, capable of classifying the behaviour as legitimate or malicious. The detection model was trained with the MalMem dataset developed by [3], which contains 9,996 memory dump samples from Windows 10 systems.

To evaluate the solution in a realistic scenario, experiments were conducted considering factors such as extraction, compression, and analysis time in computational environments that follow the configurations of real clients (such as hardware configuration) of Centro de Pesquisa Desenvolvimento e Inovação (CPDI)[1]. The results demonstrate that it is possible to adopt this approach as a practical and effective alternative for malware detection in real environments.

Finally, regarding innovation concerning the state of the art, when considering recent works (such as [1,2,5,12,13], among others), it is observed that they aim to evaluate the efficiency and effectiveness in applying AI to malware detection databases. However, these publications do not focus on evaluating the possibility of using these databases in real, scalable solutions with reduced sample evaluation time, which is the focus of this work.

2   Proposed Solution

This work proposes a solution for malware detection in Windows systems, based on the combination of Artificial Intelligence techniques and process analysis through memory dump extraction, as illustrated in Fig. 1. For this purpose, the following requirements were defined:

- Use of Artificial Intelligence in the malware detection process
- Implementation of a portable service independent of proprietary solutions
- Exclusive adoption of open-source libraries
- Guarantee of compatibility with the Windows 10 operating system
- Minimal need for user intervention
- Execution time compatible with immediate corrective actions after detection

The architecture is composed of two main components: the device and the service. The device component is responsible for periodically extracting RAM memory dumps from the monitored Windows machine using open-source tools (such as WinPmem). These memory dumps are then compressed to reduce data volume and transmitted securely via HTTPS to a remote service component. The service component operates in a Dockerized environment with a Flask server and a PostgreSQL database. It decompresses and analyzes the received memory

---

[1] https://cpdi.com.br/.

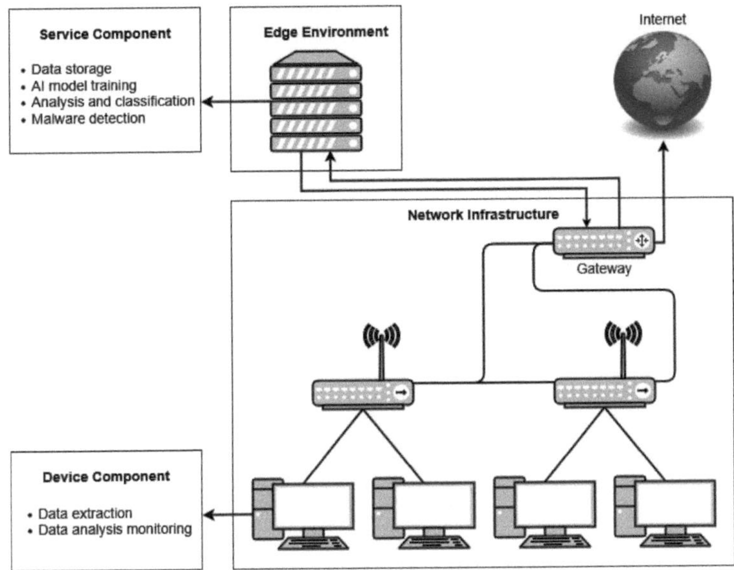

Fig. 1. Overview of the Solution.

dumps using VolMemLyzer and Volatility, extracting process features that are then classified by pre-trained AI models (CART, KNN, MLP, RF) to determine whether the behavior is benign or malicious.

Figure 2 presents the execution flow of the proposed solution, detailing the end-to-end process. It starts with the scheduled execution of a PowerShell script on the monitored Windows machine, which triggers the memory extraction using WinPmem. The generated RAW memory dump is compressed using the zip-file library and sent to the remote service with an associated unique identifier. Once received, the service decompresses the file, processes the memory data, and extracts behavioral features from the active processes. These features are passed to trained AI classifiers, which return a prediction (malicious or legitimate). The result is logged and can be retrieved by the device using the unique identifier. This workflow ensures automation, minimal user intervention, data confidentiality, and real-time malware detection.

2.1   Device Component

The device is implemented through PowerShell[2] and Python[3] scripts, requiring only the initial execution of a configuration script by the user, which automatically schedules periodic execution of the tool through Task Scheduler, in addition to ensuring that all prerequisites for execution are met. For proper application

---

[2] https://learn.microsoft.com/en-us/powershell/.
[3] https://docs.python.org/3.10/.

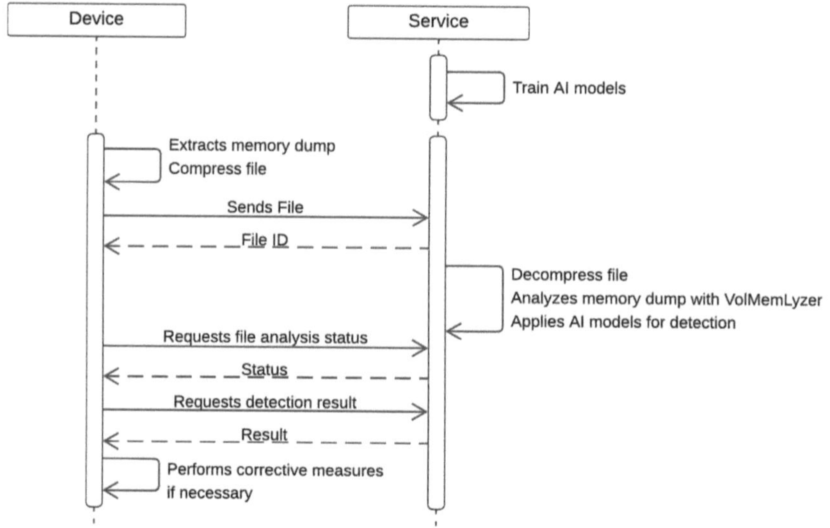

Fig. 2. Diagram of Execution Flow.

functioning, it needs to be executed with administrator privileges, Python 3 must be installed, and all necessary files and directories must exist. Processor architecture verification is also performed.

During operation, the device performs memory dump extraction with the memory acquisition tool WinPmem[4], generating a RAW file. This file is then compressed using the zipfile[5] library, aiming for sending efficiency, since the generated file can be very large and generate network overhead. After that, it is transmitted to the remote analysis service through an HTTPS connection with TLS encryption, ensuring data confidentiality and integrity during transmission, using data present in the INI format configuration file. Each file transmitted to the analysis service is associated with a unique identifier, which is returned to the monitored device in case of successful sending. This identifier allows tracking all processing stages, including execution status, time markers, and finally, the classification result, which informs the detection or non-detection of malware. This approach allows adopting corrective measures and auditing, if necessary.

2.2   Service Component

The service consists of Docker[6] containers with a Flask[7] server and a PostgreSQL[8] database. The function of this component is to train AI models for

---

[4] https://github.com/Velocidex/WinPmem/releases/tag/v4.0.rc1.
[5] https://docs.python.org/3.10/library/zipfile.html.
[6] https://docs.docker.com/.
[7] https://flask.palletsprojects.com/en/3.0.x/.
[8] https://www.postgresql.org/docs/17/index.html.

malware detection, process data received from the monitored device, store it in a structured way, analyse it, and classify it using previously trained models. When started, the service processes and adds data from the database developed by [3]. From this information, initial AI model training is performed, using CART (Classification and Regression Tree), KNN (K-Nearest Neighbors), MLP (Multi-Layer Perceptron), and RF (Random Forest) algorithms. Each generates a Pickle format file, and all are stored in the database.

The analysis flow begins with the decompression of the received file, followed by the analysis of the RAW content with VolMemLyzer[9], a volatile memory analysis tool, which, with the help of Volatility[10], extracts process characteristics from memory. These characteristics are processed by AI models previously trained with the scikit-learn[11] library, which perform behavior classification as malicious or not.

3 Industrial Implementation and Experiments

The experiments were conducted in partnership with CPDI, using a computational environment representative of configurations commonly employed by their clients. Virtual machines running the Windows 10 operating system with 2 GB, 4 GB, and 8 GB of RAM were created, simulating the computational environments of client devices.

3.1 Memory Extraction and Analysis Efficiency

This experiment aimed to evaluate the efficiency of different existing RAM memory dump extraction tools, such as DumpIt[12] and WinPmem[13], which are subsequently analysed by VolMemLyzer.

Table 1. Comparação entre ferramentas de extração de memória

RAM (GB)	DumpIt		WinPmem	
	Extraction (s)	Analysis (s)	Extraction (s)	Analysis (s)
2	16 ($\pm$1.8)	365 ($\pm$32.9)	6 ($\pm$0.6)	360 ($\pm$31.7)
4	62 ($\pm$8.1)	670 ($\pm$53.6)	23 ($\pm$2.1)	679 ($\pm$55.3)
8	235 ($\pm$23.5)	894 ($\pm$116.2)	88 ($\pm$7)	890 ($\pm$117.2)

Values in parentheses indicate 95% confidence interval. Results demonstrate that the WinPmem tool presented the lowest average extraction times. Regard-

---

[9] https://github.com/ahlashkari/VolMemLyzer/releases/tag/V2.0.0.
[10] https://github.com/volatilityfoundation/volatility3.
[11] https://scikit-learn.org/1.6/index.html.
[12] https://www.magnetforensics.com/resources/magnet-dumpit-for-windows/.
[13] https://github.com/Velocidex/WinPmem/releases/tag/v4.0.rc1.

ing analysis, dumps generated by both tools demanded, on average, similar processing times. Considering the preference for open-source solutions, WinPmem was adopted in the proposed architecture.

3.2 Data Compression Optimization

This experiment aimed to evaluate the execution time and compression rate of different tools, focusing on efficient file sending from the monitored device to the remote service, using virtual machines with 2 GB RAM memory.

Table 2. Comparação entre ferramentas de compressão

Tool	Duration (s)	Compression Rate (%)
shutil + bz2	152.50	69.30
shutil + gzip	308.39	70.09
shutil + lzma	660.19	77.94
tarfile + bz2	190.07	69.30
tarfile + gzip	355.30	70.09
tarfile + lzma	702.91	77.94
zipfile	131.90	69.94

Based on obtained results, although shutil + lzma and tarfile + lzma methods achieved the highest compression rate, execution time was significantly elevated, making them unfeasible for applications demanding quick response. The zipfile tool, in turn, presented the lowest execution time with a satisfactory compression rate, very close to other alternatives. Considering the balance between performance and efficiency, the zipfile library was chosen as the compression solution in the proposed architecture.

3.3 Malware Detection Performance

This experiment evaluates classification performance using four different ML algorithms selected for their complementary characteristics: KNN (instance-based learning), CART (decision tree with interpretability), MLP (neural network for complex patterns), and RF (ensemble method for robustness). The MalMem dataset was split using stratified sampling with 80% for training (7,997 samples) and 20% for testing (1,999 samples), maintaining class balance in both sets. Cross-validation with k = 5 folds was employed to ensure robust evaluation and prevent overfitting.

It is important to note that these results reflect performance on the controlled MalMem dataset. The high accuracy values, while promising, should be interpreted cautiously as the dataset's balanced nature and limited malware diversity may not fully represent real-world conditions where class imbalance and novel malware variants are common.

Table 3. Desempenho de Detecção de Malwares e Processos Benígnos

Method	Recall	Accuracy	AUPRC	Detection Time (ms)	CV Score (± std)
KNN	0.97	0.96	0.96	171.88	0.95 (±0.02)
CART	0.96	0.95	0.95	15.66	0.94 (±0.03)
MLP	0.95	0.95	0.97	31.25	0.94 (±0.02)
RF	0.97	0.96	0.96	78.09	0.96 (±0.01)

4 Industrial Impact and Business Value

The proposed solution addresses critical cybersecurity challenges faced by organizations using Windows environments. The partnership with CPDI allowed for real-world validation under conditions that mirror actual client deployments, ensuring practical applicability.

The architecture's modular design enables horizontal scaling, allowing organizations to monitor multiple devices simultaneously without proportional infrastructure cost increases. The 60% data compression achievement significantly reduces network bandwidth requirements, making the solution economically viable for large-scale deployments.

The minimal user intervention requirement and automated scheduling capabilities reduce operational overhead for IT departments. The solution's compatibility with existing Windows 10 environments eliminates the need for costly system migrations or extensive reconfigurations.

The 99% detection accuracy with millisecond response times enables real-time threat mitigation, crucial for maintaining business continuity and regulatory compliance. The auditable analysis process supports forensic investigations and compliance reporting requirements.

5 Conclusion

Motivated by the relevance of malware detection, this work proposed an AI-based malware detection solution with process analysis for Windows Operating Systems. The proposed solution relies on these paradigm characteristics to propose a scalable solution with lower impact on user experience and that allows containment actions in adequate time.

Based on results, it was possible to evaluate the feasibility of the malware detection solution. The compression rate superior to 60% in data demonstrates communication bandwidth savings, enabling system efficiency and scalability, even with multiple devices monitored simultaneously. The proposed solution achieved detection rates above 95% across different ML algorithms, with CART providing the best balance between accuracy and processing speed.

The industrial partnership with CPDI validated the solution's practical applicability within the constraints of the evaluation dataset. However, real-world deployment will require addressing the identified limitations, particularly regarding dataset diversity, processing latency, and scalability considerations.

The modular, extensible architecture supports integration with existing security infrastructure while providing the flexibility needed for future enhancements and adaptations to evolving threat landscapes.

Acknowledgment. The authors would like to thank the CNPq (N° 303877/2021-9 and N° 405940/2022-0) and CAPES (N° 88887.954253/2024-00 and N° 88887.972043/2024-00) of Brazil for the financial support.

References

1. Alani, M.M., Mashatan, A., Miri, A.: Xmal: A lightweight memory-based explainable obfuscated-malware detector. Comput. Secur. **133**, 103409 (2023)
2. Alsmadi, I., Al-Ahmad, B., Alsmadi, M.: Malware analysis and multi-label category detection issues: Ensemble-based approaches. In: 2022 International Conference on Intelligent Data Science Technologies and Applications (IDSTA). pp. 164–169. IEEE (2022)
3. Carrier, T.: Detecting Obfuscated Malware Using Memory Feature Engineering (2021)
4. Costa, M.A., Costa, Y.M., Almeida, Y.O., Cardoso, F.J., Gomes, R.L.: Connection management using automated firewall based on threat intelligence. In: Proceedings of the 2024 Latin America Networking Conference. p. 32–37. LANC '24, Association for Computing Machinery, New York, NY, USA (2024)
5. Djenna, A., Bouridane, A., Rubab, S., Marou, I.M.: Artificial intelligence-based malware detection, analysis, and mitigation. Symmetry **15**(3), 677 (2023)
6. Ferdous, J., Islam, R., Mahboubi, A., Islam, M.Z.: A review of state-of-the-art malware attack trends and defense mechanisms. IEEE Access **11**, 121118–121141 (2023)
7. Ferreira, M.C., Ribeiro, S.E., Nobre, F.V., Linhares, M.L., Araújo, T.P., Gomes, R.L.: Mitigating measurement failures in throughput performance forecasting. In: 2024 20th International Conference on Network and Service Management (CNSM). pp. 1–7 (2024). https://doi.org/10.23919/CNSM62983.2024.10814394
8. Gomes, R.L., da Ponte, F.R.P., Urbano, A.C., Bittencourt, L.F., Madeira, E.R.M.: Strategies for daytime slicing in future internet service providers. Transactions on Emerging Telecommunications Technologies **31**(1), e3727 (2020)
9. Maniriho, P., Mahmood, A.N., Chowdhury, M.J.M.: A systematic literature review on windows malware detection: Techniques, research issues, and future directions. J. Syst. Softw. **209**, 111921 (2024)
10. Monnappa, K.: Learning Malware Analysis: Explore the Concepts, Tools, and Techniques to Analyze and Investigate Windows Malware. Packt Publishing Ltd. (2018)
11. Nobre, F.V.J., Silva, D.d.S., Ferreira, M.C.M.M., Brito, M.L.M.L., de Araújo, T.P., Gomes, R.L.: Time-weighted correlation approach to identify high delay links in internet service providers. J. Int. Serv. Appl. **16**(1), 419–430 (2025). https://doi.org/10.5753/jisa.2025.5218, https://journals-sol.sbc.org.br/index.php/jisa/article/view/5218

12. Onoja, M., Jegede, A., Mazadu, J., Aimufua, G., Oyedele, A., Olibodum, K.: Exploring the effectiveness and efficiency of lightgbm algorithm for windows malware detection. In: 2022 5th Information Technology for Education and Development (ITED). pp. 1–6. IEEE (2022)
13. Pimenta, I., Silva, D., Moura, E., Silveira, M., Gomes, R.L.: Impact of data anonymization in machine learning models. In: Proceedings of the 13th Latin-American Symposium on Dependable and Secure Computing. p. 188–191. LADC '24, Association for Computing Machinery, New York, NY, USA (2024)

Risk Classification of IP Addresses Using Machine Learning with Weighted Voting Approach

Francisco V. J. Nobre, Davi O. Alves, Ramon S. Araujo, Gustavo A. Campos, and Rafael L. Gomes[✉]

State University of Ceará (UECE), Fortaleza, CE, Brazil
{valderlan.nobre,dav.oliveira,ramon.araujo}@aluno.uece.br,
{gustavo.campos,rafa.lopes}@uece.br

Abstract. The growing complexity of cyberattacks demands intelligent and adaptive security solutions, one of which is the detection of malicious IP addresses. This paper presents a novel approach for classifying IP addresses by integrating Machine Learning (ML) with data from multiple public threat intelligence databases, where a novel dataset was built. The proposed solution applies a weighted voting mechanism to enhance interpretability and robustness by combining diverse data sources through a multi-criteria weighting strategy. The experimental results, in a real network environment, indicate that the solution enables scalable and automated risk classification of IP addresses.

Keywords: Cybersecurity · Machine Learning · Threat Intelligence · IP Reputation

1 Introduction

The increasing sophistication of cyberattacks demands proactive, intelligent, and adaptable security solutions. Artificial Intelligence (AI) emerges as a fundamental tool for automating threat detection and classification, enabling rapid and precise responses in complex network environments [11,13]. Resilient security solutions capable of anticipating emerging threats become crucial for network connection management, ensuring security, performance, and availability while optimizing resource usage [5,6].

The application of Machine Learning (ML) techniques for analyzing IP address behavior represents a promising area in cybersecurity research [12]. Traditionally, the classification of malicious IPs relies on static lists (denylists) or manual analyses performed by security experts[3]. However, these approaches present significant limitations in terms of scalability, response time, and adaptability to new threats.

The integration of advanced technologies and proactive strategies are critical for ensuring data integrity, confidentiality, and availability. Responsive firewalls

L. A. Rodrigues and R. Oliveira (Eds.): LADC 2025, CCIS 2697, pp. 320–328, 2026.
https://doi.org/10.1007/978-3-032-11539-3_19

dynamically block low-reputation IPs based on behavioral analyses, representing an evolution in network protection. Cyber Threat Intelligence (CTI) focuses on collecting, analyzing, and interpreting information about malicious activities [17]. Using connection logs, CTI identifies suspicious traffic and attack origins [8], enabling more effective responses.

Automated threat response allows rapid reactions in critical environments. Techniques such as real-time log analysis [19] and automatic packet filtering [14] demonstrate how firewalls can proactively identify and respond to threats. Strategies such as denylists and IP reputation management are essential, enabling the pre-filtering of traffic based on public lists of malicious IP addresses [1]. Thus, it becomes necessary to develop solutions that automate these analyses, prioritizing efficiency, scalability, and response agility.

Within this context, this paper proposes using ML on Threat Intelligence data for IP address classification. To train the ML model, a dataset was built from features extracted from four public threat databases: *AbuseIPDB*[1], *Virus-Total*[2], *Pulsedive*[3], and *IPVoid*[4]. Regarding ML models, supervised techniques including *Random Forest, SVM, Neural Network, Extra Trees, Decision Tree, K-nearest Neighbors*, and *Convolutional Neural Network* were analyzed, creating an adaptive system capable of identifying complex patterns to classify IPs into three categories: Malicious (denylist), Trusted (allowlist), or Suspicious (suspect).

Thus, this work provides the following contributions: (1) Definition of the most suitable ML model for malicious IP detection, enabling its integration into cybersecurity tools to detect malicious activities in network infrastructure; and (2) Creation of a dataset with features from IPs reported in public cyber threat databases, allowing other researchers to develop new information security solutions.

2 Proposal

The proposal operates as a network infrastructure attachment without affecting operation or performance. It uses containers, APIs, and Threat Intelligence tools to ensure scalability, portability, and efficient communication with the Firewall, data collection, and ML model processing. The execution flow includes connection detection, data storage, denylist queries, and reputation score definition through public databases and ML model classification. Each module operates in an integrated manner, forming a cohesive system as illustrated in Fig. 1. Within this organization, the following modules and functionalities are implemented:

- **Threat Detection**: This module uses a machine learning model to classify IPs. The steps involve: (i) Feature extraction collecting relevant data from

---

[1] abuseipdb.com.
[2] virustotal.com.
[3] pulsedive.com.
[4] ipvoid.com.

connections, including external reputations obtained via API; and (ii) Classification where the model returns one of the following results: *denylist* (malicious IP), *allowlist* (trusted IP), or *suspect* (suspicious IP requiring continuous monitoring). The decision is then forwarded to the *Connection Management* module, which executes the corresponding action (blocking or using *Tarpit*) on network devices.

- **Reputation Check**: Responsible for querying public threat databases based on recorded connection attempts. Performs requests to services providing data on IPs listed in denylists, reputation reports, geolocation, and malicious behavior scores. This information directly feeds the AI model of the *Threat Detection* module. Main sources include: *AbuseIPDB* (reputation and denylists), *VirusTotal* (malicious behaviors), *Pulsedive* (threat modeling), and *IPVoid* (cyber threat detection). Data is integrated into the API's *denylist* table for analysis and future queries.

- **Connection Management**: Based on classifications provided by the *Threat Detection* module, this module updates routing tables and firewall rules on devices. Additionally, it executes: (i) Temporary Connection Degradation suspicious IPs have reduced priority and limited speed, mitigating risks; and (ii) Periodic IP Re-evaluation performed based on new data from public sources: every 3 days (*suspect*), weekly (*allowlist*), and monthly (*denylist*).

Fig. 1. Solution Overview.

2.1 Dataset Formation

To enable training an effective ML model, it was necessary to generate a dataset composed of information from the aforementioned public databases. Thus, a set of 2,992 IP addresses was automatically collected through a specialized bot from the four public databases mentioned. The dataset consists predominantly of denylist IPs from AbuseIPDB, complemented by allowlist addresses from trusted sources (Google, Amazon, Microsoft). This "ground truth" base ensures reliability in training and evaluation by selecting IPs with consensus classification among multiple sources, minimizing noise in supervised learning.

The dataset was formed using the following features from public databases:

- **abuseipdb_confidence_score** (0-100): Confidence index for IP malicious activity probability based on report history.

- **abuseipdb_total_reports** (0-85,000): Total malicious reports registered against the IP.
- **abuseipdb_num_distinct_users** (0-2,000): Unique users who reported the IP, strengthening credibility.
- **ipvoid_Detection_Count** (0-93): Number of detection services identifying the IP as a threat.
- **risk_recommended_pulsedive** (*critical, high, medium, low, unknown, none*): Consolidated risk classification from multiple analysis sources.
- **virustotal_reputation** (-127 to 565): Reputation score where negative values indicate poor IP reputation.
- **virustotal_malicious** (0-20): Number of engines considering the IP as malicious.
- **virustotal_suspicious** (0-5): Number of engines categorizing the IP as suspicious behavior.
- **virustotal_undetected** (0-91): Number of engines detecting no threats.
- **virustotal_harmless** (0-86): Number of engines considering the IP as harmless.

The dataset reveals distinct patterns across sources. AbuseIPDB shows confidence scores mostly at 100, indicating strong evidence of malicious activity, while reports and reporting users vary widely (0–74,906 and 0–1,135). VirusTotal reports 0–21 malicious detections (median 9), few suspicious detections, many undetected counts, and harmless ratings up to 65, suggesting most engines miss threats; reputation scores range from -127 to 549, with negative or near-zero values prevailing. Pulsedive risk levels are mostly low ($\sim 47\%$), followed by medium/none ($\sim 24\%$ each), with high-severity flags rare. IPVoid shows 0–24 detections (typically 4–11), indicating partial consensus among engines.

After collecting this data, a preprocessing step involved removing rows with missing values from at least one database, removing duplicate data, and normalizing the numeric features (using min-max scaling, where each attribute was proportionally resized based on its observed minimum and maximum values), as well as categorizing the non-numeric features. For class balancing, the SMOTE (Synthetic Minority Oversampling Technique) generated 2,469 synthetic samples, expanding the training set from 2,232 to 4,701 and equalizing the three classes (1,567 instances each). The test set (559 samples) remained unchanged. The balanced data was then used for ML model training (Sect. 2.2).

2.2 Multi-criteria Weighted Voting for Malicious IP Classification

Classifying malicious IP addresses from multiple threat intelligence sources requires approaches that balance accuracy, interpretability, and robustness. This research proposes a model grounded in weighted voting, a technique recognized in ensemble learning [4] that offers significant advantages in terms of interpretability, robustness, and flexibility. Unlike traditional ensemble methods that combine multiple machine learning models, our approach combines multiple heterogeneous data sources using domain-specific voting logic. The formulation is based on three fundamental pillars: (1) the classifier combination theory [9], which demonstrates how different classifiers can be optimally combined; (2) the mathematical foundations of weighted voting [7], which establish the basis for empirical weight assignment; and (3) its application in cybersecurity [2], which evidences the effectiveness of collaborative approaches in threat detection.

Our motivation stems from the practical limitations of approaches based on complex statistical *scores*, such as low interpretability, sensitivity to *outliers*, inflexibility for dynamic adjustments, and inability to capture the degree of consensus between sources [15].

Multi-criteria Weight Determination. The assignment of weights to each threat intelligence source is performed through three complementary metrics that capture different aspects of performance and utility in the classification task. Each metric is described below:

Individual Performance (P_i): Evaluates the discriminative capability of source i in isolation. It is measured by the accuracy observed when this source is used individually to classify validation set examples. This metric is grounded in the principle that sources with better individual performance should receive greater weight in the final decision [7]. The metric is defined in Eq. 1:

$$P_i = \frac{\text{CorrectClassifications}_i}{\text{TotalSamples}} \quad (1) \qquad C_i = |\text{corr}(\text{output}_i, \text{ground\_truth})| \quad (2)$$

where Correct Classifications$_i$ represents the number of correct classifications made by source i, and the denominator is the total evaluated samples.

Correlation with Ground Truth (C_i): Measures the degree of alignment between the outputs of source i and true labels [9]. The absolute value of Pearson's correlation between the source's output vector and the true label vector is used, as shown in Eq. 2. This captures both strong positive and negative correlations, as both indicate informative relationships [9].

Inter-Source Consensus (S_i): We propose an innovative metric that quantifies informational complementarity between sources [9], focusing exclusively on agreements that lead to correct decisions. The Inter-Source Consensus is defined by Eq. 3. Where Correct Agreements$_{i,j}$ represents the count of instances where both source i and source j are classified correctly, and Total Comparisons$_{i,j}$ is the number of comparable instances between sources i and j. This metric differs from traditional diversity approaches by prioritizing positive synergies rather than merely reducing overlapping errors [9].

$$S_i = \frac{\sum_{j \neq i} \text{Correct Agreements}_{i,j}}{\sum_{j \neq i} \text{Total Comparisons}_{i,j}} \quad (3) \qquad w_i = \frac{\alpha P_i + \beta C_i + \gamma S_i}{\sum_{j=1}^{n}(\alpha P_j + \beta C_j + \gamma S_j)} \quad (4)$$

These three metrics are then combined to form the final weights for each source using a weighted average as previously defined by Eq. 4, where $\alpha = 0.5$, $\beta = 0.3$, and $\gamma = 0.2$ (determined through empirical optimization as previously described). Experimental validation on the dataset confirmed the suitability of this configuration, reflecting the relative importance of each component [7].

Formulation of Weighted Voting. Our approach extends classical weighted voting theory [18] to the specific context of threat intelligence. For an IP x, the Class is given by Eq. 5, where X is the space of IP addresses to classify, $\mathcal{C}$ (i.e., allowlist, suspicious, or denylist) is the risk classes, $S = \{s_1, \ldots, s_n\}$ is the intelligence sources with weights $W = \{w_1, \ldots, w_n\}$, $\sum w_i = 1$, and $V_j(x)$ is $\{i : s_i$ voted for $j\}$.

$$\text{Class}(x) = \arg\max_{j \in \mathcal{C}} \sum_{i \in V_j(x)} w_i \tag{5}$$

This multi-criteria weighted voting represents a natural evolution in cybersecurity classification methods, providing a practical and theoretically grounded alternative to complex scoring approaches. It maintains high accuracy while delivering the interpretability and operational flexibility essential for critical production environments, establishing a new paradigm for multi-source threat detection systems.

3   Experiments

Experimental validation assessed threat classification effectiveness through ML metrics. Code and datasets are available in the repository[5] for experiment reproducibility. Analyzed metrics included: Precision (true positive rate), Recall (detection capability), F1-Score (harmonic mean between Precision and Recall), Accuracy (correct classifications), Harmonic Mean (consolidated measure), and execution time for tri-modal classification (*denylist, allowlist, suspect*). Seven ML algorithms were analyzed: Decision Tree (DT), Random Forest (RF), Extra Trees (ET), Convolutional Neural Network (CNN), Support Vector Machines (SVM), K-Nearest Neighbors (KNN), and Neural Networks (NN), representing established techniques in AI applications for cybersecurity [10,16]. The model evaluation used hyperparameters optimized via Grid Search with cross-validation, complexity balancing, and generalization capacity. The hyperparameters used can be found in the project repository.

Additionally, we deployed the solution on the CS Building's network gateway (TP-Link TL-SG105E switch) to assess real-world performance. Results demonstrated that the high-frequency monitoring stage executes efficiently ($\sim$7 ms), while threat intelligence database queries constitute the primary latency source ($\sim$3 s). Crucially, since each IP undergoes only a single check, these queries occur

---

[5] github.com/valderlan/LADC-IT-2025-RCIP.

infrequently. Consequently, the solution introduces negligible operational overhead to network applications.

Results in Table 1 demonstrate classification performance exceeding 88% for all algorithms. RF achieved the highest accuracy (99.64%), followed by CNN (99.28%) and ET (97.67%). However, execution time (Table 1) revealed a significant trade-off: RF requiring 13.72 ms versus DT with only 0.38ns.

Table 1. Performance of ML Models

Model	Accuracy	F1-Score	Precision	Recall	H. Mean	Time (ms)
RF	0.996422	0.996424	0.996448	0.996422	0.996435	13.72
CNN	0.992844	0.992926	0.993236	0.992844	0.993040	3.95
ET	0.976744	0.976552	0.977184	0.976744	0.976964	3.65
NN	0.962433	0.963117	0.964405	0.962433	0.963418	2.90
DT	0.949911	0.951516	0.955624	0.949911	0.952759	0.38
SVM	0.912343	0.912233	0.914102	0.912343	0.913222	9.67
KNN	0.887299	0.893027	0.902677	0.887299	0.894922	0.45

The comparative analysis reveals that, although RF achieves the highest accuracy (99.64%) in the balanced data scenario, its execution time (13.72 s) can limit real-time applications. For contexts where speed is critical, the DT model stands out as an optimized solution with the fastest execution time, being 97.23% faster than RF and 90.38% faster than CNN. Despite the lower accuracy (94.99% balanced), these differences represent reductions of only 4.67% and 4.32% compared to RF and CNN, respectively. Therefore, DT is best suited for applications that require immediate response while maintaining good detection accuracy. Its performance makes it the most balanced choice between efficiency and performance.

4   Conclusion

The evolving nature of contemporary cyber threats demands intelligent and adaptive security solutions. This research presents an innovative architecture that integrates Artificial Intelligence with multiple threat intelligence sources and IP reputation systems to classify IPs into allowlist, denylist, and suspicious. The solution incorporates a multi-criteria weighted voting mechanism to enhance robustness and interpretability. Among the evaluated models, the Decision Tree was selected for real-time scenarios due to its fast execution and competitive accuracy compared to more complex models like Random Forest. Experimental results confirmed high classification performance with low overhead. Future work includes optimizing the fusion of heterogeneous threat data to improve model adaptability and precision.

Acknowledgments. The authors would like to thank the CNPq (N° 305946/2025-0 and N° 405940/2022-0) and CAPES (N° 88887.954253/2024-00 and N° 88887.972043/2024-00) of Brazil for the financial support.

References

1. Afzaliseresht, N., Miao, Y., Michalska, S., Liu, Q., Wang, H.: From logs to stories: human-centred data mining for cyber threat intelligence. IEEE Access **8**, 19089–19099 (2020). https://doi.org/10.1109/ACCESS.2020.2966760

2. Buczak, A.L., Guven, E.: A survey of data mining and machine learning methods for cyber security intrusion detection. IEEE Commun. Surv. Tutor. **18**(2), 1153–1176 (2016). https://doi.org/10.1109/COMST.2015.2494502

3. Costa, M.A., Costa, Y.M., Almeida, Y.O., Cardoso, F.J., Gomes, R.L.: Connection management using automated firewall based on threat intelligence. In: Proceedings of the 2024 Latin America Networking Conference, LANC 2024, pp. 32–37. Association for Computing Machinery, New York (2024)

4. Dietterich, T.G.: Ensemble methods in machine learning. In: Multiple Classifier Systems, pp. 1–15. Springer, Heidelberg (2000)

5. Ferreira, M.C., Ribeiro, S.E., Nobre, F.V., Linhares, M.L., Araújo, T.P., Gomes, R.L.: Mitigating measurement failures in throughput performance forecasting. In: 2024 20th International Conference on Network and Service Management (CNSM). IFIP (2024)

6. Gomes, R.L., da Ponte, F.R.P., Urbano, A.C., Bittencourt, L.F., Madeira, E.R.M.: Strategies for daytime slicing in future internet service providers. Trans. Emerg. Telecommun. Technol. **31**(1), e3727 (2020)

7. Kittler, J., Hatef, M., Duin, R., Matas, J.: On combining classifiers. IEEE Trans. Pattern Anal. Mach. Intell. **20**(3), 226–239 (1998)

8. Komosny, D.: Evidential value of country location evidence obtained from IP address geolocation. PeerJ Comput. Sci. (2023)

9. Kuncheva, L.I.: Combining Pattern Classifiers: Methods and Algorithms. Wiley, Hoboken (2004). https://doi.org/10.1002/0471660264

10. Lazar, D., Cohen, K., Freund, A., Bartik, A., Ron, A.: IMDoC: identification of malicious domain campaigns via DNS and communicating files. IEEE Access **9**, 45242–45258 (2021). https://doi.org/10.1109/ACCESS.2021.3066957

11. Nobre, F.V.J., Silva, D.d.S., Ferreira, M.C.M.M., Brito, M.L.M.L., de Araújo, T.P., Gomes, R.L.: Time-weighted correlation approach to identify high delay links in internet service providers. J. Internet Serv. Appl. **16**(1), 419–430 (2025). https://doi.org/10.5753/jisa.2025.5218

12. Pimenta, I., Silva, D., Moura, E., Silveira, M., Gomes, R.L.: Impact of data anonymization in machine learning models. In: Proceedings of the 13th Latin-American Symposium on Dependable and Secure Computing, LADC 2024, pp. 188–191. Association for Computing Machinery, New York (2024). https://doi.org/10.1145/3697090.3699865

13. Portela, A., Linhares, M.M., Nobre, F.V.J., Menezes, R., Mesquita, M., Gomes, R.L.: The role of TCP congestion control in the throughput forecasting. In: Proceedings of the 13th Latin-American Symposium on Dependable and Secure Computing, LADC 2024, pp. 196–199. Association for Computing Machinery, New York (2024). https://doi.org/10.1145/3697090.3699869

14. Rizkilina, T.M., Rosyid, N.R.: Packet filtering automation system design based on data synchronization on IP profile database using python. J. Internet Softw. Eng. (JISE) **3**, 12–19 (2022)
15. Sommer, R., Paxson, V.: Outside the closed world: on using machine learning for network intrusion detection. In: 2010 IEEE Symposium on Security and Privacy, pp. 305–316 (2010). https://doi.org/10.1109/SP.2010.25
16. Tosun, A., De Donno, M., Dragoni, N., Fafoutis, X.: RESIP host detection: identification of malicious residential IP proxy flows. In: 2021 IEEE International Conference on Consumer Electronics (ICCE), pp. 1–6 (2021)
17. Wagner, T.D., Mahbub, K., Palomar, E., Abdallah, A.E.: Cyber threat intelligence sharing: survey and research directions. Comput. Secur. **87**, 101589 (2019)
18. Xu, L., Krzyzak, A., Suen, C.: Methods of combining multiple classifiers and their applications to handwriting recognition. IEEE Trans. Syst. Man Cybern. Part B (Cybern.) **22**, 418–435 (1992)
19. Yadav, M., Mishra, D.S.: Identification of network threats using live log stream analysis. In: 2023 2nd International Conference on Paradigm Shifts in Communications Embedded Systems, Machine Learning and Signal Processing (PCEMS), pp. 1–6 (2023)

Student Forum

Improving Safety in Industry 4.0 Using an IoT-Helmet

Evellin S. de Moura, Antônio M. B. Neto, and Rafael L. Gomes[✉]

State University of Ceará (UECE), Fortaleza, CE, Brazil
{evellin.moura,mozar.braga}@aluno.uece.br, rafa.lopes@uece.br

Abstract. Safety in industrial environments, such as construction and factories, is a daily concern for companies, since it directly affects the workers and reputation. One existing approach to improve safety in Industry 4.0 is the integration of the Internet of Things (IoT) and Decision-Making methods, enabling continuous monitoring and risk situation detection. However, it is necessary to deploy these modern solutions in the usual equipment of workers without harming their daily tasks. Within this context, this paper presents an integrated solution comprising a monitoring IoT-helmet and edge computing, which increases occupational safety and reduces response time in risk situations. The IoT-helmet collects data about the current status of the worker (including eye movement, body position, and others), while the station consolidates and displays this information for alert situations (such as falling, drowsiness, fainting, etc.) detected by AI models. This paper presents preliminary results of the development of the solution, encompassing the experiments related to posture monitoring and events of falls and drowsiness. The results indicate the capacity of the solution to identify risk situations with a suitable response time.

Keywords: IoT · Safety · Industrial Environments

1 Introduction

High-risk work environments, such as construction sites and factories, continue to pose serious safety challenges, as evidenced by 742,200 occupational accidents and 2,400 fatalities recorded in Brazil in 2024, according to the Occupational Safety and Health Observatory (2024) [12]. While preventive measures have been in place since the Industrial Revolution, recent technological advances, particularly in the Internet of Things (IoT), Decision-Making methods, and Artificial Intelligence (AI), have emerged as essential tools for improving these statistics [3,10]. AI has been recognized by institutions such as the European Parliament and the European Commission as a strategic resource for tackling occupational safety issues, with applications ranging from predictive monitoring to automated

E. S. de Moura and A. M. B. Neto—Undergraduate Students of Computer Science in UECE.

© The Author(s), under exclusive license to Springer Nature Switzerland AG 2026
L. A. Rodrigues and R. Oliveira (Eds.): LADC 2025, CCIS 2697, pp. 331–341, 2026.
https://doi.org/10.1007/978-3-032-11539-3_20

risk management [5]. Nowadays, connected devices and smart sensors enable real-time analysis of critical variables such as air quality, noise levels, and temperature, creating safer operational environments [8]. These technologies have established a new paradigm in accident prevention, with systems capable of continuously monitoring environmental conditions and operational parameters, and delivering immediate responses to emerging risks [9]. However, connectivity in IoT solutions still faces limitations due to low transmission power and environmental interference, which can reduce efficiency in scenarios that require long-range communication [4,11]. To address this point, Low Power Wide Area Network (LPWAN) technologies such as LoRa, Sigfox, NB-IoT, and LTE have been adopted, with LoRa standing out for its long range, low power consumption, ease of implementation, and ability to receive simultaneous data streams [13]. For applications that require high data rates in real-time (such as video and image transmission), the combination of Wi-Fi with the WebSocket protocol enables persistent, bidirectional connections that reduce latency and support continuous, responsive monitoring in critical environments. Within this context, this paper presents an integrated IoT- and wireless-based safety solution composed of a Monitoring Helmet and a Mobile Station at Edge Computing. The helmet includes an ESP-32 LoRa/Wi-Fi module, an ESP-32 Cam, a Li-Ion battery, an infrared sensor, and an MPU6050 gyroscope and accelerometer, enabling the collection of data such as eye openness, body posture, and distance estimation, along with real-time video capture. The Mobile Station includes a LoRa/Wi-Fi communication module, a portable computer (e.g., a Raspberry Pi), and a display screen. It receives the data transmitted by the helmet, consolidates the information, and presents it to the strategic team to support fast and effective decision-making. The main innovation of this proposal lies in the use of a hybrid communication protocol combining LoRa and Wi-Fi/WebSocket. LoRa offers advantages in terms of range and energy efficiency, especially in industrial environments where long-distance data transmission is required. Meanwhile, Wi-Fi and WebSocket support high-bandwidth data transfer, such as real-time video, with reduced latency. This hybrid architecture ensures robust connectivity and low latency even in scenarios involving multiple communication hops and environmental interference. Additionally, risk situations are detected by an entropy-based approach by quantifying the variability or unpredictability in sensor data streams, especially from inertial and environmental sensors. Compared to existing tools, the proposed solution is more accessible and cost-effective, relying on widely available and easy-to-implement technologies. LoRa, for instance, requires no complex communication infrastructure, whereas the WebSocket protocol simplifies system configuration and maintenance, eliminating the need for expensive centralized platforms or proprietary protocols. As a result, the proposed solution is well-suited for industrial environments, offering a practical and economical alternative to more infrastructure-intensive systems. The remainder of this paper is organized as follows. Section 2 describes the existing solution, highlighting the innovation of the proposal in front of them. Section 3 details the proposal, while Sect. 4 discusses the experiments and results. Finally, Sect. 6 presents the conclusions and directions for future work.

2   Related Work

Campero-Jurado et al. [2] developed an intelligent helmet using environmental and inertial sensors combined with a CNN-based model that achieved 92% accuracy in classifying occupational risks. Despite its effectiveness in anomaly detection, the system presents critical limitations for industrial use: reliance solely on Wi-Fi (with 23% connectivity failures due to electromagnetic interference), centralized processing via ThingsBoard (causing 450 ms latency), and absence of communication redundancy, reducing reliability in emergencies. In contrast, our solution proposes a hybrid architecture that combines LoRa for critical safety data and Wi-Fi/WebSocket for video transmission, ensuring robust connectivity even in multi-device scenarios. Local preprocessing of sensor data has the potential to significantly reduce both latency and bandwidth usage compared to centralized solutions.

Bavaresco et al. [1] conducted a systematic review of 127 studies on using IoT to monitor workers' physical and psychological conditions, highlighting the importance of integrating IoT with classification algorithms and data fusion to enhance safety and reduce risks in industrial settings. However, the study has key limitations: it lacks practical implementation, does not specify suitable communication protocols for industrial scenarios, and overlooks critical factors such as latency, energy consumption, and scalability in real-world applications. Our proposal aims to overcome these limitations by implementing a functional prototype with experimental validation, specifying optimized protocols for each type of data, and evaluating scalability concerns.

Li et al. [7] reviewed the use of AI in workplace accident prevention, focusing on PPE detection and unsafe behavior using deep learning. While highlighting AI's potential, the study identifies key limitations: reliance on limited datasets unrepresentative of real industrial settings, centralized processing that hampers real-time response, and lack of integration across sensory modalities such as visual, inertial, and environmental data. On the other hand, the proposed solution applies a distributed multimodal system that processes data from cameras, inertial sensors, and environmental sensors locally on the device, using AI models optimized for microcontrollers to ensure real-time detection.

Kanan et al. [6] proposed an autonomous safety system for construction sites using RF, ultrasonic sensors, and directional antennas, achieving 94% accuracy in detecting worker proximity to hazards. However, the system has key limitations: it only supports static hazard detection without analyzing dynamic behavior, relies on unidirectional GPRS communication with 2âĂŞ3 s latencies, and lacks local intelligent processing, depending entirely on external infrastructure. Differently, the proposed IoT-Helmet integrates multiple sensory modalities (MPU-6050 for inertial detection, ESP32-CAM for visual analysis, HW-201 for drowsiness monitoring) with machine learning algorithms executed locally.

The references presented in this section highlight IoT- and AI-based solutions aimed at improving workplace safety in industrial or high-risk environments. However, unlike the approach proposed in this paper, these studies exhibit converging limitations: (1) dependence on centralized infrastructure, undermining autonomy and reliability; (2) reliance on single communication protocols, limiting adaptability across different scenarios; (3) lack of intelligent distributed processing, which can lead to latencies unsuitable for critical applications; and (4) absence of comprehensive experimental validation in real industrial settings. This work seeks to address these gaps by proposing an integrated solution that combines IoT, AI, embedded systems, and a hybrid communication architecture, with the aim of enhancing latency, energy autonomy, scalability, and offline operation.

3   Proposed Solution

The system is composed of two main modules, as illustrated in Fig. 1: the Monitoring Helmet and the Mobile Station. The helmet integrates key components such as an ESP-32 Cam, MPU-6050 and HW-201 sensors, an ESP-32 LoRa/Wi-Fi module, a Li-Ion battery, and an infrared sensor. These elements enable live data collection, including eye openness, body posture, distance estimation, and video capture, providing a rich stream of information for proactive safety measures.

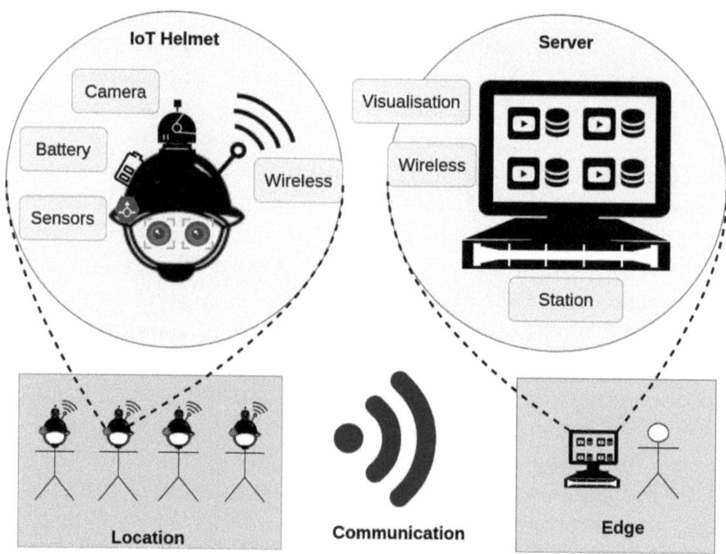

Fig. 1. Overview of the solution.

The Mobile Station includes a LoRa/Wi-Fi module, a portable computer (e.g., a Raspberry Pi), and a display interface. It receives and consolidates incoming data from the helmet, prepares it for analysis, and presents it in a clear and actionable format, enabling quick and informed decision-making by safety teams. The interface supports intuitive understanding of incoming data, enhancing real-time situational awareness.

Data transmission between the helmet and the Mobile Station is handled using LoRa and Wi-Fi protocols, with WebSocket ensuring a persistent, low-latency, bidirectional connection. This hybrid communication architecture is essential in high-risk settings, where accuracy and speed are crucial for immediate decisions. The system is engineered for robustness and efficiency, even under challenging conditions involving multiple devices or environmental interference.

To support long-term analysis and data availability, a Django-based server was developed to store and manage incoming data. An SQL database ensures persistent storage, enabling historical queries, trend analysis, and report generation. The architecture is scalable, allowing new sensors or features to be added as operational needs evolve.

Beyond improving worker safety in hazardous environments, the solution establishes a solid and flexible technological platform for intelligent decision-making. By combining smart sensing, embedded processing, and a dual-protocol communication strategy, it aims to reduce risk exposure and enhance operational efficiency across diverse industrial scenarios.

The system workflow, shown in Fig. 1, includes the following steps:

- **Data Collection by the Helmet:** The helmet gathers environmental and operational data using embedded sensors, including a gyroscope (MPU-6050) for detecting body posture, an infrared sensor (HW-201) for estimating distance, and a camera (ESP-32 Cam) for continuous video capture. The data are transmitted via ESP-32 LoRa/Wi-Fi modules, ensuring stable connectivity in high-risk environments.
- **Local Processing on the Helmet:** Sensor data are preprocessed directly on the helmet to minimize redundancy and optimize transmission. This includes sending structured packets with relevant information.
- **Data Transmission:** LoRa and Wi-Fi protocols are used for communication between the helmet and the Mobile Station. In scenarios requiring low latency and persistent data flow, the WebSocket protocol is applied to ensure fast and stable bidirectional communication.
- **Data Consolidation at the Mobile Station:** The Mobile Station receives and organizes the data using a portable computer (e.g., Raspberry Pi), preparing it for visualization and further analysis.
- **Data Visualization:** Information such as posture, eye openness, and video feed is displayed on an integrated screen, allowing the safety team to monitor conditions in real time and respond immediately to critical events.
- **Remote Monitoring:** Consolidated data is also made available for remote access, allowing external teams to monitor field conditions and provide support as needed in high-risk scenarios.
- **Data Storage and Retrieval:** A Django-based server stores the collected data in an SQL database, enabling historical tracking, report generation, and real-time queries during operations.

- **Risk Analysis:** In parallel to the execution flow, this module is running, being responsible for identifying risk conditions in real time based on collected sensor data.

3.1   Data Collection and Sensor Integration

The ESP-32 Cam is a microcontroller with an integrated camera, designed for video capture and real-time data transmission. In this project, the device plays a key role in gathering both visual and operational information. In addition to the camera, the system integrates the MPU-6050 and HW-201 sensors to enhance its monitoring capabilities. The MPU-6050, a combined gyroscope and accelerometer sensor, captures data related to rotation and acceleration across the three spatial axes (X, Y, and Z). This data includes: Rotation (X, Y, Z), which indicates changes in the helmet's orientation in real time; Acceleration (X, Y, Z), it measures the intensity of motion along each axis, allowing detection of sudden movements or falls; and temperature, which reflects the internal temperature, which can be used for equipment diagnostics or environmental assessment.

The HW-201 infrared sensor complements the system by providing distance estimates based on proximity detection. This feature is useful for environmental mapping and identifying nearby hazards. The sensor data is integrated into the ESP-32 and undergoes a preprocessing stage. During this process, the data is organized into packets that separate rotation, acceleration, and temperature information. This organization ensures efficient communication and reduces redundancy, enabling faster and more accurate analysis at the receiving server.

3.2   Eye Monitoring

In addition to capturing acceleration, rotation, and temperature data, the HW-201 infrared sensor was configured to monitor eye movement, as illustrated in Fig. 2. This feature helps detect potential risk conditions. During testing, a 10-second response threshold was defined: if prolonged eye closure is detected, an audible alarm is triggered. This functionality was designed to help prevent accidents caused by fatigue or inattention in hazardous work environments.

3.3   Data Reception and Visualization

The Mobile Unit, equipped with a visualization system, is responsible for receiving and processing data sent by the Monitoring Helmet. This data includes sensor readings such as rotation (X, Y, Z), acceleration (X, Y, Z), temperature, and visual data captured by the camera. Images are transmitted in Blob (Binary Large Object) format—a binary data structure designed to store large files, such as images or videos, compactly and efficiently. This approach ensures secure and optimized transmission.

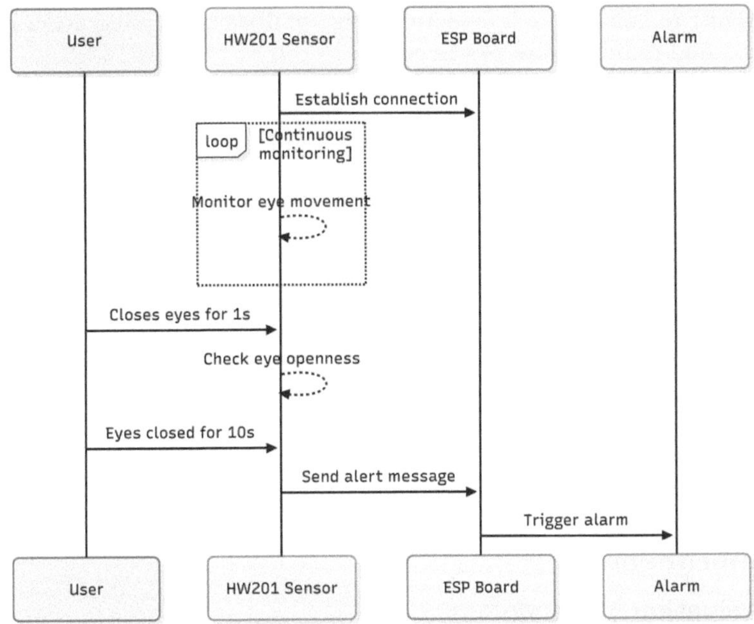

Fig. 2. Ocular anomaly detection flow.

3.4   Risk Situation Detection

The Risk Situation Detection is a crucial feature of the IoT-Helmet solution. It analyzes inputs from inertial sensors (MPU-6050), eye-tracking (HW-201), and visual streams (ESP-32 Cam), enabling timely detection of events such as falls, prolonged drowsiness, and abnormal postural shifts. A key feature of this module is the incorporation of an entropy-based analysis, which quantifies the variability in motion patterns to flag unpredictable or unstable behavior (often indicative of risk). By combining entropy metrics with threshold-based rules (e.g., eye closure duration) and future AI models trained on labeled activity data, the module ensures robust detection with minimal latency. Its distributed architecture enhances responsiveness and reliability, making it suitable for deployment in dynamic and high-risk industrial environments.

Regarding entropy, it measures the uncertainty or randomness in a dataset. In industrial safety monitoring, abrupt changes or irregular patterns in a worker's movement or posture can lead to increased entropy in sensor data. For example, the system already collects acceleration, rotation, and temperature data using the MPU-6050 sensor. In this way, lying posture was associated with higher entropy ($mean = 1.69$) compared to standing ($mean = 1.59$), indicating more unpredictable movement patterns. This implies that entropy can be a proxy for instability or abnormal behavior, flagging potential risk situations like collapses or unconsciousness. Additionally, the entropy analysis is combined with other features such as eye closure duration (from HW-201) or visual cues (from

ESP32-Cam) to enhance risk detection. This multisensory integration increases robustness and reduces false positives.

The entropy $H(S)$ of sensor data is calculated according to Eq. 1, where p_i is the probability of values falling into case i and k is the possible cases (i.e., risk situation or not). This quantifies the degree of unpredictability or variability in the data. A higher $H(S)$ indicates more randomness, potentially signaling an abnormal or risky event.

$$H(S) = -\sum_{i=1}^{k} p_i \log_2(p_i) \tag{1}$$

Regarding risk thresholding, it is detected if $H(S) > \theta$, where θ was defined by a practical experiment. Ten volunteers performed the following activities: (1) Keeping their eyes closed for 10 s; (2) Walking in a straight line for 5 min; (3) Lying down for 10 min; and (4) Standing and sitting for 5 min each. These tasks simulate typical postures and movements found in real work environments.

4   Experiments

4.1   Evaluation Methodology

Figure 3 shows the final prototype, in which all components are embedded into the helmet to optimize data collection and processing in a single unit. Data was sampled every 100 ms and transmitted to the Mobile Station via LoRa and Wi-Fi. Volunteers performed activities such as walking, standing, sitting, and lying down to generate data representing different postures and movements according to alert situation and usual behavior in industrial environments.

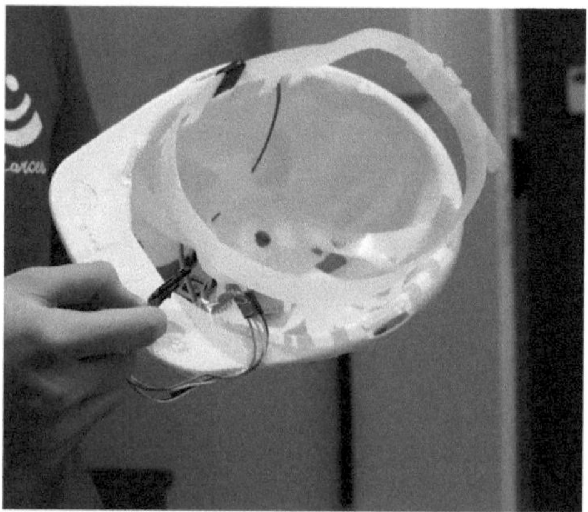

Fig. 3. Prototype of the proposed solution.

Regarding the test environments, two scenarios were deployed: (A) Indoor Environments, laboratories and classrooms at the State University of Ceará

(UECE); and (B) Outdoor Environments, open areas on campus, simulating outdoor work conditions. These environments represented different real-world use scenarios.

4.2   Results

From the experiments performed, the system accurately identified user postures, particularly using the **AccY** parameter, which showed strong statistical significance ($p < 0.001$) between standing and lying down. Drowsiness detection was successful in 85% of prolonged eye-closure cases. However, fall detection exhibited a false positive rate for abrupt movements, such as stumble while walking.

The independent samples Student's t-test confirmed that five out of six sensor parameters exhibited statistically significant differences between the standing and lying postures ($p < 0.05$). The only exception was **RotZ**, which showed no significant variation ($p = 0.617$). In addition, **entropy analysis** indicated that the lying posture generated higher data variability (mean entropy: 1.69) compared to the standing posture (*mean entropy*: 1.59). This increase in entropy suggests a greater degree of head movement freedom when lying down, reflecting increased postural unpredictability. In contrast, the standing posture demonstrated greater stability, with more consistent patterns.

The findings provide a solid foundation for using multiple sensor parameters in the automatic classification of body postures. Acceleration on the Y-axis (AccY) proved to be the most discriminative parameter, showing a significant difference between postures. This suggests that the proposed system is effective in detecting postural variations, particularly in dynamic and high-risk environments. Entropy analysis reinforces the idea that the lying posture involves greater postural variability, which may indicate an increased risk in terms of postural control. Conversely, the standing posture exhibited higher predictability, which may be advantageous for safety, as real-time posture monitoring can enable prompt intervention in hazardous situations.

Finally, compared to the studies by Campero-Jurado et al. [2] and Li et al. [7], the proposed solution offers a clear advantage by integrating various types of sensors (inertial, visual, environmental) along with a hybrid communication infrastructure (LoRa + Wi-Fi/WebSocket). Postural differences were detected more robustly, and latency was minimized through local data processing on the helmet, unlike centralized approaches that rely heavily on Wi-Fi connectivity and typically introduce higher delays.

5   Future Directions

Based on the results obtained, several improvements and expansions are planned to enhance the solution in future steps of development:

- Inclusion of Additional Postures: The analysis will be extended to include additional postures such as sitting, squatting, and other positions commonly encountered in industrial environments. This expansion will improve the system's classification accuracy across a wider range of body configurations.

– Industrial Validation: The system will be validated in actual industrial environments to test its resilience to electromagnetic interference (EMI) and its ability to operate with multiple devices in adverse conditions.
– Implementation of Alert and Fall Detection using AI: Future versions of the system will incorporate real-time alert and fall detection algorithms based on AI. These features will enhance emergency responsiveness and improve overall safety in high-risk work settings.

6   Conclusion

With the advancement of IoT and AI technologies, the development of intelligent systems to enhance safety in high-risk work environments has become increasingly viable. These technologies enable continuous monitoring of operational conditions and rapid response to hazardous situations, thereby reducing the risk of accidents and improving worker protection. Nonetheless, challenges remain in the literature, particularly regarding real-time connectivity and automated behavioral analysis for risk detection.

This study presents an integrated occupational safety solution based on IoT, consisting of a Monitoring Helmet and a Mobile Station for data reception and processing. The combination of technologies such as ESP-32, LoRa, Wi-Fi, and WebSocket enables efficient data transmission and continuous monitoring of workers' conditions, with particular emphasis on drowsiness detection and posture identification. Although the initial results are promising, this system version serves as a foundation for future enhancements, particularly through the integration of AI techniques for automated behavioral pattern analysis and anomaly detection. These advancements are expected to further enhance accident prevention capabilities and promote safer and smarter work environments.

Acknowledgment. The authors would like to thank the CNPq (N° 305946/2025-0 and N° 405940/2022-0) and CAPES (N° 88887.954253/2024-00 and N° 88887.972043/2024-00) of Brazil for the financial support.

References

1. Bavaresco, R., Arruda, H., Rocha, E., Barbosa, J., Li, G.P.: Internet of things and occupational well-being in industry 4.0: a systematic mapping study and taxonomy. Comput. Ind. Eng. **161**, 107670 (2021). https://doi.org/10.1016/j.cie.2021.107670. https://www.sciencedirect.com/science/article/pii/S036083522100574X
2. Campero-Jurado, I., et al.: Smart helmet 5.0 for industrial internet of things using artificial intelligence. Sensors **20**(21), 6241 (2020). https://doi.org/10.3390/s20216241
3. Gomes, R.L., Júnior, J.J., Abelém, A.G., Júnior, W.M.: QoE and QoS support on wireless mesh networks. In: Proceedings of the XV Brazilian Symposium on Multimedia and the Web. WebMedia 2009. Association for Computing Machinery, New York (2009). https://doi.org/10.1145/1858477.1858479

4. Gomes, R.L., Moreira, W.A., Ferreira, J.J.H., Abelém, A.J.G.: Providing QoE and QoS in wireless mesh networks through dynamic choice of routing metrics. IEEE Lat. Am. Trans. **8**(4), 454–462 (2010). https://doi.org/10.1109/TLA.2010.5595137

5. Jarota, M.: Artificial intelligence in the work process. A reflection on the proposed European Union regulations on artificial intelligence from an occupational health and safety perspective. Comput. Law Secur. Rev. **49**, 105825 (2023). https://doi.org/10.1016/j.clsr.2023.105825. https://www.sciencedirect.com/science/article/pii/S0267364923000601

6. Kanan, R., Elhassan, O., Bensalem, R.: An IoT-based autonomous system for workers' safety in construction sites with real-time alarming, monitoring, and positioning strategies. Autom. Constr. **88**, 73–86 (2018)

7. Li, Y., Wei, H., Han, Z., Huang, J., Wang, W.D.: Deep learning-based safety helmet detection in engineering management based on convolutional neural networks. Adv. Civil Eng. **2020**, 1–10 (2020). https://doi.org/10.1155/2020/9703560

8. Maia, E., Wannous, S., Dias, T., Praça, I., Faria, A.: Holistic security and safety for factories of the future. Sensors **22**(24), 9915 (2022)

9. Patel, V., Chesmore, A., Legner, C.M., Pandey, S.: Trends in workplace wearable technologies and connected-worker solutions for next-generation occupational safety, health, and productivity. Adv. Intell. Syst. **4**(1), 2100099 (2022)

10. Pimenta, I., Silva, D., Moura, E., Silveira, M., Gomes, R.L.: Impact of data anonymization in machine learning models. In: Proceedings of the 13th Latin-American Symposium on Dependable and Secure Computing, LADC 2024, pp. 188–191. Association for Computing Machinery, New York (2024). https://doi.org/10.1145/3697090.3699865

11. da Silva, M.D.V.D., Rocha, A., Gomes, R.L., Nogueira, M.: Lightweight data compression for low energy consumption in industrial internet of things. In: 2021 IEEE 18th Annual Consumer Communications & Networking Conference (CCNC), pp. 1–2 (2021). https://doi.org/10.1109/CCNC49032.2021.9369520

12. Smartlab: Frequência de notificações previdenciárias de acidentes (2024). https://smartlabbr.org/sst/localidade/0?dimensao=frequenciaAcidentes. Accessed 16 June 2025

13. Trajano, A.F., Andrade, P.C., Pimenta, I.A., Cavalcante, J., de Souza, J.N.: Delivering wifi connectivity to remote locations through lora mesh networking. In: NOMS 2022-2022 IEEE/IFIP Network Operations and Management Symposium, pp. 1–6. IEEE (2022)

Forecasting-Oriented Management of Software-Defined Fabric Environments

Ariel L. C. Portela, Maria C. M. M. Ferreira, and Rafael L. Gomes[✉]

State University of Ceará (UECE), Fortaleza, CE, Brazil
{ariel.portela,clara.mesquita}@aluno.uece.br, rafa.lopes@uece.br

Abstract. The growing adoption of programmable network architectures, such as ONF's SD-Fabric, has introduced new levels of flexibility, automation, and control into modern infrastructures. Leveraging P4-programmable data planes, centralized SDN control, and in-band telemetry, these architectures are well-suited to meet the stringent requirements of dynamic, cloud-native, and edge computing environments. However, ensuring service reliability, performance, and compliance with strict Service Level Agreements (SLAs) remains a complex challenge, particularly under high traffic dynamics and resource variability. Within this context, this paper presents a PhD research project that proposes a Forecasting-Oriented Management framework for SD-Fabric environments, combining in-band telemetry, AI-based forecasting, and a hierarchical distributed control strategy to anticipate and mitigate SLA violations. The solution proactively identifies network risks, such as failures, bottlenecks, and resource constraints, enabling intelligent decisions on traffic engineering and resource reallocation. Initial experiments, conducted in an emulated environment using P4-programmed switches and a simulated control layer, allowed comprehensive testing under varied traffic and failure scenarios. These preliminary results demonstrate the potential of the proposed approach to enhance SLA compliance and improve the resilience and efficiency of programmable network fabrics.

Keywords: P4 · Programmable Network · SLA Compliance

1 Introduction

In recent decades, reliance on communication networks to support critical societal activities has grown exponentially [7,12]. From banking systems and transportation networks to healthcare, manufacturing, and education infrastructures, connectivity has become essential for the operation of services that directly impact quality of life. This dependence underscores the need for more resilient networks, capable of operating with high availability and avoiding interruptions that could compromise these services [5,8].

Ariel L. C. Portela—PhD Candidate (1st Year) in Computer Science in UECE.

L. A. Rodrigues and R. Oliveira (Eds.): LADC 2025, CCIS 2697, pp. 342–352, 2026.
https://doi.org/10.1007/978-3-032-11539-3_21

However, the increasing complexity of modern networks has introduced new challenges. The adoption of technologies such as the Internet of Things (IoT), 5G networks, and cloud-native infrastructures has led to a massive volume of connected devices, generating heterogeneous and unpredictable data flows [2,16]. This scenario significantly increases the likelihood of network failures, which may result in service disruptions, financial losses, and negative impacts on user experience [9]. Common causes include traffic congestion, hardware failures, cyber-attacks, and configuration errors, as well as performance degradation due to bottlenecks in critical communication paths.

To address these challenges, recent advances in programmable networking, particularly the advent of Software-Defined Fabric (SD-Fabric) [13], offer a promising foundation. SD-Fabric, an open-source full-stack solution developed by the Open Networking Foundation (ONF), provides a programmable leaf-spine architecture that integrates P4-programmable switches, in-band telemetry (INT), and centralized control through ONOS and Stratum [3,18]. This architecture enables precise control over the data plane while supporting fine-grained, real-time monitoring, making it particularly suitable for critical, dynamic environments such as data centers, edge computing platforms, and 5G infrastructure.

This scenario is directly related to Software-Defined Networking (SDN), which remains a revolutionary model by separating the control and data planes, thus allowing centralized, dynamic, and policy-driven network management [6]. However, SD-Fabric extends this concept by embedding programmability and observability directly into the fabric of the network, enabling high-performance telemetry and control while preserving scalability and resilience. Even so, centralized control models still present challenges related to latency, scalability, and fault tolerance in large-scale environments. These issues are especially pronounced in time-sensitive systems such as smart factories, autonomous networks, and cyber-physical infrastructures [4].

The integration of in-band telemetry (INT) into SD-Fabric represents a significant step forward in monitoring capabilities. Unlike traditional methods, INT enables real-time capture of metrics such as delay, packet loss, queue depth, and path traversal by embedding them directly in transit packets. This continuous and low-latency visibility into the network state is fundamental for performance assurance, congestion avoidance, and anomaly detection. Moreover, the telemetry data produced by INT offers a rich basis for intelligent analytics, particularly when combined with machine learning techniques for network management.

Despite these advancements, leveraging INT for predictive failure detection and SLA assurance remains a relatively nascent field. The integration of AI-based forecasting mechanisms with data collected through programmable pipelines poses challenges in terms of model generalization, data distribution, and real-time inference [14,15]. However, it also unlocks new possibilities for developing autonomous, context-aware management strategies capable of anticipating risks and reallocating resources accordingly.

To further enhance agility and responsiveness, the adoption of hierarchical and distributed control architectures within SD-Fabric environments becomes essential. These architectures combine global oversight with localized decision-making, reducing control overhead, improving scalability, and accelerating responses to performance anomalies or threats.

Within this context, this paper describes a PhD project that proposes an integrated solution to address these gaps. Its objective is to develop an architecture that combines in-band telemetry, machine learning, and hierarchical distributed control to anticipate failures in programmable networks and enable proactive, context-sensitive decision-making. This approach seeks to reduce the impact of interruptions, ensure the continuity of critical applications, and optimize network resource usage. When embedded within a forecasting-oriented management framework, such architectural choices can significantly improve SLA compliance by enabling the network to self-adjust based on predicted failures, congestion trends, or resource shortages.

In addition, the same framework can be extended to the detection of performance bottlenecks and early threat identification, expanding its applicability beyond fault tolerance to encompass holistic network resilience. By combining the visibility provided by in-band telemetry, the programmability of P4-based data planes, and intelligent forecasting models under a distributed control strategy, this proposal aims to build a comprehensive solution for proactive and SLA-aware network management in SD-Fabric environments.

The remainder of this paper is organized as follows: Sect. 2 describes the related works. Section 3 presents the proposed solution, while Sect. 4 describes the results of the preliminary experiments carried out. Finally, Sect. 5 concludes the paper, presenting future research directions.

2   Related Work

This section summarizes related works that address network management solutions, highlighting the goals of these proposals in comparison to our proposal.

Borsatti et al. [1] propose a hierarchical and distributed approach to reliability management in 6G industrial networks, where collaboration between humans and robots demands highly reliable communication channels. The system divides the environment into subareas managed by distributed control elements, coordinated by a centralized component that dynamically adjusts redundancy allocation based on local criticality. Simulations demonstrate that it is possible to reduce resource consumption and response time without compromising required reliability levels.

Tang et al. [18] introduce Policy-Aware In-band Network Telemetry (PAINT), an approach that uses programmable in-band telemetry to locate failures in SDN networks. Network operators define and implement services via a high-level service provisioning language, allowing more precise and efficient fault identification. In the same way, Duan et al. [3] present MFGAD-INT, a method using graph deep learning with multi-feature fusion to process spatiotemporal correlations in telemetry data. Based on INT, the approach effectively identifies network anomalies, including microbursts and QoS deviations, enhancing anomaly detection accuracy in cloud data center networks.

Mayer et al. [10] proposed an experimental demonstration of a machine learning-based system to locate minor faults in optical networks controlled by SDN. The system uses streaming telemetry data collected via the gNMI protocol and artificial neural networks to locate failures, validated on an emulated NSFNet topology. Similarly, the authors in another study [11] explore a machine learning-based framework to locate minor faults using partial telemetry data in SDN environments. Their study shows that even with incomplete telemetry information, the proposed model can effectively identify and locate faults, improving network reliability.

Although several recent studies have explored the use of INT and machine learning for fault forecast and anomaly detection in programmable networks, significant gaps remain regarding realistic, large-scale, and heterogeneous environments, particularly those with stringent reliability requirements, such as industrial, edge, and carrier-grade applications.

3   Proposed Solution

This project proposes the development of a framework that integrates in-band telemetry, advanced machine learning algorithms, and hierarchical distributed control mechanisms to proactively and adaptively forecast failures, detect performance bottlenecks, and identify potential threats in programmable networks. The approach seeks to overcome the limitations of traditional monitoring and forecasting solutions, offering a robust and scalable system capable of dynamically adapting reliability levels based on network context. As illustrated in Fig. 1, the proposed framework has the following modules in their respective layers:

- Access Layer (SD-Fabric):
  - INT for Data Collector: Gathers and normalizes metadata embedded in packets (via INT), aggregating metrics like latency, loss, and queue depth, and so on, in real time.
  - Stratum Agent: Acts as the interface between P4 switches and the SDN control plane, facilitating rule deployment, telemetry access, and device configuration through standardized APIs (e.g., P4Runtime).
- Edge Layer:
  - Data Forecaster: Forecasting module using ML/DL models, trained on INT data to forecast failures or degradations.
  - SLA Monitor: Continuously checks compliance with SLA parameters, triggering mitigation actions when violations are anticipated.
  - Decision Agent: Makes autonomous decisions locally, based on real-time forecasts, following global policies set by the orchestrator.
- Cloud Layer:
  - Policy Orchestrator: Defines adaptive response policies (e.g., rerouting, load balancing, prioritization, and others) based on forecast risk and service criticality.
  - Model Trainer: Trains and updates forecasting and detection models using historical and recent data trends.

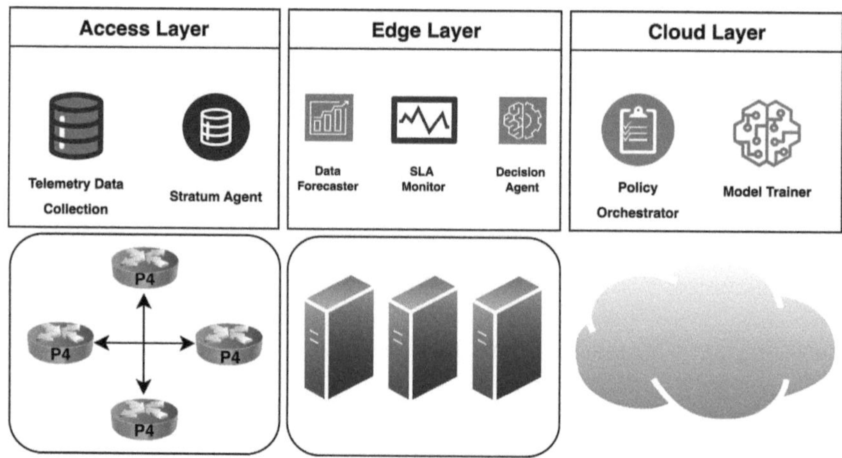

Fig. 1. Overview of the solution.

The access layer is the foundation of the architecture and consists of P4-enabled switches (such as Tofino, BMv2, or NetFPGA devices). These switches serve as the leaf nodes in the SD-Fabric topology, handling the actual forwarding of packets across the network. Their programmability is a critical feature, enabling the implementation of custom forwarding logic and telemetry mechanisms through P4 pipelines.

One of the most important capabilities at this layer is the use of INT. By embedding telemetry instructions directly into data plane operations, these switches can collect detailed, per-packet metrics such as latency, queue occupancy, packet loss, and timestamps (with minimal overhead and without the need for external monitoring probes). This real-time visibility is essential for detecting anomalies and supporting proactive network management.

To ensure smooth integration with higher layers, these programmable switches operate under the Stratum agent, which acts as a standardized abstraction layer. Through interfaces like P4Runtime (gRPC-based APIs), Stratum allows the SDN controller to configure and manage the data plane devices efficiently. This modular and programmable setup at the access layer is crucial for enabling fine-grained observability and control, which serve as the raw inputs for the AI-driven decision-making processes in the upper layers.

The edge layer serves as an intermediate intelligence tier within the architecture, designed to bring processing and decision-making closer to the data sources. It hosts local forecasting modules capable of performing low-latency inference, using real-time telemetry data received from the access layer. These forecasts enable quick reactions to emerging issues such as congestion, service degradation, or SLA violations. Thus, this layer acts as a mini-controller, embodying the principles of distributed control. Instead of relying solely on cloud-based decisions (which can introduce latency and increase bandwidth usage), edge components can take autonomous, near-instantaneous actions in response to local conditions. This enhances the resilience and responsiveness of the network, particularly in scenarios where milliseconds matter, such as in industrial automation, autonomous systems, or 5G edge applications. Additionally, the edge layer maintains synchronization with the cloud, regularly updating its models and receiving global policy adjustments. This bi-directional relationship ensures that local decisions remain aligned with broader SLA goals and network strategies, combining the best of both autonomy and coordination.

Finally, the cloud layer has the centralized control and orchestration hub of the SD-Fabric environment. One of the key roles of the cloud layer is to conduct large-scale data processing. It aggregates telemetry data collected over time and performs model training and validation for machine learning modules used in the edge. The availability of large historical datasets allows for the development of highly accurate forecasting models, capable of identifying subtle trends or early signs of degradation that would be difficult to detect with local data alone. Additionally, this layer is responsible for the definition and coordination of global policies. It sets adaptive reliability levels based on service context and criticality, distributing these configurations to the edge. This central coordination ensures a cohesive SLA enforcement strategy, allowing the system to maintain consistency while still embracing local adaptability.

3.1   In-Band Network Telemetry (INT)

The in-band telemetry implementation will use programmable switches configured with the P4 Behavioral Model (bmv2), enabling data packets to carry performance information directly within the data plane. P4 code will be developed to insert telemetry headers into packets in transit, storing relevant metrics such as ingress and egress delay at each switch, buffer utilization, number of lost packets, and timestamps. Each switch will capture these metrics in real-time, updating the packets at each hop. The SDN controller, based on open-source solutions, will coordinate the switches and define telemetry policies. At the end of the path, data will be extracted and stored in time series databases such as InfluxDB to support efficient and continuous analysis.

To ensure efficiency, telemetry will be activated only on selected flows, based on configurable criteria defined by the controller. Data will be collected at scheduled intervals to balance precision and performance. The collected metrics will be made available in real-time to the machine learning modules, which will be responsible for analysis, failure forecasting, bottleneck detection, and threat identification. This integrated flow will provide a continuous view of network behavior, enabling rapid and context-aware decisions.

3.2   Data Forecasting

The data forecasting process will be based on the data collected, which will build a time series of each type of data collected (such as latency, loss, queue depth, etc.). A time series is a sequence of data points collected at consistent, evenly spaced time intervals in chronological order. The forecasting task consists of building a model capable of forecasting future values based on patterns and dependencies identified in historical observations. Additionally, our solution utilizes the Seasonal-Trend Decomposition using LOESS (STL) to separate a time series into its seasonal, trend, and residual components. This robust approach enhances resistance to outliers, improving the reliability of the decomposition. By uncovering the underlying structure of the data, STL provides deeper insight into patterns and trends, which supports more accurate forecasting and facilitates the detection of potential anomalies or irregularities.

After the time series processing, several models may be used in time series forecasting, such as ARIMA, Holt-Winters, and Neural Network Autoregression (NNAR). However, in this PhD project, we considered LSTM and GRU [17]. LSTM is a more complex architecture compared to GRU and may offer superior performance on certain tasks, particularly those involving long-term dependencies. In contrast, GRU is simpler and faster, making it well-suited for smaller datasets or less complex problems. Ultimately, the choice between the two models should be guided by the specific requirements of the application and the characteristics of the time series under analysis.

4   Preliminary Results

This section presents the preliminary experiments done to evaluate the performance of the proposed solution in the forecast of network data and the capacity to perform data collection in programmable networks. Section 4.1 describes the experiments related to data collection, while Sect. 4.2 shows the forecasting results obtained from the experiments using real network measurements.

4.1   Data Collection in Programmable Networks

In our initial experiments, we employed Mininet-WiFi to emulate a 4-switch mesh network topology interconnected with 4 hosts, forming a representative multi-hop SDN scenario. This topology was chosen for its ability to emulate a diverse and realistic traffic environment, including redundant paths, cross-traffic, and variable congestion patterns, which are commonly observed in modern programmable networks. By generating traffic across multiple paths and monitoring real-time performance metrics at each switch (e.g., throughput, packet rate), we aim to create a comprehensive dataset reflecting realistic operational contexts. Although throughput forecasting has not yet been fully integrated into the system, this setup lays the foundation for future data collection and analysis. It provides a controlled and extensible environment to support the development and validation of predictive models in scenarios with realistic spatial and temporal network behaviors.

Figure 2 presents the packet measurements collected from each switch interface during the experimental period. The data reveals significant temporal variations in network activity, with packet rates ranging from near-zero to peaks

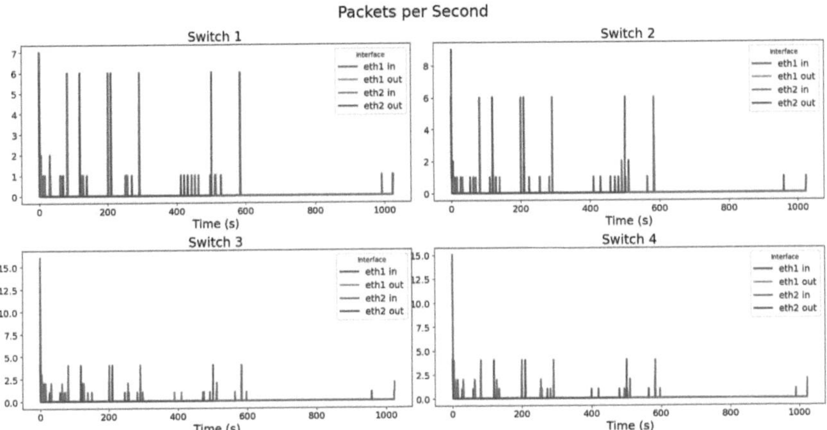

Fig. 2. Packet measurements collected from each switch interface.

of approximately 15 packets per second on Switch 3. The traffic patterns show characteristic burst behavior typical of real network scenarios, with periods of high activity followed by relative quiescence. Switch 1 and Switch 2 exhibited more moderate traffic levels (0–7 packets/second), while Switches 3 and 4 demonstrated higher variability in their traffic patterns.

4.2   Network Data Forecasting

To evaluate the feasibility of real-time network performance forecasting, we implemented and compared LSTM and GRU using the collected network data. The models were trained to forecast future throughput values based on historical traffic patterns. The results presented stem from experiments conducted using data from RNP's MonIPÊ monitoring service[1], which follows the international monitoring standard perfSONAR. In particular, we used network throughput information measured every four hours between specific links within the RNP backbone network.

Figure 3 illustrates the Root Mean Square Error (RMSE) comparison between LSTM and GRU models across different communication points in the network topology. The results demonstrate remarkably similar performance between both architectures, with RMSE values ranging from approximately 1.05×10^9 depending on the specific network segment analyzed. Both models achieved their best prediction accuracy on communication points with more stable traffic patterns, showing RMSE values below 0.15×10^9. The highest prediction errors occurred for points with highly variable traffic characteristics, where RMSE reached approximately 1.05×10^9. This suggests that traffic predictability varies significantly across different network segments and congestion control algorithms.

---

[1] www.rnp.br/en/ipe-network.

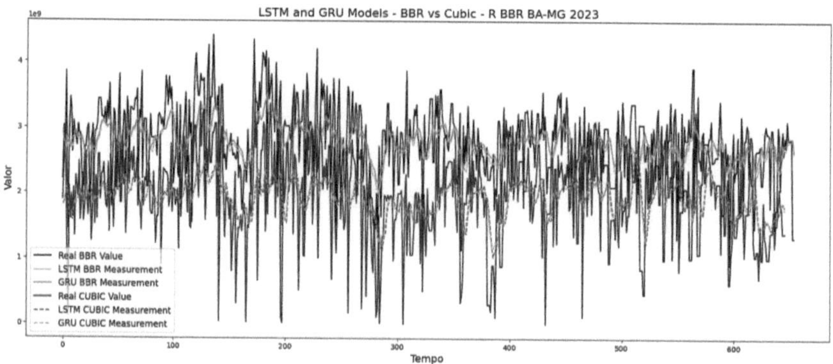

Fig. 3. Forecasting Network Data.

The comparable performance between LSTM and GRU models indicates that the simpler GRU architecture could be preferred for real-time P4-based implementations due to its lower computational complexity while maintaining prediction accuracy. These preliminary results support the feasibility of integrating machine learning-based traffic forecasting into programmable data plane switches for proactive network management and quality of service optimization.

These initial findings demonstrate the potential for implementing intelligent traffic prediction directly within P4-programmable switches. The observed traffic patterns and prediction accuracies provide a foundation for developing real-time network performance forecasting.

5   Future Research Directions

This paper presents the initial stage of an ongoing PhD research project aimed at developing intelligent, forecasting-oriented mechanisms for proactive management of programmable network fabrics. Building upon the preliminary results, several research directions have been identified to further advance the solution and address key challenges in the field:

- Execution of Lightweight Forecasting Models within the Data Plane: Inspired by emerging trends in in-network computing, future work will explore the implementation of lightweight ML models directly in the P4-programmable data plane. The goal is to enable first-stage inferences for failure prediction or anomaly detection without requiring full telemetry export to the control or edge layers. This approach will be evaluated with reference to recent efforts such as NetWasm and P4-ML [3, 18].
- Integration with Intent-Based Networking (IBN) and SLA-Aware Orchestration: The proposed framework will be extended to integrate with IBN platforms, enabling intent-based orchestration and automatic adjustments triggered by forecasted SLA violations, aligning with the vision of autonomous networks.

– Dynamic Model Adaptation via Continual Learning: To maintain forecasting accuracy over time, especially in dynamic traffic scenarios, we plan to explore online and continual learning techniques to incrementally update the ML models at the edge and cloud layers. This will reduce model drift and allow the system to adapt to new patterns, anomalies, or traffic shifts without retraining from scratch.

These research directions reinforce the project's contribution to proactive and SLA-driven network management in programmable environments. By combining distributed intelligence, in-network processing, and real-time forecasting, the framework aims to advance the resilience, scalability, and autonomy of next-generation communication infrastructures.

Acknowledgment. The authors would like to thank the CNPq (N° 305946/2025-0 and N° 405940/2022-0) and CAPES (N° 88887.954253/2024-00 and N° 88887.972043/2024-00) of Brazil for the financial support.

References

1. Borsatti, D., et al.: Hierarchical management algorithms for highly reliable communication in 6g industrial environments. IEEE Netw. Lett. **6**(1), 36–40 (2023)
2. Chauhan, P., Atulkar, M.: A framework for DDOS attack detection in SDN-based IoT using hybrid classifier. In: Machine Learning, Image Processing, Network Security and Data Sciences, pp. 889–900. Springer, Cham (2023)
3. Duan, Y., et al.: Mfgad-int: in-band network telemetry data-driven anomaly detection using multi-feature fusion graph deep learning. J. Cloud Comput. **12**(1), 126 (2023)
4. Ferreira, M.C., Ribeiro, S.E., Nobre, F.V., Linhares, M.L., Araújo, T.P., Gomes, R.L.: Mitigating measurement failures in throughput performance forecasting. In: 2024 20th International Conference on Network and Service Management (CNSM), pp. 1–7 (2024). https://doi.org/10.23919/CNSM62983.2024.10814394
5. Gomes, R.L., Bittencourt, L.F., Madeira, E.R.M.: A virtual network allocation algorithm for reliability negotiation. In: 2013 22nd International Conference on Computer Communication and Networks (ICCCN), pp. 1–7 (2013). https://doi.org/10.1109/ICCCN.2013.6614097
6. Gomes, R.L., da Ponte, F.R.P., Urbano, A.C., Bittencourt, L.F., Madeira, E.R.M.: Strategies for daytime slicing in future internet service providers. Trans. Emerg. Telecommun. Technol. **31**(1), e3727 (2020). https://doi.org/10.1002/ett.3727
7. Gomes, R.L., Júnior, J.J., Abelém, A.G., Júnior, W.M.: Qoe and qos support on wireless mesh networks. In: Proceedings of the XV Brazilian Symposium on Multimedia and the Web. WebMedia 2009, Association for Computing Machinery, New York, NY, USA (2009). https://doi.org/10.1145/1858477.1858479
8. Gomes, R.L., Moreira, W.A., Ferreira, J.J.H., Abelém, A.J.G.: Providing qoe and qos in wireless mesh networks through dynamic choice of routing metrics. IEEE Lat. Am. Trans. **8**(4), 454–462 (2010). https://doi.org/10.1109/TLA.2010.5595137
9. Lopes Gomes, R., Roberto Mauro Madeira, E.: A traffic classification agent for virtual networks based on qos classes. IEEE Lat. Am. Trans. **10**(3), 1734–1741 (2012). https://doi.org/10.1109/TLA.2012.6222579

10. Mayer, K.S., et al.: Demonstration of ml-assisted soft-failure localization based on network digital twins. J. Lightwave Technol. **40**(14), 4514–4520 (2022)

11. Mayer, K.S., Soares, J.A., Pinto, R.P., Rothenberg, C.E., Arantes, D.S., Mello, D.A.: Ml-based soft-failure localization with partial SDN telemetry (2021)

12. Nobre, F.V.J., Silva, D.D.S., Ferreira, M.C.M.M., Brito, M.L.M.L., de Araújo, T.P., Gomes, R.L.: Time-weighted correlation approach to identify high delay links in internet service providers. J. Internet Serv. Appl. **16**(1), 419–430 (2025). https://doi.org/10.5753/jisa.2025.5218

13. Osiński, T., Palimąka, J., Kossakowski, M., Tran, F.D., Bonfoh, E.F., Tarasiuk, H.: A novel programmable software datapath for software-defined networking. In: Proceedings of the 18th International Conference on Emerging Networking EXperiments and Technologies, pp. 245–260. CoNEXT '22, Association for Computing Machinery, New York, NY, USA (2022). https://doi.org/10.1145/3555050.3569117

14. Pimenta, I., Silva, D., Moura, E., Silveira, M., Gomes, R.L.: Impact of data anonymization in machine learning models. In: Proceedings of the 13th Latin-American Symposium on Dependable and Secure Computing, pp. 188–191. LADC '24, Association for Computing Machinery, New York, NY, USA (2024). https://doi.org/10.1145/3697090.3699865

15. Portela, A., Linhares, M.M., Nobre, F.V.J., Menezes, R., Mesquita, M., Gomes, R.L.: The role of TCP congestion control in the throughput forecasting. In: Proceedings of the 13th Latin-American Symposium on Dependable and Secure Computing, pp. 196–199. LADC '24, Association for Computing Machinery, New York, NY, USA (2024). https://doi.org/10.1145/3697090.3699869

16. da Silva, M.D.V.D., Rocha, A., Gomes, R.L., Nogueira, M.: Lightweight data compression for low energy consumption in industrial internet of things. In: 2021 IEEE 18th Annual Consumer Communications & Networking Conference (CCNC), pp. 1–2 (2021). https://doi.org/10.1109/CCNC49032.2021.9369520

17. Sone, S.P., Lehtomäki, J.J., Khan, Z.: Wireless traffic usage forecasting using real enterprise network data: analysis and methods. IEEE Open J. Commun. Soc. **1**, 777–797 (2020). https://doi.org/10.1109/OJCOMS.2020.3000059

18. Tang, Y., Wu, Y., Cheng, G., Xu, Z.: Intelligence enabled SDN fault localization via programmable in-band network telemetry. In: 2019 IEEE 20th International Conference on High Performance Switching and Routing (HPSR), pp. 1–6. IEEE (2019)

Service Level Agreements Compliance in 5G Network Slicing: An Analysis of Resource Allocation Strategies

Wanderson L. Costa and Rafael L. Gomes^(⊠)

State University of Ceará (UECE), Fortaleza, CE, Brazil
wanderson.leonardo@aluno.uece.br, rafa.lopes@uece.br

Abstract. 5G networks are designed to support a wide range of applications and services with heterogeneous performance requirements, where Network Slicing enables the creation of logically isolated slices to meet specific Service Level Agreements (SLAs). Resource allocation strategies ensure that the network dynamically and intelligently provisions bandwidth, computing, and storage resources to each slice based on its SLA constraints. However, there is an existing gap in the literature regarding the systematic and comparative evaluation of the performance implications of resource allocation strategies. Within this context, this paper presents a comprehensive and comparative evaluation of SLA compliance for service delivery slices in 5G networks, from the perspective of resource allocation strategies. Results of the experiments performed, using TCP and UDP traffic and KPI collection, show how different policies affect SLA compliance in terms of throughput, delay, and jitter, highlighting the trade-offs between priority, fairness, and spectral efficiency.

Keywords: Network Slicing · SLA · QoS · 5G · Resource allocation

1 Introduction

The evolution toward fifth-generation (5G) networks and the vision of beyond 5G (B5G) architectures promise to revolutionize connectivity, supporting a wide range of applications and services with drastically heterogeneous performance requirements [12]. From enhanced Mobile Broadband (eMBB) communications, which demand high throughput, to Ultra-Reliable Low-Latency Communications (URLLC), essential for critical applications such as healthcare and industrial automation, and massive Machine-Type Communications (mMTC), aimed at connecting billions of IoT devices, 5G networks must be inherently flexible and adaptable [5]. To accommodate this diversity over a shared physical infrastructure, the concept of Network Slicing has become a fundamental pillar of the 5G architecture [3].

W. L. Costa—PhD Candidate (2nd Year) in Computer Science in UECE.

© The Author(s), under exclusive license to Springer Nature Switzerland AG 2026
L. A. Rodrigues and R. Oliveira (Eds.): LADC 2025, CCIS 2697, pp. 353–363, 2026.
https://doi.org/10.1007/978-3-032-11539-3_22

Network Slicing enables the creation of multiple isolated and customized logical networks, where each slice is configured to meet the specific Service Level Agreements (SLAs) of a given service type or vertical. Ensuring Quality of Service (QoS) for these different slices in terms of throughput, delay, and jitter is a complex and critical challenge for the successful deployment of 5G [4]. For instance, healthcare services such as emergency telemedicine require strict QoS guarantees, including high data rates and ultra-low latencies for real-time video transmission [6,7].

Recent research on Network Slicing has predominantly focused on the development of dynamic and intelligent resource allocation strategies, often leveraging Artificial Intelligence (AI) and Machine Learning (ML) techniques [3,8,11,12]. Solutions based on Open Radio Access Network (O-RAN), for example, employ RAN Intelligent Controllers (RICs) and xApps to optimize RAN resource allocation in near real-time, aiming for adaptability and efficiency in the face of traffic demand fluctuations. Works such as references [10,14] demonstrate the potential of Deep Reinforcement Learning (DRL) for QoS-aware resource allocation and variable SLA assurance, optimizing performance and resource utilization in O-RAN environments. Similarly, Yeh et al. [18] also propose Deep Learning-based solutions for RAN slicing, targeting intelligent automation.

However, amid the race for dynamic and autonomous solutions, there is an existing gap in the literature regarding the systematic and comparative evaluation of the performance implications of resource allocation policies for SLA fulfillment in Network Slicing. Although studies such as Abbas et al. [1] point out that manual static resource allocation in the RAN is not the optimal approach, a quantitative understanding of how fixed parameters (such as bandwidth, channel width, and numerology) directly impact QoS metrics for different slice types is essential. This foundational analysis serves as a critical performance baseline for quantifying the real gains and complexity introduced by more sophisticated allocation schemes and for validating the suitability of simulation tools for such detailed evaluations.

Within this context, this paper presents a comprehensive and comparative evaluation of SLA compliance for eMBB, URLLC, and mMTC slices in 5G networks, from the perspective of static resource allocation strategies. Using the Network Simulator 3 (NS-3) platform integrated with the 5G-LENA module, we investigate the direct impact of bandwidth allocation, channel width, and numerology allocation policies on key metrics (such as throughput, delay, and jitter) and, consequently, the impact on the SLA. By focusing on resource allocations, the work aims to establish a rigorous performance baseline that complements existing studies focused on dynamism. Furthermore, this research validates and extends the use of NS-3 with 5G-LENA for in-depth analysis of 5G network slicing scenarios, offering practical insights into fundamental slice-level design trade-offs, including the mMTC slice, which is often underexplored in quantitative detail by studies focused on dynamic allocation.

The main contributions of this paper are: (i) an evaluation of SLA compliance across eMBB, URLLC, and mMTC slices in 5G networks under distinct resource allocation policies; (ii) the design and implementation of a reproducible simulation framework, enabling controlled experiments on bandwidth distribution, numerology, and channel width; (iii) the quantitative assessment of how allocation strategies impact throughput, delay, and jitter for each slice type, highlighting key trade-offs between priority, fairness, and spectral efficiency; and (iv) the validation of slicing configurations as a performance baseline for future studies focused on dynamic and AI-driven resource management in Open RAN-based architectures.

The remainder of this paper is organized as follows: Sect. 2 presents a review of related work, highlighting existing approaches and the gap addressed by our research. Section 3 describes the simulation methodology, including the network architecture, configuration parameters, and allocation policies. Section 4 presents and discusses the results obtained. Finally, Sect. 5 suggests directions for future research.

2   Related Work

The proliferation of applications and services in 5G networks has highlighted Network Slicing as a central technology to meet heterogeneous performance requirements, such as throughput, delay, and jitter [2,10,13,17].

The ability of Network Slicing to provision multiple isolated logical networks over a shared physical infrastructure allows for service customization tailored to specific use cases, such as eMBB, URLLC, and mMTC [1,13,16]. Many works have focused on ensuring QoS and meeting SLAs for different slice types. Wang et al. [17], for example, presented the SliceNet framework to enable network slicing with QoS requirements in 5G networks, focusing on media use cases for emergency services (eHealth). Their work experimentally validated end-to-end QoS guarantees, such as throughput of 10 Mbps or higher and latency of up to 30 ms, using a low-latency MEC platform and a programmable data plane with hardware acceleration [17]. Marinova and Leon-Garcia [9], in more recent research, explore the O-RAN architecture and its RICs to optimize RAN performance and ensure slice SLAs, including data rate and latency requirements. They highlight the importance of optimizing the resource allocation of the Network Slice Subnet Instance (NSSI) based on historical data and ML models [9].

However, a predominant trend in recent research has been the exploration of dynamic and intelligent resource allocation strategies, often based on Artificial Intelligence (AI) and Machine Learning (ML). Cheng et al. [2] developed ORANSlice, an open-source 5G network slicing platform for O-RAN, which features programmable RAN slicing compliant with 3GPP and scheduling capabilities. They use xApps in the Near-RT RIC to control and optimize RAN slicing, validating their approach in O-RAN testbeds for use cases such as slice prioritization and minimum radio resource guarantees [2]. Similarly, Yeh et al. [18] focus on RAN intelligence, introducing a Deep Learning (DL)-based solution for RAN network slicing aimed at dynamically ensuring SLAs. They implemented intelligent radio resource management algorithms as O-RAN-compliant xApps, using

DL for traffic load prediction and radio resource planning [18]. Raftopoulos et al. [14] further this line by proposing a new DRL agent design for O-RAN applications, capable of learning control policies under variable SLAs with heterogeneous minimum performance requirements, focusing on latency and minimizing SLA violation rates [14]. Mhatre et al. [10] also introduce a DRL strategy for QoS-aware intra-slice resource allocation in B5G-based O-RAN architectures, optimizing for eMBB and URLLC slices. Their approach demonstrates significant improvements in eMBB throughput and URLLC latency reduction, employing intelligent agents to learn the importance of user association parameters [10].

In contrast to the prevailing emphasis on dynamic and AI-driven allocation, the present study aims to fill a fundamental gap by systematically evaluating and comparing SLA compliance of eMBB, URLLC, and mMTC slices using static resource allocation policies. By employing the NS-3 simulation platform equipped with the 5G-LENA module, this study provides a controlled and reproducible analysis of the impact of fundamental parameters such as bandwidth, channel width, and numerology on slice throughput, delay, and jitter. While works such as Mhatre et al. [10] explore dynamic intra-slice resource allocation and user association parameterization with DRL, our focus is on providing a quantitative understanding of the performance implications of static slice-level configurations, including the mMTC slice, which often receives less detailed attention compared to eMBB and URLLC in dynamic allocation studies.

In this way, our research complements existing studies by establishing an essential baseline for evaluating the performance of static allocations. This is crucial for quantifying the actual benefits and added complexity introduced by dynamic and AI-based resource allocation schemes. Furthermore, by employing NS-3 with 5G-LENA, we validate the capability of this specific simulation tool for detailed and comparative analysis of 5G slicing strategies, an aspect that is not the main focus in most related works relying on other testbeds or simulators.

3   Methodology

The performance evaluation of the slices was carried out through computer simulations using the NS-3 simulator (version 3.42) in conjunction with the 5G-LENA module (version v3.3.y), developed by CTTC. The modeled scenario represents a 5G topology with logical slicing, as illustrated in Fig. 1, in which three distinct types of services are simulated in an isolated and controlled manner: eMBB, URLLC, and mMTC.

The configuration of the parameters in Table 1 was defined to represent a controlled, reproducible scenario aligned with the typical requirements of each slice type. The use of a single gNB and three UEs per slice simplifies the topology and facilitates isolated analysis of the effects of resource allocation. The traffic models reflect expected behavior: continuous traffic for eMBB (TCP), small and frequent transmissions for URLLC (UDP every 1 ms), and sporadic low-rate traffic for mMTC (UDP every 100 ms).

The use of Round Robin scheduling and fixed MCS (256-QAM) ensures predictability, while the RMa LoS channel model and ideal beamforming avoid

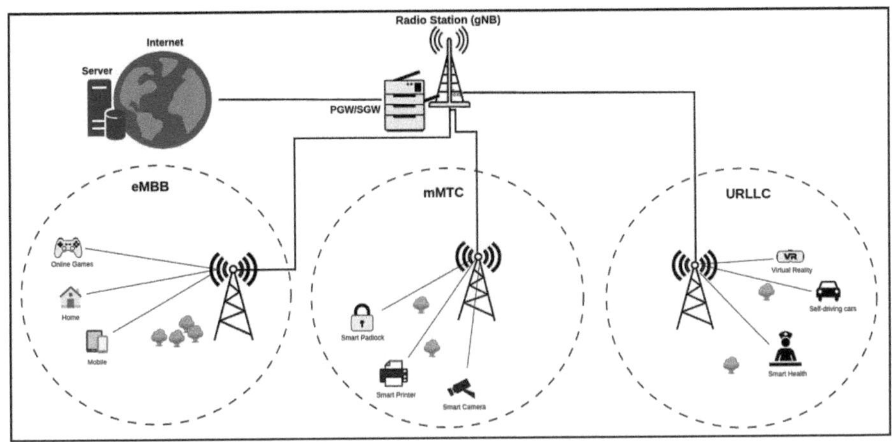

Fig. 1. Slicing scenario.

external variability. FlowMonitor was configured with 1 ms resolution to accurately capture delay and jitter indicators. This configuration ensures the validity of the results obtained for evaluating the allocation policies.

Table 1. Main simulation parameters

Parameter	Value
Simulation duration	10 s
Number of gNBs	1
UEs per slice	3
Traffic model for eMBB	TCP (BulkSend)
Traffic model for URLLC	UDP (1 ms, 100 bytes)
Traffic model for mMTC	UDP (100 ms, 50 bytes)
Scheduler	OFDMA Round Robin
MCS	Fixed (MCS 28, 256-QAM)
Beamforming	Directional (IdealBeamforming)
Channel model	3GPP RMa LoS (no shadowing)
Monitoring	FlowMonitor (DelayBin = JitterBin = 1 ms)

Regarding slice configuration, each slice was associated with a BWP configured with distinct bandwidth and frequency, as defined by the allocation policy under evaluation. The four tested policies were:

- Policy A: Priority to URLLC: 50 MHz (URLLC), 30 MHz (eMBB), 20 MHz (mMTC).

– Policy B: Equal allocation with 30 MHz for all.
– Policy C: Priority to eMBB: 50 MHz (eMBB), 20 MHz (URLLC), 10 MHz (mMTC).
– Policy D: Equal allocation with 20 MHz for all.

These configurations were applied using the `OperationBandConf` class, by initializing three operational bands in the `NrHelper` object. The association of UEs to the nearest gNB was performed automatically using the `AttachToClosestGnb` function, and each slice was assigned a dedicated bearer with a TFT (Traffic Flow Template) configured for port-based differentiation.

Finally, performance metrics were collected using the `FlowMonitor` module, configured with a temporal resolution of 1 ms. The main metrics analyzed for each slice were: Throughput (Mbps), which is the average data reception rate; Delay (seconds), which is the average packet delivery delay; and Jitter (seconds), which is the variation in delay between consecutive packets.

The metrics were automatically exported to CSV files, named according to the policy identifier (`simTag`), facilitating subsequent analysis using external tools. The code was designed to enable replication of tests with different parameters through the `CommandLine` interface.

4   Experiments

4.1   Results

This section presents the results obtained from experiments using the four resource allocation policies. The analyzed metrics include *throughput* (Mbps), average *delay* (seconds), and average *jitter* (seconds), collected for each slice (eMBB, URLLC, and mMTC) using the NS-3 `FlowMonitor` module. The values were automatically exported to CSV files and visualized graphically to facilitate comparison (Table 2).

Table 2. Comparison of Throughput, Delay, and Jitter by Slice and Policy

Metric	Slice	Policy A	Policy B	Policy C	Policy D
Throughput (Mbps)	URLLC	1.0234	1.0234	1.0234	1.0234
	eMBB	19.1619	19.1619	21.4297	17.4682
	mMTC	0.0063	0.0063	0.0063	0.0063
Delay (s)	URLLC	0.0072	0.0072	0.0072	0.0072
	eMBB	0.0114	0.0114	0.0108	0.0120
	mMTC	0.0090	0.0090	0.0090	0.0090
Jitter (s)	URLLC	0.0008	0.0008	0.0008	0.0008
	eMBB	0.0000	0.0000	0.0000	0.0001
	mMTC	0.0000	0.0000	0.0000	0.0000

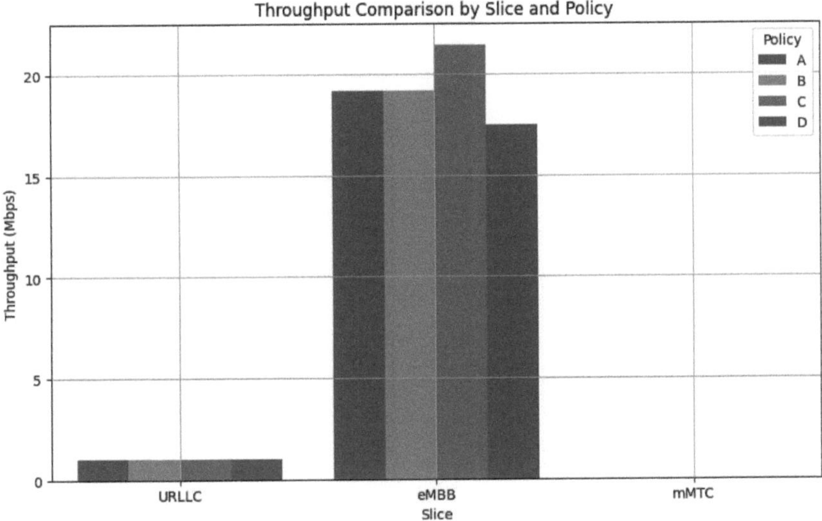

Fig. 2. Throughput Comparison by Slice and Policy.

Figure 2 shows that the eMBB slice achieved the highest throughput among the three slices. In Policy C, eMBB reached its maximum performance due to the larger bandwidth allocation (50 MHz), while the other slices (particularly mMTC) showed very low throughput values.

In Policy B, which distributes resources equally among the slices, a more balanced performance was observed, although eMBB maintained an advantage due to the nature of its traffic (TCP with high bandwidth usage). Policy D, with an equal 20 MHz allocation, resulted in an overall degradation of throughput, especially for eMBB.

Figure 3 presents the average delay observed per slice. As expected, the URLLC slice maintained the lowest delay across all policies, with Policy A standing out for its ideal performance (lowest delay) due to its priority bandwidth allocation. The eMBB slice exhibited slightly higher delay values, consistent with the use of TCP. Despite its light traffic load, the mMTC slice also showed acceptable delay performance, with a noticeable increase only in Policies C and D, where its bandwidth was more limited.

In Fig. 4, the jitter values show a trend similar to the delay. The URLLC slice again delivered the best performance. The jitter of the eMBB slice remained stable and low across all policies, demonstrating good predictability even under different bandwidth configurations. On the other hand, the mMTC slice showed more sensitivity to variation, indicating that slices with very limited bandwidth tend to suffer from greater instability, even with sparse traffic.

This experiment highlights the trade-offs between priority, fairness, and spectral efficiency. As future work, we propose the adoption of dynamic strategies based on network demand and behavior, as well as the integration of intelli-

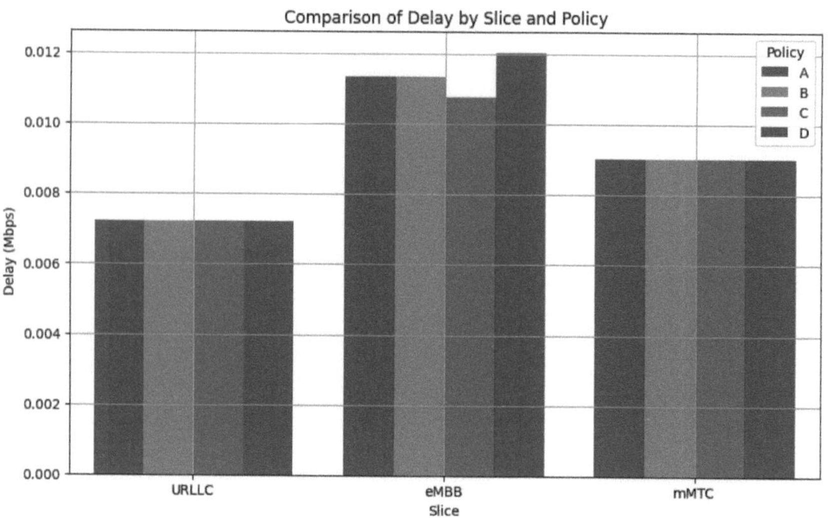

Fig. 3. Delay Comparison by Slice and Policy.

gent orchestrators in the context of *Open RAN*, capable of adapting resource allocations in real time.

4.2 Final Discussion

The results demonstrated that the bandwidth distribution among slices has a direct impact on the performance of each service. Quantitatively, it was observed that Policy C, which prioritized eMBB with 50 MHz, led to an approximate 11.8% increase in throughput for that slice compared to Policy D (21.43 Mbps vs. 17.46 Mbps), while the throughput for URLLC and mMTC remained constant. However, this prioritization resulted in a slight increase in delay for mMTC.

Policy A, which favored URLLC, ensured the lowest observed delay for that slice (0.0072 s), while maintaining jitter stability (0.0008 s), but reduced the throughput for eMBB by approximately 10.6% compared to Policy C. Policy B, with an equal allocation of 30 MHz for all slices, provided a balanced bandwidth distribution and good overall performance, though it did not optimize any specific slice. Policy D, with an equal allocation of only 20 MHz, resulted in the lowest overall efficiency, especially for eMBB, which experienced up to 18.4% reduction in throughput compared to Policy C.

Moreover, delay and jitter values remained stable for URLLC across all policies, indicating that the adopted slicing architecture is capable of ensuring ultra-low latency even under moderate bandwidth variations (a positive indicator for mission-critical services). However, the mMTC slice showed consistently low throughput across all scenarios (±0.0063 Mbps), highlighting the need for adaptive strategies in large-scale, low-data-rate deployments.

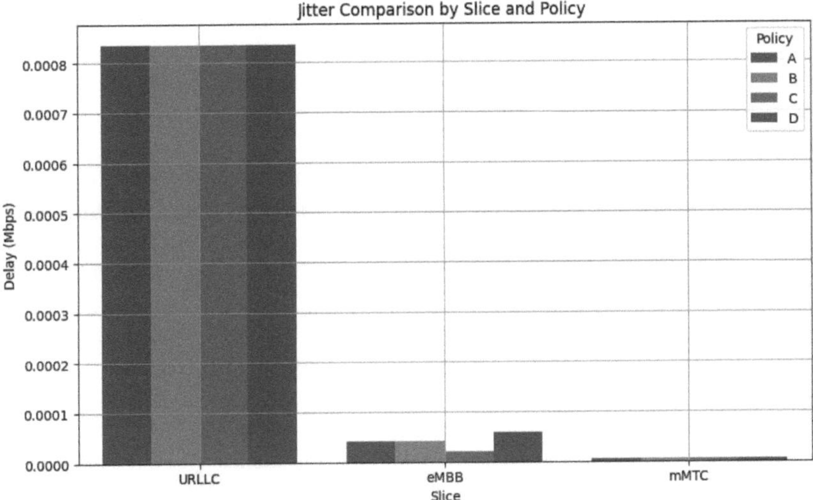

Fig. 4. Jitter Comparison by Slice and Policy.

With the evolution of infrastructure and the advancement of open architectures, it is expected that data-driven and automated approaches will play a central role in ensuring quality of service in next-generation mobile networks. The experiments and findings documented here provide a solid quantitative baseline for this transition, serving as a reference for the development of more sophisticated, dynamic, and context-aware allocation policies.

The results demonstrated that bandwidth allocation plays a decisive role in balancing efficiency and compliance, with trade-offs emerging between prioritizing individual slice performance and ensuring fairness. This analysis supports future exploration into dynamic, context-aware strategies, offering a solid reference for the design and optimization of next-generation network slicing solutions.

5   Future Research Directions

This study represents an initial stage of an ongoing PhD research project whose central objective is the development of intelligent mechanisms for resource management and SLA enforcement in 5G networks and future Open RAN-based architectures. Based on the results obtained, several research directions have been identified as continuations of this work:

– Exploration of dynamic allocation policies: Given the limitations observed in static policies, future work will explore adaptive dynamic strategies based on traffic behavior and real-time SLA violations. This line follows approaches such as those proposed by Raftopoulos et al. [14] and Mhatre et al. [10], who advocate the use of reinforcement learning for continuous resource allocation optimization.

- Integration with xApps and intelligent controllers: In line with the trend presented by Chen et al. [2] and Yeh et al. [18], this work intends to develop xApps embedded in the Near-RT RIC controller for slicing decision-making based on heuristics, fuzzy logic, and machine learning. This will enable rapid reactions to network changes and improved SLA compliance.
- Modeling of the Open RAN architecture: Inspired by the principles discussed by Rost et al. [15] and the functional split in RAN design, future steps will include modeling the explicit separation of RU, DU, and CU units. This will allow for the evaluation of slicing behavior in a modular architecture aligned with Open RAN.
- Mobility and handover evaluation: Following the experimental approach of Wang et al. [17], upcoming simulation scenarios will introduce user mobility and handover events between cells, enabling analysis of how slicing policies perform under more realistic user movement conditions.
- Expansion of analyzed Key Performance Indicators (KPIs): Following the perspectives of Abbas et al. [1] and Rafique et al. [13], the set of performance indicators will be expanded to include spectral efficiency, packet loss rate, energy consumption, and fairness index. This will allow for a more comprehensive assessment of slice behavior.
- Coordinated and Intelligent Orchestration of Multi-Domain Slices in B5G/6G Scenarios via O-RAN: This future work aims to deepen the research on coordinated resource orchestration across multiple domains, including the RAN, Transport Network, and Core Network, and using the O-RAN architecture in B5G and 6G scenarios [9].

These research directions reaffirm the project's commitment to advancing the state of the art in mobile network slicing, promoting solutions aligned with the principles of distributed intelligence, adaptability, and openness as advocated by the Open RAN architecture.

Acknowledgment. The authors would like to thank the CNPq (N° 305946/2025-0 and N° 405940/2022-0) and CAPES (N° 88887.954253/2024-00 and N° 88887.972043/2024-00) of Brazil for the financial support.

References

1. Abbas, K., Khan, T.A., Afaq, M., Song, W.C.: Network slice lifecycle management for 5g mobile networks: an intent-based networking approach. In: IEEE (2021)
2. Cheng, H., et al.: Oranslice: an open-source 5g network slicing platform for o-ran. In: Proceedings of the 30th Annual International Conference on Mobile Computing and Networking (MobiCom 2024), pp. 1–6. ACM, New York (2024)
3. Ferreira, M.C., Ribeiro, S.E., Nobre, F.V., Linhares, M.L., Araújo, T.P., Gomes, R.L.: Mitigating measurement failures in throughput performance forecasting. In: 2024 20th International Conference on Network and Service Management (CNSM), pp. 1–7 (2024). https://doi.org/10.23919/CNSM62983.2024.10814394

4. Gomes, R.L., Bittencourt, L.F., Madeira, E.R.M.: A virtual network allocation algorithm for reliability negotiation. In: 2013 22nd International Conference on Computer Communication and Networks (ICCCN), pp. 1–7 (2013). https://doi.org/10.1109/ICCCN.2013.6614097

5. Gomes, R.L., da Ponte, F., Urbano, A.C., Bittencourt, L.F., Madeira, E.R.M.: Strategies for daytime slicing in future internet service providers. Trans. Emerg. Telecommun. Technol. **31**(1), e3727 (2020). https://doi.org/10.1002/ett.3727, https://onlinelibrary.wiley.com/doi/abs/10.1002/ett.3727, e3727 ett.3727

6. Gomes, R.L., Júnior, J.J., Abelém, A.G., Júnior, W.M.: Qoe and qos support on wireless mesh networks. In: Proceedings of the XV Brazilian Symposium on Multimedia and the Web. WebMedia '09, Association for Computing Machinery, New York, NY, USA (2009https://doi.org/10.1145/1858477.1858479

7. Gomes, R.L., Moreira, W.A., Ferreira, J.J.H., Abelém, A.J.G.: Providing qoe and qos in wireless mesh networks through dynamic choice of routing metrics. IEEE Lat. Am. Trans. **8**(4), 454–462 (2010). https://doi.org/10.1109/TLA.2010.5595137

8. Lopes Gomes, R., Roberto Mauro Madeira, E.: A traffic classification agent for virtual networks based on QoS classes. IEEE Lat. Am. Trans. **10**(3), 1734–1741 (2012). https://doi.org/10.1109/TLA.2012.6222579

9. Marinova, S., Leon-Garcia, A.: Intelligent o-ran beyond 5g: architecture, use cases, challenges, and opportunities. In: IEEE (2024)

10. Mhatre, S., Adelantado, F., Ramantas, K., Verikoukis, C.: Intelligent QoS-aware slice resource allocation with user association parameterization for beyond 5g o-ran-based architecture using DRL. IEEE Trans. Veh. Technol. (2024)

11. Nobre, F.V.J., Silva, D.D.S., Ferreira, M.C.M.M., Brito, M.L.M.L., de Araújo, T.P., Gomes, R.L.: Time-weighted correlation approach to identify high delay links in internet service providers. J. Internet Serv. Appl. **16**(1), 419–430 (2025). https://doi.org/10.5753/jisa.2025.5218. https://journals-sol.sbc.org.br/index.php/jisa/article/view/5218

12. Portela, A., Linhares, M.M., Nobre, F.V.J., Menezes, R., Mesquita, M., Gomes, R.L.: The role of TCP congestion control in the throughput forecasting. In: Proceedings of the 13th Latin-American Symposium on Dependable and Secure Computing, pp. 196–199. LADC 2024, Association for Computing Machinery, New York (2024). https://doi.org/10.1145/3697090.3699869

13. Rafique, W., Barai, J.R., Fapojuwo, A.O., Krishnamurthy, D.: A survey on beyond 5G network slicing for smart cities applications. IEEE Commun. Surv. (2024)

14. Raftopoulos, R., D'Oro, S., Melodia, T., Schembra, G.: DRL-based latency-aware network slicing in O-RAN with time-varying slas. In: IEEE Wireless Communications and Networking Conference (WCNC) (2024)

15. Rost, P., Mannweiler, C., Michalopoulos, D.S., Wiethölter, S., Droste, H., Anthapadmanabhan, S.: Network slicing to enable scalability and flexibility in 5g mobile networks. IEEE Commun. Mag. (2017)

16. Singh, V.P., Singh, M.P., Hegde, S., Gupta, M.: Security in 5g network slices: concerns and opportunities. In: IEEE (2024)

17. Wang, Q., et al.: Enable advanced QoS-aware network slicing in 5g networks for slice-based media use cases. IEEE Trans. Broadcast. (2019)

18. Yeh, S.P., Bhattacharya, S., Sharma, R., Moustafa, H.: Deep learning for intelligent and automated network slicing in 5g open ran (o-ran) deployment. IEEE Open J. Commun. Soc. (2023)

Towards Hierarchical Byzantine Distributed Replication

Gabriela Stein[1,2](✉) [ID], Luiz Antonio Rodrigues[2] [ID], and Elias P. Duarte Jr.[1] [ID]

[1] Western Parana State University (UNIOESTE), Cascavel, Brazil
elias@inf.ufpr.br
[2] Federal University of Parana (UFPR), Curitiba, Brazil
gstein@inf.ufpr.br, luiz.rodrigues@unioeste.br

Abstract. State Machine Replication has been widely employed to implement fault- and intrusion-tolerant distributed applications. The seminal PBFT (Practical Byzantine Fault Tolerance) algorithm ensures replica consistency even in the presence of Byzantine faults. However, PBFT is computationally and communication-intensive, and its performance degrades as the number of replicas increases. In this work, we take the first steps toward developing a hierarchical version of the PBFT algorithm that preserves its Byzantine fault tolerance while improving scalability, such that the cost of executing the algorithm grows more moderately with the number of replicas. Our proposal is based on the VCube, a virtual topology that is scalable by definition. We present preliminary results that suggest how this hierarchical version can enhance the original algorithm, most notably by reducing the number of messages exchanged as the system size grows. While promising, further work is required to fully specify and comprehensively evaluate the hierarchical PBFT algorithm.

Keywords: State Machine Replication · Scalability · Byzantine Fault Tolerance

1 Introduction

The concept of State Machine Replication (SMR) was first introduced in the seminal work of [17], which describes a technique for implementing fault-tolerant applications by replicating servers and coordinating the interactions between the client and server replicas [24]. That is, a set of replicas of a process is defined and they perform the same set of actions in the same order to ensure consistency between the replicas. In this case, each replica is a state machine that starts in the same state and executes the same sequence of operations, so all state machines progress identically. Clients generate requests for operations that must be executed by the server; multiple clients can send multiple requests; these cannot be executed by the server replicas in different orders. There must be an agreement as to which request should be executed at which time.

L. A. Rodrigues and R. Oliveira (Eds.): LADC 2025, CCIS 2697, pp. 364–375, 2026.
https://doi.org/10.1007/978-3-032-11539-3_23

One of the most important breakthroughs to the field is presented in [4] which introduces the PBFT (Practical Byzantine Fault Tolerance) algorithm. PBFT addresses the challenge of maintaining state consistency among replicas even in the presence of Byzantine faults affecting system processes.

PBFT implements atomic broadcast [14] which ensures that messages are delivered by all processes in the system in exactly the same order. The atomic broadcast algorithm is organized in rounds. A consensus instance is executed to define the next operation in the SMR in each round, thus deciding which message will be delivered in that round, and the messages are delivered in a deterministic, predefined order. In this way, atomic broadcast will ensure that the sequence of operations executed by all processes is the same.

Despite its undeniable importance, PBFT is known to be computationally and communication-intensive. The present work aims to develop a scalable version of the algorithm, using the VCube virtual topology. VCube was first described in the context of a distributed system-level diagnosis, and has recently been specified as a unreliable failure detectors [10]. Although processes forming a VCube can communicate directly with each other (fully-connected topology), they form a virtual topology that is scalable by definition. VCube has been used to implement scalable versions of several distributed abstractions, such as a blockchain [12], a scalable network fault management system [9], a publish-subscribe system [1], atomic broadcast [23], reliable broadcast [15], and distributed mutual exclusion [22].

The remainder of this paper is organized as follows. Section 2 presents the background concepts and related work, including an overview of the PBFT algorithm and VCube. Section 3 describes our proposal for a scalable version of PBFT using the VCube virtual topology, detailing its design and operational workflow. Section 4 reports the results of simulation experiments, evaluating the performance of the proposed solution in terms of scalability, latency, and message complexity. Finally, Sect. 5 summarizes the main contributions, discusses limitations, and outlines directions for future work.

2   Background

This section provides the background to our proposal. We begin by describing the PBFT (Practical Byzantine Fault Tolerance) algorithm, highlighting its operational model and scalability issues. We then introduce the VCube virtual topology, originally proposed for distributed system diagnosis [7,8,11,18] and later adapted for various scalable distributed abstractions.

2.1   PBFT

PBFT (Practical Byzantine Fault Tolerance) is a distributed algorithm for State Machine Replication (SMR) [4]. A state machine is a representation of a process that consists of the set of states and a set of transitions - a transition between states is caused by an *"event"*. The main idea of state machine replication in the context of PBFT is the replication of a server where multiple clients make requests to multiple processes representing the same service. The operations are assumed to be deterministic, i.e. the execution of an operation by a replica in a certain state and with a certain set of arguments must always produce the same result. Furthermore, the replicas start in the same state. The solution to maintaining consistency between the replicas available on the server is to ensure that all operations requested by the clients are executed by all replicas in the same order.

Clients make requests for operations to be executed by the servers. The system must provide access control for clients. Clients are authenticated and access is denied if the client making a request is not authorized to invoke the operation. The consistency of such operations is guaranteed by PBFT: all replicas execute exactly the same operations in the same order. PBFT assumes an asynchronous system and Byzantine faults. Thus a faulty process can fail by crashing, omitting messages or presenting any arbitrary behavior. Nonetheless, PBFT assumes that the messages exchanged between the processes are authenticated. That prevents message forgery, corruption and repetition. At most f faulty replicas are supported. If the service is replicated with n replicas, the number of failures supported by the system is $f = \lfloor \frac{n-1}{3} \rfloor$.

The algorithm proposed in [4] provides both of the two classical properties —*safety* and *liveness*—as long as the system respects the maximum number of failures. According to the safety property, the replicated service behaves like a centralized (non-replicated) implementation that performs operations atomically and sequentially. If the number of faulty replicas is not greater than f, safety is guaranteed. According to the liveness property a client request is eventually executed.

The maximum number f of replicas that can fail ($n = 3f+1$) [3] is necessary first because it is important to ensure a decision with $n-f$ replies, since f replicas may simply omit their messages. However, since the system is asynchronous, it is possible that those f replies are simply delayed, and that among the $2f + 1$ replies received f are from faulty (Byzantine) replicas. In that case the majority of replies is still from correct replicas ($f + 1$) allowing a majority function to be correctly applied.

In PBFT each replica is a state machine that maintains the state and implements the operations provided by the service. The set of replicas is denoted by R and each replica has an identifier within $\{0, ..., |R| - 1\}$. Given the assumption described above, $|R| = 3f + 1$.

Among the replicas one works as a leader and is called the *primary*, the others are *backups*. Replicas keep *views* of the system. The view remains the same for a given primary. The view changes as the primary is suspected of having failed and replaced by another primary. Thus if the leader fails, a new vision is started. The replicas (both primary and backups) maintain an up-to-date view of the composition of the system. The views are numbered consecutively. The primary of view v is replica p, where $p = v \bmod |R|$. The basic operation of the algorithm is as follows:

1. The client sends an operation request to the primary replica.
2. After three-rounds of communication between the primary and backups, the replicas either execute the operation or not and send the response back to the client.
3. The client expects to receive $f + 1$ identical responses from different replicas to define the result of the operation.

The algorithm begins with client c requesting the execution of operation o with message $\langle \text{REQUEST}, o, t, c \rangle \, \sigma_c$; t is the unique timestamp of the request. Timestamps are ordered in such a way that later requests have higher timestamps than earlier requests. It can be implemented as a local counter by each replica.

Each message sent from the replicas to the client contains the current view number so that the client receives information about who the current primary process is. The client sends a request to the process it believes is the primary. The primary then broadcasts the request to all backups. In the end, each replica sends the response to the request directly to the client. The response is sent as follows: $\langle \text{REPLY}, v, t, c, i, r \rangle \, \sigma_i$, where v is the number of the current view, t is the timestamp of the request to which the response refers, i is the number of the replica and r is the result of the execution of the requested operation. As mentioned before, client c waits for $f + 1$ responses with valid signatures from different replicas that contain the same t and r before accepting the result r as correct.

If the client does not receive the responses quickly enough, it broadcasts the request to all replicas. If the request has already been processed, the replicas send the response again. If the request has not yet been processed and the replica is not the primary one, it forwards the request to the primary. If the primary is suspected of having failed, a view change is triggered.

Each replica maintains a log of messages, that contains the request messages received as well as those already executed.

The three phases defined in the PBFT protocol are *pre-prepare*, *prepare* and *commit*, described next.

The primary p sends a message $\langle \text{PRE-PREPARE}, v, n, d \rangle \, \sigma_p$ via broadcast to the backups. Here v stands for the view in which the message is sent, m for the client request message, n for the sequence number that the primary assigns to the request and d for the hash of the message. A backup replica accepts the **pre-prepare** message as long as:

1. The signatures of the request and the **pre-prepare** messages are correct, and d is the hash of the m message.
2. The *backup* is in view v.
3. The backup has not accepted another **pre-prepare** message from the same view with the same sequence number and a different d (i.e. a different message).
4. The sequence number of the message **pre-prepare** is between the specified lower limit h and upper limit H.

The last criterion is intended to prevent a primary replica from failing and exceeding the limits of the sequence number representation. If the backup i

accepts the message $\langle \text{PRE-PREPARE}, v, n, d \rangle \; \sigma_p$, it enters the *prepare* phase and thus broadcasts the message $\langle \text{PREPARE}, v, n, d \rangle \; \sigma_p$ to all other replicas (including the primary) and includes the messages in its log.

The replicas that receive the **prepare** message from a *backup* only accept this message if:

1. The signatures are correct.
2. The view number of the **prepare** message matches the current view number of the replica.
3. The sequence number is within the specified limits.

When replica **i** has received $2f$ valid **prepare** messages, those messages match the **pre-prepare** message stored in its log, and it has received the **pre-prepare** message from the primary, the request can be considered *prepared* at replica **i**. It is important to note that all earlier requests must also already be in the log.

Replica **i** then broadcasts message $\langle \text{COMMIT}, v, n, D(m), i \rangle \; \sigma_i$ to the others. This begins the *commit* phase. The replicas accept the **commit** messages and add them to their log, provided that the messages are properly signed, the number of the view matches that of the replica and the sequence number is within the limits.

After replica **i** received $2f + 1$ valid **commit** messages from different replicas, including itself, and the request is already *prepared*, then replica **i** executes the request and returns the result to the client.

The view change protocol is triggered by the failure of the primary replica; the system implements timeouts which prevents backups from waiting indefinitely for requests to be executed.

A backup is in the waiting state if it has received a valid request and it has not yet been executed. A replica starts a timer when it receives a request. The timer stops when the replica is no longer waiting for execution. If the timer of backup i for the view v expires, the replica initiates the change of the system view to the view $v + 1$.

The replica does not accept any messages while it performs the view change, with the exception of *checkpoint, view-change* and *new-view* messages. Messages of type **checkpoint** are used for garbage collection and state transfer during the view change. A *checkpoint* is considered to be stable when at least $2f + 1$ matching **checkpoint** messages are received. In addition, a message <VIEW-CHANGE $v + 1, n, C, P, i$> σ_i is broadcast to all replicas. Here n is the sequence number of the last stable checkpoint known to i, C is a set of $2f + 1$ valid **checkpoint** messages, and P is a set of sets Pm containing the m request messages prepared by i with a sequence number greater than n. Each set Pm contains the message **pre-prepare** and $2f$ **prepares** coming from different replicas with the same view, sequence number and hash.

If the primary p of view $v + 1$ receives $2f$ valid view change messages for view $v + 1$ from other replicas, it broadcasts the message $\langle \text{NEW-VIEW}, v + 1, V, O \rangle \; \sigma_p$ to the other replicas. Where V is a set containing the valid **view-change** messages received from the primary plus the **view-change** messages sent by the primary, and O is a set of `pre-prepare` messages - without the requests, only the *headers* - and is computed as follows:

1. The primary determines a sequence number *min-s* of the last stable checkpoint in V and the largest sequence number *max-s* in a *prepare* message in the V view.
2. The primary creates a new `pre-prepare` message for view $v + 1$ for each sequence number n between *min-s* and *max-s*. There can be two cases:
   (a) If sequence number **n** already appears in P: in this case, the primary generates a message $\langle \text{PRE-PREPARE}, v + 1, n, d \rangle \, \sigma_p$.
   (b) Otherwise: a new message $\langle \text{PRE-PREPARE}, v + 1, n, d^{null} \rangle \, \sigma_p$ is generated, where d^{null} is the hash of a special request null.

The primary then inserts all messages from O into its log. It proceeds to view **v + 1**, where it can again accept all types of messages. A backup replica accepts a `new-view` message if it is properly signed, if it is valid for view $v + 1$ and if the set O is correct - it verifies O in a way that is similar to how the primary creates of O. It then updates its log and broadcasts the `pre-prepare` messages for each message in O to the other replicas. Furthermore, it adds these messages to its log and in view $v + 1$.

The replicas need to go through the *prepare* and *commit* phases after receiving the `pre-prepare` messages from set O. However, they avoid re-executing operations and re-sending the client responses.

It is possible that a replica have missed some of the requests. After the replica receives V, it can determine if it has missed any requests and from which replica it can retrieve the required information.

2.2   VCube

VCube [10] is a virtual topology that includes a built-in failure detector. The virtual topology is hierarchical, corresponding to a hypercube when all processes are correct and the number of processes is a power of 2. VCube has several logarithmic properties that remain valid along time, regardless of the number of processes that fail or recover.

The processes of a VCube with dimension $d > 0$ have identifiers consisting of d bits. VCube is a pull-based failure detector, in which processes monitor each other by executing tests. Processes are organized into progressively larger clusters $s = 1, .., \log_2 n$ of 2^{s-1} [6] defined for each process i as function $c_{i,s}$ (Eq. 1), where $\oplus$ is the bitwise exclusive (XOR) operator. Table 1 shows function $c_{i,s}$ for 8 processes.

$$c_{i,s} = \{i \oplus 2^{s-1}, c_{i \oplus 2^{s-1}, 1}, ..., c_{i \oplus 2^{s-1}, s-1}\} \tag{1}$$

The virtual edges of a VCube correspond to the tests that correct processes perform on each other. After a process is tested to be correct, the tester can obtain new information from the tested process. VCube is executed in testing rounds. In each round the testers of process j are the first correct processes in each $C(j,s), s = 1...\log_2 n$. A testing round occurs when all correct processes have executed their assigned tests.

Table 1. Function $c_{i,s}$ for 8 processes.

s	$c_{0,s}$	$c_{1,s}$	$c_{2,s}$	$c_{3,s}$	$c_{4,s}$	$c_{5,s}$	$c_{6,s}$	$c_{7,s}$
1	1	0	3	2	5	4	7	6
2	2,3	3,2	0,1	1,0	6,7	7,6	4,5	5,4
3	4,5,6,7	5,4,7,6	6,7,4,5	7,6,5,4	0,1,2,3	1,0,3,2	2,3,0,1	3,2,1,0

The status of each monitored process is maintained as a counter, which allows processes to differentiate recent events from older ones. Initially, all processes are considered to be correct and the corresponding counters are all zero. After an event is detected, i.e. a correct node has become faulty or vice versa, the corresponding counter is incremented by one. Thus an even counter indicates a correct process and an odd counter indicates a faulty process.

The failure detection latency of VCube is $\log_2 n$ testing rounds in the worst case. Thus if a correct process fails (or is suspected of having failed) or recovers, this information takes at most $\log_2 n$ testing rounds to reach all correct processes. Furthermore, as each process is tested by the first correct process of each of its clusters, there are at most $\log_2 n$ testers per process, at most $n \log_2 n$ tests are executed per round.

3   Our Proposal

This section describes our research plan to implement a hierarchical version of PBFT with VCube. From the description of PBFT in Sect. 2, it is possible to see that in some cases replicas communicate among themselves using broadcast, i.e. a message is sent by all processes to all others, involving a quadratic number of messages. That represents a significant cost.

We plan to use VCube in order to disseminate the messages with a lower cost. VCube has been used to implement broadcast abstractions, including Best-Effort Broadcast and Reliable Broadcast [20,21]. A process that broadcasts a message to all other only communicates with the first correct processes of its $\log_2 n$ clusters. In this way, the processes form an autonomic spanning tree. The root of the tree propagates a message to all its clusters, and at each subsequent level one less cluster is required. Best-Effort Broadcast is accomplished with n messages.

In the original PBFT algorithm, when the primary receives a request from a client, it relays that request to all the other replicas. In our proposed algorithm, the primary receives the request, broadcasts the request to the other replicas, and waits for $2f + 1$ replies to confirm the operation. In the proposed approach, broadcasting means propagating the information through the spanning tree. Figure 1 illustrates how this is done for 8 processes, a primary and 7 replicas.

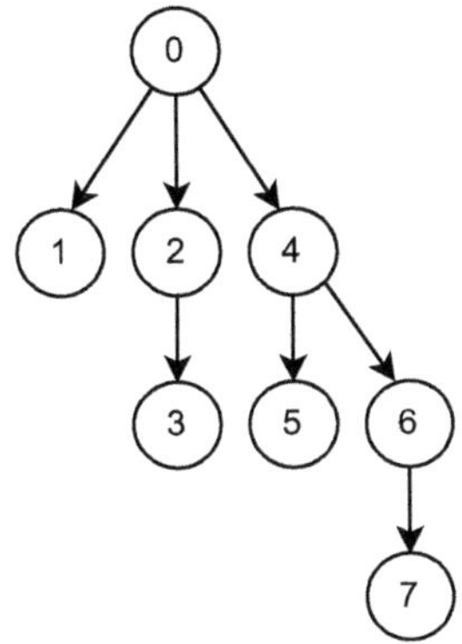

Fig. 1. Propagation of messages in the system being sent by primary 0.

This modification of the algorithm can improve the scalability, specially when the number of process in the system grows. However, it does come with a cost. The latency is slightly larger than in the original approach, as in the original algorithm the sender sends the message to all other processes at once, in our approach this involves communicating along a tree that has height $\log_2 n$.

In the next section we show simulation results comparing regular quadratic broadcast with our proposed logarithmic broadcast based on the VCube.

We are also planning other contributions that should improve the scalability of PBFT.

4   Preliminary Results

PBFT was developed on the basis of an already existing algorithm, ViewStamped Replication [19] that does not assume Byzantine—only crash faults. As an initial effort, we have proposed a hierarchical version of the Viewstamped Replication algorithm which we call HyperViewStamped Replication, published in a preliminary version in Portuguese [25].

In a nutshell, the Viewstamped Replication algorithm is a leader-based replication algorithm that uses timestamps (which are view identifiers) as a way to recover from failures. The primary replica is responsible for processing client requests and forwarding them to the other replicas. Each replica maintains the following information: a counter for the requests received, the number of the last operation committed, a log keeping the sequence of operations, a client table, information on the current composition of the system, the state of the replica (normal, view-change, recovering) and the view-change number.

Every message exchanged in the system contains the view number, and this number is only increased when the replicas perceive that the primary failed. In a fault-free scenario, the primary broadcasts the request received from the client to the other replicas via a PREPARE message. The replicas process those messages in order, ensuring that when the reply message PREPARE_OK is sent, all earlier messages had already been confirmed. As soon as the primary receives f PREPARE_OK messages, it considers the request to be confirmed and replies to the client. Once again, those messages are sent via broadcast - the same way that PBFT does.

Our first efforts towards using VCube to implement hierarchical State Machine Replication, consisted of using the topology provided by VCube to broadcast messages throughout the system, as well as also using VCube as a failure detector. We compare our HyperViewStamped Replication algorithm with the regular Viewstamped replication algorithm using a regular failure detector: all processes monitor all other processes.

In Fig. 2 we show the total number of messages exchanged by both solutions, including the messages employed by the replication algorithms themselves, as well as the monitoring messages employed by failure detectors. In the following Table 2 it is easier to discern that most messages employed by ViewStamped Replication are from the failure detector - recall that in this version, a all-to-all approach, where each process monitors all other processes in the system. The number of messages shown in the table were obtained in a normal-case operation scenario where all process in the system are correct.

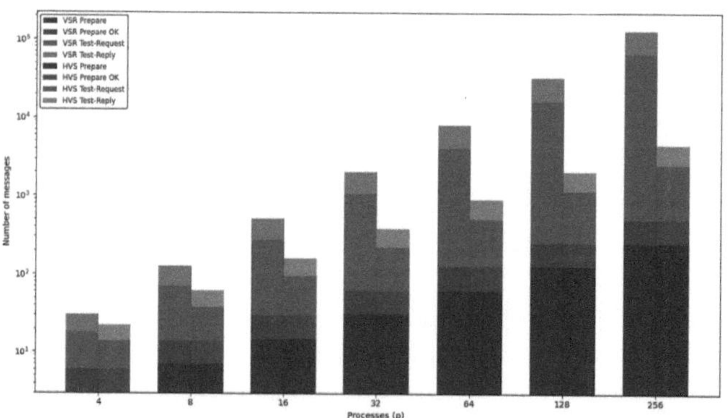

Fig. 2. Total of messages in the system per number of processes in logarithmic scale.

Table 2 shows only PREPARE and TEST-REQUEST messages. Recall that this refers to a normal-case operation case and there are no faulty processes. The number of PREPARE_OK messages matches the number of PREPARE messages exchanged. The same for TEST-REQUEST and TEST-REPLY messages. Both in HVS (HyperViewStamped Replication) and in VSR (ViewStamped Replication) the number of **PREPARE** messages that the algorithms use remains the same. However, the number of **TEST-REQUEST** messages increases substantially faster for VSR than for HVS.

Table 2. Number of **PREPARE** and **TEST-REQUEST** messages.

p	VSR		HVS	
	PREPARE	TEST-REQUEST	PREPARE	TEST-REQUEST
4	3	12	3	8
8	7	56	7	24
16	15	240	15	64
32	31	992	31	160
64	63	4,032	63	384
128	127	16,256	127	896
256	255	65,280	255	2,048

5   Conclusion

This work presented our first efforts towards a hierarchical SMR algorithm that combines VCube and PBFT which aims to be a scalable distributed replication strategy that withstands Byzantine faults. The proposed algorithm will rely on a hierarchical broadcast strategy to reduce the number of messages required by PBFT, which is quadratic. Preliminary simulation results of the crash-tolerant Viewstamped Replication are also presented. Results show that using VCube as a failure detector also has advantages instead of using an all-to-all strategy.

Future work includes a thorough survey of the several strategies that have been proposed to improve the performance of PBFT, such as [2,5,13,16]. Furthermore, we believe that several other optimizations can be devised for the hierarchical version of PBFT.

Acknowledgments. This research was partially supported by Coordination for the Improvement of Higher Education Personnel (CAPES) - Program of Academic Excellence (PROEX).

References

1. de Araujo, J.P., Arantes, L., Duarte, E.P., Jr., Rodrigues, L.A., Sens, P.: VCube-PS: a causal broadcast topic-based publish/subscribe system. J. Parallel Distrib. Comput. **125**, 18–30 (2019)

2. Bessani, A., Sousa, J., Alchieri, E.E.: State machine replication for the masses with BFT-smart. In: 44th Annual IEEE/IFIP International Conference on Dependable Systems and Networks, pp. 355–362. IEEE (2014)
3. Castro, M., Liskov, B.: Practical byzantine fault tolerance and proactive recovery. ACM Trans. Comput. Syst. (TOCS) 4, 398–461 (2002)
4. Castro, M., Liskov, B., et al.: Practical byzantine fault tolerance. In: OsDI, vol. 99, pp. 173–186 (1999)
5. Distler, T.: Byzantine fault-tolerant state-machine replication from a systems perspective. ACM Comput. Surv. (CSUR) 54(1), 1–38 (2021)
6. Duarte, E.P., Albini, L.C., Brawerman, A., Guedes, A.L.: A hierarquical distributed fault diagnosis algorithm based on clusters with detours. In: 2009 Latin American Network Operations and Management Symposium, pp. 1–6. IEEE (2009)
7. Duarte, E.P., Nanya, T.: A hierarchical adaptive distributed system-level diagnosis algorithm. IEEE Trans. Comput. 47(1), 34–45 (2002)
8. Duarte, E.P., Weber, A., Fonseca, K.V.: Distributed diagnosis of dynamic events in partitionable arbitrary topology networks. IEEE Trans. Parallel Distrib. Syst. 23(8), 1415–1426 (2011)
9. Duarte, E., dos Santos, A.L.: Network fault management based on SNMP agent groups. In: Proceedings 21st International Conference on Distributed Computing Systems Workshops, pp. 51–56. IEEE (2001)
10. Duarte, E.P., Jr., Rodrigues, L.A., Camargo, E.T., Turchetti, R.C.: The missing piece: a distributed system-level diagnosis model for the implementation of unreliable failure detectors. Computing 105(12), 2821–2845 (2023)
11. Duarte, E.P., Nanya, T., Noguchi, S., Mansfield, G.: Non-broadcast network fault-monitoring based on system-level diagnosis. In: Lazar, A.A., Saracco, R., Stadler, R. (eds.) Integrated Network Management V. ITIFIP, pp. 597–609. Springer, Boston, MA (1997). https://doi.org/10.1007/978-0-387-35180-3_44
12. Freitas, A.E.S., Rodrigues, L.A., Duarte, E.P., Jr.: vcubechain: a scalable permissioned blockchain. Ad Hoc Netw. 158, 103461 (2024)
13. Giridharan, N., Suri-Payer, F., Abraham, I., Alvisi, L., Crooks, N.: Autobahn: Seamless high speed BFT. In: Proceedings of the ACM SIGOPS 30th Symposium on Operating Systems Principles, pp. 1–23 (2024)
14. Hadzilacos, V.: Fault-tolerant broadcasts and related problems. Distrib. Syst. 97–145 (1993)
15. Jeanneau, D., Rodrigues, L.A., Arantes, L., Duarte Jr., E.P.: An autonomic hierarchical reliable broadcast protocol for asynchronous distributed systems with failure detection. J. Braz. Comput. Soc. 23(1), 1–14 (2017). https://doi.org/10.1186/s13173-017-0064-9
16. Kotla, R., Alvisi, L., Dahlin, M., Clement, A., Wong, E.: Zyzzyva: speculative byzantine fault tolerance. In: Proceedings of Twenty-First ACM SIGOPS Symposium on Operating Systems Principles, pp. 45–58 (2007)
17. Lamport, L.: Time, clocks, and the ordering of events in a distributed system. Commun. ACM 21(7), 558–565 (1978). https://doi.org/10.1145/359545.359563
18. Nassu, B.T., Duarte Jr, E.P., Ramirez Pozo, A.T.: A comparison of evolutionary algorithms for system-level diagnosis. In: Proceedings of the 7th Annual Conference on Genetic and Evolutionary Computation, pp. 2053–2060 (2005)
19. Oki, B.M., Liskov, B.H.: Viewstamped replication: a new primary copy method to support highly-available distributed systems. In: Proceedings of the Seventh Annual ACM Symposium on Principles of Distributed Computing, pp. 8–17 (1988)

20. Rodrigues, L.A., Arantes, L., Duarte, E.P.: An autonomic implementation of reliable broadcast based on dynamic spanning trees. In: 2014 Tenth European Dependable Computing Conference, pp. 1–12. IEEE (2014)
21. Rodrigues, L.A., Duarte, E.P., de Araujo, J.P., Arantes, L., Sens, P.: Bundling messages to reduce the cost of tree-based broadcast algorithms. In: 8th Latin-American Symposium on Dependable Computing (LADC), pp. 115–124. IEEE (2018)
22. Rodrigues, L.A., Duarte, E.P., Jr., Arantes, L.: A distributed k-mutual exclusion algorithm based on autonomic spanning trees. J. Parallel Distrib. Comput. **115**, 41–55 (2018)
23. Ruchel, L.V., de Camargo, E.T., Rodrigues, L.A., Turchetti, R.C., Arantes, L., Duarte, E.P., Jr.: Scalable atomic broadcast: a leaderless hierarchical algorithm. J. Parallel Distrib. Comput. **184**, 104789 (2024)
24. Schneider, F.B.: Implementing fault-tolerant services using the state machine approach: a tutorial. ACM Comput. Surv. (CSUR) **22**(4), 299–319 (1990)
25. Stein, G., Rodrigues, L.A., Duarte Jr, E.P.: Hyperviewstamped replication: Uma estratégia para replicação distribuída hierárquica. In: Workshop de Testes e Tolerância a Falhas (WTF), pp. 15–28. SBC (2025)

Author Index

A
Abelém, Antônio 133
Abreu, Diego 133
Alchieri, Eduardo A. P. 148
Alpos, Orestis 163
Alves, Davi O. 320
Amaral, Paulo 201
Andrade, Rossana M. C. 3
Araujo, Jean 94, 201
Araujo, Ramon S. 320

B
Barbaraci, Mariarosaria 163
Bentes, Daniel C. 3
Borges, Ivson 275
Brito, Andrey 20

C
Cachin, Christian 163
Callou, Gustavo 275
Campos, Francisco R. M. 3
Campos, Gustavo A. 320
Campos, João R. 37
Cialdini, Alexandre S. 3
Costa, Wanderson L. 353

D
da Rocha, Gabriel Faustino Lima 148
de Moura, Evellin S. 331
Duarte Jr., Elias P. 148, 364

F
Faísco, Miguel 238
Fealey, Kevin 112
Ferreira, Maria C. M. M. 342
Fonseca, Henrique A. 37
Freitas, Allan 133
Fulber-Garcia, Vinicius 148

G
Gomes, Rafael L. 3, 311, 320, 331, 342, 353

I
Ivaki, Naghmeh 54

J
Jananloo, Saeed Javani 75

L
Lelis, Claudio A. S. 112, 255
Lima, Eduardo 94
Lima, João C. C. 3
Lima, Vanessa C. 311
Lins, Luan 275

M
Maciel, Paulo 275
Marcondes, Cesar A. C. 112, 255
Medeiros, Ibéria 238
Melo, Carlos 291
Mendizabal, Odorico Machado 183
Moraes, Regina 37, 54

N
Neto, Antônio M. B. 331
Nobre, Francisco V. J. 320
Nuutinen, Niku Waltteri Saulinpoika 238

P
Paiva, Carlos H. 311
Patricio, Jessica C. C. 311
Pedrazoli, Aldrey 54
Peixoto, Diogo Canut Freitas 183
Pereira, José D'Abruzzo 75
Petrusic, Milan 238
Pires Correia, Jorge 221

Pontes, Davi 20
Portela, Ariel L. C. 342

R
Ramalho, Jamilson 291
Reiser, Hans P. 238
Rodrigues, Emanuel B. 3
Rodrigues, Luiz Antonio 364
Rodrigues, Renan L. 311

S
Schmid, Noah 163
Senn, Michael 163
Silva, Clenival L. 3
Silveira, Leonardo 255

Sousa, Jeffson 133
Stein, Gabriela 364

T
Trajano, Raquel F. 291

V
Vanderlei, Igor 94
Veloso, Alan 133
Venâncio, Giovanni 148
Verri, Filipe A. N. 255
Vieira, Marco 75

Z
Zola, Wagner Machado N. 221

MIX
Papier aus verantwortungsvollen Quellen
Paper from responsible sources
FSC® C105338

If you have any concerns about our products,
you can contact us on
ProductSafety@springernature.com

In case Publisher is established outside the EU,
the EU authorized representative is:
Springer Nature Customer Service Center GmbH
Europaplatz 3, 69115 Heidelberg, Germany

Printed by Libri Plureos GmbH
in Hamburg, Germany